Advances in Econometrics, Income Distribution and Scientific Methodology

Daniel J. Slottje (Ed.)

Advances in Econometrics, Income Distribution and Scientific Methodology

Essays
in Honor
of Camilo Dagum

With 23 Figures
and 31 Tables

Physica-Verlag
A Springer-Verlag Company

Prof. Daniel J. Slottje
Department of Economics
Southern Methodist University
Dallas, Texas 75275-0496, USA

H B
5 2 3
. A 3
1 9 9 9

ISBN 3-7908-1226-9 Physica-Verlag Heidelberg New York

Cataloging-in-Publication Data applied for
Die Deutsche Bibliothek – CIP-Einheitsaufnahme
Advances in econometrics, income distribution and scientific methodology: essays in honor of Camilo Dagum; with
31 tables/Daniel J. Slottje (ed.). – Heidelberg; New York: Physica-Verl., 1999
ISBN 3-7908-1226-9

© Physica-Verlag Heidelberg 1999
Printed in Germany

The use of general descriptive names, registered names, trademarks, etc. in this publication does not imply, even in the absence of a specific statement, that such names are exempt from the relevant protective laws and regulations and therefore free for general use.

SPIN 10732625   88/2202-5 4 3 2 1 0 – Printed on acid-free paper

PREFACE

Camilo Dagum was born in Rosario de Lerma, Salta, Argentina on August 11, 1925. He was educated at the National University of Cordoba, Argentina and the University of Rome, Italy, where he wrote his Ph.D thesis in economics, under the direction of Professor Corrado Gini, in 1956. His long and outstanding career in teaching and research started in 1949 at the Faculty of Economic Sciences of the National University of Cordoba where he became full professor in 1956. Having being awarded a fellowship from the Argentine National Research Council of Science and Technology, in 1960 he went to the London School of Economics as a Visiting Research Economist and worked with Professors M.G. Kendall and A.W. Phillips. Upon his return in 1962, he was elected Dean of the Faculty of Economic Sciences, a position he renounced in 1966 due to the Army's Coup d'Etat that eliminated the university's autonomy and destroyed the Argentinean constitutional and democratic order for seventeen years.

Forced to leave the country, he accepted an invitation from Professor Oskar Morgenstern to join the Econometric Research Center of Princeton University for the period 1966-68. From Princeton he went on to Mexico as a Visiting Professor of the National University of Mexico and later joined the faculty of the University of Iowa. He was appointed Full Professor at the University of Ottawa, Canada, in 1972 where he taught for 19 years. In 1992 he was designated Professor of Economics Emeritus. In 1990, at the invitation of the University of Milan, based on a 1980 Italian law that allows universities to invite a foreign professor of internationally recognized academic excellence, the Italian government created and funded for life the Chair of Statistics and Economics that Camilo occupied at the University of Milan until 1994. He then moved, by invitation to the University of Bologna where he is currently a Faculty member.

In recognition of his contributions to economic science, Camilo received Honorary Doctorates from the University of Bologna and the National University of Cordoba in 1988, and the University of Montpellier in 1996. Camilo's strong scientific association with outstanding French scholars spans many years and can be viewed through some of his most important contributions. By special invitation of his colleague and friend, the late Professor Francois Perroux, he traveled often to Paris during the 1965-1987 period to teach and to do research at the Institut des Sciences Economiques et

Mathematiques Appliquees (ISMEA), and at the Institut d'Etude du Developement Economique et Social (IEDES) of the University of Paris. In 1988, his long time friend Professor Maurice Allais invited him as one of his ten companions on the occasion of receiving the Nobel Memorial Prize in Economic Science. It should be apparent then, that Camilo's long and rich academic career was greatly influenced by his global experiences.

Camilo Dagum is one of the few economists who has worked and written in an overwhelming number of areas of diverse interests. He is the consummate eclectic academic. During a fifty year period he has published books as author, co-author and editor, in English, French and Spanish, and over 200 papers, as listed in the bibliography of his works presented here, in English, French, Spanish, Italian, German and Polish. It would be impossible to represent Camilo Dagum's contributions in a single volume, so we have chosen to deal primarily with three main areas, statistics and econometrics, income distribution, and philosophy of science.

At the young age of 24 years, he published an important contribution in Spanish on the demand function and continued with several other papers, also in Spanish, on topics such as, the Poisson distribution, the quantitative theory of money, structural and cyclical price flexibility, and the role of the statistical method in the modeling of economic agents behavior. After a stimulating research experience at the University of Rome in 1956-1957, Camilo Dagum made further contributions to econometrics and statistics, particularly on the transvariation method introduced by Gini in 1916. He demonstrated the relationship of the simplest transvariation measure or probability of transvariation to both Wilcoxon and Mann-Whitney statistics developed in the 1940's. He extended further the transvariation method to cover k-dimensional random vectors and, for the first time, applied the method to solving discrimination problems in economics. He would later make use of the first order transvariation statistic to prove how to decompose the Gini ratio between groups in an original article published in 1997.

During his two years at the Econometric Research Center of Princeton University in 1966-1968, Professor Dagum worked on fundamental problems of structural stability, structural change and econometric model building. The main results of his research were published later in various scientific journals in France, Germany, Spain and Mexico. It was during his stay at Princeton University that he also began his involvement with the problems on functional and personal income distributions, topics to which he was to return to in later years, making innovative contributions.

Professor Dagum has published at least three seminal papers on the topics of personal income distribution, inequality measures between income distributions and the relationship between income inequality measures and social welfare functions. His 1977 income distribution model(with three and four parameters)is widely applied to developed and developing economies with excellent results. He has recently generalized it to deal with the fundamental problem of personal human capital estimation and distribution. He is currently working on a new method to estimate national human capital from surveys of income and wealth distributions.

In 1980, Professor Dagum published another seminal paper where he introduced, for the first time in the literature, a measure of the directional economic distance *between* income distributions to assess the relative economic affluence between the underlying populations. One important property of his economic distance measure is that it is *directly* calculated from the *observed* income distributions contrary to other methods which get a measure from the disaggregation of a given total income distribution. The Dagum economic distance measure is relevant to evaluate the directional economic distance between, say, male and female income distributions, or that between young and adults or between incomes by levels of education; issues that are all of great social concern and that have significant policy implications. Traditionally, those measures were done by taking into account only the means or medians of the distribution considered. His work generated a stream of new ideas and spurred further developments on the subject.

In another 1990 seminal paper, extended further, Professor Dagum proved the dual relationship between social welfare functions and income inequalities. He deduced the utility function and corresponding social welfare foundation of several important income inequality ratios, such as, Theil, Atkinson, Bourguignon and others. He also proved, that contrary to common belief, the Gini ratio has a social welfare foundation and that its utility function is the only one to admit interpersonal comparisons of utility. Another important consequence of his theorem is that the utility function, being non-observable, need not to be arbitrarily specified, but can be derived as a proposition from any well accepted measure of income inequality.

Two disciplines that have fascinated Camilo Dagum since he was a student are history and philosophy. He later directed these interests, particularly towards philosophy (as in philosophy of sciences) in the context of economics. He culminated a long series of contributions on this later topic with an article published in 1995 where he addressed the scope and method of economics as a science. There, he discussed the ontology, methodology and epistemology of economics, assessing the limits and validity of some schools of economic thought.

The topics and contributions in this book are a very good representation of

Camilo Dagum's astounding diversity of interests and overall eclecticism. Remarkably, Camilo has published at least one paper per year, in every year since 1951. This is an astounding record, that may well be unmatched in the field of economics. Several of the authors in this book are leading pioneers in econometric methodology. Several others are pioneers in economic theory and several others are the leading applied economists in income distribution analysis in the world. The topics accurately reflect Camilo Dagum's breadth of understanding across various economic sub-fields, all complex in nature. What no book can capture is the person and character of the man himself. Camilo Dagum is a man of the utmost integrity, impeccable character and unparalled kindness. It is impossible not to like him for his gentleness and to not admire him for his intellectual prowess. It is with great pleasure that I present these essays to you, in honor of Professor Camilo Dagum. Special thanks must be given to Jianshan Xu for his incredible effort in getting this book into publishable form and for doing so in good humor.

Daniel J. Slottje
Dallas, Texas
1999

Table of Contents

Chapter 1

ABOUT THE CONTRIBUTION OF ECONOMETRICS TO THE ADVANCEMENT OF KNOWLEDGE: THE MACROECONOMIC RELEVANCE OF MICROECONOMIC DATA

Edmond Malinvaud

Batiment Malakoff 2-Timber J310, 15, Boulevard Gabriel Peri,
92245 Malakoff Cedex, France

1.1   Introduction

On several occasions throughout the years I had the pleasure of discussions with Camilo Dagum. They always concerned the state of our common discipline, economics, of which the two of us were not always criticizing the same theoretical developments. But we shared a common interest for quantitative methods and for their role in the advancement of economic knowledge. This book gives me an excellent opportunity for looking again into the methodology of that role. In order to avoid long repetitions with what I already wrote elsewhere on the same broad issue, I shall more precisely consider here the interplay between the systematic use of microeconomic data and the continual respecification of models of aggregate phenomena.

Economic methodology directly leads us to intensify such an interplay, without which our knowledge would remain too vague. But there are various ways to proceed from microeconomic observation to macroeconomic theory. The simplest one consists in drawing from available results of applied econometrics the "calibration" of the few parameters present in an aggregate model derived from the study of a representative agent. We shall see why such a practice is exposed to serious risks. The reference ought rather to be an explicit specification, validation and estimation of a microeconomic model, simultaneously with the revision or consolidation of the macroeconomic theory for which the microeconomic data are perceived as containing useful information.

A lucid examination of the approach suggests that it might have to take different forms, depending on the macroeconomic phenomena concerned and on the available data bases. The methodology of the interplay will most probably have to become quite complex if it wants to cover all interesting cases. This article cannot claim to offer even a bird's eye view of what such a comprehensive methodology ought to be. It aims more modestly at making readers aware of the interest of a new line of relevant research. Some applied econometricians are already engaged into this research line for the particular projects they are involved in. But few economists realize the importance for their discipline of progress in a direction that is not in any of the main focuses of attention.

The first section of this article will recall the main principles concerning the empirical foundations of economics and will point to their direct implication for the role of microeconomic data in macroeconomics. The second section will offer a formal framework for the study of the interplay in question ; although already limitative the general specification of this framework will still be too broad to be enlightening ; this is why a narrower but often more useful specification will also be presented. The third section will discuss the practices of thinking in terms of representative agents and of calibrating our models ; it will show why such practices are exposed to aggregation pitfalls ; but it will also suggest that the pitfalls are less frequently dangerous than we could have imagined.

1.2   Underlying Principles

Many economists, from far in the past to the present, have been or are taking the option of building macroeconomic knowledge exclusively from macroeconomic observation, as it appears in the statistics or national accounts. But there are two difficulties with such a direct inductive approach. In the first place, macroeconomic data do not come from controlled experiments but from observation of actual evolutions as they occur. One may suspect these evolutions result from many causes, often interfering with one another. The economist or econometrician who wants to learn from the data has a difficult time in identifying all the main factors, so as not to be misled by the spurious effects coming from omitted factors. In the second place, the data base provided by macroeconomic observations is fairly poor, particularly so when considered against the complexity and possible lack of permanence of economic phenomena occurring in societies where institutions evolve and behaviour may change. Any rough comparison with natural sciences shows how handicapped economists are because of these two difficulties.

Fortunately, economists have an advantage over their colleagues specializing in those sciences : they have direct knowledge of economic agents and of the institutional framework in which they operate. The nature of the constraints restricting actions of firms and households is known and can be specified in the situations considered by a particular theory. The same applies to the objectives agents are trying to achieve. It is thus required for scientific efficiency that, when macroeconomic data are analysed, our direct knowledge of institutions and behaviours is also taken into account. This is naturally done by modelling at the microeconomic level.

The art of macroeconomics is indeed to take advantage of all relevant observations and to best combine their information contents. Direct knowledge "from the inside" is never negligible but may be fuzzy when it concerns complex structures of interactions, aggregation across heterogeneous groups, relative importance of conflicting effects or even forms of rationality in individual behaviour. A third source of information then becomes relevant, namely observations collected at the microeconomic level, mainly from individuals, households or firms, either by statistical censuses, or by sample surveys, even in some cases by experiments on groups of students or other subjects.

It is typical for knowledge of a macroeconomic behavioural law to result from many investigations led within an overall framework implying three steps : (i) modellization of what we directly know about the autonomy and objective of the individual agent, (ii) econometric inference, from microeconomic data, about unknown parameters of the model, (iii) aggregate analysis transposing the results of the two first steps, then testing and estimating on macroeconomic data the specification derived from the transposition.

This convenient scheme well applies only to truly behavioural laws, those concerning clearly identified actions of clearly identified agents, whose autonomy can be unambiguously characterized, whose significant interactions with other agents are well captured through easily observable variables. Macroeconomic theory involves other kinds of relations, which are neither defining identities, nor simple transpositions of budgets constraints, nor still market equilibrium equations. Remaining relations may be called *"adjustment laws. "* Typical cases are equations applying to changes in the general levels of wage rates or prices. For adjustment laws macroeconomic data provide by far the main source of information, because direct inside knowledge concerning the phenomena involved is particularly fuzzy. Our knowledge for such a case rather is the outcome of a bulk of empirical fits performed on many data sets, for many countries, regions and industries, and concerning different periods. Empirical exploration then is inspired by simple-minded ideas that seem likely to agree with many potential explanations of the changes in question.

Since the article deals only with the use of microeconomic data, we shall restrict attention to behavioural laws, where this use is most direct. No doubt, what will be learned in such applications will later have a somewhat more general validity and contain lessons for future research on some adjustment laws. But, for the time being, let us focus on the domain in which the econometrics of microeconomic data for macroeconomics is most active.

1.3   A Convenient Framework

1. Prior to econometric issues a natural general question is to know how macroeconomics knowledge available at the microeconomic level ought to used. Such is precisely "the aggregation problem". We shall not consider here all its aspects, but rather focus on the most significant one for our present purpose[1].

In its purest form the problem arises when prior knowledge rests on the study of the rational behaviour of an agent supposed to be representative of a large class of active units ; the agent studied is meant to be representative with respect to the conditions in which those units are placed and to the objectives they pursue. The study is intended to be later transposed so as to provide the laws representing how the set of all units in the class, taken as a whole, operates on the markets. But such laws would be much too imprecise if the information content of statistics and of other relevant observations was not used in order to restrict the unpleasant lack of specificity of the laws. Econometric estimation then comes into play, applied at the level of individual agents when microeconomic data are processed, and at the level of aggregates in case of macroeconomic data processing. In other words, econometric contributions are brought both before and after the transposition from the micro to the macro.

---

[1]A fuller discussion is available in E. Malinvaud, "A framework for aggregation theories", *Ricerche Economiche*, University of Venice, vol 47 (1993), p. 107-135.

It has been long recognized that the transposition is most often the weakest part of the procedure, in the sense that its logical foundations are more fuzzy or inappropriate than those of either the initial study of rational behaviour or the econometric estimations. This is why more attention should be given to a close study of the transposition. In this respect an abstract general model provides a convenient reference.

2. For simplicity the model will be written here in a particular case ; but it is easily made much more general. There will be just two observed microeconomic variables, one x taken as exogenous in the analysis of the phenomenon under examination, the other y taken as endogenous. The values taken by x and y for agent i will be denoted x_i and y_i (with $i = 1, 2,...n$). The behaviour of agent i will determine y_i from x_i and from the value of a macroeconomic exogenous variable z. The function representing the determination will differ from one agent to another (the population of agents is heterogeneous). However, the differences will be characterized by the values of just one parameter t_i, so that y_i will be determined according to :

$$y_i = f(x_i, z; t_i) \qquad (1.1)$$

the function f being assumed smooth.

A full description of the microeconomic situation and of the behaviour in question would require knowledge of the function f, of the value of the macroeconomic variable z and of the $2n$ values of the microeconomic variables x_i and t_i. But for describing the macroeconomic situation and the macroeconomic phenomenon less is required. Indeed, we then need not determine all the n values of the y_i, but usually just the value of an aggregate indicator. Let us assume the indicator is the arithmetic mean :

$$\bar{y} = \frac{1}{n}\sum_{i=1}^{n} y_i \qquad (1.2)$$

To find how $\bar{y}$ varies as a function of exogenous variables, we have to look at the variations of the average of the values taken by the right-hand member of equation (1).

For computing this average, we may take advantage of the fact that the same function f and the same value of variable z apply to all agents. Computation may then proceed from the statistical distribution, over all agents, of the couple (x_i, t_i). The way to proceed is well known and will not be explained in detail here. It can be summarized in a formula involving the proportions of agents with approximately equal values of x_i and t_i.

Let indeed $G(\xi, \theta; \gamma)$ be the proportion of agents i for which :

$$x_i \leq \xi \qquad t_i \leq \theta \tag{1.3}$$

The "joint cumulative distribution function" G is written as depending on γ, a vector of parameters, and this for an important reason which will be explained in a moment, but to which we need not pay attention at this moment. The values of the function G for different values of ξ and θ might be given by statistics in which the identities of agents i would not be recorded. A table might give the number of agents in cells, each one concerning those agents with x_i belonging to a small interval of values of ξ and with t_i belonging to a small interval of values of θ. Since the function f is smooth, its value is about the same for all agents belonging to the same cell. In order to compute $n\bar{y}$ we should sum, over all cells, the product of the value of f for the cell by the number of agents in the cell. The sum of products, divided by n, is convenient written as a "Stieljes integral :

$$\bar{y} = \int f(\xi, z; \theta) dG(\xi, \theta; \gamma) \tag{1.4}$$

3. The important point is to realize that the result of the computation will depend only on z and γ. We may then write it as :

$$\bar{y} = F(z; \gamma) \tag{1.5}$$

It is precisely the "macroeconomic behaviour law" derived from the microeconomic behaviour represented by equation (1) and from the statistical distribution G. The explanatory variables are the common exogenous macroeconomic variable z and the vector of parameters γ in the statistical distribution function, which concerns simultaneously the microeconomic exogenous variables x_i and the behavioural parameters t_i.

Given this conceptual framework, the econometrician who has to process microeconomic data in order to determine F must, first, estimate f, usually starting from a microeconomic analysis providing a model of the behaviour in question, second, study the statistical distribution G and characterize its dependence on a few parameters. The second phase is not emphasized in econometric textbooks and deserves attention.

Actually, it often takes place under favourable conditions, because many statistical distributions are empirically found to be fairly invariant through time and space. Pareto was probably the first economist to draw attention to the fact, which was sometimes called "structural stability". For instance the lognormal distribution was found to perform well for the representation of many economic variables. In such cases, concerning not a couple (x_i, t_i) but just one variable like x_i, two parameters suffice : one for the median value of the x_i, another one for the standard deviation of log x_i. Such then are the proper aggregate indicators corresponding to the exogenous variables x_i.

Like many other stylized facts in economics, the invariance in question is only approximate. Moreover, it has not been investigated yet for many variables of interest and for most of the relevant joint distributions. Thus, a large field of research is open for statistical studies, which should keep pace with the development of estimation from microeconomic data.

4. An important refinement of the framework follows from the observation that, depending on the form of the microeconomic behavioural function f, a smaller or larger number of parameters may be needed in the representation of changes in the statistical distribution. An extreme case occurs when f is linear with the same slope for all agents :

$$y_i = ax_i + b_i \tag{1.7}$$

Then clearly just the first moment $\bar{x}$ of the statistical distribution of x_i matters because (7) implies :

$$\bar{y} = a\bar{x} + \bar{b} \tag{1.8}$$

This macroeconomic equation applies, no matter how much the distribution of the variable x_i may otherwise change. Even if a large number of components of the vector γ is found necessary for an accurate description of observed changes in the distribution, only the mean $\bar{x}$ will feature in the aggregate relation.

More generally the use of microeconomic data leads us to pay attention to functions f that have "a finite basis." The expression means that there are J

couples of function $a_j(z)$ and $\varphi_j(x,t)$ such that, identically in x, z and t, the function f may be written as :

$$f(x,z;t) = \sum_{j=1}^{J} a_j(z)\varphi_j(x,t) \qquad (1.9)$$

This is a special form, but also a convenient form for aggregation. Indeed, it implies that the average $\bar{y}$ is given by :

$$\bar{y} = \sum_{j=1}^{J} a_j(z)\bar{\varphi}_j \qquad (1.10)$$

where the $\bar{\varphi}_j$ are the mean values of the φ_j. If these values can be observed, equation (10) gives precisely the wanted macroeconomic equation (5), with the vector γ needing no other component than the $\bar{\varphi}_j$, no matter how much the distribution G may otherwise change.

If for instance the functions $\varphi_j(x,t)$ are polynomials of degrees zero, one and two, then the $\bar{\varphi}_j$ will be constants, mean values of the x_i and t_i, and second order moments of these variables (perhaps up to linear transformations, some $\bar{\varphi}_j$ being linear combinations of the first and second order moments).

The refinement of our framework, which so leads to aggregation of the form (10) was found to be empirically relevant. For example, studying US and UK family expenditure survey data, A. Lewbel showed that individual Engel curves could be said to have a finite basis of order 3, although there was a high degree of heterogeneity among these curves. So, aggregate Engel functions involving up to the third moment of the income distribution were accurate[2].

The main conclusion to be drawn here of recent investigations about aggregation that improved knowledge of macroeconomic laws will come from empirical research that will operate at the microeconomic level and there combine the study of behavioural functions (here f) with that of the statistical distribution characterizing microeconomic heterogeneity (here G). The conclusion is also well conveyed by the recent book of W. Hildenbrand about the properties of aggregate demand functions[3].

---

[2]A Lewbel, "The rank of demand systems : theory and non parametric estimation", *Econometrica*, May 1991.

[3]W. Hildenbrand, *Market Demand*, Princeton University Press, 1994.

1.4 About Specification and Calibration of a "Representative" Behaviour

1. With respect to the framework just exposed, most of the current practice in macroeconomic modelling is objectionable in principle, but may often happen to be nevertheless reliable in practice. Such is the paradox I should like to now discuss, so as to put in their proper perspective the recommendations I just made about the use of microeconomic data. I shall focus in succession on the two main phases of macroeconomic theory building: the specification of the models, the quantification of the parameters contained in the models. In both cases I shall begin with objections and then move on to somewhat mitigate them.

It is hardly a caricature to say that a powerful movement in academic circles has been promoting the following approach to macroeconomics: (i) specify the dynamic model of a rational "representative individual" who would alone decide the intertemporal allocation of resources, under physical constraints and abiding by simple rules supposed to represent the working of the market economy ; (ii) "calibrate" the parameters that are still undetermined in the model and, for so doing, draw from the stock of available econometric estimates ; (iii) solve the calibrated model in order to find evolutions it generates for the variables it contains under alternative circumstances labelled "shocks," characterize the common features of these evolutions; (iv) check that these features well portray "stylized facts" found in aggregate statistical time series.

Such a practice is, of course, very objectionable on two main counts : the theoretical specification and the appeal to empirical evidence. It is an extreme case of objectionable practices, but one that is revealing of more widespread habits in the profession. Exhibiting the objections is therefore a way to allude to much more common difficulties. Among the many theoretical objections to be raised against some of the models most popularized by the movement, attention must here concern the role given to the representative individual. Among the objections against the way in which empirical evidence is called in, calibration will be considered here because it often draws from microeconomic data.

2. The role played by the representative individual, as described above in step (i), is sometimes claimed to be justified by the hypothesis that there are many individuals, but all alike. However, the statement of an hypothesis that is so obviously in contradiction with the observed microeconomic heterogeneity cannot be a serious justification.

Speaking of identical individuals is also hiding what has all chances to be a still more serious fault of the specification. There are in fact several kinds of agents ; at least two have to be recognized in any macroeconomic model that does not limit its scope to long-run trends only: households and enterprises. In the short and medium run, we cannot neglect the autonomy of enterprises, which have their own functions and are subject to their own constraints ; this is why they are reacting somewhat differently from individuals, who act as consumers, workers and wealth owners. The point is so clear that it should be distinguished and taken for granted; methodological discussions about the presence of representative agents should rather concentrate on models with at least a representative household and a representative firm[4]. The following discussion will concern such a set-up, with no further reminder; it will thus have to face only the problems raised by heterogeneity as usually perceived. Even so circumscribed the problems may seem to be quite challenging.

Anyone studying the main body of the literature on aggregation can only find it worrisome and distressing. Most results are negative; it is just in exceptional cases that we can find affirmative answers to such questions as: do individual demand functions aggregate into market demand functions having similar properties?[5] Do microeconomic production functions aggregate into similar macroeconomic production functions ?[6]

The negative results are so pervasive that they apply whatever the levels of disaggregation that macroeconomists can consider to apply. This remark is of course not an argument against disaggregation, which is in some cases imposed by the question at issue, and which is more generally likely to reduce the impact of aggregation pitfalls (at the often important cost, however of a more cumbersome modellization). But distinguishing several social classes or several industries does not remove the effects of heterogeneity within the classes or industries.

3. What conclusion ought to be drawn from such difficulties? Is it simply to say that "anything can happen" at the macroeconomic level? Certainly not. We must, of course, respect the decision of a young economist who, realizing the difficulty of clear-cut answers in macroeconomics, decides to specialize in

---

[4]In any case, the use of the representative agent fiction raises different problems from those introduced by the confusion between households and firms. We blur the issues if we do not distinguish the two kinds of problems. This is one of the reasons why I do not fully endorse the position expressed by A. Kirman in "Whom or what does the representative individual represent ?", *Journal of Economic Perspectives*, Spring 1992, p. 117-136.

[5]The conclusions to be derived from the literature on this question are presented in A. Kirman, op.cit.

[6]For a discussion of answers to this broad question see for instance E. Malinvaud, op.cit.

another field. But the whole profession of economists cannot think and do the same: macroeconomic phenomena affect too much the life of people around us; economic history and analysis of business trends should suffice to persuade us that those phenomena are not purely random and that a good part of them can be explained. Moreover, as was reminded in section 1, progress of knowledge in macroeconomics would be very slow if we should never use for it what we know about microeconomic realities. Thus, there is no alternative but to face the aggregation problem.

In practice the situation is much less hopeless than would seem to be implied by the aggregation literature referred to above. Think of any example, such as what we know about the effects of changes in real wage rates on the aggregate supply of, and demand for, labour. This knowledge is not so precise, but mainly because of an imprecise estimation of effects on individual supplies and demands in the labour market ; uncertainty about aggregation effects does not seem to be relatively so troublesome.

At the present state of evaluation of the practical importance of the problem, we may be fairly sure that aggregation will overturn or destroy only few, if any, of the insights coming from the two sources discussed in this paper : (i) the theoretical analysis of a representative household supplying labour and a representative firm demanding labour, (ii) the econometric analysis of microeconomic data. The problem is more modestly that we are uncertain about the biases resulting from direct transpositions to the macro-level.

The framework presented in section 2 explains why those biases are likely to be small in many cases[7]. Firstly, individual behaviours will often be fairly well represented by functions with a "basis" involving only few factors, the most important ones of which having averages $\overline{\varphi}_j$ closely correlated with corresponding macro-variables (for example with individual labour demand, a mean factor $\overline{\varphi}_j$ will be correlated with the aggregate demand for goods

---

[7]In many cases, but not always. For instance a serious examination of the aggregation of production functions suggests that the common elasticity of substitution of the most appropriate macroeconomic function has little chance to be well estimated by an average of the corresponding elasticities of the microeconomic functions. Indeed, the aggregate production function is meant to serve in the representation of constraints linking quantity and price changes (inputs, ouput, real wage and interest rates) as a consequence of technical constraints, the behaviour of firms and the market conditions in which they operate. Aggregation is more complex in this case than in the framework of section 2. See in particular E. Malinvaud, *Macroeconomic Theory : A Textbook on Macroeconomic Knowledge and Analysis*, Elsevier, Amsterdam, 1998 ; chapter 4, part 6.

addressed to firms). Secondly, "structural stability" will often be such that other mean factors $\overline{\varphi}_k$, such as those concerning second and higher order moments of the statistical distributions, will change little in the applications of the aggregate analysis: the aggregation biases will then be small, for the same reason explaining why only small biases are entailed in regressions by omitted variables that little vary.

The route to follow in order to reduce uncertainty about possible aggregation biases is also well indicated by the framework of section 2. On each type of behaviour or constraint, we need (i) a proper microeconomic representation, (ii) a good characterization of the nature and extent of heterogeneity, (iii) a good knowledge of the factors leading to changes in the statistical distributions representing this heterogeneity. If and when we know all that, deducting assessments about the biases should be rather easy.

4. When calibrating the values of parameters of their models, macroeconomists claim to use all available information about these values. Since the relevant empirical evidence contains an increasing proportion of estimates coming from econometric fits using microeconomic data, such data also receive an increasing weight in what macroeconomists say.

But the practice of calibration is dangerous and objectionable because it lacks standards of rigour ; it is so exposed to subjectivity or even to the temptation of selecting values that are systematically favourable to a particular thesis (I happened to read sentences written in an authoritative tone and asserting, for some elasticities, values which were supporting a point, but were also quite different from what I inferred from econometric sources). Unavoidably econometricians are worried when they see that this practice is spreading ; they perceive it as a regression in the accepted norms of economic research.

There would be no more to say if econometricians had an alternative practicable and better procedure to offer to macroeconomists. Econometric teaching concerns the treatment of a new data set. But in most cases the macroeconomist does not see why he or she should bring in the argument, or use in the application, results from new data whereas so many data have already been treated for similar purposes. Focusing on a new econometric fit might even amount to unduly disparage the information contained in the stock of pre-existing econometric results[8]. In the real context of macroeconomic research,

---

[8]Some of my Bayesian friends will probably frown when reading this paragraph. Bayesian econometricians indeed teach how treatment of a new data set should aim at tranforming a prior uncertain knowledge into a posterior uncertain knowledge. Good for understanding the

imposing everywhere econometric estimations abiding by the rules taught in econometric lectures would be a worse course of action than accepting a part for calibration.

But a discipline must be defined and implemented, even simply by ethical norms. The discipline ought to give a central part to surveys on the results of econometric studies. Authors of surveys, rather than macroeconomists involved in specific projects, ought to provide the values to be used in calibrations ; the macroeconomists ought then to give precise references to those surveys or at least to explain why they do not do so, and then indicate the sources they are drawing from.

Because they have enough room, authors of surveys can properly deal with a difficulty frequently occurring when an econometric result is used beyond the case considered by the producer of this result. The estimates provided by the econometrician in question convey a relevant information content of the data set used, but relevant with respect to a particular model, and this model has little chance to exactly coincide with that to be calibrated. For instance the macroeconomist needs a value for a particular elasticity; a survey reviews the estimates found for similarly denominated elasticities; but these elasticities do not all concern exactly the concept to which the macroeconomist really refers; perhaps none of them exactly does ; indeed practically any elasticity involves a partial derivative and is not defined unless are also defined all variables appearing in the function that the partial derivative concerns. Now, the exact values of the various, but similarly denominated, elasticities may not be very different. The survey has to discuss whether such is the case, so as to suggest within which family of models the quoted results might serve for calibration.

Authors of surveys, who now have at their disposal a lot of estimates obtained from microeconomic data and who will be read by macroeconomists searching for numerical values to insert in their models, should nowadays also try and discuss the aggregation biases that might concern such uses. This is, of course, more easily said than done. But it is so important for the progress of our macroeconomic understanding! I believe that the framework exposed in the second section of this article might help to clarify issues.

But even if authors of surveys in applied econometrics tackle the task I am here assigning to them, macroeconomists also ought to pay serious attention to the aggregation problem that can otherwise undermine or restrict the relevance

---

underlying methodology, this teaching unfortunately does not lead to a practicable procedure, especially when account is taken of a feature to be reminded in a moment.

of their models. Indeed, as I mentioned but perhaps too quickly, the framework of section 2, fairly often adapted to the aggregation of behavioural laws, does not cover all forms of complexities that can affect transpositions from a microeconomic to a macroeconomic model.

Considering more fully those issues here would unfortunately lead us away from our present topic for long: the use of microeconomic data.

Chapter 2

TWO ASPECTS OF THE METHODOLOGY OF MODELING DETERMINISTIC PROCESSES AND EVALUATION

Clive W.J. Granger[1]

Department of Economics, University of California, San Diego, La Jolla,
CA 92093-0508, USA

2.1   Introduction

A continuing interest of Camilo Dagum has been with the methodology of economics and of econometric modeling as seen in Dagum (1968), (1985) and (1989). Since the appearance of that work two areas of possible importance that have been developed concern the re-emergence of deterministic processes and relationships and the new, growing emphasis on the evaluation of theories and models. In this essay I will discuss these topics and their inter-action. It builds on the work by Camilo but I will not attempt to discuss it, as mainly I would be taken too far from my theme, although into interesting and important topics concerning methodology.

The basic paradigm of scientific research is that one starts with a well constructed theory, internally consistent, that suggests a specification for an empirical model. The econometrician takes this specification, which will involve some unknown coefficients, and estimates these coefficients from a relevant data set by a respected estimation procedure, and so the completed empirical model is achieved. This model is then interpreted, possibly in terms of the original theory, by asking if certain coefficients are significantly different from zero and "of the correct sign." The econometricians role here is the traditional one, as exemplified by the quotations "Econometrics is concerned with the estimation of relationships suggested by economic theory" (opening sentence of Harvey (1990)) and "econometrics basic task is to put empirical

---
[1]Witten under NSF Grant SBR-9708615

flesh and blood on theoretical structures" (Johnson (1984)). Although these statements certainly represent views once widely held they do not capture the opinion of most currently active econometricians. The basic paradigm has too many practical difficulties. For example:

(i) Many theories are too simplistic and do not fit the properties of actual data such as seasonality, trends, unit root or long-memory properties, and various other aspects of the actual dynamics and structural breaks. The distance between the specification given by the theory and the actual data is too great for the model to be fitted in a plausible fashion. The basic specification has to be changed to fit the data but may then not be in accord with the theory. If the differences were subtle, the specification based on the theory can be easily nested or embedded in a realistic specification. However, this is much more difficult if the differences are large, if the theory calls for a stationary (short-memory) process but the data appears to be integrated (long-memory), for example. The case discussed in Section 2 has theory giving a deterministic process but reality is stochastic. In a few special cases, it is possible to nest, if the theory calls for a certain type of equilibrium (as in the form of cointegration) then it can be (in fact, will be) embedded in a stationary, stochastic vector autoregressive model of a particular form known as an error-correction model.

(ii) The basic paradigm does not include a procedure for evaluating the quality of the embedded empirical model. The question of evaluation is discussed in Section 3.

(iii) If there are several competing models, the paradigm does not help one decide if one model is superior to the others on some acceptable metric. For example, if a model is designed to explain a given set of "stylized facts" then it may not be unique, in which case one needs some way to decide which is the best based on a criterion not using these "facts."

Partly because of these difficulties, econometricians now often find themselves involved in "specification searches," usually starting with a model suggested by one of the available theories, but not always so. As the information in the data gets used up in the process of comparing specifications and estimating models, it may be inappropriate to use the same data to evaluate a model or to compare competing models. Thus "out-of-sample" and cross-validation techniques have been devised. The question of evaluation is considered further in Section 3.

2.2 Singularities and Deterministic Processes

The so-called soft-sciences, such as economics, have often looked for guidance to the hard-sciences, such as physics and chemistry, for advice about sound methodology. However the primary objects with which they deal are quite different, from the raw, unyielding atoms of the physical world to the decision making, free-thinking individuals populating the social sciences, and so basic differences exist. The old debate of "is Economics a science?" outlined in Blaug (1992) holds little interest today.

The hard scientists have developed various strategies and attitudes that are not found in the soft sciences, and vice-versa. One example is the idea that relationships should fit exactly, if it were not for a small error described as "measurement error," due to poor experimental design or quality of equipment. Thus, for a linear relationship

$$Y_t = \underline{\beta}' \underline{X}_t + e_t \tag{2.1}$$

the belief is that if enough *observable* X variables are added to the regression, the variance of the residual can be made very small, giving an R^2 value of, perhaps, 0.99. The relationship will usually be thought of as an instantaneous, or structural one. Economists would no longer expect such a good fit for their models, particularly if the dependent variable is a growth rate, as they expect there to be many important but *unobservable* explanatory variables that comprise Y_t. If X_t is replaced by its expectation based on a prior information set, the resulting reduced form can be used for forecasting and the new equation will not fit anywhere near as well. The new errors will be larger because of the information loss, so the equation becomes

$$Y_t = \underline{\beta}' E[X_t | I_{t-1}] + \tilde{e}_t \tag{2.2}$$

Thus, the near singularity of (2.1) does not necessarily lead to perfect forecastability unless each explanatory variable can be perfectly forecast.

If (2.1) fitted without error it would represent a singularity within the joint distribution of the group of random variables (Y_t, X_t). There are some examples, in theory, of such singularities, particularly identities, but they do not play a major role in modern dynamic econometrics. The same cannot be said for near singularities, where a group of I(1) variables, with large and growing variances, have a linear combination that has a relatively small and a stable variable, in I(0) variable, which is the case when cointegration occurs. Although originally cointegration was thought to be a surprising event, unlikely to be found with much frequency, it appears to be "found" remarkably often.

A consequence of the reduced form, or VAR model (2.2), is that the effect, if certain shocks on the variable can be discussed, such as "supply shocks", "output shocks", "consumption shocks" and "technology shocks", with the help of an impulse response formulation. If a non-linear model is used one can further ask if negative and positive shocks have the same effects or large and small shocks. The discussion of this type of "shocking economics" has become a widespread pre-occupation, although its benefits have not been evaluated very carefully. No similar discussion, I believe, will be found in the physical sciences as their attitude to residuals, rather than unexpected shocks, is very different.

2.3   Chaos

The possibility that processes can be forecast perfectly, at least in the short-run, is viewed as being plausible in some hard sciences but would not be taken seriously by most econometricians, however short the forecasting interval and especially for variables measured with high frequency. The advent of the class of processes known as "chaotic" has produced series with interesting, in fact highly complicated, properties whilst being generated by a deterministic mechanism, so that if this mechanism is known, perfect forecatability is a consequence. A simple, and familiar example, is

$$X_{t+1} = \alpha X_t (1 - X_t) \tag{2.3}$$

For values of   between 0.38 and 4 and a starting value in (0,1) the sequence generated by this "map", of X_t onto X_{t+1} the series has the appearance of a stochastic series, with continual changes in direction. Further, if $\alpha = 4$, X_t has the properties of a white noise series, with mean ½, have estimated autocorrelations all very near zero and thus a flat spectrum. Such a process will be called "white chaos." It is important to note that even though a white chaos has the linear properties of an iid process it does not contain all the properties, as $g(X_t)$ will not necessarily be white chaos. For examples, whereas $g(\varepsilon_t)$ is iid if ε_t is iid, it has been found that if X_t is generated by (3.1) with $\alpha = 4$, X_t is white chaos but X_t^2 has a first-order autocorrelation significantly different from zero. Surveys of chaos and their uses in economics are provided by Brock, Hsiao, and LeBarron (1991) and Day and Chen (1993).

Chaos produces deep and sophisticated mathematics with some charming theorems and some of the most compelling multi-dimensional diagrams from anywhere in mathematics. The belief in perfectly fitting relationships plus the attraction of the technical aspects of the theory has resulted in a wide-spread use of chaos models in the hard-sciences, where a "non-linear model" has become virtually equated with chaos. The availability of a wide range of non-linear stochastic models, which embed chaos models, is largely ignored, possibly because of the belief in the deterministic fit of relationships. An equation such as (3.1), with $\alpha = 4$, gives the forecast of X_{t+1}

$$f_{t,1} = 4X_t(1 - X_t) \tag{2.4}$$

and the forecast error will be zero. However, if one repeats this process several times to get h-step forecasts eventually $f_{t,h}$ will have to be approximated due to rounding-off on the computer, and as h becomes large, these errors blow up at an exponential rate for an interval and poor forecasts result. In comparison, the linear forecast, based just on the autocorrelations, will be just $f_{t,h} = 1/2$ for all h and the variance of the forecast error will be a constant, equal to the variance of X_t

The existence of white chaos led to the obvious question - how do we know if the residuals of economic relationships that have been considered to be stochastic white noise (zero autocorrelated) series are not really deterministic white chaos series? An interesting statistical test, known as the BDS test (Brock, Duchert, and Scheinkman (1987)) was constructed from chaos arguments but had as its null hypothesis that the process was iid. Although the test was designed to have power against an alternative of chaos it was also found to have power against various other alternatives, such as stochastic non-linearity (White et.al. (1993)), heteroskedasticity and autocorrelations. Other tests, such as those based on the Lyapunov exponent assume the process is deterministic and then ask if it is chaos or not, and may require the process to be bounded. Overall, I think that it is fair to say that no convincing evidence of economic variables being chaotic has been discovered. There are two mitigating reasons for this. The tests proposed in physics require very large data sets and for economics these are, so far, mostly found in finance. It seems that the least likely place to find deterministic behavior is on a speculative market driven by many thousands of independent decision makers maximizing utility or wealth using heterogeneous information sets. Secondly, if an economic variable consisted of a chaotic component plus a substantial stochastic element, where the "variances" of the two components were comparable in size, it is very difficult to observe or find the chaotic part.

If data were generated from (3.1), or any one of several other possible simple chaos producing maps, then experience suggests that if, say, 400 terms were available a technique such as artificial neural network modeling will produce a very close approximation to the true map, and this will result in one-step forecasts with very small errors. The quality of the multi-step forecasts will degrade quickly compared to the case where the map is known exactly. Of course if the data is observed with an added stochastic noise, the neural net will have difficulty in estimating a good approximation to the map.

Economic theorists have asked the question - can one take fairly standard models and find cases where these models produce chaos. It has been found quite possible for models to give chaos, although not necessarily white chaos. A number of examples are given in Benhabib (1992). A critical review of this book appears in Granger (1994). The book consists of 21 chapters by distinguished contributors and the editor concludes that "cycles and chaos are perfectly compatible with a wide variety of standard equilibrium models." Of course, to get to a chaos model, which is deterministic, one has to start with a deterministic economic theory. It is a long-standing tradition that economic theories are presented deterministically, with stochastic residuals later added to them almost as an after-thought when the theory is found not to exactly fit some economic data. This is a similar attitude to that taken in the exact sciences, where relationships hold exactly part from measurement error. Although it is found that standard theory models could produce chaos, there is little evidence that they actually do so. In a chapter in Benhabib (1992), Brock and Sayers discuss statistical evidence and conclude "The search for evidence of low dimensional chaos in business cycle data has provided evidence in favor of non-linearity in employment, unemployment, industrial production, and pig iron production. Little evidence of low dimension chaos was found ..." Three other chapters find evidence of non-linearity in economic data but little or none for chaos, particularly white chaos.

The continual use of deterministic models by economic theorists creates a substantial problem for econometricians who want to use them to specify empirical models and thus to evaluate the work of the theorists. If economic data is actually stochastic it is unclear how one can evaluate a deterministic model other than just rejecting it. Embedding a deterministic component within a stochastic framework is inherently difficult. The best understood case is where a deterministic equilibrium relationship is embedded within a stochastic dynamic environment, but special tests are required. However this case does not include chaos, which cannot represent an equilibrium as it is inherently a dynamic relationship.

Naturally, anyone can perform virtually any research they want to, but my belief is that economics as a profession would benefit if theorists concentrated on producing more realistic models, which here means truly stochastic relationships between random variables, represented by a joint probability distribution, rather than deterministic relationships.

2.4 Evaluation

The use of evaluation varies considerably across a modern society. Some books, films and music are criticized in newspapers and specialty journals, doctors and dentists evaluate patients, engineers evaluate bridges and teachers evaluate students. On the other hand there is little evaluation, at least in public, of newspaper critics, doctors, lawyers, judges, or bridge engineers. In economics, evaluation plays a central role in basic theory, as consumers are assumed to compare alternative bundles of goods in terms of utility and companies compare alternative investments in terms of potential profitability. The survival of the fittest in a competitive market place is an extreme form of evaluation. However the sales of a product is not an unambiguous measure of quality, even after allowing for price differences between brands. An example is provided by the most popular films, as measured by box-office sales, "ET" and the "Star Wars" trilogy, which did not win Oscars.

In the competition for space on supermarket shelves evaluations of a product are undertaken by the original producer, the store buyer, and by the eventual consumer. Although in practice all three evaluations will have impact on sales of the product, the economist will prefer to emphasize the desires of the consumer. Similarly, university students are now asked to evaluate their teachers whereas a more suitable group of evaluators of the teachers would be those who eventually employ the students!

Most of the criteria available for evaluating econometric models, or provided by econometricians for evaluating empirical models, are derived from statistics, such as R^2 or likelihood values or possibly values of model selection criteria such as AIC or BIC. Of course, these are not absolute values but they can be used to compare alternative specifications or empirical models. However, a number of economists have argued that an economic measure should be used to evaluate economic products. Of course, these measures have to be observable, so that "utility" is not acceptable, but an unobserved, positive multiplicative constant does not matter, so that a cost function of the form ae^2
where e is an error, can be used for any positive a, as the same ranking of procedures is obtained regardless of a.

Two parts of economics have paid particular attention to evaluation, finance and forecasting. Both have developed economic measures and sophisticated testing procedures. Finance considers returns from a portfolio, after consideration of risk and transactions costs.

Forecasts are evaluated by sequences of the following form. For a variable and horizon of interest X_{n+h}, make, at time n, a point forecast $f_{n,h}$ which results in an error $e_{n,h}$. Assume that the forecasts are used by a decision maker and that a sub-optimal forecast leads to costs, which take the form $C(e)$ for error e. (A more complicated form of cost function can be used but will not be considered here.) $C(e)$ will have the properties that $C(0) = 0$, and increases away from zero. The forecasts $f_{n,h}$ will be derived from a model whose coefficients are estimated to minimize the expected value of $C(e)$ in sample. Out of sample a pair of specifications or models can be compared by statistics based on C (errors) where the errors occur post-sample. A variety of results about the properties of certain functions of these errors have been reviewed in Granger (1999) and Christoffersen and Diebold (1996) and statistical tests can be derived from them.

Some other parts of economics could also be evaluated by considering the outcomes of a model in terms of their effects on a decision maker who bases a decision on the outcome but this is rarely done. The evaluation will often depend on the objective of the model, assuming that this is specifically stated. A particularly difficult class of models to evaluate are those claiming to be useful for policy determination. A discussion can be found in Banerjee and Hendry (1997).

The evaluation sequence, forecast $\rightarrow$ error $\rightarrow$ cost to decision maker $\rightarrow$ statistical test completely breaks down for deterministic theories and models if the optimum forecast is used, rather than an approximating linear forecast. There will be virtually no error, thus no cost and thus no test and there will be no thought of an alternative specification or competing model. Development in economics would die. Of course, in practice, the model does not fit exactly. There is an error but how big this error has to be to reject the idea of a "deterministic law for variables measured with errors" rather than inherently stochastic variables is completely unclear.

2.5 Conclusions

It is my personal belief that chaos models will prove to be a fad in economics and will soon vanish just as catastrophe theory and many parts of control theory taken from engineering have already passed through. On the other hand I also believe the economic and, particularly econometric, methodology will not be complete until strong emphasis is given to evaluation of all models, using economic rather than simple statistical measures as the criteria. This is not going to be an easy task but by requiring modelers to state the purpose of the model and how it should be evaluated, the quality of models will certainly improve. I would hope that the same requirements will hold for economic theorists, and I believe that this will make theorists more interested in developing the bridges between their theories and the actual data available from the economy, so that the theories can be correctly tested and compared to alternatives.

REFERENCES

[1]   Banerjee, A. and D.F. Hendry (1997) ed.: *The Econometrics of Economic Policy*. Blackwell, Oxford.

[2]   Benhabib, J. (1992): *Cycles and Chaos in Economic Equilibrium*. Princeton University Press.

[3]   Brock, W.A., W.D. Dechart, and J. Scheinkman (1987): "A Test for Independence Based on the Correlation Dimension." SSRI Working Paper 8702, University of Wisconsin, Madison.

[4]   Brock, W.A., D.A. Hsieh, and B. LeBaron (1991): *Nonlinear Dynamic, Chaos and Instability*. MIT Press, Cambridge, MA.

[5]   Christoffersen, P.F. and F.X. Diebold (1996): "Further Results on Forecasting and Model Selection Under Asymmetric Loss," *Journal of Applied Econometrics* 11, 561-571.

[6]   Dagum, C. (1968): "On Methods and Purposes on Econometric Model Building." *Zeitschrift für Nationalökonomie* 28, 381-398.

[7]   Dagum, C. (1985): "Structural Stability, Structural Change and Economic Forecasting" in P. Tschopp (ed.) *Optimality at Structures*, Economica, Geneva.

[8]   Dagum, C. (1989): "Scientific Model Building: Principles, Methods and History" in H. Wold *Theoretical Empiricism*. Paragon House: New York.

[9]   Day, R.H. and P. Chen (1993): *Non-linear Dynamics and Evolutionary Economics*. Oxford University Press.

[10] Granger, C.W.J. (1994): "Is Chaotic Economic Theory Relevant For Economics? A Review Essay." *Journal of International and Comparative Economics* 3, 139-145.

[11] Granger, C.W.J. (1999): "Forecasting With Generalized Cost Functions." To appear, *Spanish Review of Economics.*

[12] Harvey, A. (1990): *The Econometric Analysis of Time Series* 2nd Edition. MIT Press, Cambridge, MA.

[13] Johnson, J. (1984): *Econometric Methods* 3rd Edition. McGraw Hill: New York.

[14] White, H., T.-H. Lee, and C.W.J. Granger (1993): "Testing for Neglected Nonlinearity in Time Series Models," *Journal of Econometrics* 56, 269-290.

Chapter 3

AN EXTENSION OF THE GAUSS-MARKOV THEOREM FOR MIXED LINEAR REGRESSION MODELS WITH NON-STATIONARY STOCHASTIC PARAMETERS[*]

Estela Bee Dagum
Statistical Sciences, University of Bologna, Via delle Belle Arti 41,
40126 Bologna, Italy

Pierre A. Cholette
Time Series Research and Analysis Centre, Statistics Canada, Ottawa,
K1A 0T6, Canada

3.1   Introduction

The presence of fixed and stochastic parameters in a mixed linear regression model has been dealt with for the case where the stochastic parameters follow a stationary process. The solution is given either by Generalized Least Squares (e.g. Rao, 1965, p. 192) or by a recursive state space estimation procedure such as the Kalman filter and smoother (e.g. Sallas and Harville 1981). The estimation of non-stationary stochastic parameters has been mainly approached in the state space framework, either as an initial condition problem (see among others, Ansley and Kohn, 1985, 1989; Kohn and Ansley, 1986; Bell and Hillmer, 1991 and De Jong, 1989, 1991); or as a hierarchical model with "fixed" effects in the hierarchy given a flat prior distribution (see Sallas and Harville, 1981, 1988; Tsimikas and Ledolter, 1994).

In this paper, we present a mixed linear model, where the parameter space consists of fixed and non-stationary stochastic parameters. We prove that the usual

[*]This paper provides a proof of the Extended Gauss-Markov theorem to show that Generalized Least Squares gives the Minimum Variance Linear Unbiased Estimator for models where the parameter space contains fixed and non-stationary stochastic parameters. This approach avoids the problem of initial conditions encountered in state space modelling as well as the need for a two-step solution, filtering and smoothing. We discuss various applications of the theorem.

non-recursive Generalized Least Square (GLS) solution of the model provides the Minimum Variance Linear Unbiased Estimator of both fixed and non-stationary stochastic parameters. This solution circumvents the problem of initial conditions and avoids the need for a two-step solution encountered in the state space approach, i.e. filtering and smoothing.

Section 2 gives the theorem and section 3 presents different cases where the theorem applies.

3.2　　　Extension of the Gauss-Markov Theorem

Let the mixed linear model consist of the following two equations:

$$y = X_1 \beta + X_2 \theta + e, \ E(e) = 0, E(e\,e') = V_e \tag{3.1a}$$

$$D \ \theta = \eta, \ E(\eta) = 0, E(\eta\,\eta') = V_\eta \tag{3.1b}$$

where β is a vector of p unknown fixed parameters and θ is a vector of T non-stationary stochastic (random) parameters. After applying an appropriate linear operator D of dimension qxT ($q \leq T$), the stochastic parameters have mean 0 and positive definite covariance matrix V_η. Typically θ is a time series, D is a regular and/or seasonal differencing operator, and V_η is the covariance matrix corresponding to an Autoregressive Moving Average (ARMA) process.

Model (1) can be written in a condensed form as

$$\begin{bmatrix} y \\ r \end{bmatrix} = \begin{bmatrix} X_1 & X_2 \\ 0 & D \end{bmatrix} \begin{bmatrix} \beta \\ \theta \end{bmatrix} + \begin{bmatrix} e \\ \eta \end{bmatrix}, \quad \begin{matrix} E(ee') = V_e \\ E(\eta\eta') = V_\eta \end{matrix}, \ E(e\eta') = 0 \tag{3.2a}$$

or

$$\tilde{y} = Z \alpha + u, \ E(u) = 0, \ E(u\,u') = V_u = \begin{bmatrix} V_e & 0 \\ 0 & V_\eta \end{bmatrix} \tag{3.2b}$$

where r in $\tilde{y}$ is 0 for the non-stationary case, but not necessarily for some variants treated as a particular case in section 3.

Theorem: The Generalized Least Square (GLS) solution of model (2),

$$\hat{\alpha} = (Z'V_u^{-1}Z)^{-1}(Z'V_u^{-1}\tilde{y}) = \begin{Bmatrix} X'_1 V_e^{-1} X_1 & X'_1 V_e^{-1} X_2 \\ X'_2 V_e^{-1} X_1 & X'_2 V_e^{-1} X_2 + D'V_\eta^{-1}D \end{Bmatrix}^{-1} \begin{Bmatrix} X'_1 V_e^{-1} y \\ X'_2 V_e^{-1} y + D'V_\eta^{-1}r \end{Bmatrix}$$

$$, \quad (3.3a)$$

$$V_{\hat{\alpha}} = (Z'V_u^{-1}Z)^{-1} = \begin{Bmatrix} X'_1 V_e^{-1} X_1 & X'_1 V_e^{-1} X_2 \\ X'_2 V_e^{-1} X_1 & X'_2 V_e^{-1} X_2 + D'V_\eta^{-1}D \end{Bmatrix}^{-1} \equiv \begin{bmatrix} V_{\hat{\beta}} & V_{\hat{\beta},\hat{\theta}} \\ V_{\hat{\theta},\hat{\beta}} & V_{\hat{\theta}} \end{bmatrix}, \quad (3.3b)$$

is the *Minimum Variance Linear Unbiased Estimator of both fixed and stochastic parameters in* α.

To prove the theorem we start from the well known result (see Whittle, 1963) that for any two random vectors α and y, the minimum variance unbiased linear estimate of α using data y is given by:

$$\hat{\alpha} = E(\alpha) + V_{\alpha,y}V_y^{-1}(y - E(y)), \quad (3.4a)$$

with covariance matrix

$$V_{\hat{\alpha}} = E(\hat{\alpha} - \alpha)(\hat{\alpha} - \alpha)' = V_\alpha \ V_{\alpha,y} V_y^{-1} V_{y,\alpha} \quad (3.4b)$$

where V_y is the covariance matrix of y and $V_{\alpha,y}$ is the covariance matrix of α and y. For stationary stochastic parameters α this result applies directly. For non-stationary parameters, however the covariance matrix V_α is not uniquely defined, which is one motivation for this theorem.

First we establish the particular form of (4) under model (1a), which can be written as

$$y = X\alpha + e, \ E(e) = 0, \ E(ee') = V_e \quad (3.5)$$

where $X = [X_1 \ X_2]$ and $\alpha = [\beta' \ \theta']$. Under a model such as (5), we have $E(y) = X E(\alpha)$, $V_y = (X V_\alpha X' + V_e)$, $V_{\alpha,y} = V_\alpha X'$. Substituting these in (4) yields:

$$\hat{\alpha} = E(\alpha) + V_\alpha X'(X V_\alpha X' + V_e)^{-1}(y - X E(\alpha)) = V_{\hat{\alpha}}V_\alpha^{-1}E(\alpha) + V_{\hat{\alpha}}X' V_e^{-1} y, \quad (3.6a)$$

$$V_{\hat{\alpha}} = V_\alpha - V_\alpha X'(X V_\alpha X' + V_e)^{-1}X V_\alpha = (V_\alpha^{-1} + X' V_e^{-1} X)^{-1}, \quad (3.6b)$$

where we use the identity $(A + BCB')^{-1} = A^{-1} - A^{-1}B(B'A^{-1}B + C^{-1})^{-1}B'A^{-1}$ to derive (6b). Result (6a) can be easily derived backwards by showing $V_{\hat{\alpha}}V_\alpha^{-1}E(\alpha) =$

$E(\alpha)-$ $[V_\alpha X'(X V_\alpha X' + V_e)^{-1}]X E(\alpha)$ and   that $V_{\hat{a}}X' V_e^{-1} y =$
$[V_\alpha X'(X V_\alpha X' + V_e)^{-1}] y$, which in turn imply the first expression of $\hat{a}$ in (6a) :

$V_{\hat{a}}V_{\hat{a}}^{-1}E(\alpha)= (V_\alpha - V_\alpha X'(X V_\alpha X' + V_e)^{-1}X V_\alpha) V_{\hat{a}}^{-1} E(\alpha)$
$\qquad = E(\alpha) - [V_\alpha X'(X V_\alpha X' + V_e)^{-1}]X E(\alpha);$
$V_{\hat{a}} X' V_e^{-1} y = (V_\alpha - V_\alpha X'(X V_\alpha X' + V_e)^{-1}X V_\alpha) X' V_e^{-1} y$
$\qquad = \{ V_\alpha X V_e^{-1} - V_\alpha X' [(X V_\alpha X' + V_e)^{-1} (X V_\alpha X' + V_e - V_e)] V_e^{-1} \} y$
$\qquad = \{ V_\alpha X V_e^{-1} - V_\alpha X' [(X V_\alpha X' + V_e)^{-1} (X V_\alpha X + V_e)-(X V_\alpha X' + V_e)^{-1} V_e] V_e^{-1} \} y$
$\qquad = \{ V_\alpha X V_e^{-1} - V_\alpha X' [I - (X V_\alpha X' + V_e)^{-1} V_e] V_e^{-1} \} y$
$\qquad = \{ V_\alpha X V_e^{-1} - V_\alpha X' V_e^{-1} + V_\alpha X' (X V_\alpha X' + V_e)^{-1} V_e V_e^{-1} \} y = [V_\alpha X'(X V_\alpha X' + V_e)^{-1}] y.$

Next, under commonly used assumptions, we prove the following three propositions: (a) $V_{\hat{a}}$ of (6b) is equal to $(Z'V_u^{-1}Z)^{-1}$ of (3b), (b) the first term in $E(\alpha)$ of (6a) is zero and (c) the second term of (6a) can be expressed as $(Z'V_u^{-1}Z)^{-1} (Z'V_u^{-1} \tilde{y})$ of (3a). This will complete the proof.

$$\text{Let us define,} \quad \zeta = \begin{bmatrix} \beta \\ \theta_0 \\ \eta \end{bmatrix} = \begin{bmatrix} I_p & 0 & 0 \\ 0 & I_d & 0 \\ 0 & D_1 & D_2 \end{bmatrix} \begin{bmatrix} \beta \\ \theta_0 \\ \theta^* \end{bmatrix} = K \begin{bmatrix} \beta \\ \theta \end{bmatrix} = K\alpha , \qquad (3.7)$$

where θ_0 contains the $d = T - q$ initial conditions of θ, where θ^* contains the last q values of θ, and where D_1 and D_2 are respectively the first d and the last q columns of D (of (1b)).

Because the stochastic parameters are non-stationary, the variance is not uniquely defined; the common treatment in the literature is to assume diffuse and orthogonal initial conditions (see e.g. Ansley and Kohn 1985). We assume diffuse and orthogonal priors for β and θ_0 as follows:

$$E(\begin{bmatrix} \beta \\ \theta_0 \end{bmatrix}[\beta' \ \theta'_0]) = h \ I_{p+d} , \ h \rightarrow \infty ; \ E(\beta \ \eta')=0, E(\theta_0 \ \eta')=0 . \qquad (3.8)$$

For a given value $h > 0$, the covariance matrix of ζ is given by $V_\zeta(h)=block(h I_{p+d}, V_\eta) = K V_\alpha(h) K'$. The identity $(ABC)^{-1} = C^{-1}B^{-1}A^{-1}$ implies $V_\zeta^{-1}(h)= (K V_\alpha(h) K')^{-1}= (K')^{-1} V_\alpha^{-1}(h) K^{-1}$. Pre- and post-multiplying the latter expression of $V_\zeta^{-1}(h)$ by K' and K, and substitution of K defined in (7) yields:

$$V_{\bar{\alpha}}^{-1}(h) = K' \, V_{\zeta}^{-1}(h) \, K \; = block \, (\, h^{-1} \, I_{p+d} \, , \, 0_N \,) + block \, (\, 0_p \, , \, D' \, V_{\eta}^{-1} D \,). \tag{3.9}$$

Replacing $V_{\bar{\alpha}}^{-1}$ by $V_{\bar{\alpha}}^{-1}(h)$ and X by $[X_1 X_2]$ in the last expression, $(V_{\bar{\alpha}}^{-1} + X' \, V_e^{-1} \, X \,)^{-1}$, of (6b), and a few re-arrangements yield

$$V_{\hat{a}}(h) \;=\; \left\{ \begin{bmatrix} X'_1 \, V_e^{-1} X_1 & X'_1 \, V_e^{-1} X_2 \\ X'_2 \, V_e^{-1} X_1 & X'_2 \, V_e^{-1} X_2 + D' V_{\eta}^{-1} D \end{bmatrix} + \begin{bmatrix} h^{-1} I_{p+d} & 0 \\ 0 & 0 \end{bmatrix} \right\}^{-1}, \tag{3.10}$$

which after letting $h \to \infty$ becomes identical to $V_{\hat{a}} = (Z' V_u^{-1} Z \,)^{-1}$ of (3b). This proves proposition (a).

Replacing $V_{\bar{\alpha}}^{-1}$ by $V_{\bar{\alpha}}^{-1}(h)$, the first term, $V_{\hat{a}} V_{\bar{\alpha}}^{-1} E(\alpha)$, of (2.6a) can be written as

$$V_{\hat{a}} K \; V_{\zeta}^{-1}(h) \, K' \begin{bmatrix} E(\beta) \\ E(\theta) \end{bmatrix} = \; V_{\hat{a}} K \begin{bmatrix} h^{-1} I_{p+d} & 0 \\ 0 & V_{\eta}^{-1} \end{bmatrix} \begin{bmatrix} E(\beta) \\ E(\theta_0) \\ E(\eta) \end{bmatrix}, \tag{3.11}$$

which converges to zero, because $h^{-1} \to 0$ and $E(\eta) = 0$. This proves proposition (b) and also shows that the generalized least square solution does not have the problem of the initial conditions.

The last term $V_{\hat{a}} X' \, V_e^{-1} \, y$ of (6a) is equal to (3a) because $V_{\hat{a}} = (Z' V_u^{-1} Z \,)^{-1}$ as demonstrated by (2.10) and $X' \, V_e^{-1} \, y$ is equal to $Z' \, V_u^{-1} \, \tilde{y}$ for $r = 0$:

$$X' \, V_e^{-1} \, y \;=\; \begin{bmatrix} X'_1 V_e^{-1} y \\ X'_2 V_e^{-1} y \end{bmatrix} \;=\; Z' \, V_u^{-1} \, \tilde{y} \;=\; \begin{bmatrix} X'_1 V_e^{-1} y \\ X'_2 V_e^{-1} y + D' V_{\eta}^{-1} 0 \end{bmatrix}, \tag{3.12}$$

which proves proposition (c) and completes the proof.

Solution (3) can be applied as such but depending on the size of the matrices involved, it may be appropriate to invert matrix $(Z' V_u^{-1} Z)$ by parts, under *any* convenient partitioning. Matrix $V_{\hat{a}} = (Z' V_u^{-1} Z \,)^{-1}$ is then repartitioned according to (3b), i.e. with parts $V_{\hat{\beta}}$, $V_{\hat{\beta},\hat{\theta}}$, $V_{\hat{\theta},\hat{\beta}} = V_{\hat{\beta}',\hat{\theta}}$ and $V_{\hat{\theta}}$. A generic expression for (3) is then:

$$\hat{\beta} \;=\; (V_{\hat{\beta}} \, X'_1 + V_{\hat{\beta},\hat{\theta}} \, X'_2 \,) \, V_e^{-1} \, y + V_{\hat{\beta},\hat{\theta}} \, D' \, V_{\eta}^{-1} \, r, \tag{3.13a}$$

$$\hat{\theta} = (V_{\hat{\theta},\hat{\beta}} X'_1 + V_{\hat{\theta}} X'_2) V_e^{-1} y + V_{\hat{\theta}} D' V_\eta^{-1} r. \tag{3.13b}$$

where r is 0 in the non-stationary cases. The usual corollary to the Gauss-Markov theorem holds: the Minimum Variance Linear Unbiased Predictor of any linear combination of the parameters, $w = W \alpha$, is given by:

$$\hat{w} = W \hat{\alpha} = [W_1 W_2] \hat{\alpha} = W_1 \hat{\beta} + W_2 \hat{\theta} \tag{3.13c}$$

$$V_{\hat{w}} = W V_{\hat{\alpha}} W' = W_1 V_{\hat{\beta}} W'_1 + W_2 V_{\hat{\theta},\hat{\beta}} W'_1 + W_1 V_{\hat{\beta},\hat{\theta}} W'_2 + W_2 V_{\hat{\theta}} W'_2 \tag{3.13d}$$

However, when V_e is not of full rank, the above formulae containing its inverse are no longer valid. This problem can be solved by applying the same derivation but where V_e is replaced by $V_e + \delta I$ ($\delta > 0$). Then, $\hat{\alpha}$ and $V_{\hat{\alpha}}$ in (6) can be interpreted as the limits to which the resulting equations converge when $\delta > 0$. Note that the first expression of $V_{\hat{\alpha}}$ in (6b) and $\hat{\alpha} = V_\alpha X'(X V_\alpha X' + V_e)^{-1} y$ from (6a) (the terms in $E(\alpha)$ cancel out) remain valid for $\delta = 0$.

3.3 Applications of the Extended Gauss-Markov Theorem

Mixed linear models are often encountered in time series analysis to deal with various problems, such as, signal extraction, constrained forecasting, interpolation, extrapolation and benchmarking. This section discusses some of these applications.

3.3.1 Signal extraction

In the context of time series data, signal extraction refers *broadly* to the estimation of the "signal" from the data, the signal being the target variable of interest. In a *strict sense*, signal extraction assumes an explicit model for the signal. Two common types of models are: simple regression models to capture deterministic components like trend and trading-day variations; and autoregressive integrated moving average (ARIMA) models (Box and Jenkins, 1970). Under both the wide and strict definitions of signal extraction, the signal is at least partly concealed by noise and some nuisance fluctuations need to be removed.

For signal extraction, model (2a) can be as follows:

$$\begin{bmatrix} y \\ 0 \end{bmatrix} = \begin{bmatrix} R & I_T \\ 0 & D \end{bmatrix} \begin{bmatrix} \beta \\ \theta \end{bmatrix} + \begin{bmatrix} e \\ -\eta \end{bmatrix}, \quad \begin{matrix} E(ee')=V_e \\ E(\eta\eta')=V_\eta \end{matrix}, \quad E(e\eta')=0, \tag{3.14}$$

where vector y of dimension $Tx1$ contains a monthly (say) time series w observed with error and to be estimated, i.e. $y = w + e$. The underlying time series signal w consists of a deterministic part $R\beta$ and a non-stationary stochastic part θ. The deterministic part $R\beta$ can be trading-day variations or some other intervention effect, where R of dimension Txp contains the appropriate regressors. The non-stationary stochastic part θ of dimension $Tx1$ follows an ARIMA model. For example, matrix D is the product of the first regular and seasonal difference operators of dimension $(T-13)xT$, $r=0$ and matrix V_η is such that η follows an ARMA model (i.e. θ follows the corresponding ARIMA model).

The estimates can be obtained from (13) with the appropriate substitutions. The following analytical solution given by Dagum, Cholette and Chen (1998) can also be used:

$$\hat{\beta} = (R'D' V^{-1} DR)^{-1} R' D' V^{-1} [0 - D y], \quad V_{\hat{\beta}} = (R'D' V^{-1} DR)^{-1},$$

$$\hat{\theta} = y^* + V_e D' V^{-1} [0 - D y^*], \quad V_{\hat{\theta}} = V_{\hat{\theta}_0} + H V_{\hat{\beta}} H',$$

$$\hat{w} = R \hat{\beta} + \hat{\theta}, \quad V_{\hat{w}} = V_{\hat{\theta}_0} + (R - H) V_{\hat{\beta}} (R - H)',$$

where $y^* = y - R\hat{\beta}$, $H = R - V_e D' V^{-1} DR$, $V_{\hat{\theta}_0} = V_e - V_e D' V^{-1} DV_e$, $V = DV_e D' + V_\eta$. This analytical solution requires only V to be invertible instead of V_e and V_η as in (13).

3.3.2 ARIMA interpolation and extrapolation with intervention

Problems often encountered in time series analysis are those of interpolation and extrapolation. Interpolation refers to producing estimates for *missing* observations *within* the sample period; and extrapolation, *outside* the sample period. Both can be viewed as a form of signal extraction, where the signal is the "true" series for these periods.

For ARIMA interpolation and extrapolation with intervention effects, model (2a) takes the form:

$$\begin{bmatrix} y \\ 0 \end{bmatrix} = \begin{bmatrix} J R & J \\ 0 & D \end{bmatrix} \begin{bmatrix} \beta \\ \theta \end{bmatrix} + \begin{bmatrix} e \\ -\eta \end{bmatrix}, \quad \begin{matrix} E(ee') = V_e \\ E(\eta\eta') = V_\eta \end{matrix}, \quad E(e\eta') = 0 \tag{3.15}$$

where vector y of dimension $Nx1$ is a mixture of monthly, quarterly and annual values of a monthly (say) time series w observed with error and to be estimated, i.e. $y = Jw + e$, where J is a NxT matrix of 0s and 1s. For example y may contain "irregularly spaced" data on the time series. This time series $w = R\beta + \theta$ consists of a deterministic part $R\beta$ and a non-stationary stochastic part θ, which are as in equation (14). The observations y are related to β and θ by $y = JR\beta + J\theta + e$.

The estimates of β and θ are then given by (13a) and (13b), with $X_1 = JR$ and $X_2 = J$; and the estimates of the times series w are given by (13c) and (13d) with $W_1 = R$ and $W_2 = I_T$.

For the months outside the range of periods covered by any y_n ($n = 1,...,N$), the $\hat{w}_t$ s are extrapolations (forecasts) and/or backcasts; for the months embedded but not directly covered by the time periods of any y_n, the $\hat{w}_t$ s are interpolations; and for the months directly covered by the time periods of some y_n (i.e the observation is monthly), the $\hat{w}_t$ s are fitted values. (The specification of which months are covered is governed by the placement of the 1's in J; the periods covered can be calendar or fiscal years, quarters, etc.; more details are given by Cholette and Dagum, 1994).

Note that some of the $\hat{w}_t$ s can be viewed as constrained ARIMA forecasts (Pankratz 1989, Guerrero 1989, Trabelsi and Hillmer 1989), if some of the "observations" y_n pertain to the future, although these authors used a slightly different approach mentioned later.

The Boot, Feibes and Lisman (1967), the Cohen, Müller and Padbergh (1971) and the Stram and Wei (1986) methods to interpolate more frequent series between less frequent series easily emerge as special cases of model (15), where the deterministic part is absent. This is achieved by eliminating from (15) the first column (JR and 0) of the regressor matrix and the first row (β) of the parameter vector.

3.3.3 Interpolation and extrapolation by means of related series

Interpolations and extrapolations at higher frequency (e.g. monthly) can also be obtained by using related series available at the same higher frequency. The latter are specified as regressors for the target variable of interest which is measured at the lower frequency (e.g. annually).

For this case, model (2.2a) takes the form:

$$\begin{bmatrix} y \\ 0 \end{bmatrix} = \begin{bmatrix} JR & J \\ 0 & I_T \end{bmatrix} \begin{bmatrix} \beta \\ \theta \end{bmatrix} + \begin{bmatrix} e \\ -\eta \end{bmatrix}, \quad \begin{matrix} E(ee')=V_e \\ E(\eta\eta')=V_\eta \end{matrix}, \quad E(e\eta')=0 \tag{3.16}$$

where y contains the low frequency measurements and the remaining vectors and matrices are as in (15). If R contains the high frequency related time series deemed to behave like the target series $w = R\beta + \theta$, the Chow and Lin (1971, 1976) interpolation method is obtained. As a particular case, R may contain functions of time, so that $R\beta$ models a time trend plus trigonometric seasonality, etc.

The estimates can be obtained from (13) with the appropriate substitutions. The following analytical solution given by Dagum, Cholette and Chen (1998) can also be used:

$$\hat{\beta} = (R'J' V^{-1} JR)^{-1} R'J' V^{-1} y, \quad V_{\hat{\beta}} = (R'J' V^{-1} JR)^{-1},$$

$$\hat{\theta} = V_\eta J' V^{-1} [y - JR\hat{\beta}], \quad V_{\hat{\theta}} = V_{\hat{\theta}_0} + H V_{\hat{\beta}} H',$$

$$\hat{w} = R\hat{\beta} + \hat{\theta}, \quad V_{\hat{w}} = V_{\hat{\theta}_0} + (R-H) V_{\hat{\beta}} (R-H)',$$

where $H = V_\eta J' V^{-1} JR$, $V_{\hat{\theta}_0} = V_\eta - V_\eta J' V^{-1} J V_\eta$ and $V = J V_\eta J' + V_e$.

3.3.4 Benchmarking

Benchmarking is widely used in statistical agencies. Benchmarking situations arise whenever two (or more) sources of data are available for the same target variable, observed at different frequencies, e.g. monthly versus annually, monthly versus quarterly. Generally, the two sources of data do not agree and one source, typically the less frequent, is more reliable than the other because it originates from a census, exhaustive administrative records or a larger sample. Traditionally, benchmarking has consisted of adjusting the less reliable series to make it consistent with the more reliable observations known as *benchmarks*. However, benchmarking can be defined more broadly as the process of optimally combining two sources of measurements, in order to achieve improved estimates of the series under investigation (Cholette and Dagum, 1994).

For benchmarking, model (2a) can take the form:

$$\begin{bmatrix} y_s \\ y_a \end{bmatrix} = \begin{bmatrix} R & I_T \\ 0 & J \end{bmatrix} \begin{bmatrix} \beta \\ \theta \end{bmatrix} + \begin{bmatrix} e \\ \eta \end{bmatrix}, \quad \begin{matrix} E(ee')=V_e \\ E(\eta\eta')=V_\eta \end{matrix}, \quad E(e\eta')=0 \tag{3.17}$$

where y_s and y_a respectively stand for "sub-annual" (e.g. monthly) time series and "annual" benchmarks with relatively small error η. Vector $R\beta$ is a constant or linear bias parameter, which can be viewed as the systematic discrepancy between y_a and the corresponding sums of y_s.

The estimates can be obtained from (13) with the appropriate substitutions. The following analytical solution given by Dagum, Cholette and Chen (1998) can also be used:

$$\hat{\beta} = -(R'J'V^{-1}JR)^{-1}R'J'V^{-1}[y_a - Jy_s], \quad V_{\hat{\beta}} = (R'J'V^{-1}JR)^{-1},$$

$$\hat{\theta} = y^* + V_e J'V^{-1}[y_a - Jy^*], \quad V_{\hat{\theta}} = V_{\hat{\theta}_0} + H V_{\hat{\beta}} H',$$

where $\quad y^* = y_s - R\hat{\beta}, \quad H = R - V_e J'V^{-1}JR, \quad V_{\hat{\theta}_0} = V_e - V_e J'V^{-1}JV_e$ and $V = JV_e J' + V_\eta$.

In Pankratz (1989), Guerrero (1989) and Trabelsi and Hillmer (1989), y_s is a series of forecasts, with covariance matrix V_e, obtained from an econometric model or a time series model; and the second equation of (17), $y_a = J\theta + \eta$, is a set of constraint ("extra-model information") to be imposed on the forecasts. In the absence of bias, the formulae above reduce to $\hat{\theta} = y_s + V_e J'V^{-1}[y_a - Jy_s]$ and $V_{\hat{\theta}} = V_e - V_e J'V^{-1}JV_e$ and are those discussed by those authors.

Note that y_s could contain interpolations to be benchmarked.

Acknowledgement
We are very thankful to our colleague Zhao-Guo Chen for many valuable comments which improved the demonstration of the theorem.

REFERENCES

[1] Ansley, C.F., Kohn, R. (1985) "Estimation, Filtering, and Smoothing in State Space Models with Incompletely Specified Initial Conditions", *The Annals of Statistics*, Vol. 13, No. 4, pp. 1286-1316.

[2] Ansley, C.F. and Kohn, R. (1989), "Filtering and Smoothing in State Space Models with Partially Diffuse Initial Conditions", *Journal of Time Series Analysis*, Vol. 11 pp. 275-293.

[3] Bell, W.R. and Hillmer, S.C.(1991), "Initializing the Kalman Filter for Nonstationary Time Series Models", *Journal of Time Series Analysis*, Vol. 12, pp. 283-300.

[4] Boot, J.C.G., Feibes, W. and Lisman, J.H.C. (1967), "Further Methods of Derivation of Quarterly Figures from Annual Data", *Applied Statistics*, Vol. 16, no. 1, pp. 65-75

[5] Box, G.E.P. and Jenkins, G.M. (1970) *Time series Analysis, Forecasting and Control*, Holden-Day.

[6] Chen, Z. G., Cholette, P.A. and Dagum, E. B. (1997), "A Nonparametric Method for Benchmarking Survey Data via Signal Extraction", *Journal of the American Statistical Association*, Vol. 92, No. 440, pp. 1563-1571.

[7] Cholette, P.A and Dagum, E. B. (1994), "Benchmarking Time Series with Autocorrelated Sampling Errors", *International Statistical Review*, Vol. 62, pp. 365-377.

[8] Chow, G.C. and Lin, A.-L. (1971), "Best Linear Unbiased Interpolation, Distribution and Extrapolation of Time Series by Related Series", *Review of Economics and Statistics*, Vol. 53, No. 4, pp. 372-375.

[9] Cohen, K.J., Müller, W. and Padberg, M.W. (1971) "Autoregressive Approaches to the Disaggregation of Time Series Data", *Applied Statistics*, Vol. 20, pp 119-129.

[10] Dagum, E. B., Cholette, P.A. Chen, Z.-G. (1998), "A Unified View of Signal Extraction, Benchmarking and Interpolation of Time Series", forthcoming in *International Statistical Review*.

[11] De Jong, P. (1991), "The Diffuse Kalman Filter", *The Annals of Statistics*, Vol. 19, pp. 1073-1083.

[12] Duncan, D.B. and Horn, S.D. (1972), "Linear Dynamic Recursive Estimation from the Viewpoint of Regression Analysis", *Journal of the American Statistical Association*, Vol. 67, pp. 815-821.

[13] Guerrero, V. M. (1989) "Optimal Conditional ARIMA Forecast", *Journal of Forecasting*, Vol. 8, pp. 215-229

[14] Kohn, R. and Ansley, C.F. (1986), "Estimation, Prediction and Interpolation for ARIMA Models with Missing Data", *Journal of the American Statistical Association*, Vol. 79, pp. 125-131.

[15] Pankratz, A. (1989), "Time Series Forecasts and Extra-Model Information", *Journal of Forecasting*, Vol. 8, pp. 75-83.

[16] Rao, C.R. (1965), *Linear Statistical Inference and its Applications*, John Wiley.

[17] Robinson, G.K. (1991), "That BLUP Is a Good Thing: The Estimation of Random Effects", *Statistical Science*, Vol. 6, No. 1 pp. 15-51.

[18] Sallas, W.M., Harville, D.A. (1981), "Best Linear Recursive Estimation for Mixed Linear Models", *Journal of the American Statistical Association*, Vol. 76, pp. 860-869.

[19] Sallas, W.M. and Harville, D.A. (1988), "Noninformative Priors and Restricted Maximum Likelihood Estimation in the Kalman Filter" in *Bayesian Analysis of Time Series and Dynamic Models* (J.C. Spall ed.), New York: Marcel Dekker.

[20] Stram, D.O. and Wei, W.W.S. (1986), "A Methodological Note on the Disaggregation of Time Series Totals", *Journal of Time Series Analysis*, Vol. 7, pp. 293-302.

[21] Trabelsi, A. and Hillmer, S.C. (1989), "A Benchmarking Approach to Forecast Combination", *Journal of Business and Economic Statistics*, Vol. 7, pp. 353-362.

[22] Tsimikas, J., Ledolter, J. (1994), □REML and Best Linear Unbiased Prediction in State Space Models□, *Communications in Statistics, Theory and Methods*, Vol. 23, No. 8, pp. 2253-2268.

[23] Whittle, P. (1963), *Prediction and Regulation*, New York, D. Van Nostrand.

Chapter 4

COMPUTATION IN MACROECONOMETRIC MODEL-BUILDING: SOME HISTORICAL ASPECTS

Ronald G. Bodkin[*]

200 Wilbrod St. University of Ottawa, Ottawa, Ontario K1N6N5, Canada

4.1 Introduction

The subject of this paper is some computational aspects of macroeconometric models, over a period of roughly sixty years that such models have been in existence. Ironically, my presentation will be mainly in literary terms, with no proofs and only passing references to algorithms.

I shall begin by considering an analogous question, namely how the technology of putting word to paper -- writing -- has evolved over the past two centuries. Recently, my dear wife brought me back a small present from one of her many business trips, namely a goose quill pen set with accoutrements. (The accoutrements included a holder with a small container for the liquid ink.) This got me to thinking. In fact, the technology of writing has evolved considerably over recent history. Consider what an improvement a steel-tipped pen is over a goose-quill pen! Now add fountain pens, ball-point pens, mechanical typewriters, electronic typewriters, and then word-processors (or personal computers, on one of which the written version of this presentation was

---

[*]I should like to thank my co-authors of the joint works cited in the bibliography, namely Professors Cheng Hsiao, Michael D. Intriligator, Kanta Marwah, and especially Lawrence R. Klein. Also, the diagram of this paper is an adaptation of one in Chapter 12 of my book with Intriligator and Hsiao. In addition, Joel Popkin is warmly thanked for sharing his reminiscences of our graduate school days at Penn. The late Michael D. McCarthy is enthusiastically thanked for both his comments on an early draft of this paper and for pointing me to his writings. Finally, Charles Renfro is thanked warmly for his comments and suggestions on various drafts of this paper. Of course, all of the above are absolved from any errors of omission or commission which remain. This paper was originally presented to the Second International Conference on Computing in Economics and Finance of the *Society of Computational Economics*, in Geneva, Switzerland, on June 28, 1996.

fashioned). The progress has been enormous in the past two centuries, and the difference is reflected in the typical office of today and even thirty years ago. (When was the last time that you had to fuss with carbon papers?)

I should argue that the progress in computation has been even more rapid. When Tinbergen and the other first model-builders went to work in the mid-1930s, computation methods were primitive, and obtaining computed results was incredibly slow, by our standards. A standard computational device was the slide rule, while the desk calculator, a relatively new device, was (while quite rapid compared to hand computation) still not of a nature to permit the kind of calculations that we take for granted today.[1] After World War II, the electronic computer (with its vacuum tubes) came along, and the speed of computation increased manyfold. Various generations of mainframe computers increased speed and ease of handling, all the while decreasing in size, so that huge rooms were no longer required to house these computational beasts. Perhaps the most stunning development of the past 15 years has been the development of the personal computer or microcomputer (I shall use these terms synonymously), made possible by the micro-chip. Indeed, I have been informed by individuals more knowledgeable than I on this subject that a present-day (mid 1990s) pentium can be adapted to possess, in some respects, the computational capacity and speed of a typical mainframe computer of the beginning of the 1980s! So the progress has been astounding. Even for much smaller quantities of calculations, the progress has been impressive. Roughly 30 years ago, I bought a very fine slide rule at the Yale Co-op in New Haven for $35 U.S. (Let us estimate the price paid, in 1996 dollars, at over $100; it also represented *more than* ? of 1 per cent of my *annual* starting salary at Yale in 1962-63.) Today such a piece of equipment would be a museum piece, if I had not lost it on one of my many moves, because there are pocket desk calculators that can do everything which that slide rule could do (with considerable more accuracy; even the best slide rules were only accurate to three significant figures) and which cost only a fraction of the purchase price, in nominal or constant dollars. Nevertheless, at the time, it was a reasonable purchase.

Indeed, it can be argued that progress in computation has been essential to progress in macroeconometric model-building, as Klein has argued on a number of occasions[2] and as Professor T.W. Anderson confirmed in an interview with

---

[1] And what clunkers these early desk calculators were! Heavy and noisy, they had little resemblance to the calculators that every student takes for granted today. As they were also quite expensive, they were generally reserved for offices and statistical laboratories.
[2] See, in particular, Chapter 15 of Bodkin, Klein, Marwah (1991).

Professor Phillips a decade ago (Phillips, 1986). Computation has always been of great importance for macroeconometric (and microeconometric) model-building and other applications, yet research achievement was hindered because computation facilities were not powerful, even though computational demands were heavy. Often, research and problem formulation were adjusted ("bent," in the words of T.W. Anderson) to fit the rudimentary computer facilities available, particularly in older applications, as we shall see. Moreover, as indicated by the homely slide rule example, the real (and nominal) cost of computing via the personal computer has also dropped phenomenally.

The plan of this presentation is as follows. In the following section, I review some computational aspects of the early days, focussing in particular on the Tinbergen Model of the U.S. economy produced for the League of Nations (right in Geneva, where this paper was first delivered). Section 3 considers computational aspects over the immediate postwar period (roughly to the end of the 1970s). In Section 4, I consider the impact of the personal computer and the micro-chip on econometric modelling during the 1980s, while Section 5 considers briefly some developments in the current decade. The concluding section presents one or two philosophical thoughts about the nature of computation and whether it should be regarded as only a support activity to model-building. In addition, I hazard some cautious guesses about developments to the new millennium and slightly beyond.

4.2   The Pre-Computer Era

4.2.1   Computational issues in Tinbergen's model

The first working econometric model of the U.S. economy is generally considered to have been Tinbergen's 1939 model, constructed in Geneva for the League of Nations just before the outbreak of World War II.[3] This model consisted of 31 behavioural equations and 17 identities, at least enumerated in Bodkin, Klein, Marwah (1991). A modern reader is struck by a number of features of Tinbergen's 1939 model. Thus all the equations are linear, as even those which are naturally nonlinear have been linearized. Also, distributed lags

---

[3]See Tinbergen (1968) or the summary in Bodkin, Klein, Marwah (1991), Chapter 2. An interesting alternative retelling of this story may be found in Mary S. Morgan (1990, pp.108-130), which also outlines some contemporary reactions to Tinbergen's pioneering efforts. Parenthetically, I am assuming a background in econometric model building such as one might obtain from a text such as Intriligator, Bodkin, and Hsiao (1996).

are represented as fractional lags. It is clear that these approximations have been made for the ease of computation.

The limited computational power available to Tinbergen is even more evident both in the ways in which he used his model and in which he did not use the model. First, the omissions. There are no full model simulations over the sample period, nor are there any block simulations. Thus the manner in which the model (or subsections of it) hangs (hang) together cannot be judged. Similarly, there are no direct multiplier calculations, although Tinbergen did derive (by throwing away terms judged to be of second order of importance) a linear relationship between real private production and the autonomous component of housing expenditures. From this approximate relationship, he calculated the impact multiplier of a rise in autonomous spending on housing to be 4.4, while the long-term multiplier was estimated to be roughly 5.4. (That both figures are probably much too high, according to more refined, recent estimates, even of this historical period, is probably beside the point.) The basic use that Tinbergen made of his model was to attempt to say something about the fundamental stability or instability of the U.S. economy. To do this, he reduced one endogenous variable (Tinbergen chose corporate profits) to a linear difference equation; in other words he expressed, again after some approximations, the current value of this variable as a function of its own lagged values and some exogenous variables. The homogeneous portion of this difference equation can be examined to see whether its structure generates cycles and, if so, whether these cycles are damped, neutral or explosive.[4] In the event, the difference equation in corporate profits produced damped cycles, with a periodicity of 4.8 years, which was not wildly different from the NBER's average length for the reference cycle, at least during normal times.[5]

4.2.2 Pre-computer computational issues

In those pre-electronic computer days, calculation skills were at a premium and a variety of devices were used for calculation: hand-plotted diagrams, paper and pencil, slide rules, the adding machine, manually operated desk-top calculators, electrically operated desk-top calculators, punched card tabulators,

---

[4]It will be recalled that, in a linear model, all endogenous variables have the same dynamic structure, so that one will get identical answers no matter which endogenous variable is selected for intensive examination.

[5]However, Tinbergen went on to show that, if a "boom psychology" operated through the stock market, this could easily convert a system that was normally stable into an unstable one. Indeed, this was a major part of Tinbergen's explanation of the Great Depression (at least for the U.S.A.).

and even the abacus. One computational method that was used for calculating regression coefficients (in the non-degenerate case) was the "Doolittle method." In this technique, the unknown parameters to be estimated were laid out in a manner that took advantage of the symmetry of the problem, and at the same time a check sum was carried along at each step of the way, so that the solitary researcher could easily check himself/herself at each step of the calculations. My notes from a course in regression and variance analysis given by Lawrence R. Klein in 1958 include roughly six pages devoted to the details of this routine but important task! (Of course, such techniques are completely superfluous today, although the importance of a hands-on experience in current computation techniques remains of primary importance.) Skilled operators of desk calculators could, with some practice, estimate regression coefficients of regressions with eight or nine explanatory variables in a day of intensive mental and physical labour, at least given the value of the sample moments. Even the ungifted could perform a regression with three or four explanatory variables in less than an afternoon, at least after a little practice. Of course, the capacity to withstand boredom was a formidable asset.[6]

As a related matter, there was much advance screening of data by quick graphical methods. The technique of subgroup averages was often employed to obtain a quick impression of the stochastic relationship:

$$y_i = f(x_i) + \varepsilon_i , i = 1, 2,..., n.$$

The data were first classified by the size distribution of the x_i's, and then the subgroup means for the y_i's and the x_i's were calculated. These two subgroup means were then plotted (in two dimensions, obviously) in order to obtain a visual impression of the parametric structure of the function f. Such techniques were often taken much further and used to construct graphical estimates of multiple regression equations. Indeed, a serious debate was carried out in the *Quarterly Journal of Economics* on the virtues and weaknesses of graphical versus numerical methods of regression fitting.[7]

---

[6]This technique is described in some detail in both the first and second editions of Klein's famous econometrics text, where it is termed the "Gauss-Doolittle method." See Klein (1974), pp. 282-295.

[7]See Malenbaum and Black (1937, 1940), Bean (1940), and Ezekiel (1940) A related issue was whether it made any essential difference if variables were first detrended and then employed in a simple (or multiple) regression equation, or if the time trend were just included as an explanatory variable in the corresponding multiple regression equation. Frisch and Waugh (1933) proved that these two procedures were essentially equivalent, which had the important side effect of simplifying considerably some computations.

4.2.3   Solving Macroeconometric Models on the Desk Calculator

As we have already seen, little attention was paid to system properties that we routinely examine today by means of full system simulations (either within the sample period or outside of it), dynamic multiplier properties, and more complicated policy simulation analyses. However, the computational burden that such exercises impose on desk calculators was (and still is) unbearable for even a "medium-size" macroeconometric model of roughly 50 equations. However, gradually it was realized that one could indeed solve even a working simultaneous equations model, provided its "core" of simultaneous equations was of small, manageable size, say no more than 10 equations. Thus Klein recollects being able to solve, in his youth, equation systems of 10-20 linear relations (not all in the simultaneous core) with ordinary lags in a day or less. Similarly, in writing this paper, I asked Joel Popkin to reminisce about his experience solving a truncated (a simultaneous core of 18 equations) version of Klein's Postwar Quarterly Model (1964), for the Klein-Popkin (1961) study of inventory investment fluctuations as a major cause of the short-term business cycle. The major units of the analysis were eight-quarter simulations of the estimated development of the U.S. economy during two recession periods during the 1950s. Popkin recalls that, at the end of this exercise, he was able to calculate an entire eight-quarter simulation during a working day (or even less, provided there were no arithmetical errors uncovered during the checking process).[8]

---

[8]With further simplifications, the 18 equation simultaneous core could easily be reduced to two equations in two unknowns. Popkin recalls preferring the Monroe desk calculator to the Marchand, even though the latter was quieter. The carriage return was faster with the former, and this was a non-trivial consideration when hundreds of individual calculations must be made.

A related matter is the issue of inverting a Leontief matrix, which takes the form of $(I - A)$, where A is generally quite sparse. Waugh (1950) showed that this could often be done efficiently by a power series expansion,

$$(I - A)^{-1} = I + A + A^2 + A^3 + \dots \ ,$$

to any desired degree of accuracy, under certain conditions on the technology (A) matrix, which were generally satisfied. Since matrix multiplication is a much easier operation than (direct) matrix inversion, Waugh's work provided an important computational short-cut in inverting Leontief matrices of some size. Today, such problems are far removed from our present concerns.

Nevertheless, none of the above is intended as criticism of the pioneers of econometric computation. Indeed, given the bluntness of their tools, the excellence of the results achieved is nothing short of remarkable.

4.3   The Dawn of the Computer Era

The electronic computer became available after the Second World War, but its use became diffused only gradually.[9] The first electronic computers were mainframes with vacuum tubes, and this equipment was both expensive and space-filling. (Many of us have memories of whole floors of a science building taken up by this special (and specialized) equipment. Still, research was revolutionized by this innovation. Gone was the tedium of calculation, and many alternative forms could be tried, for better or for worse! Days of computation turned into hours, if not computer-minutes, and researchers' evenings (if not late afternoons!) could be freed up for other pursuits.[10]

The diffusion of computer technology was not instantaneous. Thus the Klein-Goldberger (1955) model was first estimated and solved on the desk calculator; only at a later stage were electronic computers employed to perform the task of estimation. (Indeed, a general simulation program was being developed for this model at Michigan in the mid-1950s but was never completed.) Similarly, the Oxford model of the U.K. economy (Klein, Ball, Hazelwood, and Vendome, 1961) was handled in a similarly mixed fashion -- some of the work was done on desk calculators and some on electronic computers.

However, the computer was the wave of the future, and the trend was definitely in the direction of making the computer do the brute force labour of parameter estimation and system simulation. (Of course, the introduction of computer methods of computation varied by researcher and by institution; by the end of the 1950s the leading institutions were using the computer for routine calculations and by the mid-1960s its use was nearly universal, at least for simple regression computations.) Parameter estimation, whether by least squares or by some simultaneous equations method (say limited information

---

[9]Thus the first modern electronic computer was up and running at the University of Pennsylvania, at the Moore School of Electrical Engineering, in February 1946. Still, as a graduate student in the late 1950s and early 1960s, my contact with the computer in the early part of my graduate studies was extremely limited. Nevertheless, a research project with Lawrence R. Klein during the summer of 1960 introduced me to the power of this very useful computational servant, which certainly facilitated my dissertation shortly thereafter.

[10]Indeed, it is not too much of an exaggeration to single out this extremely versatile piece of physical capital as a separate factor of production. This idea has been forcefully expressed by Charles Renfro (1981) in a paper with the title, "The Computer as a Factor of Production." T.W. Anderson (in Phillips, 1986) has expressed similar ideas, in terms of the advantages that a current-day graduate student would have over a student trained in the immediate postwar period.

maximum likelihood or two stage least squares), was not too difficult to program. Hence it became possible to implement the simultaneous equations methods of parameter estimation that the old Cowles Commission at the University of Chicago had recommended on theoretical grounds, but which were so difficult to calculate in the practice of their time (the end of the 1940s). As well, data storage methods improved, as punch cards[11] gave way first to computer tapes and later to diskettes. Easier electronic access to raw data in turn aided computation greatly.

However, the solution of dynamic systems for simulation purposes (for checking the fit of the model as a system, in forecasts, in multiplier calculations, and/or in more complicated policy simulations) presented a whole host of additional problems. With the development of efficient programs for model solutions (often involving the inversion of a nonsingular matrix), linear, determinate econometric models could easily be solved on the computer; a solution path that might have taken a week's work on the desk calculator could be solved in a half an hour of time, on the electronic computers of the early 1960s.[12]

Of course, even by the early 1960s, most working macroeconometric models were not linear. Thus it appeared that a solution program would have to be model-specific, which appeared to be a terrible waste, given that programming was a very scarce resource and that many models were experimental, with only a short lifetime. How might one overcome such difficulties?

One immediate solution (used by Suits, 1962, in his Michigan model) was simply to linearize a non-linear model, say by using a Taylor series expansion around the sample means of the variables in question. While this generally entailed some inaccuracies (particularly as one travelled some distance from sample means), the solutions appeared to be satisfactory, at least to a first approximation.

The Brookings Model of the 1960s[13] was not completely linear either and consisted of roughly 200 or so (depending on the variant) simultaneous

---

[11]These were terribly unwieldy; Michael D. McCarthy (1992) recalls the traumatic experience of seeing his deck of punch cards run over by a delivery truck!

[12]Lagged endogenous variables presented a new complication, but not one that was very serious. All that was needed was to allow past values of system-determined variables to enter into the solution program of a current period, and indeed these past values could come from the model solutions of previous periods of the very model under consideration. This entailed introducing some logical analysis into the program, along with a routine of matrix inversion.

[13]See, e.g., Duesenberry, Fromm, Klein, and Kuh (1965) or Bodkin, Klein, Marwah (1991), Chapter 4.

equations, which at the time was considered to be very large. Klein and others found that one block of equations was linear in quantities if prices were given; in particular, this block could be represented as:

$L_1(q;\text{given } p) = 0$.

In addition, a second block was linear in prices if quantities were taken as given; the representation was:

$L_2(p;\text{given } q) = 0$.

An iteration procedure could be affected by guessing at a vector of prices (the elements of the **p** vector) and solving the linear equation $L_1 = 0$, by standard methods. The computed values of the **q** vector were then substituted into L_2 as givens, and the model then generated a solution for the **p** vector. The problem was then iterated between these two sets of linear equations. Good results were obtained, but the computer program was quite clumsy (by present standards) and so much machine time was consumed.[14] Today of course it is no problem at all to solve 200 simultaneous equations of the sort found in standard macroeconometric models, but it was considered quite an accomplishment in the mid-1960s. Also, initially the solution was presented, as a final result, simply as a set of values obtained from the solution of the simultaneous equations problem, rather than as standard tabulations in national income accounting tables. Slightly later, the solutions were displayed in standard tabulations, although these presentations were not as elegant as our current solution programs.

For some model specifications, it became necessary to introduce more than two main blocks, and the late Edwin Kuh observed that, if the blocks were to be subdivided to the limit, one equation per block, a much faster solution could be obtained. This was so because the iteration of the evaluation of single equations was much faster than matrix inversion, which the block solution procedure employed. The well-known methods of Gauss-Seidel iteration[15] were thus introduced to econometrics and have been used for decades now, all over the world, in practically every centre faced with the computational problem of solving simultaneous equation systems. Pioneering work in developing solution programs to implement this powerful technique was done by Morris

---

[14] See also the discussion in Michael D. McCarthy (1992), pp. 389-90, where some additional details of the solution process are given.
[15] See Klein (1983), especially pages 59-67.

Norman, along with Charles Holt (1965), Edwin Kuh (as already mentioned), George Schink, and Charles Renfro.

It was not only the speed and simplicity of the Gauss-Seidel algorithms that turned out to be ideally designed for the electronic computer where repeated iterations are very efficient; the programmed computer is also very efficient in constructing tables and graphics of the final results for easy presentation. Thus the solutions need not be presented to the user community as a set of solution values (for either a given variable or for a given time period); instead, the user may have standardized tables such as those that appear in official government publications. In addition, widely available graphic routines that manipulate the data as soon as the simulations are completed enable the findings to be displayed vividly for users. The generation of solutions in the form of standard accounting tables was completed as early as the mid-1960s, while computer graphics were most rapidly developed in the late 1970s and early 1980s.

Another use of the computer (its memory capacity, in particular) is that of data-banking. Large scale microeconometric and macroeconometric models make extensive use of a number of series; for every one that enters the final model as an exogenous or endogenous variable of the system, there may be three or five series that are either intermediate inputs or which do not make the final cut. Accordingly, keeping track of a large number of series (recording, performing accounting checks, calculating simple transformations and especially updating series as new data become available [or old data are revised]) is a task that is ideally suited to the modern computer (either mainframe or, increasingly, the personal computer). One of the first major computer data banks was constructed for the Brookings model by James Craig in the second half of the 1960s. Centralized coordination of data series was particularly important in the Brookings project, as the Brookings model was always a team effort. Mention may also be made of the CANSIM data bank program of Statistics Canada, which greatly facilitated econometric work on the Canadian economy, obviating a number of routine tasks of data collection, collation, and transformation. Today, an important part of econometric model-building is a data bank program (a data banking system) that will perform the tasks just outlined, calling up the appropriate series when the researchers wish to estimate a new relationship or perform some relevant simulations.[16]

---

[16]On economic data base systems, see Renfro (1980a and 1997a). Renfro argues that the importance of such systems is generally underappreciated, often by a considerable margin. Accurate, relevant and timely data are of critical importance in constructing econometric models, and without suitable data base programs, one can almost guarantee that one's data will lack at least some of these highly desirable characteristics. To use a homely analogy: although a cabinet maker would rarely underestimate the importance of the quality of the

In fact, from the use of the computer to solve models and to keep track of data banks, the next logical step was to produce comprehensive computer programs that would handle all of the routine aspects of model-building. Thus integrated programs were developed during the 1970s that would not only manage data banks, perform routine parameter estimation, and solve the dynamic equations of the macroeconometric model (including the presentation of the results in graphical and other user-friendly formats) but that would also handle some routine (but technical and essential) tasks of model-building. These tasks were (1) to compile a working model that was consistent and complete and also (2) to code the equations of the working model, for ease of handling in model applications. The comprehensive program with which I am most familiar is MASSAGER (developed by Michael C. McCracken and associates then of the Economic Council of Canada and now of Informetrica Limited), which was subsequently used when Bodkin succeeded McCracken as Director of the CANDIDE Project of the Government of Canada in the mid-1970s. Other such comprehensive programs for model development and maintenance include TROLL, developed by Edwin Kuh at MIT and others around the same time and MODLER (which stands for Modelling Language for Economic Research), developed by Charles Renfro, with the help of others, in the early 1970s.[17]

4.4   The 1980s: the Personal Computer and the Microchip

In retrospect, the invention of the 1980s has been the personal computer.

---

wood used as a raw input, an econometric model-builder may at times underestimate, with drastic consequences, the importance of the raw data employed in her/his model.

[17]For the early history of MASSAGER, see McCracken (1967) and McCracken and Sonnen (1972). On the history and uses of MODLER, see Renfro (1996a). We shall return to the MODLER and TROLL comprehensive programs when we discuss briefly in Section 5 developments in the current decade, during which MODLER appears to have assumed a leading role. A comprehensive survey of developments with regard to integrated programs, up to the beginning of the 1980s, may be found in Drud's survey article (1983a). Mention may also be made of two other comprehensive modelling programs developed during the 1970s and 1980s: AREMOS, created and maintained by the WEFA group for use on their series of models of the 1980s and EPS, developed and maintained by DRI/McGraw-Hill for use on the DRI models. In addition, two other integrated programs that are somewhat less comprehensive are RATS and TSP (for which the contribution of Robert E. Hall may be mentioned), which some consider to have been designed primarily as estimation programs, to which some model organization features were then "added on." (For a brief discussion of the combination of TSP with some model solution capabilities, see Drud (1983b).)

The invention of Steve Wozniak and Steve Jobs converted what was an expensive, esoteric tool of research into a household fixture, well within the budget of millions of middle-class households. It has increased the computer sophistication of millions of households in developed countries, to the point that internet communications have become routine. Moreover, with the personal computer the typical user had unlimited access: one could not be bumped off by "higher priority" uses.[18] Of course, associated with these technological developments was a continuing reduction in costs -- capital costs for the requisite computing equipment and current costs, in terms of the expense of producing desired calculations.

Naturally, all of this had an effect on econometric model-building. Once the technology of personal computers had become widespread (and once some of the standard model-building computer programs had became adapted to the PC), some model-builders (in particular, those who did not use them for consulting services) began to adapt their models to the personal computer. Thus, some academic scholars and some in-house researchers in non-specialist firms tended to construct relatively small models (50 to 200 equations in total), because at the time the memory capacity of the personal computers could not easily handle larger models.[19] Thus the trend towards seeking more careful explanations of the behaviour of economic agents, requiring more detailed and larger models, was for a time interrupted. On the other hand, if one still wished to use a large scale model without incurring the expenses of drastic reprogramming (500 to 2000 equations), the mainframe computer was still available.[20]

This hypothetical problem may be formalized in the following graph.

---

[18]Thus Charles Renfro recalls that, in the early 1980s, large jobs (in terms of the memory capacity required) on the mainframe computer had a very low priority, and so these operations were often limited to one or two per day, with a concomitant slow-down in research progress. The PC changed all this.

[19]However, it was possible, by the mid-1980s, with the use of MODLER and sufficiently ingenious reprogramming of the ancillary software, to increase the scale of the model handled on the personal computer, to the point where all but the largest macroeconometric models could be handled on this instrument. Nevertheless, often model-builders did not put themselves to this trouble; in other words, an apparent technological limitation was not a real one. Instead, the matter could be interpreted alternatively as a limitation arising from an academic social phenomenon.

[20]Indeed, for some uses, it might have been desirable to use the supercomputer. Thus Project LINK in its full glory in the mid-1980s was comprised of some 20,000 equations for the 80 or so countries (or geographical regions) of the system. The solution of this world model could be most easily effected on the supercomputer, due to the size of the computational problem.

Consider the problem of selecting an optimum size or scale for a micro or macroeconometric model; this variable (say as measured by the number of equations in the system) appears on the abscissa or horizontal axis. On the vertical axis or ordinate we measure (in monetary units) both the total costs of model operation (which of course includes computational costs) and the total benefits of such a model project. If the model is a commercial operation, then such benefits could be ordinary commercial revenues; if the model is a research tool or an instrument for more rational economic policy, such benefits are more problematic to measure. However, in both cases we assume that a rule of diminishing marginal benefit (with respect to model size) is valid. (If the model is simply a commercial operation, this would be equivalent to assuming diminishing marginal revenue with respect to this input.) As for the curve of total costs, it may be assumed that this curve is the envelope for two separate technologies, one employing the personal computer and the other employing the mainframe. As one approaches memory and other capacity limitations of a particular computer technology, costs rise rapidly with respect to model scale. However, if the model scale contemplated is too large to be handled efficiently on the microcomputer, there was always the mainframe as an alternative modelling instrument. Thus the appearance the total cost curve is such that its concavity shifts twice over the region contemplated; total costs, which are low on the personal computer, rise slowly at first with scale as marginal costs of computation are at first not sensitive to scale. However, once the personal computer's ordinary capacity is approached, costs begin to rise very rapidly. If one then switches the system to a mainframe computer, the whole cycle of costs with respect to model scale can be repeated. Accordingly, if one seeks to optimize with regard to model scale (setting marginal benefit equal to marginal cost), one sees immediately that there are two local optima. (See the graph.) The global optimum is easily obtained in the case: one inspects the two local optima, calculates the difference between total benefits and total costs, and then selects the *optimum optimorum*. If this global optimum occurs at scale OA, then the model is built and maintained on the personal computer. On the other hand, if it occurs at OB, then we have a mainframe econometric model. (Of course, with the capabilities of current PCs and software, the whole exercise may be "academic," in the pejorative sense of that term.)

Finally, in the 1980s, the solution of large macroeconometric models began to be combined with video teleconferencing. Once the solution programs had been developed, it was not unusual (for major econometric model projects, such as the Wharton model users or the LINK group) to have a group of model users assembled in a room, who would then suggest alternative model simulations (based on different policy proposals, alternative views of the exogenous variables, constant adjustments to be made, etc.) This was done as early as the late 1960s. However, to assemble groups of people in different geographical locations across the world and solve a world model (such as the LINK system of interrelated national and regional models) under new assumptions was an exciting new development. Klein reports such a teleconference of participants in Project LINK in the mid-1980s, with three groups of conference participants in Bedminster (New Jersey, USA), Tokyo, and Zurich. Audio-visual equipment allowed conference participants in the three sites to converse about the problem and to suggest some fresh calculations, which were effected at LINK Central (then in Philadelphia). As the time for computing turnaround on the supercomputer was approximately 15-20 minutes (with five year projections), with the raw calculations taking only roughly five minutes, several of these interactions could take place during the four hour teleconference. Such procedures for using macroeconometric models would never have been possible in the pre-computer era; in addition, modern video teleconferencing equipment was obviously another essential input.

4.5   A Brief Look at the 1990s

These remarks will be brief, for two reasons. First, this is supposed to be a survey of historical developments, and so current realities don't belong, strictly speaking, in such a survey. Indeed, historians believe that a certain lapse of time is necessary to give objectivity to striking events or personalities, who/which may have been highly controversial in the past. So two remarks will have to suffice.

The first remark is the continuing evolution of personal computers, as their capacities continue to increase (and their capital and current operating costs fall). Thus I have been told that the Pentium that sits on the desks of many of us contains potentially as much computing power as the main-frames of the early 1980s, as they were used at the time. For example, Charles Renfro reports that a solution for 12 quarters of a 650 equation version of the Wharton model took approximately four minutes of computer time on the personal computers of the mid-1980s (a Compaq 386); today, on an (IBM) Aptiva Pentium 100, he has re-calculated the solution to the same problem and shown that it could be solved (for the same number of periods, of course) in 9? seconds"! So the current-day machine is more than 25 times faster![21]

---

[21]In a recent communication by Friedman and Schwartz (1991), Milton Friedman reports in an addendum to the main article that a multiple regression that he wanted calculated in the

This leads to a second point. Since the current and capital costs of personal computers are so much less than those of main-frames, economic factors would be pushing model builders and users toward the use of micro-computers, provided that these can get the job done. With current technology, this appears to be less of an issue. Thus Charles Renfro reports that MODLER handles 500-1000 equation macroeconometric models on the personal computer with ease, although he claims that his product has the edge on its rivals in this regard, at least with regard to the adaptation to the micro-computer. (In this context, the expression "with ease" refers to the need not to use inordinate amounts of RAM [random access memory], as this has often been the limiting factor for micro-computer work.) Incidentally, Renfro even reports the case of an engineering process model-builder who, more than a decade ago, constructed and solved, on the personal computer, a model of more than 3000 equations, using the MODLER framework.[22]

In terms of the graphical optimization problem of the previous section, these remarks suggest that the *optimum optimorum* will increasingly lie with the microcomputer-constructed econometric model, whose scale itself may increase somewhat over time.   Indeed, the day of mainframe computer (in its conventional sense) may have already passed.

4.6   Concluding Remarks; the Future

As we have seen, progress in computer technology (software and hardware) has made an enormous difference to the evolution of econometric model-building in general and macroeconometric modelling in particular.[23]   It is probably fair to say that in no other sub-discipline of economics have the computer and its capabilities taken on so much importance.   Yet program development (particularly the development of comprehensive programs for the

---

1940s would have taken 3 months of skilled clerical time by the Doolittle method on a desk calculator and in fact took some 40 hours of machine time on one of the best computers of the day (located at Harvard University). On the other hand, the parameters of this regression can now be calculated on the "desktop computer" in less than 30 seconds. As Friedman reports it, this is his "favorite story to illustrate what has happened to our computer power."

[22] At the conference in Geneva (June 1996), it could be noted that the TROLL super-program had also been adapted to the personal computer, with the application freely available for sale on the floor of the conference hall itself.

[23] As Renfro (1981) has suggested, innovative computer technology has probably had its greatest importance in the sub-discipline of macroeconometric modelling. In turn, these developments may have been spurred by strong commercial demands for the related services, particularly conditional and unconditional forecasting.

management of a macroeconometric model project) has often not benefited from the prestige that it warrants, if not been subject to outright neglect! This is unfortunate. In the various fields of pure mathematics, I understand that often high credit is bestowed on the simplification of the proof of a theorem agreed to be true, or at least the rendering of such a proof more easily understandable or capable of an intuitive interpretation. This should be the case for econometric computation; the field should be recognized as a legitimate subject of intellectual endeavour, rather than seen as the construction of ever more powerful machines and techniques for "crunching" numbers.[24] Indeed, ultimately the future of applied econometrics will depend upon the profession renewing its vital resources in this area. Perhaps organizations such as the Society of Computational Economics and their associated conferences can help redress the balance.

Finally, I shall close this too long presentation with some highly speculative remarks about what the future may bring. The business climate of the first half of the 1990s in North America, Japan, and Western Europe, which some have characterized as a "controlled depression," has been very hard on the macroeconometric modelling industry. I personally do not believe that this is the end of the growth trend; economic history teaches us that even the worst depressions do not last forever.[25] Similarly, I think that the progress in computing software and hardware will continue to take place. Indeed, with the problem of rapid computation for large models generally solved, the problem may well become one of the presentation of the results of masses of data to nonspecialists. So will this continuing progress continue to spur improvements in macroeconometric model-building? This is a very difficult question to answer without a crystal ball. My own feeling is that the major innovations are behind us in these applications. However, this could simply be a failure of imagination on my part.

---

[24]On this point, see the extensive discussion by Charles G. Renfro (1980a, 1980b, 1996a, 1997a, and 1997b).

[25]Since these lines were first written (in the spring of 1996), a strong recovery has appeared in the United States of America, and some signs of life have appeared in Canada and Western Europe. As of the date of writing (December 1997), the state of the business cycle in Japan is still questionable, due to financial instability. The rapid turnaround in the United States reminds us how rapidly cyclical conditions can change.

FIGURE 4.1:

Graphical determination of the optimum scale of a macro-econometric model

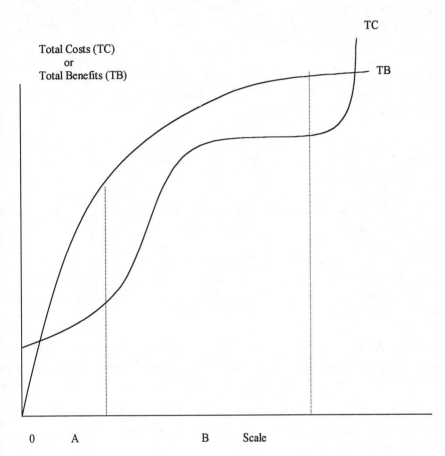

REFERENCES

[1]   Bean, Louis, "The Use of the Short-Cut Graphic Method of Multiple Correlation: Comments," *Quarterly Journal of Economics*, Vol. 54 (February 1940), pp. 318-341.

[2]   Bodkin, Ronald G., Lawrence R. Klein, Kanta Marwah, *A History of Macro-econometric Model-Building* (Aldershot, U.K.: Edward Elgar Limited, 1991), especially chapters 2 and 15.

[3]   Drud, Arne, "A Survey of Model Representations and Simulation Algorithms in Some Existing Modeling Systems," *Journal ofEconomic Dynamics and Control*, Vol. 5, No. 1 (February 1983), pp. 5-35 (1983a), "Interfacing Modeling systems and Solution Algorithms," *Journal of Economic Dynamics and Control*, Vol.5, No. 1 (February 1983), pp. 131-149 (1983b).

[4]   Duesenberry, James S., Gary Fromm, Lawrence R. Klein, and Edwin Kuh, *The Brookings Quarterly Econometric Model of the United States* (Chicago and Amsterdam: Rand McNally & Company and North-Holland Publishing Company, 1965).

[5]   Ezekiel, Mordecai, "The Use of the Short-Cut Graphic Method of Method of Multiple Correlation: Further Comment," *Quarterly Journal of Economics*, Vol. 54 (February 1940), pp. 346-358.

[6]   Friedman, Milton, and Anna J. Schwartz, "Alternative Approaches to Analyzing Economic Data," *American Economic Review*, Vol.81, No. 1, (March 1991), pp. 39-49.

[7]   Frisch, Ragnar, and Frederick V. Waugh, "Partial Time Regressions as Compared with Individual Trends," *Econometrica*, Vol. 1 (1933), pp. 387-401.

[8]   Holt, Charles C., "Validation and Simulation of Macroeconomic Models Using Computer Simulation," Chapter 16 (pp. 637-650) of Duesenberry, Fromm, Klein, and Kuh (1965).

[9]   Intriligator, Michael D., Ronald G. Bodkin, and Cheng Hsiao, *Econometric Models, Techniques, and Applications*, Second Edition

(Upper Saddle River, New Jersey, USA: Prentice-Hall, Inc., 1996).

[10] Klein, Lawrence R., "A Postwar Quarterly Model: Description and Applications," *Models of Income Determination*, Vol. 28 of *Studies in Income and Wealth* (Princeton, N.J.: Princeton University Press [for the NBER], 1964), *A Textbook of Econometrics*, Second Edition (Englewood Cliffs, New Jersey: Prentice-Hall, Inc., 1974). [The date of the first edition is 1952.], *Lectures in Econometrics* (Amsterdam/New York: North-Holland/Elsevier Science Publishers B.V., 1983).

[11] Klein, L.R., R.J. Ball, A. Hazelwood, and P. Vendome, *An Econometric Model of the United Kingdom* (Oxford: Basil Blackwood, 1961).

[12] Klein, L.R., and A.S. Goldberger, *An Econometric Model of the United States 1929-52* (Amsterdam: North-Holland Publishing Co., 1955).

[13] Klein, Lawrence R., and Joel Popkin, "An Econometric Analysis of the Postwar Relationship between Inventory Fluctuations and and Changes in Aggregate Economic Activity," pp. 69-89 in Joint Economic Committee of the 87th U.S. Congress, *Inventory Fluctuations and Economic Stabilization* (Washington, D.C.: U.S. Government Printing Office, 1961).

[14] Malenbaum, W., and J.D. Black, "The Use of the Short-Cut Graphic Method of Multiple Correlation," *Quarterly Journal of Economics*, Vol. 52 (November 1937), pp. 66-112, "Rejoinder and Concluding Comments," *Quarterly Journal of Economics*, Vol. 54 (February 1940), pp. 358-364.

[15] McCarthy, Michael D., "The Cowles Commission, The Brookings Project, and Econometric Services Industry: Successes and Possible New Directions: A Personal View," *Econometric Theory*, Vol. 8 (1992), pp. 383-401.

[16] McCracken, M.C., "A Computer System for Econometric Research," *Social Science Information*, Vol. 5 (1967), pp. 151-158.

[17] McCracken, M.C., and Carl A. Sonnen, "A system for Large Econometric Models: Management, Estimation, and Simulation," *in Proceedings of the Association for Computing Machinery*, Annual

Conference, August 1972.

[18]   Morgan, Mary S., *The History of Econometric Ideas* (Cambridge, U.K.:
       Cambridge University Press, 1990).

[19]   Phillips, Peter C.B., "The ET Interview: Professor T.W.Anderson,"
       Econometric Theory, Vol. 2, No. 2 (August 1986), pp. 249-288.

[20]   Renfro, Charles G., "Economic Data Base Systems: Some Reflections
       on the State of the Art," *Review of Public Data Use*, Vol. 8, No. 2
       (August 1980), pp. 121-139 (1980a), "Production, Distribution and Use
       of Data: An Editorial," *Review of Public Data Use*, Vol. 8 (1980),
       pp.295-306 (1980b), "The Computer as a Factor of Production in
       Economic Data Provision and Research," Paper presented at the annual
       meeting of the A.E.A., Washington, D.C., Dec. 30, 1981., Letter to
       Ronald G. Bodkin, dated April 18, 1996. , Letter to Ronald G. Bodkin,
       dated May 20, 1996, Letter to Ronald G. Bodkin, dated May 22, 1996,
       "On the Development of Econometric Modeling Languages: MODLER
       and its First Twenty-Five Years,"*Journal of Economic and Social
       Measurement*,   Vol.   22   (1996a),   pp.   241-311,   Unpublished
       Memorandum, dated August 8, 1996, "Economic Data Base Systems:
       Further Reflections on the State of the Art," *Journal of Economic and
       Social Measurement*, Vol. 23, No. 1 (March 1997), pp. 43-85 (1997a),
       "Normative Considerations in the Development of a Software Package
       for Econometric Estimation," presented to the Third conference of the
       Society for Computational Economics, Stanford University, June 30 -
       July 2, 1997 (1997b).

[21]   Suits, Daniel B., "Forecasting and Analysis with an Econometric Model,"
       American Economic Review, Vol. 52, No. 1 (March 1962), pp. 104-132.

[22]   Tinbergen, Jan, *Business Cycles in the United States of America 1919-
       1932*, Part II *of Statistical Testing of Business-Cycle Theories* (New
       York: Agathon Press, Inc., 1968) [Originally published in Geneva by the
       Economic Intelligence Service of the League of Nations in 1939.]

[23]   Waugh, Frederick V., "Inversion of the Leontief Matrix by Power
       Series," *Econometrica*, Vol. 18 (April 1950), pp. 142-154.

Chapter 5

MEASURING INFORMATIVENESS OF DATA BY ENTROPY AND VARIANCE

Nader Ebrahimi
Division of Statistics, Northern Illinois University, DeKalb, IL 60115, USA

Esfandiar Maasoumi
Department of Economics, Southern Methodist University, Dallas, TX 75275-0496, USA

Ehsan S. Soofi
School of Business Administration, University of Wisconsin-Milwaukee, WI 53201, USA

5.1 Introduction

Measuring informativeness of data or news is particularly important as it quantifies the amount of "learning'". This is central to scientific progress as well as to assessing the direction and value of "information'" and technologies. As is the case with all "indices'", the desirability of any measure of information depends on at least two considerations: First is the inference/investigative technique that would utilize the information. The second is the distributional characteristics of the information which is to be summarized. As examples, least squares techniques are, by design, incapable of utilizing any information other than the "variation'" in a distribution/data. And, the Gaussian distributions/data are entirely characterized by the first two moments; any index will thus be a function of the same moments. These two considerations need to be borne in mind when contrasting entropy and variance as indices of informativeness or uncertainty.

Bayesian learning and updating is one of the most elegant and prevalent of the formalisms in all of science. It provides for a particularly efficient means of assessing the value of new information. It is in this context that we measure informativeness. A Bayesian analysis includes a likelihood function, $f(x|\theta)$

and a prior distribution $P(\theta)$ which maps the analyst's uncertainty about the parameter θ. The prior is updated by the observed data $x = (x_1, \cdots, x_n)$ into a posterior distribution . The comparison of uncertainty before and after observing the data is of interest since it quantifies any information gain.

We are concerned with the problem of evaluating the informativeness of a given data set. Our results pertain to the post data stage; Abel and Singpurwalla (1994) provide an interesting example of the problem in a reliability analysis context. The problem of measuring the informativeness of a given data set at the post data stage is different than the more extensively analyzed pre-observation, or the design stage in which the "expected information'" relative to the variable space is measured. It is well known that, on average, samples are informative according to both variance and entropy (see, e.g., Lindley 1956). However, this may not be the case for some data configurations and prior distributions.

Entropy and Variance are "indices'" that have been used to measure dispersion, volatility, risk, uncertainty, and information. Variance has been prominent but the use of entropy is growing rapidly. This paper examines the use of variance and entropy for measuring informativeness of data in the Bayesian setting. Our main findings may be summarized as follows. For binary data, when the prior is uniform, all data are "informative'". But we find that with other conjugate priors, such as Jeffreys' prior, "surprises'" are possible since the posterior entropy may be increased while variance is always reduced. With Zellner's Maximal Data Information Prior (Zellner 1971), however, all binary sample are also informative. In our second case of exponential data, variance and entropy may differ in their verdict for finite sample sizes. For large samples, however, both will agree that the data are informative. In our last case of Gaussian data and conjugate priors, when the variance is known, the data are informative on the mean. Variance and entropy agree on their verdicts. But when the mean is known, variance and entropy may not agree on the informativeness of the data on the unknown variance in finite samples. Predictably, they do agree in large samples.

The outline of this paper is as follows. In section 2, we provide an overview of some information functions for quantifying the information content of a given data and the expected information in the data. Section 3 discusses the informativeness of binary data under two types of non-informative priors for the Bernoulli parameter. Section 4 discusses the informativeness of exponential data under the conjugate prior. Section 5 discusses the informativeness of Gaussian data under the conjugate priors for the mean and variance. Section 6 concludes.

5.2   The Role of Information Theory

The literature in economics, econometrics, and statistics has witnessed a great rise in the use of information theory concepts and measures in the last decade or so. The axiomatic appeal and the role played by entropy as a criterion function in deriving optimal measures and Maximum Entropy (ME) distributions, explain the recent abundance of entropy-based methods in econometrics and other areas; see, e.g., Soofi (1990, 1994, 1997), Zellner (1988, 1991, 1996a, 1996b, 1997), Maasoumi (1993, 1998), Ryu (1993), Golan, Judge, and Miller (1996), Fomby and Hill (1997), and references therein. Holm (1993) has recently developed ME Lorenz curves. Stutzer (1995, 1996) has introduced information theoretic financial indices. In the Bayesian Method of Moments (BMOM) approach, for example, the ME is the vehicle for generating post-data distributions for the structural parameters of econometric models and for prediction; see Zellner (1994, 1996a-b, 1997), Zellner and Sacks (1996), Zellner, Tobias, and Ryu (1997).

Entropy of a parameter θ with an absolutely continuous prior probability distribution $P(\theta)$ over the parameter space Θ is defined by

$$H(\Theta) \equiv H[p(\theta)] = -\int_{\Theta} p(\theta) \log p(\theta) d(\theta) \qquad (5.1)$$

where $p(\theta)$ is the probability density function of P.

The entropy measures the "uniformity'" of a distribution. $H(\Theta)$ increases as $p(\theta)$ approaches a uniform distribution. Consequently, the concentration of probabilities decreases and it becomes more difficult to predict θ. In this sense $H(\Theta)$ is a measure of *uncertainty* associated with $p(\theta)$. The negative entropy $-H(\Theta)$ is used as a measure of information (Zellner 1971); see Soofi and Gokhale (1997) for a justification.

A conditional entropy is obtained by using a conditional density in (1). The posterior entropy is given by the conditional entropy $H(\Theta|x) = H[p(\theta|x)]$ and the entropy of the sampling distribution is $H(X) = H[f(x|\theta)]$.

Conditioning may increase or decrease the entropy. The expected conditional entropy with respect to the sampling distribution is $E_x[H(\Theta|x)] \leq H(\Theta)$; the equality holds if and only if Θ and $\mathbf{X}$ are stochastically independent. That is, on average, conditioning decreases the entropy as is the case for variance.

In Bayesian statistics, the information about a parameter is quantified by a discrepancy measure between the posterior and prior distributions; see, e.g., Lindley (1956), Goel and DeGroot (1979), Zellner (1971, 1984), and Goel (1983). We measure the information provided by the actual data x about a parameter $\theta \in \Theta$ by the entropy difference

$$\vartheta(\Theta \mid x) = H(\Theta) - H(\Theta \mid x)$$

The informativeness of the data is indicated by the sign of $\vartheta(\Theta \mid x)$. When $\vartheta(\Theta \mid x) > 0$, the uncertainty is reduced by the data and the sample is said to be informative; otherwise the data is said to have produced a "surprise" (Lindley 1956).

Following Lindley (1956), the information function that has been widely used for comparison of experiments at the planning stage for the purpose of data collection is the mutual information defined as:

$$\vartheta(\Theta \wedge \mathbf{X}) \equiv E_x[\vartheta(\Theta \mid x)] = H(\Theta) - E_x[H(\Theta \mid x)]$$

See Soofi (1997) for details and applications. Mutual information may be written in terms of the following Kullback-Leibler discrimination information functions:

$$\vartheta(\Theta \mid x) = K[f(x,\theta) : f(x)p(\theta)] = \int\int_{R^n\Theta} f(x,\theta) \log \frac{f(x,\theta)}{f(x)p(\theta)} d\theta dx = E_x\{K[p(\theta \mid x) : p(\theta)]\}$$

The mutual information $\vartheta(\Theta \wedge \mathbf{X})$ provides a measure of expected information discrepancy between the posterior and prior distributions, which is the expected information in yet unobserved data $\mathbf{X}$ about the parameter. Note that $\vartheta(\Theta \wedge \mathbf{X}) \geq 0$, with equality if and only if. $f(\theta, x) = p(\theta)f(x)$ Accordingly, $\vartheta(\Theta \wedge \mathbf{X})$ is also a measure of stochastic dependence between the two variables.

In traditional statistics, variance is used for measuring uncertainty. The widespread use of variance for measuring uncertainty is rooted in statistical estimation (Fisher 1921). In statistical estimation, Fisher's information is defined as

$$F(\theta) \equiv F[f(x \mid \theta)] = -E_{x\mid\theta} [\frac{\partial^2}{\partial\theta^2} \log f(x \mid \theta)]$$

$F(\theta)$ is a measure of information in X, i.e., in $f(x|\theta)$, about the parameter θ in the sense that it quantifies "the ease with which a parameter can be estimated" by x (Lehmann 1983, p. 120). Inherent in this interpretation are the requirements that: (a) X be an unbiased and efficient estimator of θ, so $V(X|\theta) = [F(\theta)]^{-1}$, and (b) under $f(x|\theta)$, the probabilities are concentrated around the mean value θ.

From the information-theoretic viewpoint, the Fisher information F is a second order approximation to the discrimination information function $K[f(x|\theta):f(x|\theta+\Delta\theta)]$ where θ and $\theta+\Delta\theta$ are two neighboring points in the parameter space and the two distributions $f(x|\theta)$ and $f(x|\theta+\Delta\theta)$ are two densities in the same parametric family (Kullback 1959). Lindley (1961) showed that ignorance between two neighboring values θ and $\Delta\theta$ in the parameter space implies that $\vartheta(\Theta \wedge X) \approx 2(\Delta\theta)^2 F(\theta)$.

Ebrahimi, Maasoumi, and Soofi (1999) explore the relationship between the variance and entropy in terms of an approximation of the density, and discuss the equivalence of entropy and variance orderings implied by a more general partial order relation between random variables. They also identify a few transformations of continuous random variables that preserve the equivalence of variance and entropy orderings, and offer some results on the equivalence of entropy and variance orderings for well-known families of continuous and discrete distributions.

Zellner (1971) defined an information function for quantifying the information in the data x about a parameter θ with the prior $p(\theta)$, which may be written as:

$$G[p(\theta)] = E_\theta\{H[p(\theta)] - H[f(x|\theta)]\} = E_\theta\{K[f(x|\theta):p(\theta)]\} = \vartheta(\Theta \wedge X) + H(\Theta) - H(X)$$
(5.2)

Zellner proposed $G[p(\theta)]$ as a criterion function for developing prior distributions that are maximally committed to the data. The prior $p^*(\theta)$ that maximizes $G[p(\theta)]$ is referred to as *the Maximal Data Information Prior (MDIP)*. The first equation in (5.2) is the *a priori* expected information in the data-generating density (likelihood function) which is "purified" from the information in the prior. The second equation in (2) shows that $G[p(\theta)]$ is the *a priori* expected information for discrimination between the data-generating distribution and the prior. The MDIP gives explicit solutions in many problems and is capable of including side information in terms of moment constraints on $p(\theta)$; see Zellner (1991) for details.

We use the following notations in the sequel. Let F_1 and F_2 be two distributions with entropies H_1, H_2 and variances V_1, V_2. Then, *the Variance Ordering* $V_1 \leq V_2$ will be denoted by $P_1 \overset{V}{<} P_2$ and the *Entropy Ordering* $H_1 \leq H_2$ will be denoted as $P_1 \overset{E}{<} P_2$. When variance and entropy order the two distributions similarly, we write $P_1 \overset{EV}{<} P_2$.

5.3   Informativeness of Binary Data

The likelihood function for the Bernoulli parameter based on the binary data, $x_1, \cdots, x_n$, is

$$p(y|\theta) = \theta^y (1-\theta)^{n-y}, \ y = \sum_{i=1}^{n} x_i, \ x_i = 0,1, \ 0 \leq \theta \leq 1. \tag{5.3}$$

We wish to evaluate the informativeness of the data about the parameter θ. We consider two classes of prior distributions for θ.

5.3.1   Conjugate priors

The conjugate family of priors for the likelihood function (3) is $P(\theta) = Beta(a,b)$. The posterior distribution is $P(\theta|n,y) = Beta(y+a, n-y+b)$. Two important examples of conjugate priors are the uniform prior $P(\theta) = Beta(1,1)$ and Jeffreys' invariant prior $P(\theta) = Beta(.5,.5)$.

Under the uniform prior, the posterior distribution is $P(\theta|n,y) = Beta(y+1, n-y+1)$. It is well known that among all distributions with a given support, the uniform distribution has the maximum entropy. Thus under the uniform prior, anysample is informative due to reductions in posterior entropy and variance.

Under Jeffreys' prior, the posterior distribution is $P(\theta|n,y) = Beta(y+.5, n-y+.5)$. In this case, however, not all samples are informative about if uncertainty is measured by entropy.

Lindley (1957) showed that for the Beta family $Beta(\alpha, \beta)$, when α and β are large, entropy and Fisher information (variance) behave similarly.

Ebrahimi, Maasoumi, and Soofi (1999) showed that $P_1 \overset{EV}{<} P_2$ holds for $\alpha_1 < \alpha_2$ and $\beta_1 < \beta_2$ when $(\alpha, \beta) \in S_\alpha \cap S_\beta$, each region defined as follows:

$$S_\alpha = \{(\alpha, \beta) : \alpha > 1 - \frac{(\beta - 1)\psi_\alpha(\alpha + \beta)}{\psi_\alpha(\alpha) - \psi_\alpha(\alpha + \beta)}\}$$

(5.4)

$$S_\beta = \{(\alpha, \beta) : \beta > 1 - \frac{(\alpha - 1)\psi_\beta(\alpha + \beta)}{\psi_\beta(\beta) - \psi_\beta(\alpha + \beta)}\}$$

where $\psi_z(z)$ is the derivative of the digamma function $\psi(z)$.

When n and y are large, (4) holds. In some small samples, however, variance and entropy may give opposite assessments of informativeness of data under the Jeffreys' prior.

Table 5.1 shows $H(\theta) - H(\theta | n, y)$ and $V(\theta) - V(\theta | n, y)$ for $n \leq 5$. We note that $V(\theta) - V(\theta | n, y) > 0$ for all y, an indication of monotone decrease in spread of the posterior distribution around the mean. But for $n \leq 4$, $P(\theta) \overset{E}{<} P(\theta | n, y)$ holds only when y is near 0 or near n. For $= n/2$, $n=2,4$ and for $y=1,2$, $n=3$, $H(\theta) - H(\theta | n, y) < 0$ Thus under the conjugate family of priors, binary data can produce a "surprise'" according to entropy, but not according to variance.

TABLE 5.1:
Posterior Entropy and Variance of Binomial Experiments Based on Jeffreys' Prior, and y Successes in n Trials.

| | $H(\theta) - H(\theta | n, y)$ | | | | | $V(\theta) - V(\theta | n, y)$ | | | | |
| | n | | | | | n | | | | |
y	1	2	3	4	5	1	2	3	4	5
0	0.306	0.708	1.004	1.234	1.423	0.062	0.090	0.103	0.110	0.114
1	0.306	-0.194	-0.053	0.114	0.267	0.062	0.062	0.078	0.090	0.098
2		0.708	-0.053	-0.042	0.048		0.090	0.078	0.083	0.090
3			1.004	0.114	0.048			0.103	0.090	0.090
4				1.234	0.267				0.110	0.098
5					1.423					0.114

5.3.2   Maximal data information prior (MDIP)

The MDIP for the Bernoulli parameter is

$$p^*(\theta) = C_0\theta^\theta(1-\theta)^{1-\theta}, 0 \le \theta \le 1. \tag{5.5}$$

where the normalizing constant $C_0 \approx 1.6185$ found by a numerical evaluation; see Zellner (1984).

The density (5.5) is symmetric around $\theta=0.5$ which is the minimum. Moreover, $p(0.5) = 0.5C_0$, and $\lim_{\theta \to 0} p^*(\theta) = \lim_{\theta \to 1} p^*(\theta) = C_0$. Thus, the MDIP gives twice as much probabilities to the values near each end point, zero and one. However, the MDIP is not as extreme as the Jeffreys' prior in assigning high probabilities to the end values.

The least informative data configuration is when $n=2k$ and $y=k$, $k = 0,1,2,\cdots$. In this case, the posterior density is

$$p(\theta \mid n = 2k, y = k) = C_k\theta^{k+\theta}(1-\theta)^{k+1-\theta} \tag{5.6}$$

where C_k^{-1} must be found numerically by evaluating

$$C_k^{-1} = \int_0^1 \theta^{k+\theta}(1-\theta)^{k+1-\theta}\,d\theta$$

Note that C_k^{-1}, $k = 0,1,2,\cdots$ is a decreasing sequence, so C_k, $k = 0,1,2,\cdots$ is an increasing sequence. For $k>0$, $\lim_{\theta \to 0} p(\theta \mid n = 2k, y = k) = \lim_{\theta \to 1} p(\theta \mid n = 2k, y = k) = 0$

Entropy of (5.6) is given by

$$H(\theta \mid n = 2k, y = k) = -(\log C_k + 2C_kD_k)$$

where

$$D_k = \int (k+\theta)\log(\theta)\theta^{k+\theta}(1-\theta)^{k+1-\theta}\,d\theta$$

Although, D_k, $k = 0,1,2,\cdots$ is a decreasing sequence, it can be shown that the product C_kD_k, $k = 0,1,2,\cdots$ is an increasing sequence. Hence, $H(\theta \mid n = 2k, y = k)$, $k = 0,1,2,\cdots$ is a *decreasing* sequence.

The density (5.6) is symmetric around $\theta = 0.5$. Variance is given by

$$V(\theta \,|\, n = 2k, y = k) = C_k \int_0^1 \theta^{k+\theta+2} (1-\theta)^{k+1-\theta} d\theta - \frac{1}{4}$$

It can be shown that $V(\theta \,|\, n = 2k, y = k)$, $k = 0,1,2,\cdots$ is also a *decreasing* sequence.

Figure 5.1 shows Jeffreys' prior *Beta*$(.5,.5)$ (dash-2 points), Zellner's MDIP (dash-1 point), and the associated posterior densities for $n = 2k$, $k = 0,1,2,3$. The solid curves are the posteriors based on the MDIP. All three have less entropy and variance as compared with the prior. The two dashed curves and the dash-3 dots curve are the Beta posteriors based on Jeffreys' prior. The first two have larger entropies and the third one has smaller entropy than *Beta*$(.5,.5)$. Since under *Beta*$(.5,.5)$ the probability is heavily concentrated at the tails of the distribution, the prior has a larger variance than all posteriors. For $n = 2,4$, the probability is less concentrated under the posteriors than the prior.

We conclude that under Zellner's MDIP (5), all binary samples are informative whether measure uncertainty by entropy or by variance; i.e., under the MDIP, no sample may produce a ``surprise".

5.4 Informativeness of Exponential Data

For exponentially distributed occurrence times with rate , the conjugate prior is Gamma, $P(\theta) = G(\alpha, \beta)$. Note that θ is the precision parameter of the exponential distribution, whereas β is the scale parameter of the Gamma prior for. The posterior distribution is $P(\theta \,|\, x) = G[n + \alpha, \beta(1 + \beta T_n)^{-1}]$, where $T_n = \sum x_i$. That is, the sample increases the shape parameter and decreases the scale parameter of the prior gamma distribution.

In order to determine the informativeness of the sample, we note that $P(\theta \,|\, x) \overset{V}{<} P(\theta)$ if and only if

$$\log(1 + \beta T_n) \geq (1/2) \log(1 + n/\alpha) \tag{5.7}$$

and that $P(\theta \,|\, x) \overset{E}{<} P(\theta)$ if and only if

$$\log(1 + \beta T_n) \geq \log[\Gamma(\alpha + n)/\Gamma(\alpha)] + (1-\alpha)[\psi(\alpha + n) - \psi(\alpha)] - n\psi(\alpha + n) + n \tag{5.8}$$

Thus, $P(\theta|x) \overset{EV}{<} P(\theta)$ does not always hold. However, we can establish $P(\theta|x) \overset{EV}{<} P(\theta)$ for large samples. Using the asymptotic approximations,

$$\log[\Gamma(z)] \approx 1/2\log(2\pi) - z + (z - 1/2)\log(z) \tag{5.9}$$

and

$$\psi(z) \approx \log(z) - 1/2z^{-1} \tag{5.10}$$

the condition (5.8) reduces to

$$\log(1 + \beta T_n) \geq (1/2)\log(1 + n/\alpha) + (1 - \alpha)/(2\alpha) - (\alpha - 1/2)\log\alpha + o(n) \tag{5.11}$$

As $n_{n\to\infty}$, $T_n/n \to \theta^{-1}$ and $E_\theta(\theta^{-1}) = (\alpha - 1)\beta^{-1}$, where the expectation is taken with respect to the prior distribution $P(\theta)$. We find that for large n and $\alpha > 1$, $\log(1 + \beta T_n) \to \log[1 + (\alpha - 1)n]$. Thus, averaged over the parameter space, the conditions (5.7) and (5.11) are asymptotically satisfied.

We remark that the notion of average entropy has been used before. The prior and posterior information in the density $p(x|\theta)$ are defined by the prior and posterior average (negative) entropies $-E_{P(\theta)}[H(X|\theta)]$ and $-E_{P(\theta|x)}[H(X|\theta)]$; see Zellner (1971, 1991) and Zellner (1988, 1991). The notion of average entropy is also used in the entropy estimation context by Gill and Joanes (1979), Mazzuchi, Soofi, and Soyer (1997), and in the information theory literature by Campbell (995).

5.5   Informativeness of Gaussian Data

For samples from the Gaussian distribution, $f(x|\theta, \sigma^2)$ with σ^2 known, the conjugate family of priors for is $P(\theta) = N(\alpha, \beta^2)$. The posterior distribution is $P(\theta|x) = N[(\sigma^2\alpha + T_n\beta^2)/(\sigma^2 + n\beta^2)$. $\beta^2\sigma^2/(\sigma^2 + n\beta^2)$. Clearly, $V(\theta) > V(\theta|x)$ and $H(\theta) > H(\theta|x)$ for all samples x. Thus all samples are informative about the normal mean according to both variance and entropy. This seems to be more of an exception than a rule.

For $f(x|\mu,\theta) = N(\mu,\theta)$ with known μ, the conjugate family is the Inverse Gamma, $P(\theta) = IG(\alpha,\beta)$ and the posterior is $P(\theta|x) = IG(\alpha + n/2, \beta + Q_n)$, where $Q_n = 1/2\sum(x_i - \mu)^2$. In this case, we also note that $P(\theta|x) \overset{V}{<} P(\theta)$, if and only if

$$\log(1 + Q_n/\beta) < \log[(\alpha + n/2 - 1)/(\alpha - 1)] + 1/2\log[(\alpha + n/2 - 2)/(\alpha - 2)] \qquad (5.12)$$

and $P(\theta|x) \overset{E}{<} P(\theta)$, if and only if

$$\log(1 + Q_n/\beta) < \log[\Gamma(\alpha)/\Gamma(\alpha + n/2)] + (\alpha + 1)[\psi(\alpha + n/2) - \psi(\alpha)] + (n/2)[\psi(\alpha + n/2) - 1]$$
$$(5.13)$$

Here, we also note that $P(\theta|x) \overset{EV}{<} P(\theta)$ does not always hold.
For large n, the condition (12) reduces to

$$\log(1 + Q_n/\beta) < (3/2)\log(\alpha + n/2) - [\log(\alpha - 1) + 1/2\log(\alpha - 2)] \qquad (5.14)$$

Using the asymptotic approximations (5.9) and (5.10), the condition (5.13) reduces to

$$\log(1 + Q_n/\beta) < (3/2)\log(\alpha + n/2) + \log[\Gamma(\alpha)/\sqrt{2\pi}] - (\alpha + 1)\psi(\alpha) + \alpha - 1/2 + o(n)$$
$$(5.15)$$

As $n \to \infty$, $Q_n/n \to \theta$, and $E_\theta(\theta) = (\alpha - 1)\beta$, where the expectation is taken with respect to the prior distribution $P(\theta)$. We find that for large n and $\alpha > 1$, $\log(1 + Q_n/\beta) \to \log[1 + (\alpha - 1)n]$. Thus, averaged over the parameter space, the conditions (5.14) and (5.15) are asymptotically satisfied.

5.6   Conclusions

An important example was given of Bayesian prior distributions specifying situations in which variance and entropy may or may not agree. For binary data, under a conjugate prior, the posterior entropy may increase or decrease as compared with the prior entropy, but the posterior variance always decreases. With Zellner's Maximal Data Information Prior (MDIP), both the posterior entropy and variance decrease for all binary data. Entropy analysis shows that while the MDIP shares a feature of Jeffreys' prior which assigns relatively higher probabilities to the end points than to the middle, it is not as extreme as Jeffreys' prior under which some samples ought to be evaluated as reducing information about the Bernoulli parameter!

Entropy and variance may also give opposite assessment of informativeness of exponential data. For the Gaussian case with a *known* scale parameter, under the conjugate prior for the mean, the entropy and variance concur that every data set is informative about the mean. But for the case of unknown scale and unknown mean, the two measures may give opposite assessment.

FIGURE 5.1:
Jeffreys' and Zellner's Priors for the Bernoulli Parameter and Corresponding
Posterior Distributions for *n=2k, k=1,2,3*.

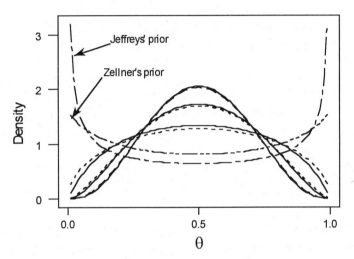

- Dash-dot curve is the Jeffreys' invariant prior *Beta(.5,.5)* for the Bernoulli
parameter θ.
  - Dot curves are *Beta(1.5,1.5)* and *Beta(2.5,2.5)* posterior densities for
  n=2k, y=k=1,2, which have higher entropies and lower variances than
  the Jeffreys' prior.
  - Dash curve is *Beta(3.5,3.5)* posterior density for *n=6, y=3* , which has
  a lower entropy and a lower variance than the Jeffreys' prior.
- Dash-2 dots curve is the Maximal Data Information Prior for the
Bernoulli parameter θ.
  - Solid curves are posterior densities for *n=2k, y=k=1,2,3*, which have
  lower entropies and lower variances than the Maximal Data

REFERENCES

[1]   Abel, P. S. and N.D. Singpurwalla (1994) ``To Survive or to Fail: That is the Question'', *The American Statistician*, 48, 18-21.

[2]   Ebrahimi, Maasoumi, and Soofi (1999) ``Ordering Univariate Distributions by Entropy and Variance'', *Journal of Econometrics*, 90, 2, 317-336.

[3]   Fisher, R. A. (1921) ``On Mathematical Foundations of Theoretical Statistics'', *Philosophical Transactions of the Royal Society of London*, Ser. A, 222, 309-368.

[4]   Fomby, T. B. and R. C. Hill (1997) Advances in Econometrics: *Applying Maximum Entropy to Econometric Problems*, Vol. 12, Greenwich CT: JAI Press.

[5]   Goel, P.K. (1983) ``Information Measures and Bayesian Hierarchical Models'', *Journal of the American Statistical Association*, 78, 408-410.

[6]   Goel, P.K. and M. H. DeGroot (1979) ``Comparison of Experiments and Information Measures'', *The Annals of Statistics*, 7, 1066-1077.

[7]   Gill, C.A. and Joanes, D.N. (1979) ``Bayesian Estimation of Shannon's Index of Diversity'', *Biometrika*, 66, 81-85.

[8]   Golan, A., Judge, G., and D. Miller (1996) *Maximum Entropy Econometrics*, New York: Wiley.

[9]   Holm J. (1993) ``Maximum Entropy Lorenz Curves'', *Journal of Econometrics*, 59, 377-389.

[10]   Kullback, S. (1959) *Information Theory and Statistics*, N.Y.: Wiley (reprinted in 1968 by Dover).

[11]   Lehmann, E. L. (1983) *Theory of Point Estimation*, N.Y.: Wiley.

[12]   Lindley, D.V. (1956) ``On a Measure of Information Provided by an Experiment'', *The Annals of Mathematical Statistics*, 27, 986-1005.

[13]   Lindley, D.V. (1957) ``Binomial Sampling Schemes and the Concept of Information", *Biometrika*, 44, 179-186.

[14]   Lindley, D. V. (1961) ``The Use of Prior Probability Distributions in Statistical Inference and Decision", *Proceedings of the Fourth Berkeley Symposium*, 1, 436-468, Berkeley: UC Press.

[15]   Maasoumi, E. (1993) ``A Compendium to Information Theory in Economics and Econometrics", *Econometric Reviews*, 12(2), 137-181.

[16]   Maasoumi, E. (1998) ``Empirical Analyses of Inequality and Welfare,", in M.H. Pesaran and P. Schmidt (eds), *Handbook of Applied Microeconometrics*, Basil Blackwell.

[17]   Mazzuchi, T. A., Soofi, E.S., and R. Soyer (1997) ``Bayesian Estimatation of Entropy and the information index", under review.

[18]   Ryu, H. K. (1993) ``Maximum Entropy Estimation of Destiny and Regression Functions", *Journal of Econometrics*, 56, 397-440.

[19]   Shannon, C. E. (1948) ``A Mathematical Theory of Communication", *Bell System Technical Journal*, 27, 379-423.

[20]   Soofi, E. S. (1990) ``Effects of Collinearity on Information About Regression Coefficients", *Journal of Econometrics*, 43, 255-274.

[21]   Soofi, E. S. (1994) ``Capturing the intangible concept of Information", *Journal of the American Statistical Association*, 89, 1243-1254.

[22]   Soofi, E. S. (1997) "Information Theoretic Regression Methods", *in Advances in Econometrics: Applying Maximum Entropy to Econometric Problems*, 12, T. B. Fomby and R. C. Hill (eds.), 25-83, Greenwich, CT: JAI Press.

[23]   Soofi, E. S. and Gokhale, D.V. (1997) "Information Theoretic Methods for Categorical Data", in *Advances in Econometrics: Applying Maximum Entropy to Econometric Problems*, 12, T. B. Fomby and R. C. Hill (eds.), 107-134, Greenwich, CT: JAI Press.

[24]   Stutzer, M. (1995) ``A Bayesian Approach to Diagnostics of Asset Pricing Models'', *Journal of Econometrics*, 68, 367-397.

[25]   Stutzer, M. (1996) ``An Information-Theoretic Index of Risk in Financial Markets'', *in Bayesian Analysis in Statistics and Econometrics: Essays in Honor of Arnold Zellner*, D.A. Berry, K.M. Chanloner, and J.K. Geweke (eds.), New York: Wiley.

[26]   Zellner, A. (1971) *An Introduction to Bayesian Inference in Econometrics*, New York: Wiley (reprinted in 1996 by Wiley)

[27]   Zellner, A. (1984) *Basic Issues in Econometrics*, Chicago: University of Chicago Press.

[28]   Zellner, A. (1988) ``Optimal Information Processing and Bayes' Theorem'' (with discussion*)*, *The American Statistician*, 42, 278-284.

[29]   Zellner, A. (1991) ``Bayesian Methods and Entropy in Economics and Econometrics'', in *Maximum Entropy and Bayesian Methods*, eds. W. T. Grandy, Jr. and L. H. Schick, 17-31, Netherlands: Kulwer.

[30]   Zellner, A. (1996a) ``Bayesian Method of Moment / Instrumental Variable (BMOM/IV) Analysis of Mean and Regression Models'', in *Modeling and Prediction*: Honoring Seymour Geisser, J. Lee, W. Johnson, and A. Zellner (eds.), Springer-Verlag.

[31]   Zellner, A. (1996b) ``Models, Prior Information, and Bayesian Analysis'' *Journal of Econometrics*, 75, 51-68.

[32]   Zellner, A. (1997) ``The Bayesian Method of Moments (BMOM), Theory and Applications'', in *Advances in Econometrics: Applying Maximum Entropy to Econometric Problems*, Vol. 12, T. B. Fomby and R. C. Hill (eds.), Greenwich CT: JAI Press, 85,106.

[33]   Zellner, A. and B. Sacks (1996) ``Bayesian Method of Moment (BMOM) Analysis of the Multiple Regression Model with Autocorrelated Errors'', H.G.B. Alexander Research Foundation, University of Chicago.

[34]   Zellner, A., J. Tobias, and H. K. Ryu (1997) ``Bayesian Method of Moments (BMOM) Analysis of Parametric and Semiparameteric Regression Models", Manuscript presented at the Fourth World Meeting of the International Society for Bayesian Analysis, Istanbul, Turkey.

Chapter 6

SIGNIFICANCE OF THE NONUNIQUENESS OF NEOCLASSICAL DIRECT UTILITY FUNCTIONS ESPECIALLY WHEN THEY ARE EMPIRICALLY CONFIRMED[*]

Robert L. Basmann
Department of Economics, Binghamton University, Binghamton, NY 13851, USA

Daniel J. Slottje
Department of Economics, Southern Methodist University, Dallas, TX 75275, USA

Whenever a neoclassical direct utility function is in close (even perfect) agreement with consumer behavior data, there is always an alternative direct utility function that agrees at least as closely with the same data. Existence of this equally well (if not better) fitting alternative to such a neoclassical direct utility function has considerable significance for the rational conduct of potential problem analysis in the policymaking arena. [We shall give an important example later in this note.] However the nonuniqueness of the neoclassical utility function on empirical data is rarely mentioned in the literature of economic theory, it appears to be little understood among economists generally, and most doctoral students are never told about it in advanced economic theory courses.

This note presents a short proof and explanation of this nonuniqueness of empirically realistic neoclassical direct utility functions. A brief description of its significance for various economic applications and an example from a current policy issue follow the proof and concludes the note.

---

[*]We are indebted W.A. Barnett, D. W. Jorgenson, P.A. Samuelson and S.N. White for helpful comments on the subject of this paper. Responsibility for errors and omissions is ours alone.

Let S be a batch of observed vectors of price, total expenditure, and quantities consumed by a group of one of more individual consumers.[1] Let $V(X;\psi)$ be a direct utility function[2] that is strictly neoclassical.[3]

Theorem 1. (Nonuniqueness): If a strictly neoclassical direct utility function $V(X;\psi)$ rationalizes the data batch S, then $V(X;\psi)$ cannot be unique.

Theorem 1 follows directly from the following theorem:

Theorem 2. (Existence of a Direct Utility Function): If X, p, and M satisfy the linear budget constraint (1), then there is a direct utility function having the form (2a-b) below that rationalizes the data batch .

The direct utility function (2a-b) may be unique for some data batches S. However notice that the second theorem implies the nonuniqueness of every other direct utility function whether or not the taste-descriptive parameter ψ is strictly independent of budget constraint prices and total expenditure.

Now let S be an arbitrarily large sample of observed vectors (X, p, M) form an exactly repeatable, absolutely flawless revealed preference experiment.[4] The subject of the experiment is an individual consumer. p is an n-vector of positive prices and is the total expenditure the consumer is allowed to make during any specified session of the experiment. Vector (p, M) is under experimental control and is changed from session to session. The consumer response is an n-vector of nonnegative quantities chosen by the consumer subject to the budget constraint determined by (p, M). Let us assume that the consumer allocates all of the expenditure on commodities X_i, $i = 1, \cdots, n$, viz,

---

[1] X is an n-vector of nonnegative quantities. p is an n-vector of positive prices. M is total expenditure on X at prices p.

[2] For the present discussion assume that all utility functions denoted in this article possess continuous second-order derivatives with respect to components of X. This assumption causes no loss of generality that is essential. A general analysis would add nothing to the main point of this article of (Samuelson and Sato 1984, p. 589).

[3] i.e., the taste-descriptive parameter-vector ψ is strictly independent of changes in total expenditure M and budget constrain price vector p. In case ψ is differentiated with respect to p and M, strict neoclassical assumptions imply that all partial derivatives are exactly zero for every <P,M>.

[4] of course, such perfection is not attained and no one would consider it wise to base any conclusions on the assumption that such perfection is even attainable . However, the flaws in "real-world" experiments cannot overturn Theorems 1 and 2. Nor a fortiori can the flaws in "real-world" aggregate time-series and cross-section data.

$$\sum_{i=1}^{n} p_i X_i = M \qquad (6.1)$$

For all observations (X, p, M) that come in question in this note,[5] a necessary consequence is that the consumer's response (demand) results in maximization of a direct utility function that has the generalized Fechner-Thurstone(GFT) form

$$U(X; \theta) = \sum_{i=1}^{n} X_i^{\theta_i}, \ X_i > 0, \qquad (6.2a)$$

$$\theta_i = \theta_i(p, M), \ i = 1, \cdots, n, \qquad (6.2b)$$

Subject to (6.1).[6] One method of determining the exponents (6.2b) from the revealed preference data can be described very briefly.

Consider any algorithm for assigning to each (p, M) in logarithmic derivatives of the quantities X_i, $i = 1, \cdots, n$, with respect to total expenditure M and budget constraint prices p_j, $j = 1, \cdots, n$. Require the algorithm to produce derivatives that are consistent with (6.1). The logarithmic derivatives are elasticities of course. Let $E_{i0}(p, M)$ be demand elasticities with respect to M, and $E_{ij}(p, M)$, $i, j = 1, \cdots, n$ be price elasticities of demand assigned to the observed vector (p, M). It is to be expected that these elasticity vary from observation to observation just as they actually do in "real world" aggregate time –series data.[7] The exponents $\theta_i(p, M)$ are then specified by[8]

---

[5]The theorem below can be restated in conditional form with (1) as the if-clause in case the reader prefers.

[6]Truth of this mathematical theorem does not imply that this result of consumer behavior id intentional (Samuelson, 1948, p.23). Nor does it imply that the consumer is conscious of the result of the choice.

[7]Of course, the GFT form of direct utility function has been designed primarily to rationalize the construction of Konyus-Fisher-Shell "True" cost-of living indexes (Konyus 1924, 1936; Fisher and Shell 1968, pp.97-101) from nonregular systems of aggregate demand or expenditure (Basmann et al 1985). Ordinarily, price and expenditure data that are aggregates over time, over grouping s of micro-commodities, and over individual consumers in a specified group, are not known to satisfy sufficient conditions for aggregate demand functions to be regular at any point (p,M) of their domain. However, even if aggregate market data do satisfy such sufficient conditions, the GFT form of direct utility function will serve its purpose. It follows that, were individual consumer's revealed preference data actually available, the GFT form would serve equally well to rationalize a

$$\theta_i(p,M) = \beta_i p_i M^{E_{i0}(p,M)} \prod_{j=1}^{n} p^{E_{ij}(p,M)} \,, \ i = 1, \cdots, n \tag{6.3a}$$

$$\beta_i > 0, \tag{6.3b}$$

$$\sum_{i=1}^{n} \beta_i = 1 \tag{6.3c}$$

The constants β_i, $i = 1, \cdots, n$ are fitted by a procedure described in (Basmann et al 1985, Appendix C.)

In other words, if revealed preference observations satisfy (6.1), then consumer behavior necessarily results in maximization of the GFT direct utility function (6.2a-b) with exponents defined by (6.3a-c). This establishes Theorem 2. It is emphasized that satisfaction of the strong or weak axioms of revealed preference is not necessary for the above results to hold. Suppose however that it is possible to infer from a strictly neoclassical direct utility function $V(X;\psi)$ that rationalizes S in the sense that to each observation in S it assigns the demand elasticity $E_{i0}(p,M)$ and $E_{ij}(p,M)$ determined by the algorithm mentioned above.

The criterion of closeness of fit to the revealed preference data in S is embedded in the algorithm, of course. Under that criterion, the GFT direct utility function (6.2a-b)-(6.3a-c) and the neoclassical direct utility function $V(X;\psi)$ just described are equally well-supported by the empirical data.[9]

One use of the notion of a strictly neoclassical direct utility function is to define the mathematical characteristics we should expect a system of demand functions to possess in case variations of the budget constraint have absolutely no effect on consumer tastes. Probably that is the most important use. A

---

single consumer's demand system even if the latter were to be globally regular (Basmann et al 1983).

[8]In actual econometric applications the exponent functions θ_i are assumed to depend also on a random variable u_i in accordance with a general theory of stochastic changes of consumer taste (Basmann 1985). The theorems presented in this note are unaffected by the presence or absence of the random variables in the exponent functions θ_i.

[9]A method of determining the exponents θ_i in (2a-b) in terms of $V(X;\psi)$ is described by (Basmann et al 1983, p. 412); see also (Basmann et al 1985, Section I.C) for a less oryptic description.

number of policy-relevant concepts and measurements necessarily presuppose specification of a direct utility function.

The empirical rationale for calculating the optimality of a policy—relevant measurement or program based on a given utility function (say) $V(X;\psi)$ is that $V(X;\psi)$ rationalizes relevant historical data batches like S.[10]

However, the optimality, or policy-relevant measurement or program rationalized by $V(X;\psi)$ is not unique on the relevant data. The data will always afford at least equal rationale for basing the policy-relevant measurement or program on (6.2a-b)-(6.3). The following example, chosen for its timeliness, suffices to illustrate the point: TCLIs, or "true"-cost-of-living indexes (Konyus 1924; 1936; Fisher and Shell 1968, pp. 97-101), are defined in terms of a presupposed direct utility function. You cannot calculate a Konyus-Fisher-Shell TCLI without specifying a form of direct utility function.[11] A COLA (cost-of living adjustment) schedule for increasing salaries and pensions of (say) federal employees might be prescribed in terms of a TCLI based on a direct utility function $V(X;\psi)$. For sake of illustration, suppose that a Leontief form of $V(X;\psi)$ is supported by "real-world" historical data on federal employees' revealed tastes. Then the modified Laspeyres forms of price-indexed currently in official use can validly be regarded as (approximate) TCLIs. However there would necessarily be at least two other TCLIs equally as well-supported as the CPI (consumer Price Index) formula by the same historical data, and equally entitled to consideration as a basis for COLAs. If the alternative TCLI based on (6.2a-b)-(6.3a-c) were to be adopted, the stream of COLA payments would differ in timing and amount from that rationalized by the TCLI base on $V(X;\psi)$.[12] Examining all TCLIs equally well-supported by empirical data is needed.[13] Examination of observationally equivalent alternatives can throw considerable light on some questions already raised in the policy process, e.g., such as whether (say) COLAs tied to the CPI under-

---

[10]To a specified degree of approximation, of course

[11]A computer algorithm may chose a form for you without revealing the chosen form to you, however. Nor would it be a simple matter for you to recover the implicit form chosen by the algorithm. As a result, analysis of the sensitivity of the algorithmic TCLI to changes in (say) price, income, and other economic factors would become impracticable.

[12]The authors' forecast of the 1984 TCLI based on (2) below is about 8% lower than the projected CPI_U.

[13]Once and agency such as the Bureau of Labor Statistics has collected and prepared the data for computation of CPI_U or CPI_W, the additional cost of computing alternative TCLIs based on (6.2a-b) above is negligible (relatively).

compensate Social Security recipients and overcompensate (say) federal employees and pensioners.

Where it is recognized, the non-testability of a strictly neoclassical direct utility function against (6.2a-c), even with flawless revealed preference data, is not a serious problem for economic analysis and econometrics. To begin with, it is not a technical problem or puzzle for either pure economic theory or econometrics. Given the sample data , estimation of (6.2a-b)-(6.3a-c) puts the smallest premium on assuming greater knowledge than one actually has. The direct utility function (6.2a-b)-(6.3a-c) will afford the closest fit to S. That does not mean that (6.2a-b)-(6.3a-c) is the "best" choice on which to base a policy, but it is a sound reason for not ruling it out in advance. If a strictly neoclassical $V(X;\psi)$–for instance, a direct implicit addilog for (Barnett 1981, pp. 262-267)—fits a sample almost as well as (6.2a-b)-(6.3a-c),[14] The different policies that would be optimal under $V(X;\psi)$ and (6.2a-b)-(6.3a-c) respectively can be described, analyzed, and disseminated to participants in the policy process to the extent resources allow. Where practical policy measures are to be based on the choice of direct utility function, that choice is inherently political, not scientific, as a consequence of the empirical not-testability described above.

The problem is chiefly one of exerting professional responsibility towards participants in the policy process. The illustration above, involving the alternative COLA programs that would be optimal under (6.2a-b)-(6.3a-c) and some alternative $V(X;\psi)$, respectively, suffices to emphasize the point. Other illustrations from applied welfare analysis and economic regulation could have been used. No sample of data can afford an objective basis for choosing (say) measures of consumer surplus, compensating variation, or equivalent variation based on (say) $V(X;\psi)$ rather that (6.2a-b)-(6.3a-c), or conversely. Mainstream tradition has treated non-testability of "seemingly alternative' economic hypotheses as matters for philosophers' concern rather than economists'. A consequence is that even major works on welfare economics fail to mention the empirical nonuniqueness 0f the most basic concept of that field, e.g., (Harberger 1971, p. 778), (McKenzie 1983, p.3).

---

[14]It is possible that the neoclassical direct utility function might fit equally as well as (6.2a-b)-(6.3a-c). Easily arranged in a simulation (not Monte Carlo!) experiment (Basmann et al 1983; 1985), the actual occurrence of such an event appears unlikely with "real-world" time-series and cross-section data.

REFERENCES

[1]   Barnett, W.A. *Consumer Demand and Labor Supply*. Amsterdam: North-Holland, 1981.

[2]   Basmann, R.L. "A Theory of the Serial Correlation of Stochastic Taste Changes in Direct Utility Functions.' *Econometric Theory*. 1 (1985): 192–210.

[3]   Basmann, R.L., Molina, D.J. and Slottje, D.J. "Budget Constraint Prices as Preference Changing Parameters of Generalized Fechner-Thurstone Direct Utility Functions." *American Economic Review*. 73 (1983): 411-413.

[4]   Basmann, R.L., Diamond, C., Frentrup, C., White, S. "Variable Consumer Preferences, Economic Inequality, and the Cost-of-Living Concept. Part Two." *In Advances in Econometrics*, Vol. IV. Eds R.L. Basmann and G.F. Rhodes, Jr. New York: JAI press, Inc. 1985.

[5]   Fisher, Franklin M. and Shell, Karl. "Taste and Quality Change in Pure Theory of the True Cost-of Living Index." in *Value, Capital, and Growth: Papers in Honor of Sir John Hicks*. Edited by J.N. Wolfe. Edinburgh: University of Edinburgh Press. 1968.

[6]   Harberger, A.L. "Three Basic Postulates for Applied Welfare Economics," in *Journal of Economics Literature*, 9 (1971), pp. 785-797.

[7]   Konyus, A.A. "The Problem of the True Index of the Cost-of-Living. *Economic Bulletin of the Institute of Economic Conjecture*. Moscow; (1924): No. 9-10; English translation Econometrica. 7 (1936); 110-129.

[8]   McKenzie, G.W., *Measuring Economic Welfare: New Methods*, Cambridge: Cambridge University Press, 1983.

[9]   Samuelson, P.A. *Foundations of Economic Analysis*. Cambridge: Harvard University Press. 1948.

[10]   Samuelson, P.A. and Sato, Ryuzo. "Unattainability of Integrability and Definiteness Conditions in the General Case of Demand for Money and Goods." *American Economic Review.* 74 (1984): 588-604.

Chapter 7

WELFARE DISPARITY AMONG SUBGROUPS OF POPULATION: THE METHOD OF ANALYSIS WITH AN APPLICATION

Nripesh Podder
&
Pundarikaksha Mukhapadhyay
The University of New South Wales, Sydney 2052, Australia

7.1 Introduction

The aim of this paper is to examine the properties and then disaggregate a social welfare function (SWF) by subgroups of population. The functional form of the SWF was axiomatically derived by Sen and has recently been given a utilitarian foundation by Dagum. Since the function contains the Gini coefficient as the inequality parameter, it could not be disaggregated by subgroups of population in the conventional manner. In this paper, using an alternative method of subgroup decomposition of the Gini coefficient recently suggested by Podder (1993), the SWF has now been disaggregated. Among other things, with the application of this method it is now possible to identify the disadvantaged groups by their relative shares in total welfare. However, the main use of the method is probably the determination of the effect of economic growth in specific subgroups on total social welfare of the society as a whole. The method has been empirically illustrated with Australian Household Expenditures data of 1988-89. The subgroups are based on the geographical region of residence. The effect of a percentage change in income of a specific group on total welfare is also computed. This information is crucially important in a variety of social decision making situations including optimum social security decisions and cost benefit analysis.

The objective of welfare economics is to provide a framework for ranking alternative social states according to the collective preference of the society. The need for such a preference ordering arises in a variety of policy situations.

However, for practical policy decisions such as poverty alleviation or taxation, alternative social states are ranked by the decision maker's social evaluation function. In such evaluation functions the policy maker strives to include widely accepted social values. Such social evaluation functions are sometimes referred to as the social welfare function (SWF). In this paper we shall use social evaluation function and social welfare function alternately and refer to it as the SWF.

We first examine the properties of an SWF in general and the Sen (1974) SWF in particular. A method of disaggregation of the Sen SWF by subgroups of population is then suggested so that the effects of changes in the economic circumstances of specific subgroups on aggregate social welfare can be examined. Such disaggregations are crucially important in determining the target groups in social policy decisions. The method is then applied to Australian Household Expenditures data for 1988-89.

In the next section the social welfare function is presented and its properties are discussed. Since the Sen SWF involves the Gini coefficient, the appropriate method of disaggregating the Gini coefficient by subgroups of population is discussed in the third section. The method of disaggregation of the SWF by population subgroups is presented in the fourth section. The fifth section contains the results of empirical applications and their interpretations. The final section includes some concluding remarks.

7.2   The Social Welfare Function and Its Properties

Although a social welfare could be thought to be a function of a variety of economic and non-economic variables, in this paper we shall restrict ourselves to a social welfare function, which is solely dependent on economic variables, namely individual incomes. Given an income vector, $(x_1, x_2, \cdots, x_n)$, representing the distribution of income in a society, the general form of the Bergson-Samuelson social welfare function can be written as

$$W = W(x_1, x_2, \cdots, x_n) \tag{7.1}$$

This function is supposed to be increasing, unique up to a monotonic transformation and sometimes permutation symmetric in incomes. Sometimes, it is called a social welfare functional because it is argued that W depends on the individual utilities which, in turn, are the functions of real incomes. Thus if we denote $u_i = u_i(x_i)$ as the utility of the ith person, then we get the utilitarian form of the SWF as

$$W = W[u_1(x_1), u_2(x_2), \cdots, u_n(x_n)]$$ (7.2)

The form of the SWF as given in (7.2) is branded as welfarist by Sen because of its sole dependence on individual utilities. The most common utilitarian forms of (7.2) are

$$W = \sum_i u_i(x_i),$$ (7.3)

$$W = \sum_i a_i u_i(x_i), \text{ and}$$ (7.4)

$$W = \prod_i [u_i(x_i)]^{a_i}$$ (7.5)

where a_i's are positive weights attached to individual utilities. The above forms are all additive separable. Ng (1981) identifies the first two forms as Benthamite and the third one as Nash and rejects the third form on legitimate grounds. In practice, the first form is used assuming that everyone has the same utility function. Thus, the most popular form is

$$W = \sum_i u(x_i)$$ (7.6)

Since the utilitarian social welfare function depends only on individual utilities which in turn depend on the consumption bundle, or real income of each person, it does not allow for any externalities. While the level of utility of a person may depend on his/her consumption bundle or income, some disutility may be generated due to inequity in the society as a whole. For a given size of total income the utilitarian form (7.6) is maximised when income is equally divided among the individuals. This result is solely due to the concavity of the individual utility function. In general, the utilitarians do not have any direct concern for equality. Since equity and efficiency are the main concerns of a social planner or decision-maker, we believe, like many non-utilitarians, that these two arguments should enter the SWF directly. Therefore, a common non-utilitarian form of the of the Bergson-Samuelson SWF may be written as

$$W = W(S, \theta)$$ (7.7)

where S stands for total or average income representing efficiency and θ denotes a measure of inequality representing inequity. Since both of these arguments are symmetric functions of incomes, W itself is symmetric in the income vector. A SWF of the above type must satisfy the following properties.

$$\frac{\partial W}{\partial S} > 0, \text{ and } \frac{\partial W}{\partial \theta} < 0 \qquad (7.8)$$

In other words an increase in average income will increase SWF and an increase in inequality will decrease SWF. In addition, if the SWF is assumed to be Paretian it must also satisfy the additional property

$$\frac{\partial W}{\partial x_i} > 0 \text{ for all } i. \qquad (7.9)$$

This means that any addition to anyone's income including that of the richest person, must increase social welfare. Since Pareto improvement implies that at least one person is made better off without making anyone else worse off, this property may appear to be non-controversial. Yet there is considerable disagreement about Paretianity. If an extra dollar goes to a poor person then inequality will reduce and the mean income will increase. In such a case, both of these changes will have positive effects on social welfare. On the other hand if the extra dollar goes to the richest person both inequality as well as mean income will increase. Many may consider it indecent to make the richest person twice as rich without affecting anyone elses' income. However, for a Paretian SWF, the increase in welfare due to the increase in total income must be more than compensated by the decrease in welfare due to the increase in inequality. This means that (7.9) implies

$$\frac{\partial W}{\partial S}\frac{\partial S}{\partial x_i}dx_i + \frac{\partial W}{\partial \theta}\frac{\partial \theta}{\partial x_i}dx_i > 0 \text{ for all } i. \qquad (7.10)$$

Obviously, the set of admissible SWFs satisfying these properties is enormous. In order to narrow down the set, further restrictions are needed. These restrictions may be specified in terms of a number of axioms. On the basis of a set four axioms Sen (1974, 1976) arrived at a specific form of the Bergson-Samuelson class of SWFs which is

$$W = \mu(1-G) \tag{7.11}$$

where G is the Gini coefficient of inequality. Dagum (1990, 1993), from a somewhat different premise, arrived at the general form of a special type of utilitarian SWF as

$$W = \mu(1-\theta). \tag{7.12}$$

(7.12) contains any inequality measure. Dagum makes individual utility depend on the person's income as well as the whole income distribution. This makes Dagum's approach different from that of orthodox utilitarians. It is evident that by replacing θ by G we get the Sen SWF, as Dagum himself has done.

Now let us consider the properties of the SWF as given in (11). Many of these properties have not yet been explored.

1. It should be obvious that the function satisfies the Pigou-Dalton condition of transfer. For a given total (or mean) income if a small amount of income is transferred from a rich to a poor person, social welfare must increase. This is because such a transfer will lead to a reduction in the Gini coefficient while leaving average income unchanged, which is a well-known result.

2. The marginal rate of substitution between the Gini coefficient and the mean income is given by

$$\frac{dG}{d\mu} = -\frac{\partial W/\partial \mu}{\partial W/\partial G} = \frac{1-G}{\mu} \tag{7.13}$$

This shows that the SWF is highly sensitive to the mean income and less sensitive to inequality.

3. The social welfare function given in (7.11) is Paretian. This can be proved by the positivity of the direct partial derivative of the function in (7.10). Derivation of this result becomes quite complex if we try to find the partial derivative by the function of a function rule. However, it is much easier if (7.10) is first expressed in terms of the observed x's in ascending order. In that case we can obtain the derivative as

$$\frac{\partial W}{\partial x_i} = \frac{2(n-i)+1}{n^2} \tag{7.14}$$

It is obvious that this derivative is positive for all possible values of i. An increase in any individual's income will definitely lead to an increase in the mean income. However, it may either increase or decrease inequality depending on who gets the extra dollar. The lowest value of the derivative is $/n^2$ which is attained when the extra dollar goes to the richest person. As we well know, the maximum increase in inequality occurs when the extra dollar goes to the richest person. This increase in inequality decreases social welfare but it is more than compensated by the increase in social welfare due to the corresponding increase in the mean income. On the other hand if the extra dollar goes to the poorest individual, social welfare will increase by the increase in the mean income as well as the decrease in inequality.

4. The elasticities of the social welfare function with respect to the mean income and to the Gini coefficient can be derived as

$$\eta_\mu = 1 \text{ and, } \eta_G = \frac{G}{1-G}$$

respectively. This means that $|\eta_G| < |\eta_\mu|$ if $G < 0.5$, and $|\eta_G| > |\eta_\mu|$ if $G > 0.5$

5. If all incomes change proportionately, the rate of change in total social welfare is the same as that of incomes. The proof is simple. Notice that proportionate changes in all incomes leave the value of the Gini coefficient unchanged. Suppose the rate of change in incomes is r. Then the new level of social welfare is $(\mu + r\mu)(1 - G)$. Therefore the rate of change in social welfare is $[\mu(1+r)(1-G)/\mu(1-G)] - 1 = r$. On the other hand, it can be proved that if every individual's income changes by a constant, say c, then social welfare will change by the proportion $\dfrac{c}{\mu(1-G)}$.

6. The social welfare function given by (7.11) can be decomposed both by factor components as well as by subgroups of population. The latter type of decomposition was thought to be an impossibility. The proposition will be demonstrated in the next section.

It may seem that the most of the properties except the first one are somewhat restrictive. However, the Sen SWF may be easily modified to make it more flexible. For example, the generalized form of (7.11) may be given as

$$W = \mu^\alpha (1-G) \tag{7.15}$$

with $0 \le \alpha \le 1$. For α strictly less than unity, (7.15) will not be Paretian everywhere and will be non-linearly homogeneous with respect to incomes.

Also, each choice of α , will give a different marginal rate of substitution between equity and efficiency.

7.3   The Disaggregation of the Gini Index

The key to the subgroup decomposition of the SWF crucially depends on the specific inequality index used in the function. In the case of the Sen SWF the relevant inequality index is the Gini coefficient. In the context of inequality, decomposition of the index into two components, one representing the weighted sum of within group inequality and the other representing between group inequality, originally suggested by Theil (1967), has attracted most attention. It was shown by Shorrocks (1980) that only the generalised class of entropy measures is amenable to this kind of decomposition. Since the Gini index does not belong to this class, it is not possible to decompose the Gini index in the same manner. However, it should be noted that this kind of decomposition of an inequality measure is not useful in the case of social welfare. Although within group welfare makes some sense, between group welfare is completely meaningless. Using a different approach Podder (1993) has recently demonstrated that a different type of decomposition of the Gini index by subgroups of population is possible, which is useful for answering important questions regarding the contributions of various subgroups to total inequality. It will be shown that the Podder type of decomposition of the Gini index is appropriate and eminently suitable in disaggregating total social welfare by subgroups. First, let us briefly describe the method of Gini decomposition.

Suppose a society consists of five (people) whose incomes are arranged in ascending order in a vector $x' = [x_1 \ x_2 \ x_3 \ x_4 \ x_5]$. Also, suppose that the society consists of two subgroups such that the first subgroup has two members whose incomes are represented by the second and the third elements of the income vector above. The remaining elements are the incomes of the three members of the second group. We shall now construct two more vectors, one for each group, and each vector will consist of five elements. The vector for the first group will contain the incomes of its members placed in positions corresponding to those in x and the remaining positions will be filled by zeros. A similar vector can be constructed for the second group also. Thus, the subgroup income vectors are

$$x^{(1)} \equiv \begin{bmatrix} 0 \\ x_2^{(1)} \\ x_3^{(1)} \\ 0 \\ 0 \end{bmatrix}, \text{ and } x^{(2)} \equiv \begin{bmatrix} x_1^{(2)} \\ 0 \\ 0 \\ x_4^{(2)} \\ x_5^{(2)} \end{bmatrix}. \text{ Therefore, } x \equiv x^{(1)} + x^{(2)} .$$

One rationale for such constructions can be provided by an example. Suppose, the groups are based on geographical regions. A member belonging to a particular region can potentially receive income from more than one region, although in practice he/she may receive income only from the region to which he/she belongs. In this way the group income vectors could be conceived as similar to vectors of income components. Thus, corresponding to each group income vector we can construct a vector of cumulative proportion of income vector and draw a curve with respect to cumulative proportions of total population. Such a curve is called the concentration curve, and one minus twice the area under the concentration curve is called the concentration index which lies in the interval [-1, 1] instead of the interval [0, 1] as in case of the Gini coefficient. Rao (1967) was the first to establish the relationship between the Gini coefficient of income and the concentration coefficients of income components. Denoting $X_1, X_2, \ldots X_g$ as the total incomes of the g groups and X as the total income of the whole society we can write the relationship as:

$$G = \sum_i \frac{X_i}{X} C_i \text{ or } XG = \sum_i X_i C_i \tag{7.16}$$

where G is the Gini coefficient of total income and C_i is the concentration coefficient of the ith group vector. Other results derived in Podder (1993) are not directly relevant in the case of welfare disaggregation. In the next section we shall use (7.16) to disaggregate the Sen social welfare function.

7.4   Decomposition of the Social Welfare Function

To utilise the decomposition (7.16) in the SWF given in (7.11), let us denote

$$X = n\bar{x} \text{ and } X_k = n_k \bar{x}_k \tag{7.17}$$

where $\bar{x}_k$ is the mean income and n_k is the size of the population of the kth subgroup. Using these we can now rewrite (7.16) as

$$\bar{x}G = \sum_{k=1}^{g} \frac{n_k}{n} \bar{x}_k C_k . \tag{7.18}$$

Also, we can rewrite (7.11) by substituting population mean μ by the sample mean $\bar{x}$ as

$$W(\mathbf{x}) = \bar{x}(1-G) = \sum_{k=1}^{g} \frac{n_k \bar{x}_k}{n}(1-C_k) . \tag{7.19}$$

The desired decomposition of total social welfare is, thus, given by (7.19). We can put expression (7.19) in a slightly more compact fashion as

$$W(\mathbf{x}) = \sum_{k=1}^{g} \frac{n_k}{n}[\bar{x}_k(1-C_k)] . \tag{7.20}$$

The term within the square bracket on the right hand side of (7.20) is an expression very similar to the social welfare function itself. As a matter of fact, $[\bar{x}_k(1-C_k)]$ can be considered as welfare within the kth group. In that case (7.20) would tell us that total social welfare is the weighted average of welfare within subgroups, weights being the population shares of the respective subgroups. One can easily see that,

$$\frac{n_k}{n}[\bar{x}_k(1-C_k)] \tag{7.21}$$

may be considered as the absolute share of the kth subgroup in total social welfare. Note that apart from the population share of the subgroup, this share crucially depends on two other parameters, the subgroup's mean income as well as its concentration coefficient. While the mean income always has a positive effect on social welfare, the concentration coefficient may have either a positive effect or a negative effect depending on its sign. We have seen that the concentration coefficient may have either a positive sign or a negative sign. If the concentration coefficient happens to be negative it implies that the members of the subgroup are mostly concentrated in the lower rungs of the income ladder of the entire society. In that case, raising their mean income (proportionately) will enhance social welfare due to increasing average income as well as the reduction in inequality of the whole society. On the other hand, if a particular subgroup has a positive concentration coefficient it means that the members of subgroup are mostly placed at the higher rungs of the society's income ladder. A rise in their mean income will be inefficient in the sense that some of the favourable effects of rising income will be lost due to rising overall level of inequality. On the whole we can expect a positive correlation between the subgroup means and the values of subgroup concentration coefficients. It is natural that the concentration of group members at lower levels of income hierarchy will be associated with lower mean group income.

The relative share of the kth subgroup in total social welfare will be

$$\frac{n_k}{n}\left[\frac{\bar{x}_k(1-C_k)}{\bar{x}(1-G)}\right]. \tag{7.22}$$

The percentage share can be obtained by multiplying the above expression by 100. How should we then determine if the kth subgroup is faring well compared to the society as a whole? To that end we can simply look at the relative welfare share of the subgroup with respect to its population share. If the welfare share happens to be higher than the population share we can safely conclude that the subgroup is doing better than the society as a whole. The converse is also true. This method also helps us to identify the target groups for social security or development policy. In addition we can evaluate the effects of economic growth in any subgroup on the total welfare of the society. Thus, if the social decision maker has a limited fund to increase average income of some subgroups; and the aim is to achieve a maximum increase in social welfare, we can easily work out the allocation of that fund by taking the partial derivatives of the social welfare function with respect to subgroup means. The partial derivative of (7.20) with respect to the mean income of the kth subgroup will be given by

$$\frac{\partial W}{\partial \bar{x}_k}=\frac{n_k}{n}(1-C_k), \qquad (k=1,\cdots,g). \tag{7.23}$$

Therefore, the elasticity of total social welfare with respect to the mean income of the kth subgroup can be obtained as

$$\eta_k = \frac{\partial W}{\partial \bar{x}_k} \frac{\bar{x}_k}{W} = \frac{n_k}{n} \left[\frac{\bar{x}_k(1-C_k)}{\bar{x}(1-G)} \right] \tag{7.24}$$

which is exactly the same as the relative share.

However it is more interesting to consider the expression

$$\frac{1-C_k}{1-G} \tag{7.25}$$

in judging the effectiveness of a dollar rise in the total income of the kth group. If the value of the expression is greater (less) than unity it means that a dollar rise in total income of the subgroup will result in more (less) social welfare than the effect of the dollar rise spread over the whole society. This will determine more readily the target groups for development policies. Here we would like to warn the reader that if we consider $\bar{x}(1-G)$ as the mean welfare per person then it will be wrong to conclude that $\bar{x}_k(1-C_k)$ is the mean welfare per person of the members of the kth subgroup. The reason for this can be explained this way. Suppose a subgroup has a lower mean income than the average of the society and its concentration coefficient is negative indicating that the members of the subgroup mostly belong to lower income ranges. Another subgroup having higher than social average income but with positive concentration coefficient may have $\bar{x}_k(1-C_k)$ lower than the former group. Would it then be correct to say that the former subgroup has a higher level of average welfare? The answer must be negative. All we can say is that the presence of income in the former group contributes more to social welfare than that of the latter. Or, better still, a small increase in income of the former group will add more to the aggregate social welfare than the same increase of the latter subgroup. The last point to make is that subgroup welfare satisfies the Pigou-Dalton condition of transfer. By this we mean that if there is small rank preserving transfer of income from a rich person to a poor person within a subgroup, welfare share of the subgroup will increase. This is due to the fact that the concentration coefficients can be shown to satisfy the Pigou-Dalton condition as shown in Podder (1996). The importance of the above techniques as analytical tools will now be demonstrated with empirical data from the Australian economy.

7.5   Empirical Applications of Welfare Decomposition

The empirical study in this section are based on data obtained from the Survey of Consumers Expenditures conducted in 1988-89 by the Australian Bureau of Statistics (ABS, 1989). The main unit of the survey is the household which may consist of more than one family. However, if we consider single member households as families, then there are only 44 households out of 7225 that consist of more than one family. Assuming that each member of a household should be given equal weight from the point of view of economic welfare, the analysis is done in terms of income per head of a household. This means that in computing the Gini or concentration indices all households are arranged in ascending order of their income per member and then the households are given weights equal to their respective sizes. Thus the analysis is in terms of per capita income. Also it is important to note that the income concept used in this study is weekly total household income received from all sources before income taxes are paid. The relevant statistics are taken from an earlier study by Podder (1992) on inequality decomposition.

Since this empirical application is intended as an illustration of the method developed above, we consider disaggregation by a single characteristic. Here, disaggregations by subgroups are performed on the basis of the state of residence of the households only. Besides the regional groups, one can consider occupational groups, groups based on the country of birth of the head of the household and the sex of the head of the household, etc.

TABLE 7.1:

Income Shares, Population Shares and Concentration Coefficients by States

	Income per Person	Population Share (%)	Income Share (%)	Concentration Coefficient
N.S.W	231.16	24.85	25.05	0.37
Victoria	239.65	18.34	19.15	0.39
Queensland	209.10	14.78	13.48	0.30
S. Australia	218.74	10.29	9.81	0.35
W. Australia	219.52	11.63	10.41	0.33
Tasmania	204.65	9.27	8.27	0.26
N. Territory	267.72	5.53	6.46	0.49
A.C.T.	279.83	6.04	7.37	0.41
Total	229.42	100	100	0.36*

* This is the Gini coefficient for the whole society

State of residence of the household

In this exercise the disaggregation of the subgroups are determined on the basis of the residence of the household. Six states and two territories are considered. They are New South Wales (N.S.W.), Victoria, Queensland (Q'ld), South Australia (S.A.), Western Australia (W.A.), Tasmania, Northern Territory (N.T.), and Australian Capital Territory (A.C.T.). Table 1 provides the relevant statistics needed for welfare decomposition by regions of Australia. It is based on a sample of 7405 households. The reason for the difference of sample size is that in the data tape sold to us by ABS, information on the state of residence was suppressed on the ground of confidentiality. Computations in the above table were done by the ABS on special request and their data set has a different sample size.

From this table we see that income per person is the highest in the Australian Capital Territory and also its concentration coefficient is the second highest. At the same time Northern Territory has the second highest income per person but the highest concentration coefficient. We get a clear picture that in these two regions most people are in the upper income strata in the context of Australia as a whole. However, we can see that both population shares and the income shares of the two regions are quite low, but the income shares are bigger than population shares. On the other hand Tasmania has the lowest per capita income and its concentration coefficient is also the lowest. By the population share New South Wales is the biggest state in Australia. Notice also that there is a significantly high positive correlation between subgroup means and the values of the subgroup concentration coefficients. However, the correlation is not perfect as observed by the case of Australian Capital Territory and Northern Territory. Note that the population shares of the states are based on the sample and therefore they may differ slightly from the census figures. In this table income shares should be compared with the respective population shares. Table 2 provides the intended decomposition by regional groups.

Now let us interpret the results presented in Table 2. We see that four regions have lower values of the concentration coefficient than the value of the Gini coefficient of income for the whole of Australia. These regions are Queensland, South Australia, Western Australia and Tasmania with Tasmania having the lowest value. From column 4 we can say that an extra dollar going to Tasmania will add the maximum amount of social welfare in Australia while the same dollar going to Northern Territory will add the minimum amount. At the same time an extra dollar going to any other region will add just about the average amount of social welfare. The last column of the table presents the relative contributions of the states to aggregate social welfare. These contributions should be judged with respect to population shares of the states.

7.6   Conclusion

This paper derived the properties of Sen-Dagum social welfare functions and obtained the subgroup decomposition of the function using the Podder method of Gini disaggregation. The method has been applied to Australian Household Expenditure Survey Data 1988-89. The welfare decomposition among population subgroups, as presented in this paper, is an important method from the point of policy prescriptions. Using this method one can determine the target groups and one can take appropriate measures to improve the aggregate social welfare of the country.

TABLE 7.2:
Welfare Decomposition by State of Residence

	C_k	$\frac{n_k}{n}\bar{x}_k(1-C_k)$	$\frac{1-C_k}{1-G}$	$\frac{n_k\bar{x}_k(1-C_k)}{n\bar{x}(1-G)}$
N.S.W	0.37	36.19	0.984	0.246
Victoria	0.39	26.80	0.951	0.183
Queensland	0.30	21.63	1.094	0.147
S. Australia	0.35	14.63	1.016	0.099
W Australia	0.33	17.11	1.047	0.103
Tasmania	0.26	14.04	1.156	0.0955
N. Territory	0.49	7.55	0.797	0.051
A.C.T.	0.41	9.97	0.922	0.068
Australia	0.36*	146.82	1	1.000

*This is the Gini coefficient for Australia

REFERENCES

[1]   ABS (1988-89) Household Expenditures Survey

[2]   Dagum, C. (1990): "Relationship Between Income Inequality Measures and Social Welfare Functions" *Journal of Econometrics*, 43 : 91-102.

[3]   Dagum, C. (1993): "The Social Welfare Bases of Gini and Other Inequality Measures", *Statistica*, 53 : 3-30.

[4]   Ng,. .Y. K. (1981). "Bentham or Nash? On the Acceptable Forms of Social welfare Functions", *Economic Records*, 57: 238-250.

[5]   Podder, N. (1992) "The Contribution of Some Socio-economic Factors to Income Inequality in Australia", in *Study of Social and Economic Inequalities*, edited by P. Raskall and P. Saunders, Social Policy Research Centre, UNSW.

[6]   Podder, N. (1993) "A New Method of Disaggregating the Gini Index by Groups" *Sankhya*, Series B, 55 : 35-48.

[7]   Podder, N. (1996) "The Disaggregation of the Gini Coefficient by Subgroups of Population: The Main Issues and Some Solutions" *Mimeo*. The University of New South Wales.

[8]   Rao, V. M. (1967) "Two Decompositions of Concentrations Ratio" *Journal of the Royal Statistical Society*, Series A, vol 132: 428-435.

[9]   Sen, A. K. (1974): "Information Bases of Alternative Welfare Approaches" *Journal of Public Economics*, 3: 387-403.

[10] Sen, A. K. (1976): "Real National Income", *Review of Economic Studies*, 43: 19-39.

Chapter 8

MEASURING WELFARE CHANGES AND THE EXCESS BURDEN OF TAXATION

John Creedy[*]

Department of Economics, The University of Melbourne, Parkville, Victoria, 3052, Astralia

8.1   Introduction

The aim of studies of the welfare change imposed by actual or hypothetical price changes is to provide a *money measure* of the change in welfare facing different types of individual. In public finance contexts the price changes are considered to arise from the imposition of, or changes in, commodity and income taxes. This gives rise to the concept of the *excess burden* resulting from taxation, reflecting the excess of the money measure of welfare change over the tax revenue, in well-specified situations. There is a corresponding concept of the marginal excess burden arising from a change in taxation. It may also be required to provide an overall evaluation of a change in taxation, using a specified social welfare, or evaluation function that reflects the value judgements of the judge.

The purpose of this paper is to provide an introductory survey of various measures of welfare change and excess burden, paying particular attention to the measurement issues involved. A glossary of terms used is given in Appendix A.   The subject of welfare changes is in many ways central to microeconomic theory and their measurement involves all the complexities of applied demand analysis; the related literature is therefore vast. This paper does not pretend to be an exhaustive survey of the huge number of contributions to this broad topic, but attempts to 'pull some of the threads' of

---

[*]I have benefited from helpful comments on an earlier draft by Lisa Cameron, Denis O'Brien, Nilss Olekalns, and Justin van de Ven. I am particularly grateful to Tom Hall, whose many detailed queries led to substantive revisions and attempts to improve the clarity of the paper.

the literature together[1]. A brief glance at this literature reveals two major features. First, the subject has been characterized by a great deal of logomachy, with consequent confusion over some of the terminology. Secondly, despite the fact that the topic provides a prime example of a 'meeting place' between theory and application which is reflected in its major contributions, there has been a strong dichotomy between theoretical and empirical studies. Few of those proposing theoretical advances have attempted to make empirical estimates while few of those producing numerical estimates have made use of the latest theoretical advances. This paper attempts to clarify the major concepts, while placing much emphasis on practical measurement issues.

The emphasis of the first five substantive sections is largely on conceptual issues and the use of approximations designed to reduce the information required for the calculation of welfare changes. Section 2 begins by summarizing the basic definitions of welfare change, in particular the compensating and equivalent variations, comparing these with the famous Marshallian measure of consumer surplus. Section 3 then presents measures of the excess burden arising from taxation that are associated with the different welfare change measures.

The standard money measures of welfare change and excess burden involve the expenditure function, defined as the minimum cost of reaching a specified indifference curve for a given a set of prices. The relevant demand concept is therefore usually that of Hicksian, or compensated, demand curves rather than the Marshallian demand curves which are sometimes very misleadingly said to be 'directly observable'[2]. The problem immediately arises that calculation of the welfare measures appears at first sight to require knowledge of the precise form of utility, and hence expenditure, functions. Several responses to this problem have been adopted. One approach is to use an approximation to the 'true' measure which involves compensated demand elasticity but does not depend on the form of utility functions; these approximations are also examined in section 3. The overall evaluation of tax changes can then be carried out in terms of aggregate values of money welfare changes.

---

[1]For a discussion of issues, concentrating on theoretical issues of consumer surplus, see Becht (1995). Broad-ranging treatments include McKenzie (1983), Auerbach (1985) and Johansson (1987). For studies concentrating more on measurement aspects, see Blundell et al. (1994).

[2]The estimation of Marshallian demands is by no means a simple matter. Furthermore, as argued below, such demands contain all the information required to evaluate welfare measures.

An alternative approach in which the overall evaluation of changes is based on the specification of a social welfare function defined in terms of individuals' utilities, and explicitly allowing for aversion to inequality on the part of the judge, is discussed in section 4. In this case, approximations depend on the values of Marshallian, rather than compensated, demand changes. The analysis of marginal tax reform using such social welfare functions also requires substantially less information, and this is also examined in section 4.

Section 5 discusses excess burdens in the special context of income taxation and labor supply variations. This context raises no new fundamental issues, but warrants special attention given the importance of income taxation, and the fact that a change in the net wage rate, the 'price' of leisure, has a more complex effect than a change in a typical commodity price.

The treatment of income taxation leads to the subject of the marginal welfare cost of taxation and of public funds, which is examined in section 6. The excess burden measures are essentially concerned with comparisons of a distortionary tax system with a non-distortionary system, or what is usually referred to as lump sum taxation, which is assumed to raise the same revenue. However, increases in taxation from an existing tax-distorted situation are often required in order to raise additional revenue which is used to finance public expenditure. Analysis of this type of 'balanced budget' operation is only similar to the excess burden calculation if the additional public expenditure is equivalent to a cash transfer. Otherwise the expenditure can have important implications for the yield of existing taxes. This also means that, starting from a tax-distorted system, lump sum taxes can affect the ability of existing taxes to collect revenue. This type of consideration leads to the concept of the 'marginal cost of funds', which is also discussed in section 6.

The emphasis of the remaining four substantive sections of the paper is on empirical measurement issues. Despite the extensive use of approximations to welfare measures, it can be argued that the information required to calculate the approximations is usually sufficient for producing 'exact' welfare measures. The term 'exact' is used to distinguish measures from 'approximations', but it is not meant to indicate any special precision. The sampling properties of all such measures need to be examined. Furthermore, in practice there is a need to allow for population heterogeneity, since individuals are in different circumstances and face different tax rates. The majority of studies using approximations typically allow for very little heterogeneity.

There are two broad approaches to providing an exact measure of welfare change for different population groups. One, discussed in section 7, is to use observed data in order to obtain the required parameters of a specified expenditure function by deriving and then estimating the associated demand functions; the analytical or formal links between the expenditure functions and the demand functions are explicitly used. The expenditure function may be obtained by first specifying the form of the direct utility function; an example using the linear expenditure system is given. Alternatively the procedure may begin by specifying a form for the indirect utility function; an example using the 'almost ideal' demand system is given. It must of course be possible to 'identify' the parameters of the expenditure function from those of the estimated demand function. In some cases (for example that of the 'almost ideal' demand model) it may be necessary to impose, rather than estimate, values of one or more of the coefficients.

The second approach involves starting from an estimated form of Marshallian demand curve and moving from this to the required Hicksian or compensated demand curve. This step can be achieved either by an algebraic method of integration or by a numerical method of integration. These two approaches are discussed in section 8. Both the algebraic and numerical integration methods discussed in this section use parametric estimates of consumer demand functions. The a priori imposition of some 'structure' makes it easier to estimate demand functions, particularly using a limited amount of data. However, numerical methods of integration can be applied to non-parametric estimates of demand functions, raising no new basic welfare measurement issues; they are therefore not discussed here.

Given a set of estimates of expenditure functions for different population groups, it may be desired to produce some kind of overall evaluation of a tax policy change. The social welfare function makes explicit the judge's or decision-maker's willingness to trade equity for efficiency. An immediate issue concerns the arguments of the specified social evaluation, or welfare, function; for example, should utilities (as in the case of most of the 'optimal tax' literature) or some income concept be used? One approach is to express the social evaluation function using the distribution of 'equivalent incomes', following the approach explored by King (1983). This has the advantage that, unlike the use of utility, it does not depend on the particular cardinalisation of the utility functions. The use of equivalent incomes in this context is discussed in Section 9. A review of alternative strategies in given in section 10, and section 11.

8.2   Defining Welfare Changes

The aim is to define a money measure of the change in welfare, experienced by a single individual, that results from a change in prices. Such a measure is provided by the change in the cost of reaching a specified indifference curve. This is appropriate because any monotonic transformation of the individual's utility function involves only a change in the (arbitrary) utility level attached to the indifference curves; it does not produce a change in the cost of reaching the curves[3].

A fundamental ingredient in the construction of measures of welfare change is the concept of the *expenditure function*, $E(p,U)$ which gives the minimum cost of achieving the utility level U for the set of prices denoted by the vector $p = (p_1,...,p_n)$ Suppose that prices and utility are initially U^0 and p^0. Prices change to p^1 which, after the associated change in consumption, results in a new utility level of U^1. The two major measures are defined in the next subsection.

8.2.1   Compensating and equivalent variations

The *compensating variation, CV*, is the amount of money that must be given to a loser, or taken from a gainer, in order to keep the individual on the initial indifference curve. In terms of the expenditure function, it can be written as:

$$CV = E(p^1,U^0) - E(p^0,U^0) \tag{8.1}$$

The term $E(p^0,U^0)$ is the total expenditure level in the initial situation, denoted by m^0.

The *equivalent variation, EV*, is defined as:

$$EV = E(p^1,U^1) - E(p^0,U^1) \tag{8.2}$$

---

[3]Reference is often made to a 'money metric' utility measure, which is a particular normalization of the utility function (although the term is sometimes used quite loosely). For more detailed discussion of money metrics, see McKenzie (1983) and Blackorby and Donaldson (1988).

FIGURE 8.1:
Compensating and Equivalent Variations

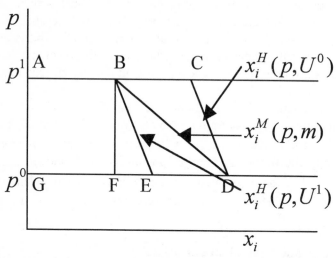

and is therefore the amount that the individual would be prepared to pay, in the new situation, to avoid the price change. The term $E(p^1, U^1)$ is the total expenditure after the price change, denoted by m^1. These welfare changes are associated with the standard decomposition of the effect of a price change into a substitution and an income effect. If $V(p,m)$ denotes the indirect utility function, then the compensating and equivalent variations are defined implicitly by $V(p^1, m^0 + CV) = V(p^0, m^0)$ and $V(p^0, m^1 - EV) = V(p^1, m^1)$. Furthermore, the equivalent variation for a change from p^0 to p^1 is equal to the (negative of the) compensating variation for a change from p^1 to p^0.[4]

Consider the case of a change in the price of a single good, good i, illustrated in Figure 1, with $m^0 = m^1$ and incomes deflated by using the price of the other goods. The points B and D show the price and consumption levels associated with, respectively, the pre- and post-change prices. The points C and E show the price and consumption levels associated with the unobserved tangency positions on, respectively, the initial indifference curve with the new prices (so that U^0 is fixed), and the new indifference curve with the old prices (so that U^1 is fixed). Hence B and D are two observed positions on the

---

[4]McKenzie (1983, p.37) prefers to think of this as another way of defining the equivalent variation, rather than an 'equivalence', in view of his objections to the compensating variation.

Marshallian demand curve, denoted $x_i^M(p,m)$, while B and E are two positions on the Hicksian demand curve (or compensated demand curve) for utility constant at U^1, denoted $x_i^H(p,U^1)$. Similarly, points C and D are two unobserved points along the Hicksian demand curve for utility constant at U^0, denoted $x_i^H(p,U^0)$.

8.2.2   Converting welfare changes to areas

The diagrammatic equivalents of the expressions in (1) and (2) are not immediately apparent. In order to describe the welfare changes in terms of Figure 1, a method is needed of converting expenditure functions into Hicksian demand functions. This is achieved by using an important property of the expenditure function whereby, from Shephard's Lemma[5]:

$$x_i^H(p,U) = \partial E(p,U)/\partial p_i \tag{8.3}$$

By integrating (3), the value of the expenditure function for a given price, say p_i^1 can therefore be regarded as an area, $\int_0^{p_i^1} x_i^H(p,U)dp_i$, for the appropriate utility level. The welfare changes defined by compensating and equivalent variations are therefore represented by areas to the left of the Hicksian demand curves, between prices p_i^0 and p_i^1, for U^0 and U^1 respectively; CV is the area ACDG, while EV is the area ABEG. For example, the equivalent variation is expressed as:

$$EV = \int_{p_i^0}^{p_i^1} x_i^H(p,U^1)dp_i = \int_{p_i^0}^{p_i^1} \frac{\partial E(p,U^1)}{\partial p_i} dp_i \tag{8.4}$$

In the case of many price changes, the welfare changes resulting from the set of price changes, where the price vector changes from p^0 to p^1, can be written:

$$CV = \sum_{i=1}^{n} \int_{p_i^0}^{p_i^1} x_i^H(p,U^0)dp_i \tag{8.5}$$

---

[5]On the expenditure function, see Diamond and McFadden (1974), and for a full-length treatment of duality see Cornes (1992).

$$EV = \sum_{i=1}^{n} \int_{p_i^0}^{p_i^1} x_i^H (p, U^1) dp_i \tag{8.6}$$

The famous measure of the change in consumer's surplus associated with Marshall (1890) is, in the case of a single price change, the area ABDG in Figure 1. It can be seen that the Marshallian measure of welfare change lies between the compensating and equivalent variations. For this reason, it is often argued that it provides a reasonable approximation where changes in a single market are being considered; see, for example, Foster and Nueuburger (1974) and Willig (1976). However, it is known that very strong and unrealistic assumptions are required for consumer's surplus to be a theoretically satisfactory measure of welfare change resulting from price changes; for a detailed statement of the conditions, see Chipman and Moore (1980).

In the case of more than one price change, the consumer's surplus measure is not well defined because its magnitude depends on the order in which the terms are evaluated in the surplus expression given by $\sum_{i=1}^{n} \int_{p_i^0}^{p_i^1} x_i^M (p, m) dp_i$ This is the 'path dependency problem', from which the compensating and equivalent variations do not suffer. See Dahlby (1977) and the references cited therein. Stahl (1985) has attempted to overcome this problem using the concept of a 'monotonic variation', defined as the Marshall integral over an operationally defined 'monotonic path'.

8.2.3   Quantity changes

The emphasis of this paper is on price changes (associated with tax changes), but it is perhaps useful briefly to indicate how welfare changes associated with quantity changes can be defined. These are required in contexts in which it is not appropriate to regard the quantity as the dependent variable. The appropriate concept is that of the *inverse demand function*, $p_i(x,m)$, where the price is expressed as a function of the budget and the vector of quantities[6]. The welfare measures for a change in a single quantity can be

---

[6]These are readily obtained from the direct utility function. From the first-order conditions, $\partial U / \partial x_i = \lambda p_i$, for maximization of $U(x)$ subject to the budget constraint, where λ is the Lagrange multiplier, then it can be shown that $p_i = m\{(\partial U / \partial x_i) / \sum_{j=1}^{n} x_j (\partial U / \partial x_i)\}$. A

expressed in terms of areas underneath the appropriate compensated inverse demand curves. The latter can be obtained from the distance function, $D(x,U)$, which represents the amount by which each element of x must be scaled (divided) in order to get onto the indifference curve associated with the utility level, U. The distance function is in fact the dual corresponding to the expenditure function, and is obtained from the direct utility function by inversion, just as the expenditure function is obtained from the indirect utility function by inversion; see, for example, Deaton (1979). Shephard's lemma applied to the distance function gives:

$$\tilde{p}_i^H = \frac{\partial D(x,U)}{\partial x_i} \tag{8.7}$$

where $\tilde{p}_i$ is the normalized price, p_i / m, and the superscript H indicates that it is the associated Hicksian or compensated inverse demand curve. When m remains unchanged, the welfare changes, ΔW, resulting from a change in quantities from x^0 to x^1, which gives rise to a utility change from U^0 to U^1, can be expressed as:

$$\Delta W = \sum_{i=1}^{n} \int_{x_i^0}^{x_{i1}} \frac{\partial D(x,U^k)}{\partial x_i} dx_i \tag{8.8}$$

and when k takes the values 0 and 1 respectively, (8) gives the compensating and equivalent variations. For further discussion of welfare changes arising from quantity changes, see Youn Kim (1997). In addition, the quantities consumed of some goods may be rationed, giving rise to further complications; see Breslaw and Smith (1995).

8.3   The Excess Burden of Taxation

The price changes that generate the welfare changes discussed above may in many contexts be regarded as resulting from the imposition of taxes. The distortions arising from taxation impose an 'excess burden' that is in addition to the revenue collected. The burden measures the cost of not being able to impose true 'lump sum' taxes. Alternative concepts of excess burden arise,

---

similar result relates ordinary demands to the indirect utility function and prices. On inverse demands, see Anderson (1980).

depending on whether compensating or equivalent variations are used. The first subsection below defines excess burdens and marginal excess burdens. The second subsection considers the use of approximations which do not require the form of the utility or expenditure function to be known, needing 'only' elasticities evaluated at current consumption levels. The final subsection considers optimal tax reform where value judgements enter explicitly but again the informational requirements are reduced.

8.3.1   Excess burden concepts

First, consider the excess burden defined as the amount, in excess of taxation paid, that the individual would give up to have all taxes removed. Hence the comparison is with respect to the absence of all taxes; marginal tax changes are considered later in this section. This definition gives an excess burden, B_E, based on the equivalent variation, as follows:

$$B_E = EV - R(p^1, m^1) \qquad (8.9)$$

where $R(p^1, m^1)$ is the revenue collected from the individual. The burden is sometimes defined in microeconomics texts so that it is negative for a tax increase, but the following uses the more common approach found in public finance studies. In the case of a set of taxes per unit of output, t_i, this is given by:

$$R(p^1, m^1) = \sum_{i=1}^{n} t_i x_i^M (p_i^1, m^1) \qquad (8.10)$$

Alternatively, the excess burden may be defined in terms of the amount, in addition to the revenue collected from the individual, that would need to be returned in order to keep utility at the pre-tax level. This gives a burden, B_c, based on the compensating variation, as follows[7]:

$$B_C = CV - R(p^1, E(p^1, U^0)) \qquad (8.11)$$

---

[7]The excess burden associated with the compensating variation is, however, sometimes defined simply by subtracting the actual revenue, as in defined in (10). The definitions given here follow those given by Auerbach (1985).

The revenue subtracted from the CV is now higher than in (10) because of the tax arising from the compensation involved in order to maintain utility at U_0. The value of R can be expressed using the relationship between the Marshallian and Hicksian demand curves such that, in general[8]:

$$x^M(p,m) = x^M(p,E(p,U)) = x^H(p,U) \tag{8.12}$$

Hence, the revenue in equation (11) can be written as:

$$R(p^1, E(p^1, U^0)) = \sum_{i=1}^{n} t_i x_i^H(p_i^1, U^0) \tag{8.13}$$

One immediate implication of the above measures is that, because of the relevance of the Hicksian demands in obtaining the EV and CV, there may be a substantial excess burden with a single tax even when the good in question has a zero own-price elasticity of demand.

The above discussion refers to the burden of taxation compared with the absence of taxes. Consider an increase in taxation, such that each tax rate increases by Δt_i, to $t_i + \Delta t_i$ per unit, and prices increase from p^1 to p^2. The marginal excess burden, ΔB_E, associated with the equivalent variation resulting from such a tax increase is the amount that the consumer would pay, in addition to the extra tax, in order to avoid the increase. Hence:

$$\Delta B_E = m^2 - E(p^1, U^2) - \{R(p^2, m^2) - R(p^1, m^2)\} \tag{8.14}$$

It is important to recognize that the change in revenue on the right hand side of (14) cannot simply be expressed, for each good, as the change in the tax rate, Δt_i, multiplied by the new quantity demanded. This is because the extra tax means that the consumption of each good falls further; this in turn means that the revenue associated with the initial tax rate of t_i falls correspondingly. This type of argument has important implications for measures of the marginal welfare cost of taxation discussed below.

Using the above approach, equation (14) can be rearranged to give:

---

[8]Movement in the other direction involves the relation:

$$x^H(p,U) = x^H(p, V(p,m)) = x^M(p,m)$$

where V denotes the indirect utility function.

$$B_E = m^2 - E(p^1, U^2) - \sum_{i=1}^{n} \Delta t_i x_i^M (p_i^2, m^2) + \sum t_i \{x_i^H (p_i^1, U^2) - x_i^M (p_i^2, m^2)\} \qquad (8.15)$$

The tax revenue measures given above are all given for a tax per unit of output, but it is often necessary to consider *ad valorem* taxes in which the tax rate is expressed as a proportion of the value of each good. Suppose that t_i now denotes the tax-exclusive rate imposed on good i. Since the prices faced by consumers are tax-inclusive, the expression for total revenue must use the equivalent tax-inclusive rate $t_i / (1 + t_i)$. Hence equation (10) becomes:

$$R(p^1, m^1) = \sum_{i=1}^{n} (\frac{t_i}{1 + t_i}) p_i x_i^M (p_i^1, m^1) \qquad (8.16)$$

The question arises of whether any particular measure of welfare change, and hence excess burden, is 'superior' to others. Several authors, for example Kay (1980), Pazner and Sadka (1980), King (1983), McKenzie (1983) and Pauwels (1986), have argued that the equivalent variation is superior. In the case of the compensating variation the welfare loss is based on the post-tax prices, whereas the tax revenue is measured in terms of values based on the pre-tax prices. If several alternative tax policies are examined, the compensating variation has the theoretically unsatisfactory property that it gives comparisons involving different prices for each policy. These problems do not arise with the use of equivalent variations. Furthermore, the excess burden based on the equivalent variation is minimized at optimal tax rates, unlike the compensating variation. A detailed comparison of alternative excess burden measures was made by Mayshar (1990). For an axiomatic treatment of alternative welfare change measures, see Ebert (1995), who showed that no measure can claim to be unequivocally superior to others and that the choice of measure cannot avoid value judgements.

8.3.2 Approximating the excess burden

One very common approach to measurement difficulties, following Harberger (1964), is to give up any attempt to provide a precise measure, requiring detailed information about utility functions and associated expenditure functions, and to employ an approximation to welfare changes. For example, following the introduction of a tax structure, taking a Taylor series expansion of $E(p^1, U) - E(p^0, U)$ and neglecting third and higher-order terms gives:

$$E(p^1, U) - E(p^0, U) = \sum_{i=1}^{n} \frac{\partial E}{\partial p_i} dp_i + \frac{1}{2} \sum_{i=1}^{n} \sum_{j=1}^{n} \frac{\partial^2 E}{\partial p_i \partial p_j} dp_i dp_j \qquad (8.17)$$

Since the tax revenue can be expressed, using $dp_i = p_i^1 - p_i^0$, as $\sum_{i=1}^{n} x_i dp_i = \sum_{i=1}^{n} \frac{\partial E}{\partial p_i} dp_i$, which is the same as the first term in (17), the excess burden is approximated by:

$$B = \frac{1}{2} \sum_{i=1}^{n} \sum_{j=1}^{n} s_{ij} dp_i dp_j \qquad (8.18)$$

where s_{ij} is the i, jth element of the symmetric matrix S, with $s_{ij} = \partial x_i^H / \partial p_j = \partial^2 E(p, U) / \partial p_i \partial p_j$. This enables the excess burden to be approximated without knowing the precise form of the utility function, so long as estimates of the compensated elasticities are available. Furthermore, for such small changes there is no distinction between the burden defined in terms of compensated and equivalent variations.

The use of such approximations makes the calculation of excess burdens relatively quick and cheap, partly because the usual approach is to obtain elasticities from other demand studies, which in turn usually means that a high level of aggregation is considered. This kind of approach gives rough illustrative calculations and sensitivity analyses are unfortunately rarely reported. A more serious use of the approximations would involve obtaining, subject to data availability, compensated demand elasticities for a range of demographic or other groups, and providing sensitivity analyses (based perhaps on the estimated standard errors of the demand function parameters).

The approximate welfare change measures may be used on the argument that, because only the first derivatives of demand functions are required, they are not likely to be very sensitive to the precise specification of the demand equations estimated. This is an important point, so long as attention is restricted to small tax changes. Critics of such an approach would argue (based on the use of methods discussed in later sections of this paper) that the additional cost of producing the 'exact' welfare measures is negligible, so that at least it would be helpful to compare results.

The approach considered in this subsection was to take a second-order approximation to the excess burden for a single individual. In evaluating the overall effect of a tax change, use is often made of the aggregate value of excess burdens in a specified population group. This is equivalent to the use of a social welfare function defined as a simple sum of such burdens, so it implies no aversion to inequality on the part of the judge. An alternative approach is to specify a social welfare function which differs in to ways from the total burden. First, the welfare function may be specified in terms of individual utilities, and secondly the form of the welfare function may allow for some aversion to inequality. This approach is considered in the next section.

8.4   Social Welfare Changes

8.4.1   A social welfare function

Instead of considering the aggregate value of welfare change measures, a social welfare function can be specified in terms of individual utilities. If V_h denotes the (indirect) utility of the *hth* household, (for $h=1,..., H$) then the welfare function, W, can be expressed in general terms as $W = W(V_1,...,V_H)$. The first derivative of W with respect to the price of the *ith* good is given by:

$$\frac{\partial W}{\partial p_i} = \sum_{h=1}^{H} \frac{\partial W}{\partial V_h} \frac{\partial V_h}{\partial p_i} \tag{8.19}$$

Use can then be made of Roy's identity[9] (the 'envelope theorem') which establishes a link between the Marshallian demands and the indirect utility function, such that (omitting the M superscript used earlier):

$$x_{hi}(p,m_h) = -\frac{\partial V_h(p,m_h)/\partial p_i}{\partial V_h(p,m_h)/\partial m_h} \tag{8.20}$$

Hence:

$$\frac{\partial W}{\partial p_i} = -\sum_{h=1}^{H} \xi_h x_{hi} \tag{8.21}$$

---

[9]Chipman and Moore (1980, p. 934) point out that the term 'identity' is inappropriate, and that the result was produced earlier by Antonelli.See also Cornes (1992, p.56-58).

with:

$$\xi_h = \frac{\partial W}{\partial V_h} \frac{\partial V_h}{\partial m_h} \qquad (8.22)$$

The term ξ_h can be interpreted as the social marginal utility of income of household h. The ξs therefore define a set of distributional weights. These weights are in general not independent of prices; for a statement of the conditions on both welfare and utility functions required for independence, see Banks et al. (1996a, pp.1230-1232). Differentiation of (21) with respect to p_i gives the second derivative:

$$\frac{\partial^2 W}{\partial p_i^2} = -\sum \left(\frac{\partial \xi_h}{\partial p_i} x_{hi} + \frac{\partial x_{hi}}{\partial p_i} \xi_h \right) \qquad (8.23)$$

8.4.2 Approximating social welfare changes

The above results can be used to obtain a second-order approximation to a change in social welfare, ΔW, resulting from a change in the price of the *ith* good of Δp_i The Taylor expansion, ignoring third and higher-order terms, gives:

$$\frac{\Delta W}{\Delta p_i} \approx \frac{\partial W}{\partial p_i} + \frac{\Delta p_i}{2} \frac{\partial^2 W}{\partial p_i^2} \qquad (8.24)$$

Substitution for the first and second derivatives, using (21) and (23) gives, as in Banks et al. (1996a, p.1229):

$$\frac{\partial W}{\partial p_i} = -\sum_{h=1}^{H} \xi_h x_{hi} \left[1 + \frac{\Delta p_i}{2 p_i} \left(\frac{\partial \log \xi_h}{\partial \log p_i} + \frac{\partial \log x_{hi}}{\partial \log p_i} \right) \right] \qquad (8.25)$$

The first point to note about this second-order approximation is that it involves the use of Marshallian own-price demand elasticities, whereas the approximation using the excess burden measure involves the use of compensated demand elasticities.

A special case of this approximation is of interest. Suppose that there is no aversion to inequality, so $\xi_h = 1$ for all h. The change in social welfare becomes, on substituting (21) and (23) into (24):

$$\Delta W = -\Delta p_i \{ \sum_{h=1}^{H} x_{hi} + \frac{\Delta p_i}{2} \frac{\partial \sum_{h=1}^{H} x_{hi}}{\partial p_i} \} \tag{8.26}$$

The first implication of equal welfare weights is that only the aggregate quantity change is relevant. If the price change arises from the introduction of a tax per unit of $t_i = \Delta p_i$, then the first term in (26), $-\Delta p_i \sum_{h=1}^{H} x_{hi}$, is the total tax revenue arising from this good, based on the pre-tax total quantity[10]. Subtracting this from the absolute value of the welfare change, and writing $\partial \sum_{h=1}^{H} x_{hi} / \partial p_i$ as $\Delta \sum_{h=1}^{H} x_{hi} / \Delta p_i$, gives the approximation to the excess welfare burden, B_W, of:

$$B_W = \frac{t_i}{2} \Delta \sum_{h=1}^{H} x_{hi} \tag{8.27}$$

Hence, in the case where a new tax is imposed on a single good, the second-order approximation to the social welfare loss, in excess of the tax revenue, is simply half the tax rate multiplied by the change in the aggregate quantity consumed. This is of course the famous measure, based on the area of a triangle associated with the market demand curve that was produced by Dupuit (1844) and Jenkin (1871). It continues to be presented in the vast majority of introductory text books, motivated simply by the use of the standard Marshallian consumer and producer surplus concepts applied to market curves.

It was mentioned earlier, when discussing Figure 1, that for a single price change the change in Marshallian consumer surplus lies between the compensating and equivalent variations, so that in some cases the Marshallian measure may provide a 'reasonable' approximation to a theoretically more appealing measure. However, the same cannot be said of the corresponding excess burden, which can differ substantially from the 'exact' measure.

The use of first- and second-order approximations, using social welfare functions based on both money welfare changes and utility for each household,

---

[10]If taxes are already imposed on other goods, then the aggregate tax revenue must allow for substitution effects. This is treated in the following subsection.

and allowing for different degrees of aversion to inequality, has been examined by Banks et al. (1996a). They found (in the context of the elimination of exemptions for value added taxation) that second-order approximations do indeed perform quite well in terms of welfare changes, but they did not report excess burdens. Obviously, the approximations perform better, the smaller is the price change examined.

8.4.3 Marginal tax reform

One approach is to concentrate exclusively on small, or marginal, tax changes. Using the above social welfare function, specified in terms of utilities, the marginal change in social welfare resulting from a change in the price of the *ith* good is given simply by the expression for $\partial W / \partial p_i$ given in equation (21) above. The method, pioneered by Feldstein (1972) and extended by Ahmad and Stern (1984), involves comparing, for each commodity, the marginal change in social welfare arising from a tax change with the marginal change in total tax revenue. The change in aggregate tax revenue arising from a marginal change in any single tax must now allow for the consequent changes in taxation arising from existing taxes on all other goods, because of substitution effects.

If, as before, t_i is the tax per unit imposed on good i, then aggregate tax revenue, R, is given by:

$$R = \sum_{h=1}^{H} \sum_{k=1}^{n} t_k x_{hk} \tag{8.28}$$

Differentiating with respect to the *ith* tax rate, and using $\partial p_i = \partial t_i$, on the assumption that the tax is fully passed on to consumers, gives:

$$\frac{\partial R}{\partial t_i} = \sum_{h=1}^{H} x_{hi} + \sum_{h=1}^{H} \sum_{k=1}^{n} t_k \frac{\partial x_{hk}}{\partial p_i} \tag{8.29}$$

The ratio, $(\partial W / \partial t_i)/(\partial R / \partial t_i) = 1/\rho_i$, measures the change in social welfare per dollar of extra tax revenue resulting from a marginal change in the tax. In order to avoid a discontinuity if the change in revenue is zero, Madden (1995) suggested taking the value of ρ_i, giving the marginal revenue cost of reform. For an optimal tax system, the marginal revenue cost of reform must be equal for all goods. Hence, the *direction* of a marginal tax reform is indicated by the relative magnitudes of this ratio for each commodity group. Furthermore, by multiplying numerator and denominator by p_i, an expression involving expenditures (rather than quantities) and cross-price elasticities is obtained. In particular, the change in revenue is $p_i X_i + \sum_k \tau_k \eta_{ki} p_k X_k$, where   is aggregate demand, X_i is the elasticity of demand for k with respect to the price of i, and τ_k is the ratio of the tax to the tax-inclusive price.

The method can be used for alternative specifications of the social welfare function, giving rise to alternative sets of the ξ_hs. In practice, it is usual to specify the social welfare function in terms of each household's total expenditure (adjusted using equivalent household scales), rather than utility. The conditions under which this is consistent are given by Banks et al. (1996a, p.1232). It does not imply price-independence.

This approach requires expenditure data to be available for each commodity group at the household level, but a useful property of (29) is that it involves only aggregate Marshallian changes in demand, evaluated at the current position. This gives a considerable reduction in information required. The approach was initially used by Ahmad and Stern (1984) in the context of a developing country where data are relatively scarce, but it has since been used in developed countries; for applications and further references see Stern and Newbery (1987), Newbery (1995), Mayshar and Yitzhaki (1995), Madden (1995, 1996, 1997) and Creedy (1997e). Deaton and Ng (1996) considered both parametric and non-parametric methods of obtaining the demand changes.

The problems of obtaining the aggregate elasticities should not of course be neglected. Comparisons of the implications of using alternative demand systems, carried out by Madden (1996), showed that similar results are obtained for different systems. This, as noted earlier, is likely in view of the fact that only demand changes at observed consumption levels are needed. He also found that the results are more sensitive to the dynamic specification of demand functions used. One practical problem is that the commodity groups which are relevant for tax purposes are not usually the same as those for which demand information is available.

8.5   Income Taxation and Labor Supply

The definitions of welfare change and excess burden given in the previous sections were discussed in the context of commodity taxes. The application of the concepts of welfare change and excess burden to the analysis of income taxation requires no new principles, but involves some subtle differences that are worth discussing. The compensating and equivalent variations resulting from an income tax change are examined in the first subsection. The special problems arising from the existence of non-linear budget constraints are discussed in the second subsection. The third subsection considers general equilibrium implications. Finally, approximations to excess burdens in the context of income taxation are presented.

The demand model can easily be extended, following the standard method of adding the consumption of leisure to the utility function and modifying the budget constraint accordingly. On tax and transfer systems with labor supply responses, and further references to the literature, see Creedy (1994, 1996). One effect of an income tax is that it affects the price of leisure, or its opportunity cost in terms of the consumption of goods. The standard demand model involves maximization of a utility function $U(x)$ subject to a budget constraint $m = \sum_{i=1}^{n} p_i x_i$, where   and   are consumption and tax-inclusive prices respectively. When the proportion of time devoted to leisure, h, is added, then the utility function becomes $U(x,h)$ and the budget constraint is changed to:

$$w(1-h) + g = \sum_{i=1}^{n} p_i x_i \qquad (8.30)$$

where g represents non-wage income and w is the net-of-tax wage rate. In some contexts, g may be influenced by a transfer system and may also depend on t. For example, if the income tax has a tax-free threshold, so that tax is a proportion of income measured in excess of the threshold, then for taxpayers this is equivalent to a proportional tax combined with a transfer payment equal to the threshold multiplied by the tax rate.

Rearrangement of (30) shows that this augmented model is equivalent to having an additional good, leisure, with a price of w, and a modified form of exogenous income, m, which is replaced by 'full income', M, where:

$$M = w + g \qquad (8.31)$$

Full income is therefore the value of earnings that would be obtained if all available time were spent working (that is, if $h=0$), plus any non-wage income, g. The expenditure function in this context gives the minimum full income needed to achieve a given utility level at a specified wage and set of goods prices.

There is not unanimity with regard to treatment of the expenditure function in this case. Some authors, for example Walker (1993, p.34-36) and Blundell et al. (1994, pp.22-27), define the expenditure function as giving the minimum non-wage income, rather than full income. In the standard indifference curve diagram of labor/leisure choice, the welfare change measures can in fact conveniently be shown in terms of changes in non-wage income. Blundell et al. (1994, p.24) do state that full income is a suitable measure if the endowment of time is given. The present approach is preferred partly because it reflects the minimum cost of consuming all goods, including leisure. It can also be adopted without modification to deal with tax changes in general equilibrium, where pre-tax factor prices also change.

A reduction in the net wage rate, resulting from an increase in income taxation, directly reduces the price of leisure and, through (31), involves a drop in the value of full income by reducing the market value of the individual's endowment of time. It is this dual effect that complicates the effect on welfare of an income tax change, and is examined in the following subsection.

8.5.1 Compensating and equivalent variations

The expressions for the compensating and equivalent variations, given earlier, need to be modified slightly in order to allow for the fact that full income and the price of leisure change in opposite directions when the income tax structure changes. The net-of-tax wage rate falls from w^0 to w^1 as a result of an income tax.

First, consider the compensating variation. The amount that an individual would need to be given to compensate for an increase in income taxation is equal to the full income that, at the new prices, would enable the old utility level to be reached, $E(w^1, U^0)$, less the full income obtained under the higher tax, M^1. Hence $CV = E(w^1, U^0) - M^1$. The former measure, the full income needed for U^0 at post tax wage w^1 is, in the case of an income tax increase, actually less than the original full income. This is because the tax increase involves a reduction in the price of a good, in this case leisure. The full income after the tax increase, M^1, is nevertheless below the amount needed to reach the appropriate point on the compensated leisure demand curve. If the standard definition of the compensating variation, as given in (1), is used along with expenditure functions defined in terms of non-wage income rather than full income, the absolute value is precisely the same as the expression given in the present paragraph.

FIGURE 8.2:
Compensated Labour Supply

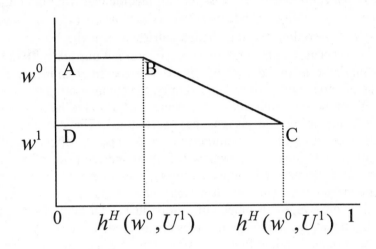

FIGURE 8.3:
Labour Supply and Welfare

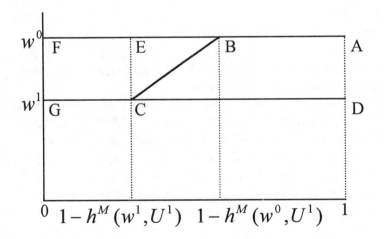

Secondly, consider the equivalent variation. The amount that the individual would be prepared to pay in the new situation in order to avoid the tax change is equal to the initial full income, M^0, less the full income that, with the initial net wage, generates the utility reached after the tax increase, $U(w^0, U^1)$. Hence $EV = M^0 - E(w^0, U^1)$ Avoiding the tax change carries with it the benefit of a higher full income (because of the higher net wage rate) but this is modified by the corresponding increase in the price of leisure. In the case of an increase in the price of a single good with a fixed labor supply, the compensating variation exceeds the equivalent variation, but in the context of variable labor supply models, the ranking for income tax changes is reversed. The complication arises essentially because of the simultaneous and opposite effect on the market value of the individual's endowment (of time) and the price of one of the goods (leisure) consumed. The above expressions can be used to examine the excess burdens arising from redistribution. This gives rise to different changes in the non-wage incomes of individuals. In the following diagrammatic treatment, the non-wage incomes are assumed to be fixed.

The above definitions do not at first sight appear to translate into areas, as in the case of a tax on a single commodity[11]. However, they are converted into areas by a simple transformation, whereby:

$$CV = \{E(w^1, U^0) - M^0\} + \{M^0 - M^1\} \tag{8.32}$$

$$EV = \{M^1 - E(w^0, U^1)\} + \{M^0 - M^1\} \tag{8.33}$$

The absolute value of the first term in curly brackets in each of the above expressions corresponds to an area to the left of a Hicksian (compensated) leisure demand curve between appropriate 'prices'.

The equivalent variation is shown in Figure 2. This shows the Hicksian demand curve for leisure which intersects the (unshown) Marshallian demand curve at $h^1 = h^M(w^1, M^1)$. The increase in welfare, the equivalent variation, arising from the reduction in the price of leisure is the area ABCD to the left of the compensated demand curve. This translates into the area, also marked ABCD, in Figure 3, which shows the corresponding labor supply curve; the relevant area is to the right of the supply curve. The change in full income,

---

[11]Some diagrammatic treatments of the burden of income tax using labor supply curves are incorrect although the correct excess burden 'triangle' is specified; see, for example, Browning (1976, p.285: 1987, p.12). Reference is often incorrectly made to areas 'underneath' the labor supply curve. The area is therefore specified in detail here.

with no change in non-wage income, is given by the area ADGF, so that the equivalent variation is the area FBCG (equal to the area ADGF less the area ABCD). The income tax revenue, the product of labor supply and the tax per unit of labor, is given by the area FECG. Hence the equivalent variation-based excess burden of the income tax is the area ECB.

8.5.2 Nonlinear budget constraints

The major practical problem when extending the model to deal with labor supply and the excess burden arising from income taxation is that the income ax system is seldom proportional. Tax and transfer systems are typically on linear, so that in practice it is necessary to deal with piecewise linear budget constraints. For each marginal tax rate, there is a separate linear section. The tax rate actually faced by each individual is therefor edogenous and depends on labor supply decisions.

In calculating the welfare changes associated with a particular tax change, t is therefore necessary to check whether the individual moves to another section of the budget constraint, so that the appropriate expenditure unction is used. For example, even with a proportional income tax the existence of non-wage income generates a corner solution corresponding to $h=1$, where the individual does not work and consumes only the non-wage income. Suppose that an increase in the tax rate is just sufficient to 'push' the individual to the corner. The equivalent variation for such a tax increase is the same as for any higher tax rise.

This point can be illustrated by the following example. Suppose the individual has Cobb-Douglas preferences $U=c^{\alpha}h^{1-\alpha}$, and $\alpha=0.7$, with non-wage income, g, equal to 25. A minimum wage of $w_{L}=g(1-\alpha)/\alpha=10.714$ is required for $h<1$. Suppose that in the absence of taxation, $w=15$, so that the individual works, $h=0.8$ and $c=28$. A tax rate of $t=0.3$ means that the net wage is 10.5 so that $h=1$ and $c=25$, giving $U'=9.518$. The expenditure function is $U(\frac{1}{\alpha})^{\alpha}(\frac{15}{1-\alpha})^{1-\alpha}$, so the equivalent variation is $40-$ $9.518(\frac{1}{\alpha})^{\alpha}(\frac{15}{1-\alpha})^{1-\alpha}$. This is the same as for a higher t because U^{1} is unaffected. Over the range where $h=1$, the expenditure function is $U^{1/\alpha}/\alpha$, so the compensating variation is given by $\frac{1}{\alpha}(28^{\alpha}0.8^{1-\alpha})^{1/\alpha}-(10.5+25)$. This is higher for a higher value of t, since the net wage would be lower than 10.5.

The implication of piecewise budget constraints that are concave is that there tends to be a 'bunching' of individuals at the corners. The use of means-testing in transfer systems means, however, that there may be convex parts of the constraint, which can generate discrete jumps at certain wage rates. On this type of phenomenon see Lambert (1985) and Creedy (1996). Furthermore, some budget constraints may not be continuous, as stressed by King (1987). Any tangency solution can be regarded as arising from an equivalent simple linear income tax with a proportional tax rate and an appropriate value of non-wage income. In econometric work, appropriate techniques have been developed to deal with such kinked budget constraints; for surveys of labor supply and taxation see, for example, Hausman (1985) and Blundell (1992).

8.5.3   General equilibrium effects

The previous discussion has been in the context of partial equilibrium where prices facing producers were assumed to be unchanged. However, a change in income and commodity taxes is likely to affect tax-exclusive prices, wages and profits, through general equilibrium effects. The expressions in (32) and (33) can nevertheless be applied directly to the general equilibrium context, given a model that allows for the interdependencies. Several such models have been developed, and these have helped to illustrate the way in which tax incidence can differ in the general, compared with the partial, equilibrium analyses, though a practical limitation is that they usually contain few individuals. One important advantage of general equilibrium models is that they force the user to be precise about the way in which the tax revenue is used.

To give an example, consider a static two-sector model with Cobb-Douglas production functions $x = L^{0.3}K^{0.7}$ and $y = L^{0.7}K^{0.3}$, where total supply of capital services is normalized to 1, and $p_x = 1$. Suppose there are two individuals with identical preferences $U = x^{0.3}y^{0.5}h^{0.2}$, and endowments of time normalized to 1 unit, where each person holds half of the available capital. Suppose the government spends 80 per cent of tax revenue on good x, and the remainder on good y (though the use of transfer payments could easily be examined in this framework). Two examples are shown in Table 1, corresponding to zero taxation and a proportional wage tax of 30 per cent. In this case, given the government's use of tax revenue, the introduction of the wage tax lead to an increase in the output of the capital-intensive good, x, so that the gross wage rate falls slightly, while the non-wage component of full income of each

TABLE 8.1:
Introduction of a Wage Tax

No.	x	y	p_y	wage	rental	revenue
1	0.469	0.818	0.954	0.50	0.562	0
2	0.526	0.703	0.944	0.49	0.567	0.187

individual increases slightly. The fall in the full income of each person is equal to 0.154, while the welfare rise associated with the fall in both p_y and the price of leisure is found to be 0.053. These results are obtained by making use of the expenditure function which is given in this case by $E(p,U) = U(\frac{1}{0.3})^{0.3}(\frac{p_y}{0.5})^{0.5}(\frac{w}{0.2})^{0.2}$, where w is the net wage. The net effect, from (33), is an equivalent variation of 0.101. Since the tax paid by each individual is 0.093, the excess burden of the wage tax is 0.008 for each person. In a partial equilibrium framework, the pre-tax wage, the prices of both goods and the capital rental would remain unchanged, giving a higher excess burden of 0.103; the proportional difference between the use of partial and general equilibrium approaches can therefore be substantial.

In practice, the general equilibrium tax models which have been constructed are at a high level of aggregation on the household side, although some of the models contain many different production sectors. It has proved to be extremely difficult to construct general equilibrium models which also handle the type of population heterogeneity that is usually required when examining the impact of detailed tax structure changes. Hence small-scale general equilibrium models have been used to examine specific issues; for an introduction to taxation in the general equilibrium framework, see Creedy (1997d). Further references to such models are made below, and for an extensive general equilibrium treatment of welfare costs of taxation, see Diewert and Lawrence (1994).

8.5.4   The welfare cost of income taxation

Several studies have focussed on measuring the excess burden, what is often called, following the terminology of Harberger (1964), the 'welfare cost' of income taxation, using an approximation to the excess burden as the measure of welfare cost: this is the area ECB in Figure 3 discussed above. The studies are typically carried out at a high level of aggregation, using a representative individual. This has the significant drawback that no attempt is made to deal with the considerable degree of heterogeneity found in practice, or to obtain econometric estimates of labor supply for different groups, allowing for the nonlinear budget constraints discussed above.

The approximation involves treating the compensated labor supply (corresponding to leisure demand) curve as linear. With a pre-tax wage of $w = w^0$ and a tax rate of t, the height of the resulting triangle is $w - (1 - t)w = tw$, the base is the change in labor supply, ΔL, so that the area of the triangle ECB is approximated by:

$$B = \frac{1}{2} t w \Delta L \tag{8.34}$$

The term ΔL is then replaced by $(\Delta L / \Delta w)tw$, using $\Delta w = tw$. If L denotes the post-tax labor supply, the compensated elasticity of labor supply with respect to the wage, η, is written as:

$$\eta = \frac{\Delta L}{\Delta w} \frac{w(1 - t)}{L} \tag{8.35}$$

and (34) becomes:

$$B = \frac{1}{2} \eta w L \left(\frac{t^2}{1 - t} \right) \tag{8.36}$$

Harberger (1964) and Browning (1976) initially evaluated the elasticity and earnings at pre-tax levels, giving a different value of L and omitting the term $(1 - t)$ from the denominator. The above approximation for the equivalent variation-based burden was given by Findlay and Jones (1982).

In obtaining numerical values, emphasis has been placed on the 'appropriate' values to use for each of the terms in (36), particularly t and η. The value of t is usually based on an average of tax rates. The resulting welfare cost measures are sensitive to these parameters.

This kind of welfare cost measure can be obtained with relatively little cost, but the practical application of this type of approximation is limited. The value of such aggregative measures is called into question, given the wide dispersion within the population, the lack of a clear link in practice between the value of t used in evaluating (36) and the tax rates that are the focus of policy debate, and the use of aggregate elasticities which ignore the important role of corner solutions. The approximation may have some pedagogic value in helping to illustrate the factors influencing the excess burden of income taxation, but aggregate measures bear no relation to practical tax structure changes that may realistically be considered. However, the use of a very high level of aggregation is not a necessary feature of studies using this approximation. For example, Wallace and Wasylenko (1992) used Browning's approach to examine the welfare effects of the 1986 tax reforms in the US. They used elasticities based on averages quoted from other studies, but applied them to individuals in micro-data sets, grouping the results into income deciles.

8.6   Marginal Welfare Cost and Cost of Funds

The previous discussion of excess burdens and marginal excess burdens, in section 3, was in terms of replacing (or partially replacing) a distorting tax with a lump sum tax involving no distortions. But this may not always be the relevant concept to examine, particularly where it is required to use an increase in tax revenue in order to finance an increase in government expenditure. The present section concentrates on the issues arising from this distinction.

The clarification of these issues actually arose from attempts to explain the substantial differences between marginal welfare cost calculations obtained by several different authors. Browning (1987) argued that these differences arose not because of the different models (for example partial and general equilibrium) or basic welfare concepts used, but because of the sensitivity of results to small differences in the various 'parameters'[12]. However, Ballard (1990) and Fullerton (1991) argued that the substantial reported differences arose also from the use of different concepts. Clarification of the marginal welfare cost concept then leads to the concept of the marginal cost of funds.

8.6.1   The marginal welfare cost

In defining his 'marginal welfare cost' of taxation measure, Browning (1987) used the difference between the equivalent variation resulting from the tax change and the change in tax revenue along the compensated demand

---

[12]An extension of the model to allow for involuntary unemployment and sticky wages was made by Freebairn (1995), who compared results using alternative models and found wide variations. His argument is that introducing these considerations shifts the emphasis of policy discussions away from the marginal tax rate. Browning's approach was applied to New Zealand by McKeown and Woodfield (1995), who used a somewhat more disaggregated approach.

curve, divided by the actual tax revenue after the tax change. Stuart (1984) used the difference between the compensating variation and the change in revenue, divided by the change in revenue. Alternatively, Ballard et al. (1985) used the difference between the equivalent variation and the change in revenue, divided by the change in revenue. Fullerton (1991) showed, for a variety of models and parameters, that the Stuart (1984) and Ballard et al. (1985) measures are generally close together, but the Browning measure is typically substantially higher. The first result is not surprising, since for a truly marginal change the equivalent and compensating variations are equal.

Ballard (1990) argued that a basic distinction needs to be drawn, following Musgrave's (1959) terminology, between differential incidence and balanced-budget analyses. In the former, comparisons are made involving the same amount of government expenditure; for example, comparisons may be made between lump sum taxation and distortionary taxes used to raise the same required revenue. This is precisely the type of comparison used when defining excess burdens. In balanced-budget analyses, government expenditure is increased and at the same time the tax system is changed in order to raise the extra revenue. This is the relevant type of analysis when the finance of a government project is being considered. In a general equilibrium analysis where an increase in taxation is used to finance higher transfer payments, the balanced budget analysis is equivalent to the differential study, since there is no change in the net tax paid. However, in most applications the distinction is important.

It seems useful, following Ballard (1990), to reserve the term 'marginal welfare cost' to refer only to balanced-budget analyses, using the same concept as in Ballard et al. (1985) mentioned above. By contrast, the 'marginal excess burden' refers to the change in welfare divided by the amount of distortionary tax revenue replaced by a lump sum tax.

The additional government expenditure involved in a balanced budget study means that, in addition to the distortionary effects of taxation considered in the differential incidence studies of excess burden, there are income effects which need to be considered. This type of argument led Atkinson and Stern (1974) to modify the standard optimality condition for a public good, in terms of equality between the marginal rate of transformation and the sum of marginal rates of substitution between the public good and private goods. The additional tax has implications for the ability of existing taxes to raise revenue. An interesting case arises if the supply of labor is backward bending, where it is possible for the marginal welfare cost to fall when income tax is increased. Ballard and Fullerton (1992, p.125) also gave an example of additional tax revenue being used to finance a road, which may give rise to an increase in the consumption of fuel. This has the effect of increasing the revenue from the existing fuel tax, irrespective of how the project is financed. These issues were also emphasized in a related paper by Triest (1990), who was concerned with the welfare cost of additional government expenditure financed from higher taxes, in a cost-benefit analyses.

These examples show that the effects of the particular new public project on behavior, especially regarding strong complements and substitutes, need to be considered. In the case of labor supply, the public project financed from the extra taxation may have significant effects depending on complementarity or substitutability with leisure. This was stressed by Snow and Warren (1996) who, allowing for this and other effects, carried out a comprehensive comparison of alternative measures of marginal welfare costs for small tax changes. They were able to show precisely why the various estimates given in the literature differ. They argued that further progress requires the inclusion of government spending as an explanatory variable in econometric studies of labor supply. Some empirical support for the including of government spending in labor supply has been provided by Conway (1997).

8.6.2   The marginal cost of funds

An important implication arising from these various studies is that while the marginal excess burden, or marginal welfare cost, is relevant for differential-incidence studies, the appropriate concept when considering the finance of a public project is the marginal cost of funds, MCF. This is defined as the change in the equivalent variation divided by the change in revenue, so that:

$$MCF = \frac{\Delta(EV)}{\Delta R} \tag{8.37}$$

The marginal welfare cost, MWC, as used in Ballard et al. (1985), is defined as:

$$MWC = \frac{\Delta(EV) - \Delta R}{\Delta R} \tag{8.38}$$

Hence the marginal welfare cost is just the marginal cost of funds, minus 1, and:

$$MWC = MCF - 1 \qquad\qquad (8.39)$$

The extended Samuelson condition requires that the sum of marginal rates of substitution should exceed the product of the marginal rate of transformation and the marginal cost of funds. As Fullerton (1991, p.306) mentioned, the marginal welfare cost can be zero even for a distorting tax, if the distortion is compensated by a positive revenue effect. Furthermore, a lump sum tax may, starting from a distorted situation, increase or decrease the excess burden, depending on whether it reduces or increases the revenue from other taxes.

Following an extensive examination of alternative excess burden measures, Mayshar (1990, p.263) concluded that the marginal cost of funds, as defined above, 'should be regarded as the most useful concept in applied tax analysis'.[13] However, this strong claim needs to be qualified: it is simply the relevant concept in balanced-budget studies, and is related in a very straightforward way to the marginal welfare cost (excess burden) that is relevant for differential incidence studies.

Related studies include Wildasin (1979) and Triest (1990). The relationship between the marginal cost of funds and tax evasion was examined by Usher (1986), and Fortin and Lacroix (1994) who compared the effects of tax increases with the use of higher penalties and a higher probability of detection. A detailed treatment of welfare costs and the cost of funds can also be found in Schob (1994), who introduced measures of the marginal benefit of public funds, along with modified measures of the marginal cost of funds, in an attempt to overcome the fact that standard measures of the marginal cost of funds require knowledge of the precise nature of the additional government expenditure. All these papers ignored distributional issues by using either identical individuals or a single individual.

The importance of the distinction between balanced budget and differential studies, along with the clarification of the role of the marginal cost of funds, are major points to arise from these analyses. The balanced budget context gives the same answer as the differential studies, corresponding to excess burden calculations, only when the extra government expenditure is equivalent to a cash transfer. A major lesson from the study of alternative models, culminating in the comparisons of Snow and Warren (1996) mentioned above, is that the form of the model can have important implications for the numerical

---

[13]Mayshar (1990, p. 267) referred to this marginal cost measure as a 'new measure', but later (1990, p. 279) he recognised that it is the measure used by Ballard et al. (1985).

orders of magnitude of the measures. Of particular importance is the issue of whether government expenditure affects labor supply.

The particular formulae used to examine marginal welfare costs for very small changes are perhaps of more practical value for the analysis of tax reforms[14]. The expressions involve elasticities and single marginal tax rates, and they do not require the form of the utility function to be specified. However, they are typically applied at the level of the representative consumer, with users taking point estimates of elasticities from other studies. In genuine applications, in contrast with theoretical comparisons, attention needs to be given to population heterogeneity. The focus on a representative consumer also means that distributional issues are entirely ignored, though such issues may be an important consideration in realistic policy considerations.

The approximations can, as mentioned above, be applied at lower levels of aggregation, given sufficient data for the estimation of demand systems. Appeal can then perhaps be made to the lack of sensitivity of the first derivatives of estimated demand equations (at observed consumption levels) to the functional form, or restrictions imposed for estimation purposes, as an argument in favor of using approximations. But it seems to be the case that those using the approximations have not been prepared, for whatever reason, to carry out the estimation themselves. Furthermore, given a set of estimates, only a small step is needed to obtain exact measures. It is also worth making the point many of the most important actual tax changes are not 'marginal'.

If it is desired to calculate 'exact' measures rather than approximations, the major requirement in practical studies is an appropriate method of obtaining either the form of the expenditure functions or their numerical values in relevant situations. The required welfare changes for a fully specified change in the tax structure can then be calculated, for each population group for which estimates are available, and the major constraint on the number of groups is imposed by data limitations. Alternative approaches are discussed in the following two sections.

---

[14]Even when using small general equilibrium models, the assumption is usually made that there is a single individual supplying labor and demanding goods. These analyses may nevertheless be useful in enabling the analysis to focus on some special cases.

8.7   Direct and Indirect Utility Functions

This section discusses approaches to the estimation of the required expenditure functions. The first approach involves starting from the direct utility function and deriving and then estimating the demand functions. The Marshallian demand functions can be derived by writing the form of the direct utility function $U(x)$ and maximizing subject to the constraint, $m = \sum_i p_i x_i$. The demand functions, and hence parameters of utility functions, are then estimated using appropriate econometric methods. The substitution of the demands $x^M(p,m)$ into $U(x)$ gives the indirect utility function $V(p,m)$. It is then only necessary to invert the indirect utility function in order to obtain the required expenditure function, $E(p,U)$. The appropriate terms required for the excess burdens can then be calculated directly[15].

The use of a direct utility function imposes a strong degree of 'structure', which is particularly useful for estimation purposes when few data are available. An early study along these lines was made by Rosen (1978), who compared results using several specifications and estimation procedures. He used the linear expenditure system estimated (for a representative consumer) using time-series data, and the constant elasticity of substitution and LES cases using household data. Rosen compared his aggregative measures with approximate measures (using approximations described above), but recognized that it is most unlikely that such approximations would actually be based on compensated elasticities calculated from a fully specified and estimated demand system. Subsection 7.1 shows how the approach via direct utility functions can be used in the context of the frequently used linear expenditure system.

One limitation of this direct utility approach is that solving the first-order conditions for utility maximization is not straightforward, or even possible, except in a few well-known cases. The second approach involves starting from a specification of the expenditure function itself, and deriving the demand functions. The demand functions can then be estimated, thereby giving the required parameters of the expenditure functions. Subsection 7.2 illustrates this approach using the almost ideal' demand model.

---

[15]However, McKenzie (1983, pp.42-44) points out that the process of inversion may not be possible in some cases.

8.7.1   The linear expenditure system

The linear expenditure system (LES) has additive utility functions of the form:

$$U = \prod_{i=1}^{n} (x_i - \gamma_i)^{\beta_i} \tag{8.40}$$

where γ_i is referred to as 'committed consumption', with $x_i > \gamma_i$, $0 \le \beta_i \le 1$; and $\sum_i \beta_i = 1$. Demand functions are given by:

$$p_i x_i = \gamma_i p_i + \beta_i (m - \sum_j p_j \gamma_j) \tag{8.41}$$

Substitution into U gives:

$$V(p,U) = (m - A)/B \tag{8.42}$$

where A and B are given by:

$$A = \sum_i p_i \gamma_i \tag{8.43}$$

$$B = \prod_i (\frac{p_i}{\beta_i})^{\beta_i} \tag{8.44}$$

The expenditure function, $E(p,U)$, is given by rearranging equation (42) to give:

$$E(p,U) = A + BU \tag{8.45}$$

Hence the compensating variation is:

$$CV = A^1 + B^1 U^0 - m^0 \tag{8.46}$$

After substituting for U^0, this can be rearranged to give:

$$CV = A^0[\frac{A^1}{A^0} + \frac{B^1}{B^0}(\frac{m^0}{A^0} - 1)] - m^0 \tag{8.47}$$

The term A^1 / A^0 is equal to $\sum_i p_i^1 \gamma_i / \sum_i p_i^0 \gamma_i$ and is therefore a Laspeyres type of price index, using the committed consumption of each good as the weight. This form can be converted to allow for taxes, or proportional changes in prices. If $\dot{p}_i$ denotes the proportionate change in the price of the *ith* good, then $A^1 / A^0 = 1 + \sum_i s_i \dot{p}_i$ where $s_i = p_i^0 \gamma_i / \sum_i p_i^0 \gamma_i$. In the case where a new *ad valorem* tax is introduced, then the proportional price change, $\dot{p}_i$, is simply equal to t_i. If a tax rate is increased by the absolute amount, Δt_i, then $\dot{p}_i = \Delta t_i / (1 + t_i)$.

The term B^1 / B^0 in (47) simplifies to:

$$\frac{B^1}{B^0} = \prod_i (\frac{p_i^1}{p_i^0})^{\beta_i} \tag{8.48}$$

which is a weighted geometric mean of price relatives. The equivalent variation is:

$$EV = m^1 - A^0[1 + \frac{B^0}{B^1}(\frac{m^1}{A^0} - \frac{A^1}{A^0})] \tag{8.49}$$

Given parameter estimates, the welfare changes can be calculated for each individual in a household expenditure survey, or for selected types of individual at specified income levels.

The linear expenditure system has been used extensively used; see, for example, Powell (1974), Lluch et al. (1977), and Dixon et al. (1982) where it forms the basis of the demand side of their multi-sector general equilibrium model. Muellbauer (1974) used the LES to examine the welfare effects of inflation in the UK, where parameters were estimated for a 'representative household', although distributional implications are implied by the changes in the two types of price index[16]. Dodgson (1983) used the LES, along with its special case of the Cobb-Douglas utility function (with parameters simply

---

[16]Stoker (1986) used the translog model to examine the welfare effects of inflation. All demand systems using a 'representative household', the total expenditure elasticities converge towards unity as total expenditure increases.

taken from average budget shares[17]) to compare the values of welfare change and excess burden, including the Harberger approximation, arising from indirect taxes in the UK. He found that for 14 commodity groups there was broad agreement between the measures of welfare change, but the Harberger approximation substantially overestimated the excess burden.

The assumption of additivity of the LES is very strong and implies, for example, that complementarity is ruled out and that own-price elasticities are approximately proportional to income elasticities; see Deaton (1974, 1975). The problems are generally thought to be less severe when broad commodity groups are used, though they are often regarded as representing the cost of overcoming data limitations. The main limitations usually relate to information about price responses at the required level of disaggregation.

When a single set of parameters is used (in a representative consumer context), one serious limitation of the LES is that its implications for indirect taxes are very strong, since it gives rise to uniform indirect taxes. However, it is possible to allow for heterogeneity. Instead of using a single set of parameters, welfare measures can be based on separate estimates of the LES for each of a range of total expenditure groups. Households within each group are assumed to have the same preferences, but these are allowed to vary with total expenditure. The uniformity of optimal indirect taxes does not arise with taste heterogeneity. It is possible to obtain estimates of the parameters of the linear expenditure system for each of a variety of total expenditure groups, using only cross-sectional budget data; see Creedy (1997a). As suggested above, the strong *a priori* restrictions underlying this type of parametric approach represent the cost of obtaining a large number of demand elasticities with limited data[18]. However, such a data limitation is a situation that faces many researchers who nevertheless need some idea of orders of magnitude in order to examine policy issues.

---

[17]The Cobb-Douglas is obtained from the LES\ simply by setting the committed expenditures to zero, so that the above results can easily be modified. Both Muellbauer and Dodgson used Deaton's (1975) estimates of the LES.

[18]The approach has been applied to the analysis of carbon taxation in Australia by Cornwell and Creedy (1996, 1997), inflation in Australia by Creedy and van de Ven (1997) and indirect tax reform in New Zealand by Creedy (1997b).

8.7.2   The almost ideal demand system

This subsection discusses the 'almost ideal' demand system, proposed by Deaton and Muellbauer (1980), which begins by specifying the form of the expenditure function rather than the direct utility function.

First, it is useful to consider the logarithmic form of Shephard's lemma, which relates budget shares to the expenditure function. From Shephard's lemma the compensated demand for the *ith* good, x^H, can be obtained using $x^H = \partial E(p,U)/\partial p_i$. Hence, it can be seen that the budget share, $w_i = x_i p_i / m$, with $m = \sum_i p_i x_i = E(p,U)$, is given by:

$$w_i = \frac{\partial \log E(p,U)}{\partial \log p_i} \tag{8.50}$$

If the expenditure function takes the form:

$$\log E(p,U) = a(p) + b(p)U \tag{8.51}$$

where a and b are general functions of the prices (that is, they are particular types of price index), the associated budget shares are:

$$w_i = p_i \frac{\partial a(p)}{\partial p_i} + U p_i \frac{\partial b(p)}{\partial p_i} \tag{8.52}$$

Writing the indirect utility as $U = (\log m - a)/b$, using (51), equation (52) can be expressed as:

$$w_i = p_i \frac{\partial a(p)}{\partial p_i} + \frac{p_i \partial b(p)}{b(p)\partial p_i} \log(\frac{m}{\exp a(p)}) \tag{8.53}$$

The 'almost ideal' demand system, proposed by Deaton and Muellbauer (1980), is obtained by specifying $a(p)$ and $b(p)$ as the following forms:

$$a(p) = \alpha_0 + \sum_k \alpha_k \log p_k + \frac{1}{2} \sum_k \sum_l \gamma_{kl}^* \log p_k \log p_l \tag{8.54}$$

$$b(p) = \beta_0 \prod_k p_k^{\beta_k} \tag{8.55}$$

The partial derivatives are therefore:

$$\frac{\partial a(p)}{\partial p_i} = \frac{1}{p_i}\{\alpha_i + \frac{1}{2}\sum(\gamma_{ik}^* + \gamma_{ki}^*)\log p_i\} \tag{8.56}$$

and:

$$\frac{\partial b(p)}{\partial p_i} = \frac{\beta_i}{p_i}b(p) \tag{8.57}$$

Defining the price index, $P = \exp a(p)$, and writing $\gamma_{ij} = \frac{1}{2}(\gamma_{ij}^* + \gamma_{ji}^*)$, the budget shares are given by:

$$w_i = \alpha_i + \sum_k \gamma_{ik}\log p_k + \beta_i \log(\frac{y}{P}) \tag{8.58}$$

Additivity requires $\sum_i \alpha_i = 1$, $\sum_k \gamma_{kj} = 0$ for all j, and $\sum_k \beta_k = 0$. In addition, homogeneity gives $\sum_k \gamma_{jk} = 0$ and symmetry gives $\gamma_{ij} = \gamma_{ji}$.

The price index, $P = \exp a(p)$, makes the budget shares highly nonlinear in the parameters, but if this can be approximated by a simple price index, the unrestricted form of the model can be estimated using ordinary least squares applied to each good in turn, using time series data[19].

Suppose prices change from p^0 to p^1. The equivalent variation, EV, is by definition $E(p^1, U^1) - E(p^0, U^1)$. Using $E(p^1, U^1) = m^1$ and:

$$U^1 = \frac{1}{b(p^1)}\log(\frac{m^1}{P^1}) \tag{8.59}$$

then, from (51):

$$EV = m^1 - \exp\{a(p^0) + b(p^0)U^1\} \tag{8.60}$$

and:

---

[19]On the use of the Stone price index suggested by Deaton and Muellbauer (1980), see Rougier (1997).

$$EV = m^1 - P^0 \exp\{\frac{b(p^0)}{b(p^1)}\log(\frac{m^1}{P^1})\} \qquad (8.61)$$

From (61), the ratio of the equivalent variation to the post-change income is given by:

$$\frac{EV}{m^1} = 1 - \exp\{\frac{b(p^0)}{b(p^1)}\log(\frac{m^1}{P^1}) - \log(\frac{m^1}{P^0})\} \qquad (8.62)$$

The price index $b(p^0)/b(p^1)$ is a weighted geometric mean of price relatives. If the price changes involve proportional changes of $\dot{p}_i$, then this index can be conveniently written as:

$$\frac{b(p^0)}{b(p^1)} = \prod_i (1 + \dot{p}_i)^{-\beta_i} \qquad (8.63)$$

It is instructive to compare the above expressions for the linear expenditure and the almost ideal demand systems. The almost ideal system has been extended in several ways; see, for example, Banks et al. (1996b). On the corresponding inverse demand system, see Eales and Unnevehr (1994).

8.8   From Marshallian to Hicksian Demands

The approaches described in the previous section involve obtaining the parameters of fully specified expenditure functions which are analytically linked to the demand functions that are estimated using available data. The imposition of a great deal of structure may often be useful, or indeed necessary, particularly where few data are available. But if there are a great deal of data, there may be circumstances in which such an approach is regarded as being too restrictive in allowing insufficient flexibility. Without the need to link demand and expenditure functions explicitly, a wider range of functional forms for the demand functions could be estimated; see, for example, McKenzie (1983, p.40). There is also the real danger that the welfare change measures obtained may depend too strongly on the form of the a priori restrictions imposed on the direct or indirect utility function[20].

This section describes two alternative approaches which begin from the specification of the Marshallian demand functions and work 'backwards' to get the information required, that is the values of the expenditure function for given prices and utility levels.

8.8.1 Algebraic integration

An approach that begins with the demand function was proposed by Mohring (1971), followed by Hause (1975) and explored further by Hausman (1981). This uses estimates of the Marshallian demand functions without reference to the direct utility function. Consider a single price change[21]. Along any indifference curve, the total differential of the indirect utility function must be zero, so that:

$$\frac{\partial V}{\partial p_i}\frac{dp_i}{dt} + \frac{\partial V}{\partial m}\frac{dm}{dt} = 0 \tag{8.64}$$

which can be re-arranged to give:

$$\frac{dm}{dp_i} = -\frac{\partial V / \partial p_i}{\partial V / \partial m} \tag{8.65}$$

But it is known from Roy's Identity that the right hand side of (65) is the Marshallian demand, $x^M(p,m)$. Hence the integration of $\partial m / \partial p_i = \partial E(p,U) / \partial p_i = x^M(p,m)$, along with an appropriate initial condition (for the constant of integration), gives the required minimum expenditure associated with any given utility level and set of prices.

Hause (1975) illustrated this approach using the cases of linear and log-linear Marshallian demands. Mohring (1971, p.352) gave an example

---

[20]It is this apparent need for a priori information about tastes that continues to stimulate the search for improved consumer surplus measures. An an example of a rather negative view, Bruce (1977, p.1037) argued that if compensating and equivalent variations, 'were operational, that would end the issue, but they are not', adding that 'market data do not reveal such relations as a matter of course'. It should be added that market demand functions are not directly observable either and that, as shown below, the welfare measures can be calculated directly from them.

[21]For more than one price change, the method raises awkward problems of integration.

142   *John Creedy*

involving demand functions of the form $x = \alpha m / p$ (which are of course known to be associated with Cobb-Douglas preferences)[22]. Hausman (1981) gave several numerical examples using the following linear case in the context of labor supply.

For a two-good model in which all quantities are deflated by the price of the second good, the Marshallian demand for good 1, is, omitting the subscript:

$$x = \gamma + \alpha p + \delta m \tag{8.66}$$

The differential equation to be solved is given by:

$$\frac{dm(p)}{dp} = r + \alpha p + \delta m \tag{8.67}$$

Giving the solution:

$$m(p) = c \exp(\delta p) - \frac{1}{\delta}(\alpha p + \frac{\alpha}{\delta} + \gamma) \tag{8.68}$$

Hausman selected the initial utility level, U, as the constant of integration, c. Substituting U for c and E for m therefore immediately gives the desired expenditure function as;

$$E(p,U) = U \exp(\delta p) - \frac{1}{\delta}(\alpha p + \frac{\alpha}{\delta} + r) \tag{8.69}$$

The term γ can be allowed to depend on various characteristics of households, so that welfare changes can be calculated for different types of household. Blomquist (1983) used this function to examine welfare changes in Sweden, and provided (pp.191-194) a detailed examination of the preferences implied by linear labor supply curves. Larson (1988) extended the basic approach to deal with supply curves and the case of the welfare changes facing producers in the face of price and production uncertainty. Larson (1992) later used the linear demand function results to illustrate how welfare changes resulting from quality changes of non-market goods could be evaluated.

---

[22]Mohring also gave numerical examples of the 'path dependency' problem, and gave what is effectively the equivalent income function (1971, p.352), discussed in section 9 below, raising the question of the set of prices to use as references prices.

Hause (1975, p.15) referred to the welfare change measures obtained by this type of approach as 'spuriously precise "exact" welfare change measures', but Hausman (1981) showed how the standard errors of the estimated parameters of the Marshallian demands can be used to attach sampling errors to the welfare changes. Criticisms of Hausman's illustrative welfare estimates were made by Browning (1985) and Haveman et al. (1987), but these did not concern the basic method of integrating from the Marshallian demands.

8.8.2 Numerical integration

In all but the simplest of cases, the explicit algebraic integration of the Marshallian demand functions is too awkward. However, it is possible to use an efficient numerical method of obtaining the Hicksian or compensated demands from the Marshallian demand function. Several procedures were suggested by McKenzie (1983), but they are rather awkward to use and seem to have received little attention. This subsection concentrates on examining a method introduced by Vartia (1983), although Balk (1995) showed that it was also contained in a rediscovered article by Malmquist (1993) that was originally written in the 1950s. The great value of a numerical procedure is that there is no need to be restricted to specifications for which explicit solutions to the integration problem can be obtained, along the lines indicated in the previous subsection.[23]

There have, however, been few applications of the technique, despite the fact that numerous references have been made to Vartia's method by critics of the continued use of approximations to welfare changes. A rare application of the method was by Hayes and Porter-Hudak (1987) who examined welfare effects of the price rise resulting from the 1973 oil embargo. Bockstael and McConnell (1993) showed in principle how the method can be use in the context of public goods. Wright and Williams (1988) examined the use of the method in the context of gains from market stabilization, allowing for various degrees of risk aversion. Creel (1997) used Vartia's method in combination with Fourier functional forms for demand.

---

[23]Hausman and Newey (1995) explored the use of nonparametric estimation procedures instead of parameterising the Marshallian demand curve, along with a numerical method of integration that differs from that of Vartia. Varian (1982) devised a nonparametric method using an approach based on revealed preferences. However, these methods, particularly the latter, require extensive data.

The method provides an extremely rapid numerical procedure that can easily be programmed and offers a great deal of potential, allowing welfare measures to be produced easily from demand functions that have been estimated without reference to an underlying (direct or indirect) utility function and which cannot be integrated analytically. For this reason and the fact that it has found so few applications, the following description states the algorithm using different notation from that of Vartia, and illustrates the use of the method for a hypothetical example.

Suppose that the Marshallian demand functions of n goods have been estimated. As before, the initial prices are denoted by p_i^0, giving rise to initial quantities demanded of x_i^0, for $i=1,...,$n. (The superscript, M, for Marshallian, has been omitted here for convenience). The level of total expenditure is m^0. A tax change leads to a new set of prices, p_i^1, for which the new demands can easily be calculated from the Marshallian demand function; but the problem is to calculate the appropriate values of $E(p,U)$. This involves moving along the required indifference curve.

The first step involves setting a number of intervals, N, into which the price ranges are to be divided. A higher value of N increases the accuracy of the procedure. Then, for each good, i, obtain the following ($N+1$ element) price vectors, for $j=1,..., N+1$:

$$p_i(j) = p_i^0 + k(j)(p_i^1 - p_i^0)$$ (8.70)

where:

$$k(j) = \frac{j-1}{N}$$ (8.71)

The technique involves repeating the following iterative procedure for values of j from $j=2$ up to $j=N+1$. For each value of j, it is required to find the 'stable' value of m, say $m(j)$, and 'stable' values of demands, say $x_i(j)$ for each good. Each stage, s, requires repeated calculation of quantities demanded, $x_i^{j(s)}$ for the jth price in the interval and the adjusted value of m, say $m^{j(s)}$, using, for each good, i:

$$x_i^{j(s)} = x_i(p_1(j),...,p_n(j), m^{j(s-1)})$$ (8.7)

with:

$$m^{j(s)} = m(j-1) + 0.5\sum_{i=1}^{n}\{x_i^{j(s)} + x_i(j-1)\}\{p(j) - p(j-1)\} \tag{8.73}$$

using $x_i(1) = x_i^0$ and $m(1) = m^0$. Furthermore, $m^{j(1)} = m(j-1)$. Equations (72) and (73) are repeated until:

$$\left| m^{j(s)} - m^{j(s-1)} \right| \leq \delta \tag{8.74}$$

with the value of δ set arbitrarily small; stability is usually achieved rapidly for each j. Equation (72) is evaluated using the estimated set of demand equations. Once this convergence has been reached, then the 'stable' value of $m^{j(s)}$ and the associated demands $x_i^{j(s)}$ are used for the next, that is the $j+1th$, set of values, $m(j+1)$ and $x_i(j+1)$. In practice, care should be taken to avoid setting δ too small, even with large N; a value of $\delta = 0.00001$ is usually appropriate. The accuracy of the method depends mainly on the number of intervals used for any particular context; experiments can quickly reveal the order of magnitude to use for N.

When the values for $j = N+1$ have been calculated, the resulting 'stable' values of and the s are the compensated values of total expenditure and demands. Hence the final x_i s correspond to those that are on the indifference surface passing through the initial consumption bundle, but with the new set of prices. Importantly, the final value of obtained corresponds to the value of the expenditure function $E(p^1, U^0)$. The compensating variation is therefore simply given by the difference between this final stable value and the initial value of total expenditure, m^0. In order to calculate $E(p^0, U^1)$, from which the equivalent variation can be calculated, it is necessary to repeat the whole exercise by going 'backwards' from the price vector p^1 to the vector p^0. The exact sampling properties of the resulting estimates have not been obtained, but their precision was examined by Porter-Hudak and Hayes (1986, 1987).

8.8.3   A three-good example

Each step of the above procedure converges rapidly, so it is possible to compute the welfare changes extremely quickly for large N. In order to demonstrate the use of the method, suppose that, for a particular type of individual, the following Marshallian demands have been obtained, using standard econometric methods. For each of three goods ($i=1,2$):

$$x_i^M = \frac{\theta_i m}{p_i} \tag{8.75}$$

Here the prices represent the tax-inclusive prices. These demands are of course known to arise from a Cobb-Douglas utility function and are chosen purely for convenience. As stated above, the value of Vartia's method is that it can be applied to any set of demands.

Suppose that $\theta_1=0.35$, $\theta_2=0.45$ and $\theta_3=0.2$, $m=100$, while the initial prices are equal to 1, 1.2 and 1.5 respectively for goods 1 to 3. Suppose that *ad valorem* taxes are imposed leading to new prices of 1.1, 1.32 and 1.8; that is, $t_i=0.1$ for all i The application of the above method (for $\delta=0.00001$ and $N=100$) gives the results shown in Table 2. The row labeled p^0 shows the Marshallian demands for the pre-tax prices, along with the Hicksian demands corresponding to post-tax utility, U^1; the latter are obviously lower than the former because $U^1<U^0$. The row labeled p^1 shows the Marshallian demands for the post-tax prices, along with the Hicksian demands corresponding to pre-tax utility U^0. The final two columns of the table give the values of minimum total expenditure for each price and utility combination.

Using the results shown in Table 2, the compensating and equivalent variations resulting from the tax change are equal to 11.931 and 10.659 respectively. Using the values in the table, it can be found that the tax revenue is equal to 10.606, while the revenue that would be obtained from the Hicksian demands, for prices p^1 and utility U^0, is equal to 11.871. Hence the excess burden based on the compensating variation, B_C, is 0.060, while that based on the equivalent variation, B_E, is 0.053.

TABLE 8.2:
Hypothetical Example of Vartia's Method

	Marshallian demands			Hicksian demands			$E(p,U)$	
	x_1^M	x_2^M	x_3^M	x_1^H	x_2^H	x_3^H	U^0	U^1
p^0	35	37.5	13.33	31.269	33.503	11.912	100	89.341
p^1	31.818	34.091	11.11	35.614	38.158	12.437	111.931	100

8.8.4   Income taxation

Consider instead an individual consuming two goods and leisure, where the demand functions take the same form as above, but respecified in terms of full income, and leisure is the third good with $\theta_3 = 0.2$. In using Vartia's approach, the value of m must of course be replaced by the sum of non-wage income and the product of the net wage and the endowment of time. In the present example, the endowment of time has been normalized to unity. Suppose that non-wage income is fixed at 20, while the prices of the two goods are fixed at 1 and 1.2 respectively, and the wage rate is initially 100. Hence full income is initially 120. The demands for goods 1 and 2, and leisure, are found to be 42, 45 and 0.24 respectively. The introduction of a proportional income tax, at the rate of 0.2, reduces the full income to 100, reduces the demands for the two goods to 35 and 37.5, and increases the
demand for leisure to 0.25.

Using Vartia's method, the (Hicksian) consumption levels giving the initial utility, after the introduction of the tax, are 40.167, 43.036 and 0.287 respectively, corresponding to a full income of 114.762. The compensation required for the tax is therefore 14.762. The (Hicksian) demands corresponding to the post-tax utility level, at the initial prices, are found to be 36.597, 39.2115 and 0.209 respectively, corresponding to a full income of 104.564. Avoiding the introduction of the tax would involve returning to the full income of 120, so in the post-tax position the individual would be prepared to pay the difference between 120 and 104.564, that is 15.436, in order to avoid the tax.

In practice, sets of demand functions, including labor supply functions, would be estimated for a large range of household types. The numerical integration method could then be applied to each of a number of hypothetical households, or to each household in a budget survey. Nonlinear budget constraints, leading to jumps and other discontinuities in labor supply functions, can be accommodated.

In some cases, the effects of specified income tax changes may be the primary focus of analysis and only a set of labor supply functions may be available. The above method can easily be carried out without the need for any information about the demand functions for commodity groups. This is because, as seen from equation (73), the demands for those goods for which there is no price change are irrelevant. Hence the above income tax example could be repeated without any consideration of the commodity demands, giving precisely the same values for the excess burdens. Care must be taken when using a given labor supply function, specified for example in terms of hours worked corresponding to a wage specified perhaps as an hourly rate, to ensure that full income is defined appropriately. This requires the maximum number of hours that can be worked (or the endowment of time) to be given. In the above example, the 'endowment' of time has been normalized to one unit. Obviously, leisure and not labor supply must be fed into the numerical procedure.

8.9   The Use of Equivalent Incomes

The previous two sections have discussed alternative methods of calculating welfare changes for particular population groups, distinguished by income and other characteristics. It may, however, be required to provide an overall evaluation of a change in the tax structure. Such an evaluation can be carried out using a specified social welfare function that reflects a judge's value judgements. Section 4 discussed the use of social welfare functions in terms of utilities. This section discusses the use of welfare functions expressed in terms of the distribution of individuals', or households', 'equivalent incomes'.

The use of the concept of equivalent income was explored in detail by King (1983). Examples using this concept, allowing for labor supply variations, include Apps and Savage (1989) who used the 'almost ideal' demand system of Deaton and Muellbauer (1980), and Fortin and Truchon (1993) who used the linear expenditure system. An early brief discussion of equivalent incomes using the linear expenditure system was provided by Roberts (1980).

8.9.1   The equivalent income function

Equivalent income is defined, following King (1983), as the value of income, m_e, which, at some reference set of prices, p_r, gives the same utility as the actual income level. In terms of the indirect utility function, m_e is therefore defined by the equation:

$$V(p_r, m_e) = V(p, m) \tag{8.76}$$

Using the expenditure or cost function gives:

$$m_e = E(p_r, V(p, m)) \tag{8.77}$$

This may be written as:

$$m_e = F(p_r, p, m) \tag{8.78}$$

where the function F is referred to as the equivalent income function. An advantage of the equivalent income concept is that comparisons are made using a fixed set of reference prices, and it does not depend on the cardinalisation of utility functions used[24].

King (1983, pp.208-210) gave the equivalent income function for the utility functions generating linear demands, loglinear demands, and the almost ideal demand system He also stated the equivalent income functions for the direct utility functions associated with the linear expenditure system and the indirect translog system. Consider, for example, the linear expenditure system. The results of section 6 can be used to show that:

$$m_e = A_r + \frac{B_r(m - A)}{B} \tag{8.79}$$

Expanding the terms in A and B gives:

$$m_e = \sum_i p_{ri}\gamma_i + \{\prod_i (\frac{p_{ri}}{p_i})^{\beta_i}\}\{m - \sum_j p_j\gamma_j\} \tag{8.80}$$

Consider the use of pre-change prices as reference prices, so that $p_{ri} = p_i^0$ for all i. Substitution into equation (80) shows immediately that pre-change equivalent income is simply the actual income (or total expenditure) and the post-change equivalent income is the value of actual income after the change less the value of the equivalent variation; that is, $m_e^1 = m^1 - EV$. In the case where $m^0 = m^1 = m$, the proportional change in equivalent income resulting from the price change is simply EV/m. If all prices change by the same proportion, then the value of EV/m is the same for all levels of m, so that any relative measure of inequality based on the distribution of equivalent incomes is unchanged.

---

[24]The use of equivalent incomes in optimal tax models has been explored by Creedy (1997c); this avoids the dependence of optimal tax rates on the particular cardinalisation of utility functions used.

Equivalent incomes are, as in the example of the linear expenditure system given here, nonlinear functions of the estimated parameters of the utility functions. Their sampling properties can therefore be examined using approximations such as that given by Goldberger (1964); the standard errors of welfare measures using this type of approach were discussed by King (1983, pp.210-212).

8.9.2   Social evaluations

The effect on a specified social welfare or evaluation function of a change in prices and incomes can be measured in terms of a change in the distribution of equivalent incomes. Values of the social welfare function can be calculated for a population group using a complete distribution of values of m_e^0 and m_e^1 so that, according to the value judgements implicit in the welfare function, a change can be judged in terms of its overall effect.

Instead of starting with an explicit form of the social welfare function, an initial analysis might, for example, first examine the generalized Lorenz curves for the distributions of m_e^0 and m_e^1 to see if standard 'dominance' results apply; for a statement of the various dominance conditions available, see Lambert (1993). These give comparisons of social welfare involving a minimum of assumptions about the precise form of welfare function. If these results do not provide a complete ordering of the distributions, then fully specified welfare functions can be evaluated using the distribution of equivalent incomes.

Consider, for example, the use of a social welfare function defined in terms of equivalent incomes, such that welfare per person, W, is given by:

$$W = \frac{1}{N} \sum_{i=1}^{N} \frac{m_{e,i}^{1-\varepsilon}}{1-\varepsilon} \qquad (8.81)$$

where ε is the degree of constant relative inequality aversion of the judge. This has the abbreviated form, expressed in terms of the arithmetic mean, $\overline{m}_e$, and Atkinson's inequality measure, I_A, of equivalent income, given by:

$$W = \overline{m}_e (1 - I_A) \qquad (8.82)$$

This conveniently reflects the trade-off between mean equivalent income and its equality, or what is often referred to as the trade-off between 'equity and efficiency', that the judge finds acceptable. Alternative forms of the welfare function may of course be used. For example, welfare rationales are available for the use of (82) along with the Gini inequality measure (or extended Gini measure) substituted for the Atkinson inequality measure; on alternative abbreviated welfare functions, see Lambert (1993). In practice it would be useful to examine the implications of adopting a range of value judgements.

8.10   Review of Strategies

It is appropriate to consider the major lessons arising from this review of concepts and methods, although dogmatism is best avoided as this is obviously an area where many issues are matters of judgement and preferences. First, and most obviously, it seems worth repeating the point that anyone who has gone to the trouble of estimating a Marshallian demand curve for a particular good has the information required for the evaluation of compensating or equivalent variations resulting from a price change. This is true even if the estimates are not based on any explicit restrictions introduced by specifying the form of direct or indirect utility functions. In some cases, algebraic integration can be carried out, but in the majority of cases (particularly when changes in several prices are considered), numerical methods of integration are needed. Having estimated the demands, this type of integration can be carried out for a small additional cost of time, given a computer program for performing the necessary iterations.

8.10.1 The level of aggregation

An important issue concerns the level of aggregation to be used. In the context of income taxation, numerous studies have attempted to measure the overall burden of taxation or the marginal welfare cost of a small change in taxation (or the associate marginal cost of funds). The methods used are usually (though not always) based on 'representative individual' models, so that a single number is produced, based on a single compensated labor supply elasticity and tax rate. In addition, the tax system is summarized by a proportional tax. Such aggregate measures are invariably based on an approximation to the welfare measure, and the value used for the elasticity is typically taken from another study. Such studies can be carried out relatively quickly at low cost, but can perhaps be regarded as providing illustrations rather than reliable estimates; in some cases they might even be described in pejorative terms as 'back of the envelope' calculations. The results are attractive to those who wish to emphasize the welfare cost of taxation in popular debate by stating that, for example, 'for every $1 of income tax revenue, there is an excess burden of x cents'. Such studies have nevertheless helped to clarify some of the concepts involved and have provided an idea of the sensitivity of results to the assumptions used. A high level of aggregation (on the consumption side) is used in general equilibrium models. These, being based on assumed preferences, produce 'exact' welfare change measures and have the advantage that they are able to allow for changes in input prices that result from the reallocation of resources consequent on the tax change. It has proved to be extremely difficult to build general equilibrium models displaying substantial heterogeneity on the household side. Hence, in practice a trade-off is involved between the level of aggregation and the desire to handle factor price changes.

Any practical policy analysis inevitably involves the more complex tax and transfer systems generally found in industrialized countries. Hence it is necessary to allow explicitly for the fact that there is a wide dispersion of welfare costs across the population. Individuals differ in the tax rates they face. Furthermore, such rates are endogenous, since they depend on labor supply decisions. It is suggested that, whenever possible, it would be best to avoid using a high level of aggregation; for strong criticisms of the use of a high level of aggregation and representative individual models, see Hammond (1990). It would be useful to attempt to examine welfare changes for a wide range of individuals or households. Policy analysis, faced with the distribution of changes, can then introduce explicitly the required value judgements in an evaluation of the overall effect of a tax change. This means a concentration on the demand side and, as suggested above, a neglect of general equilibrium considerations. It may be that progress here can be made by finding some way of linking the outputs of models developed for general equilibrium and household analyses.

8.10.2 The use of approximations

The use of approximations raises somewhat different considerations and is not necessarily linked to the level of aggregation used[25]. Such approximations

---

[25]In considering marginal indirect tax reform, it was however mentioned that consumption information is required at the household level but that only aggregate elasticities are needed. Hence the approach usually involves the use of aggregate time-series data to obtain price

are attractive because they give results that can be expressed in terms of demand elasticities which are evaluated at observed expenditure levels. It is not appropriate to think that the use of approximations is necessarily quicker or cheaper than the calculation of 'exact' measures, except of course where elasticities are taken from other studies. Determination of the elasticities requires an extensive exercise in applied demand analysis that involves estimating a set of demand functions which could in fact be used to obtain exact measures.

The use of approximations is more likely to be motivated by the judgement that the estimated demand functions may be unreliable for extrapolation purposes. This may be combined with the view that the first derivatives of demand functions are perhaps not so sensitive to the precise functional form used. Sensitivity analysis is still strongly recommended and it must always be remembered that only marginal tax changes can be examined.

The approximations relate to individuals whose positions are considered to be described by tangency solutions. They cannot handle those individuals who are at corner solutions or who, as a result of price changes, move towards or away from corner solutions. Furthermore, it has to be recognized that there is a practical need for the welfare evaluation of tax and other policy changes that cannot sensibly be regarded as marginal. Examples of non-marginal changes include a partial tax shift from direct to indirect taxation, a flattening of the income tax structure by eliminating higher marginal rates, and introducing or eliminating a tax on a particular good. It is this type of change which also gives rise to most public debate. This raises the need for an approach in which the 'exact' welfare changes imposed on different types of household, and arising from a fully specified set of tax changes, can be evaluated. The model must be able to capture, as far as possible, the complexity of actual tax and transfer systems in operation. However, the special sense in which the term 'exact' is used in this context needs to be recognized; attention needs to be given to sampling variations.

8.10.3 The importance of the demand model

As discussed in some detail in this paper, the essential ingredient for the calculation of welfare measures is a method of evaluating expenditure functions. This can be achieved either by 'moving' from the direct or indirect utility function to specification and estimation of the demand functions (and

---

elasticities which are then applied to a cross-sectional household expenditure survey (with consequent diffuculties of matching commodity groups used).

hence parameters of utility functions), or by integrating from estimated demand functions that have been obtained without imposing such strong a priori restrictions. The choice of approach will be substantially influenced by the nature of the available data.

Attempts to examine income tax changes present special problems because of the added complexity of the non-linear budget constraints, although if the focus is on income taxation it is not necessary simultaneously to model the complexity of commodity demands. As stressed by King (1987, p.62), 'the quality of the model and associated parameter estimates is the critical factor in assessing the plausibility of the simulated gains and losses'. The model provides the foundation for welfare analysis. The question of the appropriate concepts to use in measuring welfare changes has been extensively debated and does not present the major challenge.

The real problems in and costs of any practical study arise from the difficulties, relating to available data, estimation and testing, of obtaining the demand model (including leisure demand). Ideally, the construction of a suitable model would begin (in the absence of longitudinal data) with a substantial data set consisting of a time series of household expenditure surveys, where information is available about labor supply as well as the various income sources, along with a time series of price indices for the same commodity groups as used in the cross-sectional budget surveys. The resulting large data set would enable a reasonable degree of disaggregation in estimating demand and labor supply functions. The production, 'cleaning' and preparation of such a data set is an extensive and important exercise which should not be discounted. The luxury of being able to use this kind of resource is in fact available in only a few countries.

The specification and estimation of a demand and labor supply model then represents a major challenge, requiring careful judgement and a range of applied econometric skills. This usually requires a considerable degree of 'experimentation' with alternative approaches; one approach is seldom unambiguously superior to others. In general, more 'structure' has to be imposed if available data, particularly regarding price responses, are limited. For surveys of applied demand analysis see, for example, Deaton (1986), Blundell (1988), Blundell et al. (1993) and Clements et al. (1996).

Having produced and estimated a suitable demand model, the next step involves the production of computer software which is capable of applying particular tax structures to a sample of households and evaluating the welfare changes for each household. A variety of distributional analyses can then be carried out, including the study of detailed effects for particular types of household, the production of inequality measures and the examination of alternative social evaluation functions which embody explicit value judgements. This kind of project inevitably involves a certain amount of team work drawing on a range of skills, including computing skills. It is therefore not surprising that the best examples of this type of work have come from special research center or groups relying on substantial grants.

8.11   Conclusions

This paper has examined alternative concepts of the welfare cost of taxation, along with practical approaches to measurement problems. The major concepts of welfare change, including excess burdens and the marginal cost of funds, were discussed, with particular attention being paid to the case of income taxation where labor supplies are variable. Various approximations to the welfare measures were examined, including the analysis of marginal tax reforms. Alternative approaches to the practical measurement of 'exact' welfare changes were then examined. These included approaches based on the specification of either the direct or the indirect utility function, and the derivation of associated demand functions that are then estimated. Alternatively, 'unrestricted' estimates of Marshallian demand functions can be used, where the required values of expenditure functions are obtained either by algebraic or numerical integration methods. Finally, the evaluation of tax changes using social welfare functions defined in terms of equivalent incomes was discussed.

The fundamental requirement of any detailed practical analysis of welfare changes is a suitable consumer demand model, along with empirical estimates of the required demand functions including, where relevant, labor supply functions. Data constraints are therefore likely to play a crucial role in determining the choice of approach. The applied demand and labor supply analysis is also the most costly part of the exercise, and requires much judgement and skill. With a solid foundation, it is then possible to add a range of welfare analyses. Having invested in the fixed cost of producing suitable software for the analysis of alternative tax policies, reforms can be examined at relatively little additional cost.

Finally, it is perhaps worth considering whether attempts to measure welfare costs are actually worthwhile, given the difficulties faced and the data limitations facing most studies. Could it be said that the study of welfare costs represent the Holy Grail of applied microeconomics, and would it be better to avoid reporting spuriously accurate results that may be substantially influenced by a priori assumptions rather than the data used? Are such attempts actually worse than useless? It is of course not difficult to find expressions of such nihilistic views. But while the problems should certainly not be minimized, debates regarding tax reforms (particularly those of the non-marginal variety) are necessarily framed in terms of their expected effects on 'equity and efficiency'. In the absence of serious attempts to measure the orders of magnitude involved, any debate will inevitably be influenced instead only by uninformed guesses and rhetoric. It is suggested that careful studies which make the assumptions clear, stress their limitations and provide a range of sensitivity analyses, can make a valuable contribution to decision-making and the evaluation of existing tax structures.

APPENDIX: Glossary of Symbols Used

p_i Consumer price of good i ($i=1,...n$)

x_i Consumption of good i

m Budget (income) $\geq \sum_{i=1}^{n} p_i x_i$

$U(x)$ Direct utility function

$V(p,m)$ Indirect utility function

$E(p,U)$ Expenditure (cost) function

$x_i^M(p,m)$ Marshallian demand function: $x_i^M = -\dfrac{\partial V(p,m)/\partial p_i}{\partial V(p,m)/\partial m}$

$x_i^H(p,U)$ Hicksian (compensated) demand function: $x_i^H = \partial E(p,U)/\partial p_i$

CV Compensating variation for change in prices from p^0 to p^1,
$= E(p^1,U^0) - E(p^0,U^0)$. Also: $V(p^1,m^0+CV)=V(p^0,m^0)$
For fixed m, $CV = \sum_{i=1}^{n} \int_{p_i^0}^{p_i^1} x_i^H(p,U^0)dp_i$

EV Equivalent variation for change in prices from p^0 to p^1,
$E(p^1,U^1) - E(p^0,U^1)$. Also: $V(p^0,m^1-EV)=V(p^1,m^1)$
For fixed m, $EV = \sum_{i=1}^{n} \int_{p_i^0}^{p_i^1} x_i^H(p,U^1)dp_i$

$R(p,m)$ Tax revenue

B_C Excess burden based on CV, given by $CV - R(p^1,E(p^1,U^0))$

B_E Excess burden based on EV, given by $EV - R(p^1,m^1)$

$W(V)$ Social welfare function based on utitlities

ξ_h Social marginal utility of h

w_i Budget share of ith good: $p_i x_i / m = \partial \log E(p,U) / \partial \log p_i$

S Matrix of substutution terms: $s_{ij} = \partial^2 E(p,U) / \partial p_i \partial p_j$

REFERENCES

[1]   Ahmad, E. and Stern, N. H. (1984) The Theory of Tax Reform and Indian Indirect Taxes. *Journal of Public Economics*, 25, pp. 259-289.

[2]   Anderson, R. W. (1980) Some Theory of Inverse Demand for Applied Demand Analysis. *European Economic Review*, 14, pp. 281-290.

[3]   Apps, P. and Savage, E. (1989) Labor Supply, Welfare Rankings and the Measurement of Inequality. *Journal of Public Economics*, 47, pp. 336-364.

[4]   Auerbach, A. J. (1985) The Theory of Excess Burden and Optimal Taxation. In *Handbook Of Public Economics*, vol.1 (ed. by A. J. Auerbach and M. Feldstein), pp. 61-127. Amsterdam: Elsevier.

[5]   Atkinson, A. B. and Stern, N. H. (1974) Pigou, Taxation and Public Goods. *Review Of Economic Studies*, 41, pp. 119-128.

[6]   Balk, B. M. (1995) Approximating a Cost-of-living Index from Demand Functions: A Retrospect. *Economics Letters*, 49, pp. 147-155.

[7]   Ballard, C. L. (1990) Marginal Welfare Cost Calculations: Differential Analysis vs. Balanced-Budget Analysis. *Journal of Public Economics*, 41, pp. 263-276.

[8]   Ballard , C. L. and Fullerton, D. (1992) Distortionary Taxation and the Provision of Public Goods. *Journal of Economic Perspectives*, 6, pp. 117-131.

[9]   Ballard, C. L., Shoven J. B. and Whalley J. (1985) The Total Welfare Cost of the United States Tax System: A General Equilibrium Approach. *National Tax Journal*, 38, pp. 125-140.

[10] Banks, J., Blundell, R. and Lewbel, A. (1996a) Tax Reform and Welfare Measurement: Do we Need Demand System Estimation? *Economic Journal*, 106, pp. 1227-1241.

[11] Banks, J., Blundell, R. and Lewbel, A. (1996b) Quadratic Engel Curves, Indirect Tax Reform and Welfare Measurement. *Review of Economics and Statistics,*

[12] Becht, M. (1995) The Theory and Estimation of Individual and Social Welfare Measures. *Journal of Economic Surveys,* 9, pp. 53-87.

[13] Blackorby, C. and Donaldson, D. (1988) Money Metric Utility: A Harmless Normalization? *Journal of Economic Theory.* 46, pp. 120-129.

[14] Blomquist, N. S. (1983) The Effect of Income Taxation on the Labor Supply of Married Men in Sweden. *Journal of Public Economics,* 22, pp. 169-97.

[15] Blundell, R. (1988) Consumer Demand Behavior: Theory and Empirical Evidence - A Survey. *Economic Journal,* 98, pp. 16-65.

[16] Blundell, R. (1992) Labor Supply and Taxation: A Survey *Fiscal Studies,* 13, pp. 15-40.

[17] Blundell, R., Pashardes, P. and Weber, G. (1993) What do we Learn About Consumer Demand Patterns from Micro Data? *American Economic Review,* 83, pp. 570-597.

[18] Blundell, R., Preston, I. and Walker, I. (eds.) (1994) *The Measurement of Household Welfare.* Cambridge: Cambridge University Press.

[19] Bockstael, N. E. and McConnell, K. E. (1993) Public Goods as Characteristics of Nonmarket Commodities. *The Economic Journal,* 103, pp. 1244-1257.

[20] Breslaw, J. A. and Smith, J. B. (1995) Measuring Welfare Changes When Quantity is Constrained. *Journal of Business and Economic Statistics,* 13, pp. 95-103.

[21] Browning, E. K. (1985) A Critical Appraisal of Hausman's Welfare Cost Estimates. *Journal of Political Economy,* 93, pp. 1025-1034.

[22]   Browning, E. K. (1977) A Hidden Welfare Cost of Taxation. *National Tax Journal*, 30, pp. 89-90.

[23]   Browning, E. K. (1987) On The Marginal Welfare Cost of Taxation, *American Economic Review*, 77, pp. 11-23.

[24]   Browning, E. K. (1976) The Marginal Cost of Public Funds, *Journal of Political Economy*, 84, pp. 283-298.

[25]   Bruce, N. (1977) A Note on Consumers Surplus, The Divisia Index, and The Measurement of Welfare Changes. *Econometrica*, 45, pp. 1033-1038.

[26]   Chipman, J. S. and Moore, J. C. (1980) Compensating Variation, Consumer's Surplus, And Welfare. *American Economic Review*, 70, pp. 933-949.

[27]   Clements, K. W., Selvanathan, A. and Selvanathan, S. (1996) Applied Demand Analysis: A Survey. *Economic Record*, 72, pp. 63-81.

[28]   Conway, K. S. (1997) Labor Supply, Taxes, and Government Spending: a Microeconometric Analysis. *Review of Economic Studies*, LXXIX, pp. 50-67.

[29]   Cornes, R. (1992) *Duality and Modern Economics*. Cambridge: Cambridge University Press.

[30]   Cornwell, A. and Creedy, J. (1996) Carbon Taxes, Prices and Inequality in Australia. *Fiscal Studies*, 17, pp. 21-38.

[31]   Cornwell, A. and Creedy, J. (1997) *Environmental Taxes and Economic Welfare: Reducing Carbon Dioxide Emissions*. Aldershot: Edward Elgar.

[32]   Creedy, J. (1994) Taxes and Transfers with Endogenous Earnings: Some Basic Analytics. *Bulletin of Economic Research*, 46, pp. 97-130.

[33]   Creedy, J. (1996) *Fiscal Policy and Social Welfare: An Analysis of Alternative Tax and Transfer Systems*. pp. xi+260. Aldershot: Edward Elgar.

[34]   Creedy, J. (1997a) Measuring the Welfare Effects of Price Changes: A Convenient Parametric Approach. *Australian Economic Papers* (forthcoming).

[35]   Creedy, J. (1997b) *Statics and Dynamics of Income Distribution in New Zealand. Wellington*: Institute of Policy Studies.

[36]   Creedy, J. (1997c) The Optimal Linear Income Tax: Utility or Equivalent Income, Scottish *Journal of Political Economy*, (forthcoming).

[37]   Creedy, J. (1997d) Taxation in General Equilibrium: An Introduction. *Bulletin of Economic Research*, 49, pp. 177-203.

[38]   Creedy, J. (1997e) Marginal Indirect Tax Reform in Australia. *University of Melbourne Department of Economics Research Paper*.

[39]   Creedy, J. and van de Ven, J. (1997) The Distributional Effects of Inflation in Australia 1980-1995. *Australian Economic Review*, 30, pp. 125-143.

[40]   Creel, M. D. (1997) Welfare Estimation using the Fourier Form: Simulation Evidence for the Recreational Demand Case. *Review of Economics and Statistics*, LXXIX, pp. 88-94.

[41]   Dahlby, B. G. (1977) The Measurement Of Consumer Surplus And The Path Dependence Problem. *Public Finance*, 32, pp.293-311.

[42]   Deaton, A. S. (1974) A Reconsideration of the Empirical Implications of Additive Preferences. *Economic Journal*, 84, pp. 338-348.

[43]   Deaton, A. S. (1975) *Models and Projections of Demand in Post-war Britain*. London: Chapman and Hall.

[44] Deaton, A. S. (1979) The Distance Function in Consumer Behavior with Applications to Index Numbers and Optimal Taxation. *Review of Economic Studies*, 46, pp. 391-405.

[45] Deaton, A. S. (1986) Demand Analysis. In *Handbook of Econometrics*, vol. III. (ed. by Z. Griliches and M. D. Intriligator), pp. 1768-1839. New York: North-Holland

[46] Deaton, A. S. and Muellbauer, J. (1980) *Economics and Consumer Behaviour*. Cambridge: Cambridge University Press.

[47] Deaton, A. S and Ng, S. (1996) Parametric and Non-parametric Approaches to Price and Tax Reform. *NBER Working Paper*, no. 5564.

[48] Diamond, P. A. and McFadden, D. L. (1974) Some Uses of the Expenditure Function in Public Finance. *Journal of Public Economics*.3, pp. 3-21.

[49] Diewert, W. E. and Lawrence, D. A. (1994) *The Marginal Costs of Taxation in New Zealand*. Canberra: Swan Consultation.

[50] Dixon, P., Parmenter, B. R., Sutton, J. and Vincent, D. P. (1982) ORANI: *A Multisectoral Model of the Australian Economy*. Amsterdam: North Holland Publishing Company.

[51] Dodgson, J. (1988) On the Accuracy and Appropriateness of Alternative Measures of Excess Burden. *The Economic Journal*, 93 (Supp), pp. 105-113.

[52] Dupuit, J. (1844) De la Mesure de L'utilite Des Travaux Publics. *Annales Des Ponts Et Chaussees 8*. Translated and reprinted in *Readings In Welfare Economics* (ed. by K. Arrow and T.Scitovsky), London: Allen and Unwin, 1969, pp. 255-283.

[53] Eales, J. S. and Unnevehr, L. J. (1994) The Inverse Almost Ideal Demand System. *European Economic Review*, 38, pp. 101-115.

[54] Ebert, U. (1995) Consumer's Surplus: Simple Solutions to an Old Problem. *Bulletin of Economic Research*, 47, pp. 285-294.

[55]   Feldstein, M. S. (1972) Distributional Equity and the Optimal Structure of Public Prices. *American Economic Review*, 62, pp. 32-36.

[56]   Findlay, C. C. and Jones, R. L. (1982) The Marginal Cost of Australian Income Taxation. *The Economic Record*, 58, pp. 253-262.

[57]   Fortin, B. and Lacroix, G. (1994) Labor Supply, Tax Evasion and the Marginal Cost of Public Funds: An Empirical Investigation. *Journal of Public Economics*, 55, pp. 407-431.

[58]   Fortin, B., Truchon, M. and Beausejour, L. (1993) On Reforming the Welfare System: Workfare Meets the Negative Income Tax. *Journal of Public Economics*, 51, pp. 119-151.

[59]   Foster, C. D. and Neuburger, H. L. I. (1974) The Ambiguity of the Consumer's Surplus Measure of Welfare Change. *Oxford Economic Papers*, 26, pp. 66-77.

[60]   Freebairn, J. (1995) Reconsidering the Marginal Welfare Cost of Taxation. *The Economic Record*, 71, pp. 121-131.

[61]   Fullerton, D. (1991) Reconciling Recent Estimates of the Marginal Welfare Cost of Taxation. *American Economic Review*, 81, pp. 302-308.

[62]   Goldberger, A. S. (1964) *Econometric theory*. Chichester: Wiley.

[63]   Hammond, P. J. (1990) Theoretical Progress in Public Economics: A Provocative Assessment. *Oxford Economic Papers*, 42, pp. 6-33.

[64]   Harberger, A. C. (1964) Taxation, Resource Allocation and Welfare. In *The Role Of Direct And Indirect Taxes In The Federal Reserve System*. Princeton N. J.: Princeton University Press.

[65]   Hause, J. C. (1975) The Theory of Welfare Cost Measurement. *Journal of Political Economy*, 83, pp. 1145-1182.

[66]   Hausman, J. A. (1981) Exact Consumer's Surplus and Deadweight Loss. *American Economic Review*, 71, pp. 662-676.

[67]   Hausman, J. A. (1985) The Econometrics of Nonlinear Budget Sets. *Econometrica*, 53, pp. 1255-1282.

[68]   Hausman, J. A. and Newey, W. K. (1995) Nonparametric Estimation of Exact Consumers Surplus and Deadweight Loss. *Econometrica*, 63, pp. 1445-1476.

[69]   Haveman, Robert H., Gabay, M. and Andreoni, J. (1987) Exact Consumer's Surplus and Deadweight Loss: A Correction. *American Economic Review*, 77, pp. 494-495.

[70]   Jenkin, F. (1871) On The Principles Which Regulate the Incidence of Taxes. Proceedings of the Royal Society of Edinburgh. In *Readings In The Economics Of Taxation* (ed. by R. A. Musgrave and C. S. Shoup), pp. 227-239. London: Allen and Unwin.

[71]   Johansson, P-0. (1987) *The Economic Theory and Measurement of Environmental Benefits*. Cambridge: Cambridge University Press.

[72]   Kaplow, L. (1996) The Optimal Supply of Public Goods and the Distortionary Cost of Taxation. *National tax Journal*, XLIX, pp. 513-533.

[73]   Kay, J. A. (1980) The Deadwight Loss From A Tax System. *Journal of Public Economics*, 13, pp. 111-119.

[74]   King, M. A. (1983) Welfare Analysis of Tax Reforms Using Household Data. *Journal of Public Economics*, 21, pp. 183-214.

[75]   King, M. A. (1987) Empirical Analysis of Tax Reforms. In *Advances in Econometrics*, Volume II (ed. by T. F. Bewly). Cambridge: Cambridge University Press.

[76]   Lambert, P. J. (1985) Endogenizing the Income Distribution: The Redistributive Effect, and Laffer Effects, of a Progressive Tax-Benefit System. *European Journal Of Political Economy*, 1, pp. 3-20.

[77] Lambert, P. J. (1993) *The Distribution and Redistribution of Income.* Manchester: Manchester University Press.

[78] Larson, D. M. (1988) Exact Welfare Measurement For Producers Under Uncertainty. *American Journal Of Agricultural Economics*, 70, pp. 597-603.

[79] Larson, D. M. (1992) Further Results on Willingness to Pay For Nonmarket Goods. *Journal Of Environmental Economics And Management*, 23, pp. 101-122.

[80] Lluch, C., Powell, A. A. and Williams, R. A. (1977) *Patterns in Household Demand and Saving.* Oxford: Oxford University Press for the World Bank.

[81] Madden, D. (1995) An Analysis of Indirect Tax Reform in Ireland in The 1980s. *Fiscal Studies*, 16, pp. 18-37.

[82] Madden, D. (1996) Marginal Tax Reform and the Specification of Consumer Demand Systems. *Oxford Economic Papers*, 48, pp. 556-567.

[83] Madden, D. (1997) Conditional Demand and Marginal Tax Reform. *Oxford Bulletin of Economics and Statistics*, 59, pp. 237-255.

[84] Malmquist, S. (1993) Index Numbers and Demand Functions. *The Journal of Productivity Analysis*, 4, pp. 251-260.

[85] Marshall, A. (1890) *Principles Of Economics.* (9th edn (1961) ed. by C. W. Guillebaud). London: Macmillan.

[86] Mayshar, J. (1990) On Measures of Excess Burden and their Application. *Journal of Public Economics*, 43, pp. 263-290.

[87] Mayshar, J. and Yitzhaki, S. (1995) Dalton-improving Indirect Tax Reform. *American Economic Review*, 85, pp. 793-807.

[88] McKeown, P. C. and Woodfield, A. E. (1995) The Welfare Cost of Taxation in New Zealand Following Major Tax Reforms. *New Zealand Economic Papers*, 29, pp. 41-62.

[89] McKenzie, G. (1983) *Measuring Economic Welfare: New Methods*, Cambridge: Cambridge University Press.

[90] Mohring, H. (1971) Alternative Welfare Gain And Loss Measures. *Western Economic Journal*, 9, pp. 349-368.

[91] Muellbauer, J. (1974) Prices and Inequality: The United Kingdom Experience. *Economic Journal*, 84, pp. 32-55.

[92] Musgrave, R. A. (1959) *The Theory Of Public Finance*. New York: McGraw Hill.

[93] Newbery, D. M. (1995) The Distributional Impact of Price Changes in Hungary and The United Kingdom. *Economic Journal*, 105, pp. 847-863.

[94] Newbery, D. M. and Stern, N. (eds.) (1987) *The Theory of Taxation for Developing Countries*. Oxford University Press for the World Bank.

[95] Pauwels, W. (1986) Correct and Incorrect Measures of Deadweight Loss of Taxation. *Public Finance*, 41, pp. 267-276.

[96] Pazner, E. A. and Sadka, E. (1980) Excess Burden and Economic Surplus as Consistent Welfare Indicators. *Public Finance*, 35, pp. 439-449.

[97] Porter-Hudak, S. and Hayes, K. (1986) The Statistical Precision of a Numerical Methods Estimator as Applied to Welfare Loss. *Economics Letters*, 20, pp. 255-257.

[98] Porter-Hudak, S. and Hayes, K. (1987) Regional Welfare Loss Measures of the 1973 Oil Embargo: A Numerical Methods Approach. *Applied Economics*, 19, pp. 1317-1327.

[99] Powell, A. A. (1974) *Empirical Analytics of Demand Systems*. Lexington, Massachusetts: *Lexington Books*.

[100] Roberts, K. (1980) Price-Independent Welfare Prescriptions. *Journal of Public Economics*, 18, pp. 277-297.

[101] Rosen, H. S. (1978) The Measurement of Excess Burden With Explicit Utility Functions. *Journal of Political Economy*, 86, pp. S121-S136.

[102] Rougier, J. (1997) A Simple Necessary Condition for Negativity in the Almost Ideal Demand System with the Stone Price Index. *Applied Economics Letters*, 4, pp. 97-99

[103] Schob, R. (1994) On Marginal Cost and Marginal Benefit of Public Funds. *Public Finance*, 49, pp. 87-106.

[104] Snow, A. and Warren, R. S. (1996) The Marginal Welfare Cost of Public Funds: Theory and Estimates. *Journal Of Public Economics*, 61, pp. 289-305.

[105] Stahl, D. O.(1985) A Note on the Consumer Surplus Path-of-integration Problem. *Economica*, 50, pp. 95-98.

[106] Stoker, T. M. (1986) The Distributional Welfare Effects of Rising Prices in the United States: The 1970's Experience. *American Economic Review*, 76, pp. 335-349.

[107] Stuart, C. (1984) Welfare Cost Per Dollar of Additional Tax Revenue in The United States. *American Economic Review*, 74, pp. 352-362.

[108] Triest, R. K. (1990) The Relationship Between the Marginal Cost of Public Funds and Marginal Excess Burden. *American Economic Review*, 80, pp. 557-566.

[109] Usher, D. (1986) Tax Evasion and the Marginal Cost of Public Funds. *Economic Inquiry*, 24, pp. 563-586.

[110] Varian, H. (1982) The Nonparametric Approach to Demand Analysis. *Econometrica*, 50, pp. 945-973.

[111] Vartia, Y. O. (1983) Efficient Methods of Measuring Welfare Change and Compensated Income in Terms of Demand Functions. *Econometrica*, 51, pp. 79-98.

[112] Walker, I. (1993) Income Taxation, Income Support Policies and Work Incentives In The UK. *In Current Issues In Public Sector Economics* (ed. by P. M. Jackson), pp. 31-57. London: Macmillan.

[113] Wallace, S. and Wasylenko, M. (1992) Tax Reform 1986 and Marginal Welfare Changes For Labor. *Southern Economic Journal*, 59, pp. 39-48.

[114] Wildasin, D. E. (1979) Public Good Provision With Optimal and Non-Optimal Commodity Taxation. *Economic Letters*, 4, pp. 59-64.

[115] Willig, R. D. (1976) Consumer's Surplus Without Apology. *American Economic Review*, 66, pp. 589-597.

[116] Wright, B. D. and Williams J. C. (1988) Measurement Of Consumer Gains From Market Stablization. *American Journal Of Agricultural Economics*, 70, pp. 616-627.

[117] Youn Kim, H. (1997) Inverse Demand Systems and Welfare Measurement in Quantity Space. *Southern Economic Journal*, 63, pp. 663-679.

Chapter 9

DECOMPOSING THE REDISTRIBUTIVE EFFECT OF TAXES: NEW MEASURES OF VERTICAL EQUITY AND INEQUITY

John P. Formby
Department of Economics, University of Alabama, Tuscaloosa,
AL 35487, USA

Hoseong Kim
Department of Economics, University of Alabama, Tuscaloosa,
AL 35487, USA

W. James Smith
Department of Economics, University of Colorado, Denver, CO 80217, USA

9.1   Introduction

Two ethical norms, vertical equity and horizontal equity, are generally applied to assess the fairness and distributive justice of a tax system. Due to tax induced rerankings controversy surrounds the exact meaning and joint empirical application of the two equity concepts. This paper adopts Aronson and Lambert's (1994) recently proposed measure of horizontal equity and demonstrates that overall or "net vertical equity" can be additively decomposed into three separate, distinct and quantifiable terms – "vertical equity", "tax rerankings", and "post-tax income rerankings". The latter two terms involve vertical inequities that are embedded into an otherwise progressive tax system. To separate the two inequities from net vertical equity we make use of the relative deprivation interpretation of the Gini coefficient and decompose the redistributive effect of taxes into four distinct terms, three of which measure and decompose vertical equity and inequity. To illustrate the decomposition method we use individual income tax return data and measure the effects of the Tax Reform Act of 1986 on horizontal inequity, vertical equity, tax-rerankings, and post tax income rerankings. Horizontal inequity is measured using the recently developed procedure of Aronson and Lambert (1994). The remainder of the redistributive effect is decomposed using the new procedures developed in this paper.

Two ethical norms, vertical equity and horizontal equity, are often applied to assess the fairness and distributive justice of a tax system. Vertical equity (VE) requires that individuals with greater earnings and incomes pay more taxes and relies upon unequal treatment of individuals based upon the ability to pay principle of taxation. In contrast, horizontal equity (HE) is based upon a fairness principle that requires equal treatment of equals. As a consequence, in a tax system characterized by horizontal equity individuals with identical incomes and "needs" must pay the same tax.

The two ethical norms are intrinsically appealing and have unquestionably influenced the course of tax policy. However, in actually assessing the fairness and distributive justice of tax systems there is little agreement on how VE and HE are to be measured. In the absence of a consensus on measurement, it is difficult to reach agreement about the effects of substantive changes in tax policy. For example, researchers and policy analysts using different measures of vertical and horizontal equity may well reach conflicting conclusions concerning the equity effects of a major change in policy such as the Tax Reform Act of 1986.

The most popular method for identifying and applying the vertical and horizontal equity norms involves comparing pre and post-tax income distributions using Gini coefficients and Lorenz curves. This approach permits an appealing decomposition of the tax impacts of policy changes into vertical and horizontal equity effects and if there are no tax-induced rerankings of individuals, the methodology for decomposing changes in tax policy is quite simple and very compelling. In practice, however, such rerankings are always present, significantly complicating tax policy analysis. As a consequence, much of the recent work on tax fairness and distributive justice addresses the question of how best to interpret and measure the equity effects of tax induced reranking. Specifically, how do rerankings relate to VE and HE and how should the tax effects of a policy change be decomposed to provide the best insight into the issue of fairness and justice?

Significant disagreement surrounds the issue of rerankings. Feldstein (1976), Atkinson (1980) and Plotnick (1981) all suggest that rerankings are at the essence of horizontal inequity; and, thus, appropriate measures of HE must include reranking effects. However, Berliant and Strauss (1985, 1993, and

1996), Kaplow (1989), and Musgrave (1990) argue against this idea and insist that reranking should be considered as a part of vertical equity, not horizontal equity. In an important recent contribution, Aronson and Lambert (1994) address this problem by defining *HE* as the equity loss accounted for by the unequal treatment of equals and analyze rerankings as a separate criterion distinguishable from both vertical and horizontal equity. While this approach is reasonable, it rests, as most of the relevant literature does, on acceptance of the pre-tax distribution as the point of reference in discussions of fairness and tax justice. Recently, Lerman and Yitzaki (1994) argue that the post-tax ranking is just as appropriate and perhaps more appropriate than the pre-tax ranking in measuring the reranking effect.[1] Further, as emphasized by Berliant and Strauss, measures of vertical equity should not depend solely on the post-tax income distribution nor should they depend only on pre-tax income positions of individuals that are treated as equals.

A related issue centers on the connection between rerankings and tax-induced changes in income inequality. Atkinson (1980) forwarded the difference between the Gini coefficient and concentration coefficient as an index of rerankings. This prompted a number of refinements decomposing the total redistribution effect of taxes into vertical and horizontal equity. While appealing, this approach is subject to the well-known criticism that Mookerjee and Shorrocks (1982) level at the remainder (reranking) term in the decomposition of Gini coefficients by population subgroups, namely, it is difficult to decipher. Further, when rerankings are interpreted in a manner that has clear and unambiguous normative significance,[2] the widely used decomposition of the redistribution effect of taxes into vertical and horizontal equity overestimates the vertical equity effects of tax changes.

In this paper we show that the term normally referred to as vertical equity (and which we refer to as "net vertical equity") can be expressed as the additive sum of three separate, distinct and quantifiable terms – "vertical equity", "tax rerankings", and "post-tax income rerankings". The latter two terms involve distinct vertical inequities embedded into an otherwise progressive tax system.[3]

---

[1] The logic of this view is that once an individual, say A, is reranked, any additional tax on A that pushes his post-tax income further below B, is equivalent to taxing a poor person. This issue is discussed in detail below and incorporated into our tax decomposition as one aspect of vertical inequity.

[2] The relative deprivation interpretation of the Gini coefficient provides a compelling logic for decompositions of the Gini. For a recent discussion see Cowell (1997).

[3] Our measure of horizontal inequity is identical to that of Aronson and Lambert (1994).

To identify each of these terms, we make use of the relative deprivation interpretation of the Gini coefficient [Yitzhaki, (1979) and Hey and Lambert, (1980)]. Specifically, the redistributive effect of taxes is decomposed into the following four terms:

vertical equity – represents and is measured by the decrease in the deprivation of individuals with low pre-tax incomes whose relative post-tax income is improved by the tax
tax rerankings – represent and are measured by the increase in the deprivation of the individuals who have lower pre-tax incomes and are reranked by those whose taxes are smaller, and
post-tax income reranking – this represents and is measured by the increase in deprivation of individuals with higher pre-tax incomes compared to those with lower pre-tax incomes but higher post-tax incomes.
horizontal inequity – this represents and is measured by the increase in deprivation of individuals with lower post-tax incomes relative to those with higher post-tax incomes and who have the same pre-tax income.

In a tax system with progressive tax rates vertical equity is positive, but the presence of tax rerankings and post-tax income rerankings detract from vertical equity. Together, tax rerankings and post-tax income rerankings sum to provide a measure of the vertical inequity. Vertical equity and the two vertical inequities sum to "net vertical equity" (*NVE*), which is equivalent to the usual concept of vertical equity in the Kakwani decomposition.

What is new is our decomposition of net vertical equity into three additive terms -- vertical equity, tax rerankings, and post-tax income rerankings. The advantages of our decomposition procedure are threefold. First, it overcomes most criticisms leveled at existing decomposition procedures. Second, it permits changes in tax policy to be separated into progressive and regressive components. Finally, when vertical equity is combined with tax rerankings and post-tax income rerankings our approach coincides with the traditional definition of the redistributive effect of taxes into vertical and horizontal equity. To illustrate our decomposition method we use individual income tax return data and measure the effects of the Tax Reform Act of 1986 on horizontal inequity, vertical equity, tax-rerankings, and post tax income rerankings.

The remainder of the paper is organized as follows. Section II provides an historical perspective on the measurement of vertical and horizontal equity and intuitively explains our decomposition. Section III presents the formal analysis.

Section IV presents empirical measures of the decompositions for microdata from the Internal Revenue Service Statistics of Income for 1985 and 1988. The final section provides brief concluding remarks.

9.2   Historical Perspective on Horizontal and Vertical Equity

A number of investigators have stressed the fact that in practice two individuals are almost never identical; and, as a consequence, the principle of equal treatment has little empirical content unless it is extended to include "equal treatment of equals and unequals treated accordingly." [4] To address this issue Feldstein (1976) proposed the following definition of horizontal equity, "if two individuals be equally well off in the absence of taxation, they should also be equally well off if there is a tax". This naturally leads to a comparison of the ordering of utility levels before and after a tax change. Thus, horizontal equity implies that a tax should leave the relative positions of an individual in the pre and post-tax income distribution unchanged. From this perspective the criterion of equal treatment implies an absence of rank reversals. As a measure of *HE*, Atkinson (1980) and Plotnick (1981) [hereafter A-P] suggested the difference between the post-tax income Gini and concentration indices that are computed using the ranking of taxpayers in the pre-tax income distribution. Kakwani (1984) later proposed the decomposition of the total redistribution effect into horizontal and vertical components. In Kakwani's decomposition, vertical equity measures the difference of pre-tax Gini and post-tax concentration index, and horizontal inequity is the A-P index of rerankings. In this literature, the term vertical equity refers to differences in the post-tax income distribution that are generated by tax policies that are imposed on a given pre-tax income distribution. Measures of vertical equity are essentially changes of pre and post-tax income inequality.

The reranking definition of *HE* lies at the heart of the Kakwani decomposition. Several writers have taken issue with the A-P measures of horizontal equity and with Kakwani's decomposition. Berliant and Strauss (1985, 1993, and 1996), Musgrave (1990) and Kaplow (1989) all maintain that the traditional principle of horizontal equity, based upon "equal treatment of equals," is logically separate from the recent notion of no rank reversals.

---

[4]See, for example, Feldstein (1976), Atkinson (1980), Plotnick (1981, 1984), and King (1983).

Berliant and Strauss (1985) provide two counterexamples that clearly demonstrate the deficiency of the no rank reversal *HE* criterion. They show that the A-P index counts order reversal as full violations of *HE*, while ignoring substantial disturbances in the initial distribution that do not result in rerankings.

Kaplow (1989) offers an example that highlights the discontinuity of *HE* when the redistributive effect of taxes is decomposed in the manner of Kakwani. Consider two individuals, A and B, who are in two distinct situations. A's income is one cent larger than B's in the first situation with the income positions reversed in the second situation. If A's income doubles, the two situations provide radically different *VE* and *HE* measures even though the two situations are virtually identical. In the first situation the doubling of A's income is regressive in terms of *VE* while there is no change in *HE*. However, in the second situation the doubling of A's income is progressive in terms of *VE* (with the degree of progressivity being almost the same as the degree of regressivity in the first situation) and there is an almost 100 percent increase in *HE*. Thus, very small changes in income are associated with discontinuous and large changes in *VE* and *HE*. This clearly is disturbing.

Musgrave (1990) advances yet different criticisms. He argues that *HE* is not merely a mathematical concept that imposes a minimum condition for fairness, but a robust rule contained in virtually all constructs of distributive justice. Further, Musgrave insists that comparisons of pre and post-tax income differences across all individuals, a procedure proposed by Kaplow (1989), is superior to measures of reranking in that it allows for changes in the magnitude of tax induced differentials, which may occur without rank reversals.

Finally, Kakwani (1984) notes a shortcoming of the decomposition of tax effects into *VE* and *HE*, which he pioneered. Once pre and post-tax rerankings exist, changes in taxes that affect the reranked individuals lead to inevitable clashes between *HE* and *VE*. Policies aimed at promoting greater vertical equity reduce horizontal equity and vice versa. Thus, the conflict between *VE* and *HE* implies that marginal changes in tax policy lead to an ambiguity concerning how to best describe the distributional impact of the tax.

To address the criticisms of the no reranking definition of *HE*, Aronson and Lambert (1994) propose an alternative to the Kakwani decomposition. In the Aronson and Lambert [hereafter A-L] decomposition the reranking effect is identified as a component separate from *HE* where the total redistribution effect of taxes is the sum of three components, *VE*, *HE*, and a reranking effect. *VE* is the redistribution that would have occurred if equals had been treated equally and unequals treated accordingly. *HE* is the reduction in the redistribution effect accounted for by the unequal treatment of equals. The reranking effect measures the additional redistribution that arises from the differences in pretax and post-tax ranking of income units. To identify these three components, A-L considers income units with the same pre-tax incomes as being in the same subgroup and use the Gini decomposition method of Bhattacharya and Mahalanobis (1967). *VE* is the difference between the pretax Gini and the post-tax between-subgroup Gini. *HE* is the sum of the within-subgroup Ginis weighted by income and population shares. The reranking effect is the difference of post-tax income Gini and concentration coefficient with incomes ranked, first, by pretax income and then by post-tax income.

A-L's decomposition is important because it correctly identifies the impact of the *HE* component on the total redistributive effect of taxes and thereby overcomes much of the criticism of the Kakwani decomposition. A-L's measure of *VE* is simply the sum of Kakwani's *VE* and the within-subgroup Ginis. There are two difficulties with A-L's index of *VE*. First, if the tax law leads, not only to rerankings of selected individuals in the ordered income distribution, but to rerankings of subgroup mean incomes as well, then A-L's three terms, *VE* + *HE* + reranking, do not sum to the total redistribution effect of the tax. The absence of the additive property is, of course, a problem for any tax decomposition. Second, A-L's decomposition continues to lead to the inevitable clash between *VE* and the adverse equity effect caused by *rerankings*.

Lerman and Yitzaki (1994) suggest still another decomposition that focuses on rerankings. They begin by asking whether a reranking is fair. Lerman and Yitzaki (hereafter L-Y) suggest decomposing the effects of a tax into two components: a reranking effect and an income inequality effect, with the latter measured by reductions or increases in income inequality, without regard to rerankings. L-Y's work is important because they persuasively argue that rerankings are unfair and regressive in terms of *VE* when they are analyzed from the perspective of post-tax income distribution. This follows from the fact that an additional tax levied on an already reranked individual is equivalent to taxing a relatively poor individual. But in terms of the Kakwani decomposition, reranked individuals are continuously treated as if they are relatively rich. As a consequence, additional taxes on reranked individuals are counted as if they enhance progressivity. This is clearly wrong and leads L-Y to argue that post-tax ranking, in which the reranked individuals are relatively poor, is more appropriate in measuring tax progressivity. In L-Y's analysis the reranking effect is the difference in the pre-tax income Gini and concentration index based upon post-tax income rank. The second component in their decomposition, the income narrowing or gap effect, is measured by the difference between the post-tax income Gini and the pre-tax concentration index based upon the post-tax income rank.

Under the L-Y decomposition, a severe reranking reduces the income gap between the rich and poor in the pre-tax distribution and increases the reranking component. In this formulation the number of rerankings matter, but L-Y's measure is insensitive to the total amount of the marginal tax imposed on reranked individuals. This is the case because the measure is based upon differences in pretax incomes, rather than post-tax incomes. Therefore, any additional tax on the reranked individual induces a fall in the total redistribution effect, rather than an increase in the reranking effect. A second point is that the reranking and the gap narrowing effects are both measures of vertical equity; one accounts for the contribution of the reranking and the other that of the non-reranking contribution to the total redistribution effect. Thus, L-Y's decomposition ignores horizontal equity altogether.

To set the stage for our own decomposition, it is useful to begin by considering an observation by Kaplow (1989, p. 143). For any two individuals, a tax reform can have five possible effects:

1) from an unequal pre-position, the individuals move closer but remain apart,
2) from an unequal pre-position, the individuals move closer and end up at an equal position,
3) from an unequal pre-position, the individuals move further apart,
4) from an equal pre-position, the individuals move apart,
5) from an unequal pre-position, the individuals reverse ranks (cross over) and end up apart.

In cases 1 and 2 the person with the higher income pays more tax. Therefore, the difference in taxes can be considered as an indication of vertical equity. In case 3, which we describe as a "tax reranking effect," there is a violation of *VE* because the individual with higher income pays a lower tax. The difference in the tax is an indication of vertical inequity (*VI*). Case 4 represents a situation in which the individuals have the same pre-tax income, but one ends up with a higher post-tax income. Thus, case 4 involves a clear violation of the equal treatment norm and leads to horizontal inequity (*HI*). In case 5 there is a reranking in terms of pre and post-tax incomes.

It is important to realize that case 5 can be thought of as a combination of cases 2 and 4. This suggests that tax effects that lead to pre and post-tax income rerankings can be separated into two parts, one involving *VE* and the other *VI*. To clarify and illustrate this point, consider a situation in which person A has higher pre-tax income, but less post-tax income than B. The impacts of the tax can be thought of as occurring in a series of sequential marginal changes. Let B's taxes be fixed and impose additional taxes on A. These taxes are marginally progressive so long as A's post-tax income remains above B's. Clearly, such taxes contribute to greater *VE*. However, once the taxes have leveled the incomes of A and B, even a tiny amount of additional tax causes A to become poorer than B. After the reranking occurs, any additional tax on A is equivalent to a tax on the poor and is marginally regressive.

Over the progressive range in the above example, A's additional tax is equal to the sum of A's pretax income less B's post-tax income. B's total tax is given by pre-tax income less post-tax income. Therefore, in the progressive range A's pre-tax income minus B's represents the difference in the taxes of the two individuals and can be interpreted as a basic measure of vertical equity. Over the regressive range, however, the difference between A and B's post-tax income can be considered as a measure of vertical inequity, because the sum of A's additional tax is equal to the difference in their post-tax incomes. This follows since B's additional tax is zero over this range.[5] Proceeding in this manner we can separate each post-tax income reranking into *VE* and *VI* components.

The procedure we propose for decomposing the total redistribution effect is consistent with the traditional *HE* and *VE* norms and yields measures that do not obscure the five types of effects (Kaplow, 1989) that can occur when taxes are changed. Further, our measures of vertical equity and inequity do not depend solely on the post-tax income distribution nor do they depend solely on the pre-tax position of equals. Rather, they involve pre and post-tax positions as well as comparisons of reranked taxpayers that. The horizontal inequity measure in the decomposition is the same as Aronson and Lambert's (1994) and reflects only unequal treatment of equals. Rerankings violate vertical equity and we provide separate measures of *VE*, a positive concept, and *VI*, a negative concept. Net vertical equity (*NVE*) is the sum of *VE* and *VI*.

Our decomposition also overcomes Kaplow's criticism of the discontinuity of *VE* and rerankings in the Kakwani decomposition. Recall Kaplow's two

---

[5]We note that the difference in post-tax incomes could be viewed as a violation of *HE* norm. However, vertical inequity is preferred because the reranking involves the tax treatment of unequals. Like Aronson and Lambert (1994), we reserve *HE* for the differential tax treatment of equals.

situations in which the incomes of A and B differ by one cent. In the first situation A's income is greater than B's and the positions are reversed in the second situation. In our decomposition, when A's income doubles there is a tax reranking in the first situation. In contrast, in the second situation, a post-tax reranking occurs. The tax reranking and the post-tax income reranking each lead to vertical inequities. In both situations there is a small increase in vertical equity. Thus, in our decomposition Kaplow's two situations have almost the same degree of net vertical equity. The troublesome discontinuity in VE and rerankings disappears.

In the next section, we elaborate on the above intuitive explanation of the decomposition with formal definitions using Yitzhaki's (1979) relative deprivation concept of Gini coefficients. We present new concentration indices, which are somewhat different from those in the established literature, but which are consistent with the new decomposition of the redistributive effect of taxes.

9.3   A New Decomposition of Vertical and Horizontal Equity

9.3.1   Definitions and distinctions

Consider a distribution of n income units with pre-tax income X_i and population mean, μ. Denote the vector of incomes and their ranks arrayed in increasing order by $[X, R(X)] = [(X_1, 1), (X_2, 2),..., (X_n, n)]$. For a given amount of tax, T_i, on income level X_i, the post-tax income is $N_i = X_i - T_i$ with an associated population mean, ω. Let the average tax rate be denoted by τ and define the amount of tax imposed on the ith income unit, beyond a proportional tax, as $d_i = T_i - \tau X_i = (1 - \tau)X_i - N_i$. When the ith tax is compared with the jth tax, the favorable (unfavorable) tax treatment of income units depends upon the difference of their respective tax deviations away from proportionality, d_j and d_i. A positive value for $d_j - d_i$ implies that the ith income unit pays less tax than the jth income unit by $d_j - d_i$ and vice versa. If the ith pre-tax income is assumed to be less than the jth unit, the difference between the deviation, $d_j - d_i$, constitutes a measure for how much better-off the tax system makes the lower pre-tax income unit relative to the higher pre-tax income unit.[6]

---

[6]We could, of course, use the difference in taxes, $T_j - T_i$, to measure the favorable (unfavorable) treatment of the lower pretax income units. However, $d_j - d_i$ correctly incorporates the concept of progressivity into the measurement of tax treatment of the lower

Suppose the ith unit's pre-tax income is below the jth unit's and their taxes are already given. Then, the additional decline in relative deprivation of the lower pre-tax income unit can be expressed as:

$$VE_{ij} = \begin{cases} d_j - d_i, & \text{if } X_j > X_i, \ N_j \geq N_i \text{ and } d_j > d_i \\ (1-\tau)(X_j - X_i), & \text{if } X_j > X_i \text{ and } N_j < N_i \\ 0, & \text{otherwise .} \end{cases} \qquad (9.1)$$

The second expression[7] in (1) represents the progressive contribution of the reranking. Averaging the decline of relative deprivation over all relatively lower incomes, yields the average reduction in deprivation for the whole population:

$$VE = \sum_{i=1}^{n} \sum_{j=1}^{n} VE_{ij} \Big/ n^2 \omega , \qquad (9.2)$$

where the average reduction of the relative deprivation is normalized by the total post-tax income.[8] It should be noted that vertical equity requires that income units with higher income must pay more tax. We emphasize that vertical equity is defined here very differently than in the Kakwani decomposition. In our analysis vertical equity is the progressive component of a tax system that contains both progressive and regressive elements.

In an otherwise progressive tax system there are three types of inequities that can arise. The first occurs when a high income individual pays less tax than a lower income individual and the post-tax income gap increases. In Section II we referred to this as a 'tax reranking,' since it has properties similar to a post-tax income reranking (the traditional reranking emphasized in the literature), except that the reversal in rank is in terms of tax payments rather than the post-tax incomes. This inequity is vertical because the *VE* norm requires that higher income individuals pay more taxes than those with lower incomes. Thus, a tax reranking occurs when there is a reversal in tax payments relative to income. A

---

income unit. See Musgrave (1995) for a detailed statement on the logic of using tax progressivity as the base for measuring vertical equity and inequity.

[7] L-Y's reranking term is the average of twice this term normalized by the total post-tax income. Therefore, L-Y's reranking term is a measure of vertical equity.

[8] Since the total tax deviation is zero we normalize by total post-tax income rather than the total deviation of the tax away from a proportional tax.

second vertical inequity occurs because of post-tax income rerankings. The third tax inequity is horizontal and is measured by the relative deprivation experienced by the individuals with lower post-tax income compared to "equals" with the same pre-tax income, but higher post-tax incomes.

To measure tax rerankings we use a proportional tax as a reference point. For any pair of pre-tax incomes that are different, a tax that causes the smaller income to deviate further from the larger income than would a proportion tax necessarily increases the relative deprivation of the individual with the lower pre-tax income. For two taxpayers, i and j, this can be expressed as:

$$TR_{ij} = \begin{cases} d_i - d_j, & \text{if } X_j > X_i \text{ and } d_j < d_i, \\ 0, & \text{otherwise.} \end{cases} \qquad (9.3)$$

For all taxpayers, the normalized average relative deprivation caused by tax rerankings is:

$$TR = \sum_{i=1}^{n} \sum_{j=1}^{n} TR_{ij} \Big/ n^2 \omega \qquad (9.4)$$

Now consider post-tax income rerankings. The relative deprivation of the individual with a high pre-tax income compared to a person with a lower pre-tax income is zero if evaluated using the pre-tax income distribution. However, since taxes rerank individuals in the income distribution, the person with a high pre-tax income may be forced into a position where they have a lower post-tax income. When post-tax incomes are reranked, there is a clear relative deprivation of the individuals who are pushed down compared to those who were in a lower pre-tax position, but who have moved ahead in the post-tax income distribution. For two taxpayers, i and j, the relative deprivation of the reranked individual who has moved down compared to the reranked individual who has moved up is:

$$RR_{ij} = \begin{cases} N_j - N_i, & \text{if } X_j < X_i \text{ and } N_j > N_i \\ 0, & \text{otherwise.} \end{cases} \qquad (9.5)$$

The post-tax income reranking, which is the normalized average of this relative deprivation, is:

$$RR = \sum_{i=1}^{n} \sum_{j=1}^{n} RR_{ij} \Big/ n^2 \omega \,.^9 \tag{9.6}$$

The final element in our decomposition is horizontal inequity, which is measured by the tax induced relative deprivation among individuals with the same pre-tax income. Of course, there is no relative deprivation in the pre-tax income distribution. Differential tax treatment causes a separation in terms of post-tax incomes and leads to relative deprivation of those who are pushed down in the post-income distribution compared to their former equals who pay less tax. This horizontal relative deprivation is measured by:[10]

$$HI_{ij} = \begin{cases} d_j - d_i = N_i - N_j, & \text{if } X_j = X_i, \ N_j < N_i, \ \text{and } d_j > d_i, \\ 0, & \text{otherwise} \end{cases} \tag{9.7}$$

Since $d_i = (1-\tau)X_i - N_i$, the normalized average horizontal inequity is:

$$HI = \sum_{i=1}^{n} \sum_{j=1}^{n} HI_{ij} \Big/ n^2 \omega \,. \tag{9.8}$$

As noted above, *HI* in our decomposition is the same as A-L's horizontal equity.

Our decomposition reveals two regressive elements that violate the vertical equity norm in an otherwise progressive tax system. The sum of the tax rerankings and post-tax rerankings is defined to be vertical inequity (*VI*). That is,

$$VI = TR + RR. \tag{9.9}$$

We also define net vertical equity (*NVE*) to be vertical equity minus vertical inequity,

$$NVE = VE - VI. \tag{9.10}$$

---

[9]We point out that this post-tax income reranking is precisely equal to one half of A-L's reranking effect.

[10]Note that since $d_i = (1-\tau)X_i - N_i$, and $X_i = X_j$, $d_j - d_i$ becomes $N_i - N_j$ in.

Net vertical equity in our decomposition corresponds to the vertical equity measure in the Kakwani decomposition and, in turn, can be considered as a "net" measure of overall tax progressivity.

Finally, we note that there is little disagreement among researchers concerning the total redistributive effect of taxes, which is measured by the difference in inequality in the pre and post-tax income distributions. The total redistribution effect is the net vertical equity minus the horizontal inequity. That is,

$$RD = NVE - HI. \qquad (9.11)$$

We emphasize that the new decomposition allows the total redistributive effect of taxes to be meaningfully interpreted in terms of relative deprivation by comparing only pre and post-tax income distributions.   Thus, the new decomposition provides a counterargument to Berliant and Strauss (1985), who assert (p. 180) that "...the analysis of a tax system's equity is inherently a two-variable problem (economic position of taxpayers without regard to the tax system and the taxpayers' effective tax rates), rather than a single variable problem (the distribution of before and after-tax income)." Our decomposition method clearly shows that tax equity can be effectively analyzed by comparing pre and post-tax incomes, which coincide with traditional norms of the vertical and horizontal equity.

The next section explains how each element of the decomposition can be conveniently estimated using Gini and concentration coefficients expressed in terms of covariance.

9.3.2   Gini and concentration index measures of vertical and horizontal equity

Gini coefficients of pre-tax income, post-tax incomes, and tax deviations away from proportionality can all be expressed in terms of the covariance of incomes and their rank:

$$G(X, R(X)) = \frac{2}{n\mu} \ Cov(X, R(X)) = \frac{2}{n\,\omega} \ Cov((1-\tau)X, R(X)) \qquad (9.12)$$

$$G(N, R(N)) = \frac{2}{n\,\omega}\, Cov(N, R(N)), \text{ and} \tag{9.13}$$

$$G(d, R(d)) = \frac{2}{n\,\omega}\, Cov(d, R(d)). \tag{9.14}$$

We note that $G(d,R(d))$ is a Gini index by the standard definition, because it is normalized by the total post-tax income rather than the total tax deviation which is zero. For convenience, however, we refer to $G(d,R(d))$ as the Gini of tax deviations. We also define two concentration coefficients,

$$C(N, (R(X,N)+R(N))/2) = \frac{2}{n\,\omega}\, Cov(N, (R(X, N)+R(N))/2), \tag{9.15}$$

$$C(d, (R(X, d)+R(d))/2) = \frac{2}{n\,\omega}\, Cov(d,(R(X, d)+R(d))/2), \tag{9.16}$$

where $R(X,N)$ and $R(X,d)$ are rank vectors, ordered first, by pre-tax income level, and then by the post-tax income level or the deviation of taxes from proportionality. We point out that (15) and (16) are the concentration coefficients of post-tax income and tax deviations and are slightly different from the traditional concentration indices, $C(N, R(X, N))$ and $C(d, R(X, d))$. It is important to note that when individuals with the same pre-tax income are considered as the same income group, the concentration coefficient of the post-tax income is the sum of the relative deprivation of within-subgroup and of the lower pre-tax income subgroup within the post-tax income distribution.

By using the above covariance definitions we can restate each term of our tax decomposition using Gini and concentration coefficients as:

Proposition 1: The post-tax income reranking is the difference between the post-tax income Gini and the associated concentration index,

$$RR = C(N, (R(N) - R(X,N))/2) = G(N, R(N)) - C(N, (R(X,N) + R(N))/2). \tag{9.17}$$

Proof: As is well known, RR is the half of the traditional reranking, $C(N, (R(X,N)-R(N)))$. Therefore, $RR = C(N, (R(X,N)-R(N))/2)$. Adding and subtracting $R(N)$ and decomposing $C(N, (R(X,N) - R(N)))$ leads to the second relation.

Q.E.D

Proposition 2: The tax reranking index is the difference between the Gini of tax deviations and the associated concentration coefficient,

$$TR = C(d, (R(d) - R(X, d))/2) = G(d, R(d)) - C(d, (R(X, d)+R(d))/2). \tag{9.18}$$

Proposition 2 can be proved by using proposition 1. This follows since TR is the measure of tax reranking whereas RR, measures the post-tax income reranking.

Proposition 3: When all individuals are divided into the k different income subgroups by the level of their pre-tax income, the index of horizontal inequity is the sum of within-group post-tax income inequality weighted by the population and income shares. That is,

$$HI = \sum_{g=1}^{k} I_g P_g G(N_g, R(N_g)) = C(N, R(X, N)) - G(\omega, R(\omega))$$
$$= (1/2) C(N, R(X, N) - R(X, d)), \tag{9.19}$$

where $I_g = n_g \omega_g / n \omega$ and $P_g = n_g / n$ are the income and population shares of income subgroup g.

Proof: First, we prove $\sum_{g=1}^{k} I_g P_g G(N_g, R(N_g)) = C(N, R(X, N)) - G(\omega, R(\omega))$. We can construct a rank vector, $R_g(X, N) = \sum_{f=1}^{g-1} n_f + R(N_g)$, such that it is a subset of $R(X, N)$. Since $Cov(N_g, a+R(N_g)) = Cov(N_g, R(N_g))$ with any constant number(a), $G(N_g, R_g (X, N))$ is still equal to $G(N_g, R(N_g))$. Since N_g also is a subset of N, normalizing by the population mean, rather than the subgroup mean of the post-tax income, leads to $\sum_{g=1}^{k} I_g P_g G(N_g, R(N_g)) = C(N, R(X, N)) - G(\omega, R(X, N))$. Note that, since the elements of ω have the same value (ω_g) and $R_g (\omega)$ is the mean of $R_g (X, N)$ when they are the same subgroup, $G(\omega, R(X, N))$ is equal to $G(\omega, R(\omega))$. Therefore,

$\sum_{g=1}^{k} I_g P_g G(N_g, R(N_g)) = C(N, R(X, N)) - G(\omega, R(\omega))$.

Second, we note that $C(N, R(X, N)) - G(\omega, R(X, N)) = (1/2) C(N, R(X, N) - R(X, d))$. This relation holds because a higher tax deviation implies a lower post-tax income with the same pre-tax incomes and $R(X, d)$ is the reverse order of $R(X, N)$ within a same subgroup. Therefore, $C(N, R(X, N)) - G(\omega, R(X, N)) = (1/2) C(N, R(X, N) - R(X, d))$

Q.E.D

By using proposition 1, 2 and 3 and the decomposition of Gini coefficient by subgroup and relative deprivation, VE can be calculated as follows:

Proposition 4: Vertical equity can be calculated from
$VE = G(d, R(d)) - RR - TR - HI = RD + RR + TR + HI$,
where the total redistribution effect of tax is the difference in the pre-tax and post-tax income Gini coefficients, $RD = G(X, R(X)) - G(N, (R(N)))$.

Proof: To show the second relation, prove $G(d, R(d)) = RD + 2(RR + TR + HI)$. To this end,
$RD + 2 RR + 2 TR + 2 HI$
$= G(X, R(X)) - G(N, R(N)) + 2 G(N, R(N)) C(N, R(X, N) + R(N))$
$+ 2 G(d, R(d)) - C(d, R(X, d) + R(d)) + C(N, R(X, N) - R(X, d))$
$= G(X, R(X)) + G(d, R(d)) - C(d, R(X, d)) - C(N, R(X, d))$.
Substituting $d = (1-\tau)X - N$ into the concentration curve, $C(d, R(X, d))$, leads to the following result:
$G[d, R_{(d)}] = RD + 2 LH + 2 RR + 2 HI$.

Q.E.D

9.4 Decomposing the Equity Effects of the Tax Reform Act of 1986

Feldstein (1995b) describes The Tax Reform Act of 1986 (TRA86) as the most important natural experiment in public finance since the start of the income tax. The availability of large samples of microdata before and after reform provides researchers with an unparalleled opportunity to gauge both the efficiency and equity effects of fundamental changes in tax policy.[11] In this

---

[11]Feldstein (1995a, 1995b) focuses on the efficiency effects of changes in marginal tax rates on labor supply.

section we measure and decompose the total redistributive effect of federal income taxes immediately before and after TRA86. Our purpose is to illustrate the new decomposition and we forego discussion of the provisions of TRA86. We point out that knowledgeable observers were initially optimistic and believed that on balance TRA86 would lead to greater equity.[12] However, most researchers have found the effects of TRA86 to be surprisingly small and some suggest that progressivity may actually have declined. But these researchers have focused on overall measures or used the Kakwani decomposition, which nets out the effects of changes in the vertical inequities accompanying tax reform.[13] It is possible that TRA86 had significantly greater equity effects than is commonly believed and these have been obscured by summary measures that fail to distinguish between vertical equity and vertical inequity and attribute all post-tax rerankings to *HI*. The decompositions reported below shed light on this issue.

To illustrate our decompositions we use nationally representative samples of approximately 20,000 tax returns from the Ernst and Young Tax Research Database for 1985 and 1988.[14] We use the Internal Revenue Service (IRS) measures of adjusted gross income (AGI), taxes and after-tax incomes. We extract information from individual tax returns and adjust IRS values for differences in family size, composition and needs. Specifically, we restate pre-tax income, post-tax income and taxes in terms of equivalence values using the following equivalence scale (Z):

$$X = Y / Z, \tag{9.21}$$

where Y is the observed IRS value, $Z = (A + \alpha C)^{\beta}$, $0 \leq \alpha \leq 1$, and $0 \leq \beta \leq 1$, A is the number of adults and C is the number of children. The parameter α determines the importance of children and β adjusts for economies of scale due

---

[12]Most of the attention focused on overall progressivity. See, for example Pechman (1987).

[13]See, for example, Feldstein (1988), Pechman (1990), Wallace, Wasylenko, and Weiner (1991), Michael (1991) Slemrod (1990, 1992), Gravelle, (1992). Gramlich, Kasten and Sammartino (1993), Kasten, Sammartino and Toder (1994) and Bishop, Chow, Formby and Ho (1997).

[14]The sample size is 19,735 tax returns for 1985 and 21,228 for 1988. In making equivalence scale adjustments we found that the tax returns revealed a total of 46,494 persons in 1985 and 43,740 in 1988. A substantial portion of the tax returns were for the same taxpayers in both years but we do not make use of the panel feature of the data in this paper.

to family size. If $\alpha = 0$, only adults matter, but when $\alpha = 1$ children are counted as if they are equivalent to adults. The equivalence scale declines as the exponent, β, increases. For $\beta = 0$ the equivalent before tax income is merely the unadjusted IRS measure. When $\alpha = 1$ and $\beta = 1$, the equivalent income is *per capita* money income.

For any pair of parameter values, α and β, the next step in the empirical estimation requires specification of precisely what we mean when income and tax units are said to have "equal equivalent incomes". This issue must be addressed in order to calculate *HI*, *NVE* and the other elements in the decomposition. Following Lambert and Aronson (1994) we answer this question in two ways. First, equal equivalent incomes are defined as identical numbers, which means a zero band is used to calculate *HI*. Second, we select a small positive band such as the 5£ per week number used by Aronson and Lambert (1994). This is equivalent to approximately $500 US per year. Of course, choosing any positive band is somewhat arbitrary and involves a trade-off between the horizontal and net vertical equity terms in the decomposition. As the width of the income band becomes larger, *HI* grows and the post-tax income and tax rerankings become smaller.[15]

The Appendix reports detailed estimates for the zero income band (Tables A1 and A2) and a $500 "equal equivalent income" band (Tables A3 and A4) for selected equivalence scale values. A number of important results stand out. Note first that the pre-tax Gini coefficient is uniformly larger and the redistributive effect (*RE*) is uniformly smaller in 1988 compared to 1985. This is the case irrespective of the equivalence scale adjustment. Similarly, the post-tax Gini coefficient is larger and the tax deviation Gini smaller for all equivalence scale adjustments. However, the equivalence scale adjustments clearly matter when one looks at the decompositions and expresses *VE*, *TR*, *RR*, and *HI* as a percent of either the pre-tax Gini or tax deviation Gini. These results are shown Tables 1 and 2. To highlight the influence of the equivalence scale adjustment Figures 1-6 provide three-dimensional plots of the redistribution effect, vertical equity and net tax inequities (*RR* + *TR* + *HI*) in 1985 and 1988.

Two findings with respect to the decompositions warrant emphasis. First and most important, the inequities associated with tax rerankings, which are ignored in the literature, are far larger than either the post-tax income rerankings or

---

[15] As proven by Formby, Seaks, and Smith (1988), Paglin Gini confronts a similar problem in distinguishing between age groups.

horizontal inequity, which garner so much attention in policy analysis and tax research. Table 3 shows that in 1985 the tax reranking inequity was more than 15 times larger than the post-tax income rerankings for all combinations of α and β. In 1988 the differences are smaller, but *TR* remains larger than *RR* by a factor that varies between 3.7 and 6.3, depending upon the parameter values of equivalence scale adjustments. Table 3 also shows the tax rerankings as a percent of vertical equity and the redistributive effect of income taxes. Depending upon the parameter values of α and β and whether a zero or $500 income band is used, the tax reranking inequity is between 14 and 28 percent of vertical equity and accounts for between 17 to 41 percent of the overall redistributive effect. A second important result shows that horizontal inequity is quite small. Using a zero income band, *HI* it is scarcely measurable, accounting for less than 1/1000 of one percent of the redistributive effect of taxes. For the $500 income band *HI* is larger, but still extremely small. In 1985 estimates of *HI* are between 0.5 and 1.1 percent of the redistributive effect depending upon the equivalence scale adjustments. The measures are even smaller in 1988.

The decompositions also lead to insights into the effects of tax reform across time. In terms of income per tax return (parameter values $\alpha = 0$ and $\beta = 0$), nominal pre-tax income grew by 25 percent, income inequality increased and the average tax rate dropped by almost one percent. Thus, income tax rates became lower and flatter. At the same time the standard deduction and earned income credit both increased. Ceteris paribus, the change in the income tax rate schedule would reduce vertical equity, while the rise in the standard deduction and earned income credit would tend to increase vertical equity. Our results show *VE* decreased, with estimates ranging between 10 and 17 percent depending upon the parameter values for α and β and whether a zero or $500 income band is used. We find that the post-tax reranking effect, *RR*, became three times larger between 1985 and 1988 and that the tax reranking effect, *TR*, fell slightly. However, since *TR* is so much larger than *RR*, the changes in the absolute size of the two reranking effects was almost the same. As a consequence, the changes in *TR* and *RR* offset and the effects of the inequities on *VI* are inconclusive and dependent upon different parameter values. When *VE* and *VI* are combined we find that net vertical equity decreased by at least 9 percent with most estimates ranging between 14 and 20 percent. Although *HI* decreases slightly, it is so small that it has a negligible effect on tax equity. On balance, our analysis strongly indicates that TRA86 decreased the overall equity of federal income taxes.

TABLE 9.1:

The Redistributive Effect and Tax Equity Decompostions of US Income Taxes in 1985 and 1988(Expressed Relative to the Pre-tax Gini Coefficient of Income Inequality)

$500 Income Band and Selected Equivalence Scale Values

Equivalence Scale Adjustment		Year	VE as a Percent of Pre-Tax Gini Coefficient	RR as a Percent of Pre-Tax Gini Coefficient	TR as a Percent of Pre-Tax Gini Coefficient	HI as a Percent of Pre-Tax Gini Coefficient	RE as a Percent of Pre-Tax Gini Coefficient
α	β						
0.00	0.00	85	8.987	0.100	2.273	0.033	6.582
		88	10.317	0.087	2.021	0.036	8.173
0.25	0.25	85	10.662	0.078	1.753	0.045	8.786
		88	10.735	0.076	1.711	0.056	8.892
0.50	0.50	85	10.082	0.080	2.090	0.088	7.824
		88	7.166	0.315	1.979	0.025	4.847
0.75	0.75	85	8.224	0.277	1.528	0.026	6.393
		88	8.415	0.284	1.359	0.031	6.740
1.00	1.00	85	8.200	0.314	1.229	0.040	6.618
		88	7.914	0.319	1.343	0.054	6.198

TABLE 9.2:

The Redistibution Effect and Tax Equity Decompositions of US Income Taxes in 1985 and 1988(Expressed Relative to the Tax Deviation Gini Coefficient of Income Inequality)

$500 Income Band and Selected Equivalence Scale Values

Equivalence Scale Adjustment		Year	VE as a Percent of Tax Deviation Gini Coefficient	RR as a Percent of Tax Deviation Gini Coefficient	TR as a Percent of Tax Deviation Gini Coefficient	HI as a Percent of Tax Deviation Gini Coefficient
α	β					
0.00	0.00	85	78.884	0.874	19.954	0.288
		88	75.555	3.320	20.862	0.264
0.25	0.25	85	83.312	0.677	15.715	0.296
		88	81.441	2.687	15.611	0.261
0.50	0.50	85	85.036	0.624	13.984	0.356
		88	83.399	2.818	13.473	0.311
0.75	0.75	85	84.868	0.614	14.039	0.478
		88	84.146	3.055	12.410	0.388
1.00	1.00	85	81.702	0.652	16.935	0.710
		88	82.181	3.313	13.948	0.558

TABLE 9.3:

Tax Re-ranking (*TR*) as a Percent of Post-Tax Income Re-ranking (*RR*), Vertical Equity (*VE*), and Redistribution Effect (*RE*)

Equivalence Scale Adjustment		1985						1988					
		No Income Band			$500 Income Band			No Income Band			$500 Income Band		
α	β	TR/ RR	TR/ VE	TR/ RD	TR/ RR	TR/ VE	TR/ RD	TR/ RR	TR/ VE	TR/ RD	TR/ RR	TR/ VE	TR/ RD
0.00	0.00	2014	25.20	34.27	2283	25.30	34.54	607	27.57	40.62	628	27.61	40.82
	0.25	1987	19.51	24.53	2328	19.59	24.73	597	20.08	26.24	622	20.08	26.30
	0.50	1878	18.22	22.55	2328	19.59	24.73	577	18.89	24.28	608	18.94	24.42
	0.75	1799	17.64	21.68	2232	17.84	22.05	573	18.38	23.44	610	18.43	23.59
	1.00	1749	17.88	22.05	2229	18.17	22.59	588	18.65	23.86	635	18.78	24.16
0.25	0.25	1970	18.74	23.33	2321	18.86	23.59	557	19.14	24.72	581	19.17	24.83
	0.50	1848	16.77	20.38	2248	17.00	20.77	500	16.99	21.34	527	17.11	21.58
	0.75	1760	15.70	18.82	2213	16.06	19.42	461	15.59	19.24	493	15.82	19.64
	1.00	1711	15.73	18.87	2250	16.33	19.83	446	15.14	18.58	487	15.54	19.24
0.50	0.25	1957	18.27	22.61	2309	18.41	22.90	529	18.52	23.75	552	18.58	23.89
	0.50	1832	16.20	19.54	2241	16.44	19.96	453	15.98	19.85	478	16.15	20.17
	0.75	1758	15.50	18.54	2244	15.94	19.24	404	14.52	17.72	436	14.91	18.35
	1.00	1749	16.44	19.90	2347	17.14	21.04	391	14.45	17.66	433	15.10	18.68
0.75	0.25	1945	17.95	22.13	2304	18.13	22.46	508	18.07	23.06	532	18.17	23.27
	0.50	1829	16.01	19.26	2255	16.34	19.81	421	15.38	19.00	446	15.65	19.45
	0.75	1777	15.99	19.24	2285	16.54	20.13	373	14.20	17.32	406	14.75	18.17
	1.00	1819	18.05	22.29	2460	18.83	23.65	375	14.98	18.49	419	15.78	19.77
1.00	0.25	1937	17.72	21.78	2302	17.90	22.11	492	17.72	22.53	514	17.85	22.78
	0.50	1829	16.03	19.29	2262	16.40	19.89	398	15.03	18.51	422	15.30	18.97
	0.75	1812	16.79	20.41	2363	17.38	21.39	358	14.33	17.55	392	14.98	18.57
	1.00	1512	19.63	24.82	2596	20.73	26.71	377	16.11	20.24	421	16.97	21.67

FIGURE 9.1:
Tax Redistribution Effect in 1985

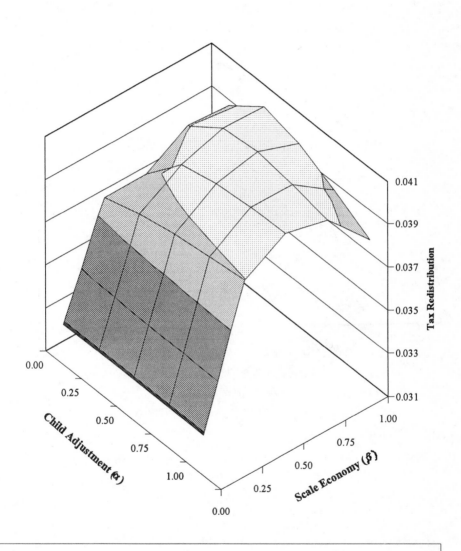

FIGURE 9.2:
Vertical Equity in 1985

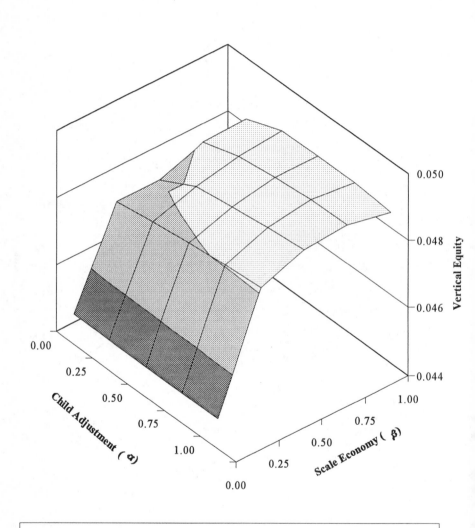

FIGURE 9.3:
Tax Inequity in 1985 (Tax Inequity is the sum of RR, TR and HI)

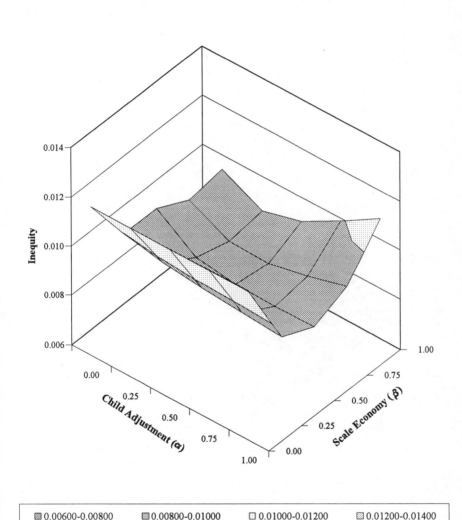

FIGURE 9.4:
Tax Redistribution Effect in 1988

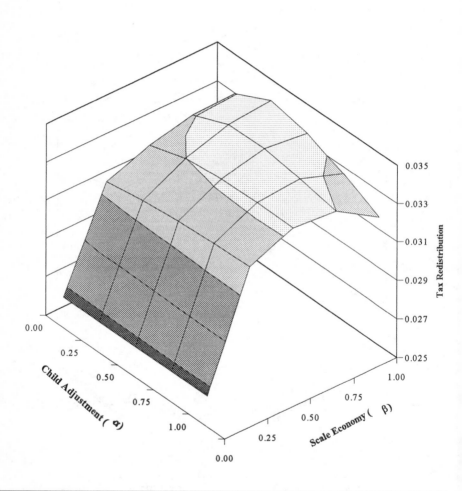

■0.02500-0.02700 ▨0.02700-0.02900 ▨0.02900-0.03100 ▨0.03100-0.03300 ☐0.03300-0.03500

FIGURE 9.5:
Vertical Equity in 1988

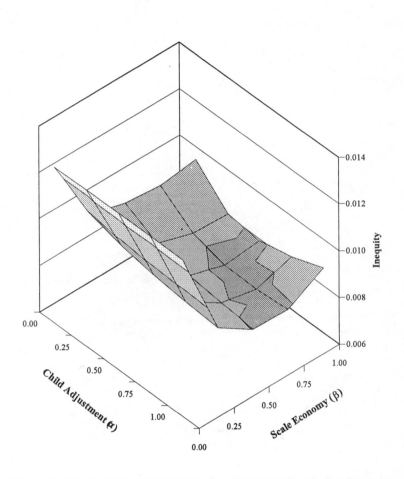

▦ 0.00600-0.00800	▦ 0.00800-0.01000	▨ 0.01000-0.01200	☐ 0.01200-0.01400

FIGURE 9.6:
Tax Inequity in 1988 (Tax Inequity is the sum of RR, TR, and HI.)

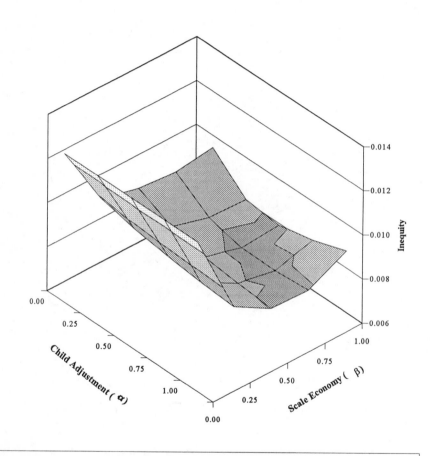

| ▨ 0.00600-0.00800 | ▨ 0.00800-0.01000 | ▨ 0.01000-0.01200 | ☐ 0.01200-0.01400 |

9.5 Conclusion

Decomposing the redistributive effect of taxes into vertical and horizontal equity is intrinsically appealing but in practice has proven to be somewhat elusive. Kakwani's (1984) extensively applied and Gini based decomposition procedure has been challenged on a number of grounds. Aronson and Lambert (1994) overcome much of the criticism by correctly identifying the horizontal inequity component and decomposing the redistributive effect into three terms *VE, HI,* and a reranking effect. These three components are measured using the Gini decomposition method of Bhattacharya and Mahalanobis (1967). But, as emphasized by Kaplow (1989), some part of the reranking term clearly involves vertical equity. Further, there are aspects of the vertical equity effects of taxes that are entirely ignored in established decomposition procedures.

This paper builds upon the work of Kakwani (1984) and Aronson and Lambert (1994) by devising a method that overcomes remaining criticisms of the Gini coefficient and concentration index approach to decomposing the equity effects of tax reform. Aronson and Lambert's (1994) method of measuring *HI* is accepted and the remainder of the redistributive effect, referred to as "net vertical equity," is shown to be the additive sum of three separate, quantifiable and meaningful terms – "vertical equity", "tax rerankings", and "post-tax income rerankings". Post-tax income rerankings, of course, are much discussed in the literature. In contrast the tax rerankings are virtually ignored. Both involve distinct vertical inequities that detract from the overall vertical equity in an otherwise progressive tax system. To identify each of these terms, we make use of the relative deprivation interpretation of the Gini coefficient and apply covariance decomposition methods.

To illustrate the new decomposition procedure we apply it to investigate the equity effects of federal income taxes in the United States before and after the Tax Reform Act of 1986. Large samples of individual tax returns are used along with several equivalence scales to make estimates of the redistributive effect of taxes, vertical equity, post-tax income rerankings, tax rerankings and horizontal inequity in 1985 and 1988. A number of important empirical results emerge. Using an income band similar in relative size to the one Aronson and Lambert (1994) apply in their study of UK tax equity we find horizontal inequity to be extremely small. It declines across time but has little measurable effect on the redistributive impact of U.S. income taxes. In contrast, the vertical inequities associated with tax rerankings are quite large; dwarfing both horizontal inequity and the vertical inequity caused by post-tax income rerankings. On balance, the evidence indicates that the redistributive effect of the US incomes was substantially reduced by the 1986 tax reform, with diminished vertical equity being the primary explanation of this change.

APPENDEX

TABLE 9.A1:

1985 Zero Income Band

α	β	Income and Taxes ($)			Mean Tax Rate	Gini Coefficients			Tax Redistributions and Decompostion						
		Pre-tax Income	Post-tax Income	Tax	Tax Rate	Pre-Tax	Post-Tax	Tax Deviation	VE	RR	TR	VI	NVE	HI	RD
1	2	3	4	5	6	7	8	9	10	11	12	13	14	15	16
0.00	0.00	24216	20639	3577	0.1477	0.4997	0.4668	0.0566	0.0448	0.0006	0.0113	0.0118	0.0329	0.00000031	0.0329
	0.25	25112	21411	3701	0.1474	0.4615	0.4238	0.0572	0.0475	0.0005	0.0093	0.0097	0.0378	0.00000017	0.0378
	0.50	21739	18547	3192	0.1468	0.4535	0.4149	0.0569	0.0477	0.0005	0.0087	0.0092	0.0386	0.00000017	0.0386
	0.75	18922	16158	2765	0.1461	0.4479	0.4089	0.0568	0.0479	0.0005	0.0084	0.0089	0.0390	0.00000017	0.0390
	1.00	16569	14162	2408	0.1453	0.4454	0.4066	0.0569	0.0479	0.0005	0.0086	0.0090	0.0388	0.00000029	0.0388
0.25	0.25	24115	20548	3567	0.1479	0.4608	0.4225	0.0570	0.0476	0.0005	0.0089	0.0094	0.0383	0.00000004	0.0383
	0.50	20081	17111	2970	0.1479	0.4528	0.4133	0.0565	0.0480	0.0004	0.0080	0.0085	0.0395	0.00000004	0.0395
	0.75	16845	14357	2488	0.1477	0.4485	0.4083	0.0561	0.0482	0.0004	0.0076	0.0080	0.0402	0.00000004	0.0402
	1.00	14243	12144	2099	0.1474	0.4486	0.4085	0.0561	0.0481	0.0004	0.0076	0.0080	0.0401	0.00000010	0.0401
0.50	0.25	23392	19923	3469	0.1483	0.4603	0.4217	0.0569	0.0478	0.0004	0.0087	0.0092	0.0386	0.00000004	0.0386
	0.50	18953	16137	2816	0.1486	0.4537	0.4138	0.0564	0.0481	0.0004	0.0078	0.0082	0.0399	0.00000005	0.0399
	0.75	15520	13213	2307	0.1487	0.4527	0.4123	0.0561	0.0482	0.0004	0.0075	0.0079	0.0403	0.00000004	0.0403
	1.00	12855	10945	1910	0.1486	0.4580	0.4183	0.0564	0.0481	0.0005	0.0079	0.0084	0.0397	0.00000013	0.0397
0.75	0.25	22823	19432	3390	0.1486	0.4601	0.4213	0.0569	0.0479	0.0004	0.0086	0.0090	0.0388	0.00000004	0.0388
	0.50	18106	15407	2699	0.1491	0.4553	0.4152	0.0564	0.0482	0.0004	0.0077	0.0081	0.0401	0.00000004	0.0401
	0.75	14571	12394	2177	0.1494	0.4582	0.4181	0.0564	0.0483	0.0004	0.0077	0.0082	0.0401	0.00000004	0.0401
	1.00	11904	10125	1780	0.1495	0.4692	0.4304	0.0571	0.0480	0.0005	0.0087	0.0091	0.0388	0.00000009	0.0388
1.00	0.25	22355	19029	3326	0.1488	0.4600	0.4210	0.0569	0.0479	0.0004	0.0085	0.0089	0.0390	0.00000004	0.0390
	0.50	17435	14829	2606	0.1495	0.4572	0.4171	0.0565	0.0483	0.0004	0.0077	0.0082	0.0402	0.00000006	0.0402
	0.75	13846	11770	2076	0.1500	0.4642	0.4245	0.0568	0.0483	0.0004	0.0081	0.0086	0.0397	0.00000005	0.0397
	1.00	12141	10367	1773	0.1461	0.4778	0.4429	0.0533	0.0441	0.0006	0.0087	0.0092	0.0349	0.00000019	0.0349

TABLE 9.A2:
1988 Zero Income Band

		Income and Taxes ($)			Mean	Gini Coefficients			Tax Redistributions and Decompostion						
α	β	Pre-tax Income	Post-tax Income	Tax	Tax Rate	Pre-Tax	Post-Tax	Tax Deviation	VE	RR	TR	VI	NVE	HI	RD
1	2	3	4	5	6	7	8	9	10	11	12	13	14	15	16
0.00	0.00	29737	25622	4116	0.1384	0.5486	0.5220	0.0518	0.0392	0.0018	0.0108	0.0126	0.0266	0.00000211	0.0266
	0.25	31874	27566	4309	0.1352	0.5022	0.4706	0.0509	0.0412	0.0014	0.0083	0.0097	0.0316	0.00000115	0.0316
	0.50	27529	23829	3700	0.1344	0.4926	0.4602	0.0509	0.0417	0.0014	0.0079	0.0092	0.0324	0.00000116	0.0324
	0.75	23899	20708	3191	0.1335	0.4849	0.4520	0.0511	0.0420	0.0013	0.0077	0.0091	0.0330	0.00000116	0.0330
	1.00	20863	18099	2764	0.1325	0.4798	0.4468	0.0515	0.0422	0.0013	0.0079	0.0092	0.0330	0.00000193	0.0330
0.25	0.25	30629	26471	4158	0.1357	0.5015	0.4696	0.0505	0.0412	0.0014	0.0079	0.0093	0.0319	0.00000022	0.0319
	0.50	25462	22010	3452	0.1356	0.4920	0.4590	0.0499	0.0415	0.0014	0.0070	0.0085	0.0330	0.00000026	0.0330
	0.75	21317	18432	2885	0.1353	0.4855	0.4517	0.0496	0.0417	0.0014	0.0065	0.0079	0.0338	0.00000023	0.0338
	1.00	17983	15556	2428	0.1350	0.4827	0.4487	0.0494	0.0417	0.0014	0.0063	0.0077	0.0340	0.00000061	0.0340
0.50	0.25	29712	25667	4044	0.1361	0.5011	0.4690	0.0502	0.0411	0.0014	0.0076	0.0091	0.0321	0.00000026	0.0321
	0.50	24032	20755	3277	0.1363	0.4927	0.4594	0.0494	0.0413	0.0015	0.0066	0.0081	0.0332	0.00000029	0.0332
	0.75	19637	16957	2680	0.1365	0.4889	0.4552	0.0487	0.0413	0.0015	0.0060	0.0075	0.0338	0.00000026	0.0338
	1.00	16222	14008	2215	0.1365	0.4907	0.4571	0.0484	0.0410	0.0015	0.0059	0.0074	0.0335	0.00000075	0.0335
0.75	0.25	28986	25032	3954	0.1364	0.5009	0.4687	0.0499	0.0411	0.0015	0.0074	0.0089	0.0322	0.00000022	0.0322
	0.50	22949	19807	3142	0.1369	0.4940	0.4607	0.0489	0.0411	0.0015	0.0063	0.0078	0.0333	0.00000022	0.0333
	0.75	18420	15891	2530	0.1373	0.4936	0.4601	0.0482	0.0409	0.0016	0.0058	0.0074	0.0335	0.00000022	0.0335
	1.00	15003	12938	2065	0.1377	0.5004	0.4676	0.0481	0.0404	0.0016	0.0060	0.0077	0.0327	0.00000052	0.0327
1.00	0.25	28386	24507	3879	0.1366	0.5008	0.4685	0.0498	0.0410	0.0015	0.0073	0.0087	0.0323	0.00000028	0.0323
	0.50	22087	19052	3035	0.1374	0.4956	0.4623	0.0486	0.0409	0.0015	0.0062	0.0077	0.0332	0.00000039	0.0332
	0.75	17486	15073	2414	0.1380	0.4987	0.4657	0.0479	0.0405	0.0016	0.0058	0.0074	0.0331	0.00000029	0.0331
	1.00	14099	12146	1953	0.1385	0.5105	0.4787	0.0480	0.0399	0.0017	0.0064	0.0081	0.0318	0.00000091	0.0318

TABLE 9.A3:
1985 $500 Income Band

α	β	Income and Taxes ($)			Mean Tax Rate	Gini Coefficients			Tax Redistributions and Decomposition						
		Pre-tax Income	Post-tax Income	Tax		Pre-Tax	Post-Tax	Tax Deviation	VE	RR	TR	VI	NVE	HI	RD
1	2	3	4	5	6	7	8	9	10	11	12	13	14	15	16
0.00	0.00	24216	20639	3577	0.1477	0.4996	0.4668	0.0569	0.0449	0.0005	0.0114	0.0119	0.0330	0.00016401	0.0329
	0.25	25112	21411	3701	0.1474	0.4615	0.4238	0.0575	0.0476	0.0004	0.0093	0.0097	0.0379	0.00016789	0.0377
	0.50	25112	21411	3701	0.1474	0.4615	0.4238	0.0575	0.0476	0.0004	0.0093	0.0097	0.0379	0.00016789	0.0377
	0.75	18922	16158	2765	0.1461	0.4478	0.4089	0.0573	0.0481	0.0004	0.0086	0.0090	0.0391	0.00023086	0.0389
	1.00	16569	14162	2408	0.1453	0.4453	0.4066	0.0576	0.0482	0.0004	0.0088	0.0091	0.0390	0.00027664	0.0387
0.25	0.25	24115	20548	3567	0.1479	0.4607	0.4225	0.0574	0.0478	0.0004	0.0090	0.0094	0.0384	0.00017003	0.0382
	0.50	20081	17111	2970	0.1479	0.4528	0.4133	0.0570	0.0482	0.0004	0.0082	0.0086	0.0396	0.00019810	0.0394
	0.75	16845	14357	2488	0.1477	0.4484	0.4083	0.0568	0.0485	0.0004	0.0078	0.0081	0.0403	0.00023571	0.0401
	1.00	14243	12144	2099	0.1474	0.4485	0.4085	0.0571	0.0486	0.0004	0.0079	0.0083	0.0403	0.00029559	0.0400
0.50	0.25	23392	19923	3469	0.1483	0.4603	0.4217	0.0573	0.0479	0.0004	0.0088	0.0092	0.0387	0.00017160	0.0385
	0.50	18953	16137	2816	0.1486	0.4536	0.4138	0.0569	0.0484	0.0004	0.0080	0.0083	0.0401	0.00020254	0.0399
	0.75	15520	13213	2307	0.1487	0.4526	0.4123	0.0569	0.0486	0.0003	0.0077	0.0081	0.0405	0.00025146	0.0402
	1.00	12855	10945	1910	0.1486	0.4579	0.4183	0.0576	0.0486	0.0004	0.0083	0.0087	0.0399	0.00033438	0.0396
0.75	0.25	22823	19432	3390	0.1486	0.4601	0.4213	0.0573	0.0480	0.0004	0.0087	0.0091	0.0390	0.00017377	0.0388
	0.50	18106	15407	2699	0.1491	0.4552	0.4152	0.0570	0.0485	0.0004	0.0079	0.0083	0.0402	0.00021061	0.0400
	0.75	14571	12394	2177	0.1494	0.4581	0.4181	0.0574	0.0487	0.0004	0.0081	0.0084	0.0403	0.00027444	0.0400
	1.00	11904	10125	1780	0.1495	0.4691	0.4304	0.0585	0.0486	0.0004	0.0091	0.0095	0.0391	0.00037895	0.0387
1.00	0.25	22355	19029	3326	0.1488	0.4600	0.4210	0.0573	0.0481	0.0004	0.0086	0.0090	0.0391	0.00017577	0.0390
	0.50	17435	14829	2606	0.1495	0.4572	0.4171	0.0572	0.0486	0.0004	0.0080	0.0083	0.0403	0.00021865	0.0401
	0.75	13846	11770	2076	0.1500	0.4641	0.4245	0.0579	0.0487	0.0004	0.0085	0.0088	0.0399	0.00029829	0.0396
	1.00	11204	9521	1683	0.1502	0.4806	0.4430	0.0593	0.0485	0.0004	0.0100	0.0104	0.0380	0.00042124	0.0376

TABLE 9.A4:
1988 $500 Income Band

α	β	Income and Taxes ($)			Mean Tax Rate	Gini Coefficients			Tax Redistributions and Decomposition						
		Pre-tax Income	Post-tax Income	Tax		Pre-Tax	Post-Tax	Tax Deviation	VE	RR	TR	VI	NVE	HI	RD
1	2	3	4	5	6	7	8	9	10	11	12	13	14	15	16
0.00	0.00	29737	25622	4116	0.1384	0.5486	0.5220	0.0520	0.0393	0.0017	0.0109	0.0126	0.0267	0.00013724	0.0266
	0.25	31874	27566	4309	0.1352	0.5021	0.4706	0.0511	0.0413	0.0013	0.0083	0.0096	0.0317	0.00013219	0.0315
	0.50	27529	23829	3700	0.1344	0.4926	0.4602	0.0512	0.0418	0.0013	0.0079	0.0092	0.0326	0.00015666	0.0324
	0.75	23899	20708	3191	0.1335	0.4849	0.4520	0.0514	0.0421	0.0013	0.0078	0.0090	0.0331	0.00018632	0.0329
	1.00	20863	18099	2764	0.1325	0.4797	0.4468	0.0518	0.0424	0.0013	0.0080	0.0092	0.0332	0.00022318	0.0330
0.25	0.25	30629	26471	4158	0.1357	0.5014	0.4696	0.0506	0.0412	0.0014	0.0079	0.0093	0.0320	0.00013205	0.0318
	0.50	25462	22010	3452	0.1356	0.4920	0.4590	0.0502	0.0416	0.0014	0.0071	0.0085	0.0331	0.00015441	0.0330
	0.75	21317	18432	2885	0.1353	0.4854	0.4517	0.0500	0.0419	0.0013	0.0066	0.0080	0.0339	0.00018146	0.0337
	1.00	17983	15556	2428	0.1350	0.4826	0.4487	0.0500	0.0420	0.0013	0.0065	0.0079	0.0341	0.00022157	0.0339
0.50	0.25	29712	25667	4044	0.1361	0.5010	0.4690	0.0504	0.0412	0.0014	0.0077	0.0090	0.0322	0.00013208	0.0320
	0.50	24032	20755	3277	0.1363	0.4926	0.4594	0.0497	0.0415	0.0014	0.0067	0.0081	0.0334	0.00015447	0.0332
	0.75	19637	16957	2680	0.1365	0.4889	0.4552	0.0493	0.0415	0.0014	0.0062	0.0076	0.0339	0.00018256	0.0337
	1.00	16222	14008	2215	0.1365	0.4906	0.4571	0.0493	0.0414	0.0014	0.0062	0.0077	0.0337	0.00023259	0.0335
0.75	0.25	28986	25032	3954	0.1364	0.5008	0.4687	0.0502	0.0412	0.0014	0.0075	0.0089	0.0323	0.00013265	0.0322
	0.50	22949	19807	3142	0.1369	0.4939	0.4607	0.0494	0.0413	0.0014	0.0065	0.0079	0.0334	0.00015506	0.0332
	0.75	18420	15891	2530	0.1373	0.4935	0.4601	0.0490	0.0412	0.0015	0.0061	0.0076	0.0336	0.00018984	0.0334
	1.00	15003	12938	2065	0.1377	0.5003	0.4676	0.0491	0.0409	0.0015	0.0064	0.0080	0.0329	0.00025237	0.0326
1.00	0.25	28386	24507	3879	0.1366	0.5008	0.4685	0.0501	0.0412	0.0014	0.0073	0.0088	0.0324	0.00013386	0.0322
	0.50	22087	19052	3035	0.1374	0.4955	0.4623	0.0491	0.0411	0.0015	0.0063	0.0078	0.0334	0.00015578	0.0332
	0.75	17486	15073	2414	0.1380	0.4987	0.4657	0.0488	0.0409	0.0016	0.0061	0.0077	0.0332	0.00019947	0.0330
	1.00	14099	12146	1953	0.1385	0.5104	0.4787	0.0491	0.0404	0.0016	0.0069	0.0085	0.0319	0.00027433	0.0316

REFERENCES

[1] Aronson, J. Richard and Peter Lambert (1994). "Decomposing the Gini Coefficient to Reveal the Vertical, Horizontal, and Reranking Effects of In come Taxation," *National Tax Journal* 47: 273-294.

[2] Aronson, J. Richard, Paul Johnson, and Peter Lambert (1994) "Redistributive Effect and Unequal Income Tax Treatment," *The Economic Journal* 104: 262-270.

[3] Atkinson, Anthony B. (1980) "Horizontal Equity and the Distribution of the Tax Burden." In the *Economics of Taxation,* edited by H. Aaron and M. Boskin. Washington, D.C.: The Brookings Institution.

[4] Berliant, Marcus C. and Robert P. Strauss (1985) "The Horizontal and Vertical Equity Characteristics of the Federal Individual Income Tax, 1966-77." In National Bureau of Economic Research, *Studies In Income and Wealth,* edited by M, David and T. Smeeding, Chicago: University of Chicago Press: 179-213.

[5] Berliant, Marcus C. and Robert P. Strauss (1993) "State and Federal Tax Equity: Estimates Before and After the Tax Reform Act of 1986," *Journal of Policy Analysis and Management* 12: 9-43

[6] Berliant, Marcus C. and Robert P. Strauss (1996) "On Recent Expositions of Horizontal and Vertical Equity," *Public Economic Review (Inaugural Issue)*: 129-150

[7] Bhattacharya N. and Mahalanobis (1967) "Regional Disparities in Household consumption in India," *Journal of the American Statistical Association* 62: 143-61.

[8] Feldstein, Martin S (1976) "On the Theory of Tax Re-form," *Journal of Public Economics* 6: 77-104.

[9] Feldstein, Martin (1995a) "Behavioral Responses to Tax Rates,: Evidence From the Tax Reform Act of 1986," *American Economic Review* 85, 170-174."

[10] Feldstein, Martin (1995b) "The Effects of Marginal Tax Rates on Taxable Income: A Panel Study of the 1986 Tax Reform Act, *Journal of Political Economy* 103, 551-572.

[11] Formby, John P., Terry G. Seaks, and W. James Smith (1988) "On the Measurement and Trend of Inequality: A Reconsideration," *American Economic Review* 79: 256-264.

[12] Gramlich, Edward (1985) "Comment," In *Horizontal Equity, Uncertainty, and Economic Well Being,* edited by Martin David and Timothy Smeeding, 264 68. Chicago: University of Chicago Press.

[13] Gramlich, E.M., Kasten R., Sammartino F. (1993) "Growing Inequality in the 1980s: The Role of Federal Taxes and Cash Transfers," in S. Danziger and P. Gottschalk, eds., *Uneven Tides: Rising Inequality in America* (New York: Russell Sage Foundation).

[14] Gravelle, J. (1992) "Equity Effects of the Tax Reform Act of 1986," *Journal of Economic Perspectives* 6: 27-44.

[15] Hayes, K., Lambert, P.J. and Slottje, D. (1995) "Evaluating Effective Income Tax Progression," *Journal of Public Economics* 56: 461-474.

[16] Hey, J. D. and P. J. Lambert (1980) "Relative Deprivation and the Gini Coefficient: Comment," *Quarterly Jourrnal of Economics* 95: 567-573.

[17] Kakwani, N.C. (1984) "On the Measurement of Tax Progressivity and Redistributive Effect of Taxes with Applications to Horizontal and Vertical Equity," *Advances in Econometrics*, 3: 149-168.

[18] Kakwani, N. C. (1994) "The Relative Deprivation Curve and Its Application," *Journal of Business and Economic Statistics* 2: 384-399.

[19] Kaplow, Louis (1989) "Horizontal Equity: Measures in Search of a Principle," *National Tax Journal* 41: 139-153.

[20] Kasten R., Sammartino F. and Toder E. (1994) "Trends in Federal Tax Progressivity, 1980-1993," in J. Slemrod, ed., *Tax Progressivity and Income Inequality* (Cambridge: Cambridge University Press).

[21] Lambert, P.J. and Pfähler, W. (1992) "Income Tax Progression and Redistributive Effect: the Influence of Changes in the Pretax Income Distribution," *Public Finance*, 47: 1-16.

[22] Lambert, Peter J. and J. Richard Aronson (1993). "Inequality Decomposition Analysis and the Gini Coefficient Revisited," *The Economic Journal* 103: 1221-1227.

[23] Lambert, P.J. (1993) *The Distribution and Redistribution of Income: A Mathematical Analysis,* 2nd ed. (Manchester: Manchester University Press).

[24] Lerman, Robert and Shlomo Yitzhaki (1994) "Changing Ranks and The Inequality Impact of Taxes and Transfers," *National Tax Journal* 36: 403-17.

[25] Michael, R.C. (1991) "Economic Growth and Income Inequality Since the 1982 Recession," *Journal of Policy Analysis and Modeling* 10: 11-28.

[26] Miller, R.G. (1981) *Simultaneous Statistical Inference*, 2nd ed. (New York: Wiley).

[27] Mookerjee, Dilip and Anthony F. Sharrocks (1982) "A Decomposition Analysis of the Trend in U,K. Income Inequality," *Economic Journal* 92: 886-902.

[28] Musgrave, Richard A. (1990) "Horizontal Equity, Once More," *National Tax Journal* 43: 113-22.

[29] Musgrave, Richard A. (1995) "Progressive Taxation, Equity, and Tax Design," In *Tax Progressivity and Income Inequality*, edited by Joel Slemrod, 341-356, Cambridge University Press.

[30] Pechman, J. (1987) "Tax Reform: Theory and Practice," *Journal of Economic Perspectives*, 1: 11-28.

[31] Pechman, J. (1990) "The Future of the Income Tax," *American Economic Review* 80: 1-20.

[32] Slemrod, J. (1990) *Do Taxes Matter? The Impact of the Tax Reform Act of 1986* (Cambridge: MIT Press).

[33] Plotnick, Robert (1981) "A Measure of Horizontal In equity," *Review of Economics and Statistics* 63: 283-288.

[34] Plotnick, Robert (1985) "A Comparison of Measures of Horizontal inequity," In *Horizontal Equity, Uncertainty and Economic Well Being*, edited by M. David and T. Smeeding, ch 8, New York: NBER.

[35] Pyatt, Graham (1976) "The Interpretation and Disaggregation of Gini Coefficients," *Economic Journal* 8 : 243-255.

[36] Slemrod, J. (1992) "Taxation and Inequality: A Time Exposure Perspective," in J. Poterba ed., *Tax Policy and the Economy* (Cambridge: MIT Press).

[37] Slemrod, J. (1995) "Transitory versus Permanent Responses to Tax rate Changes," *American Economic Review*, 85: forthcoming.

[38] Wallace, S., Wasylenko, M. and Weiner, D. (1991) "The Distributional Implications of Reforming the Personal and Corporate Income Taxes," *National Tax Journal* 44: 181-198.

[39] Yitzhaki, Shlomo (1979) "Relative Deprivation and The Gini Coefficient," *Quarterly Jorurnal of Economics 93*: 321-324.

Chapter 10

INCOME TRANSFORMATION AND INCOME INEQUALITY[*]

Yoram Amiel
Ruppin Institute, Israel

Frank A. Cowell
London School of Economics and Political Science, Houghton Street, London
WC2A 2AE, United Kingdom

10.1   Introduction

This paper is about the structure of income inequality comparisons. The analysis of income inequality is, of course, essentially about the sharing-out of a "cake" or "pie" and some of the elementary principles which apply to comparisons of alternative cake-divisions are usually assumed to be well known. However, except in the very simplest cases, more is required than these elementary principles. For inequality analysis to have economic meaning, or for it to be used as a basis for rational social decisions, it is important that judgments of alternative share-outs should conform to some sort of structure. We examine the issues that arise in connection with this structure and employ a new experimental test to investigate a specific hypothesis about the relationship between income levels and inequality orderings.

Why is structure so important to distributional judgments? In situations where a given cake is to be split between two individuals little is required other

[*]We examine the way in which across-the-board additions to incomes are perceived to change inequality. Using a questionnaire we investigate whether subjective inequality rankings correspond to the principle of scale-independence or of translation-independence, or to some generalized concept of independence which incorporates the other two principles as special cases. We find evidence that the appropriate independence concept depends on the income levels at which inequality comparisons are made. This paper is Partially supported by the Human Capital and Mobility Programme of the EU grant #ERBCHRXCT94067 and ESRC grant #R000 23 5725. We would like to acknowledge the research assistance of Ceema Namazie.

than consistency and impartiality. Beyond these simplest cases coherent inequality judgments usually require the introduction of specialized equipment – inequality measures. These are analytical devices for giving systematic answers to questions about ways of sharing a cake of given size amongst a given number of people. More formally we may characterize an inequality measure as a function which induces an ordering over a set of income vectors belonging to a simplex.

In the development of the modern theory of inequality analysis considerable attention has been devoted to the systems of contours of such measures at any particular income level - the map portraying the assessment of various distributions of a fixed cake that are regarded as "equally unequal". This is one aspect of structure. But, what would happen if we were to consider instead cakes of differing sizes? How should the tools of inequality analysis perform at different levels of overall income? It would be interesting to know the way in which one might try to "hook up" the systems of contours corresponding to each such overall income level. This is where the structure of inequality judgments involves the issue of income transformation.

In the literature there is a clear difference of opinion on the issue of income transformation. This has typically involved the relative merits of the principles of scale independence - under which measured inequality is unaffected by uniform proportional transformations of income vectors - and of translation independence under which inequality is unaffected by the addition of an identical constant to every component of the vector.[1] Some economists have suggested various compromises between the two principles.[2] In this paper we suggest a generalization of these approaches which are also supported by questionnaire evidence.

In section 2 we set out the essence of the income transformation problem and in section 3 we introduce the questionnaire study that we used to investigate this problem. Section 4 investigates a specific hypothesis on the structure of inequality orderings and section 5 concludes.

---

[1] See, for example, the illuminating discussion in Kolm (1976a, 1976b). Note also the distinction between scale (translation) independence as we have used the terms here and scale (translation) invariance in the sense that inequality orderings are preserved under rescaling (translations) of income. For example, using the notation of page 3 below, an inequality measure $I: X \mapsto R$ is scale invariant if, for any $\alpha \in R$, $x \in X$, $y \in X$, $x + \alpha x \in X$, it is true that $I(x) > I(y) \Leftrightarrow [I(x + \alpha x) > I(y + \alpha y)]$.

[2] See Bossert and Pfingsten (1990), Kolm (1968, 1976a, 1976b, 1996). See also Seidl and Pfingsten (1994) and the interesting non-linear compromise of Krtscha (1994).

10.2   The Transformation Problem

Suppose we have a fixed population of n people, each of whom has a given income $x_i, i = 1, 2, ..., n$. Write the income distribution as the vector $\mathbf{x} := (x_1, x_2, ..., x_n)$ and let the set of all income distributions be X, which we take to be a convex subset of $\mathbf{R}^n$.[3] Suppose also that we have agreed on some inequality measure as a tool for appraising income distributions. Now let us imagine that we increase (or decrease) each person's income simultaneously from the reference point $\mathbf{x}$, the original distribution. The problem is this: what kind of income change will ensure that inequality remains unchanged? In particular, would inequality remain unchanged under transformations that involved equal absolute additions to, or equi-proportionate transformation of, all incomes?

The answer to this question will depend upon the type of inequality measure employed. The literature has focused principally upon two appealing special cases: *absolute* measures which have the property that, for all $\alpha \in \mathbf{R}, \mathbf{x} \in X, \mathbf{x} + \alpha \mathbf{1} \in X$, the income-distribution vectors $\mathbf{x}$ and $\mathbf{x} + \alpha \mathbf{1}$ are regarded as equivalent by the inequality measure, and relative measures which have the property that, for all $\alpha \in \mathbf{R}, \mathbf{x} \in X, \mathbf{x} + \alpha \mathbf{x} \in X$, the vectors $\mathbf{x}$ and $\mathbf{x} + \alpha \mathbf{x}$ are regarded as equivalent by the inequality measure.[4] Obviously absolute measures remain unchanged under income additions of equal absolute amounts, and relative measures are independent under proportional income additions. However these two special types of independence can be characterized in a more general way. Let t denote the transformation type of a particular inequality comparison, and let $\mathbf{y} := t\mathbf{x}/\mu(\mathbf{x}) + [1 - t]\mathbf{1}$ be the transformation direction, where $\mu(\mathbf{x})$ is the mean of $\mathbf{x}$. Then evidently relative measures are independent of income changes in the transformation direction parallel to the original vector $\mathbf{x}$ (transformation type $t = 1$); absolute measures are independent of income changes in the transformation direction along the 45° ray (transformation type 0). The concept of transformation direction and transformation type are illustrated in Figure 1 and in the enlargement in Figure 2. Point A corresponds to $\mathbf{x}$, the current income distribution, B corresponds to $\mathbf{x} + \mathbf{x}/\mu(\mathbf{x})$, and C to $\mathbf{x} + \mathbf{1}$; the line BC is orthogonal to the ray of perfect

---

[3]It is common in the literature to take $X \subset \mathbf{R}^n_+ \setminus \{0\}$ but as we will see on page 1015(paragraph 2) this side-steps an awkward problem that is fundamental to the concept of inequality contours; moreover it sidesteps the problem only for the special case of scale independent measures.

[4]See Blackorby and Donaldson (1978, 1980, 1984)

equality. The transformation direction y is the ray from A to any point on the line BC (produced).

It is also worth noting that - except in very special circumstances - an inequality measure cannot be both relative and absolute at the same time. For, if it were to satisfy both these criteria simultaneously, then either the measure would have to be discontinuous somewhere, or it would have to be a constant function - which would of course be economically trivial.[5] So, if we consider continuity to be a desirable property that an inequality measure should possess, we must choose between relative and absolute measures - or we must introduce some other principle to characterise income transformations.

The choice between relativism and absolutism has been resolved in a variety of ways. As we noted in the introduction, many of the standard references take a clear position in favor of one principle or the other.[6] Others have expressed greater scepticism. For example, Dalton implicitly rejected both principles: he argued that proportionate additions to all incomes would reduce inequality and that proportionate subtractions will increase it; therefore, *a fortiori*, equal additions reduce inequality.[7] Sen has also argued[8] that scale independence is not defensible. As an alternative approach, Kolm (1976b) and Bossert and Pfingsten (1990) have also suggested some straightforward compromises between the principles of scale independence and translation independence. For example Bossert and Pfingsten suggest that one considers transformation types t such that $0 < t < 1$:Pfingsten (1988) has further attempted to underpin this suggested approach with an experimental test in the form of a sophisticated questionnaire.

Of course, there is a whole range of apparently reasonable views about the effect of equal and proportionate additions to incomes on inequality. Let us briefly review some of these by illustrating the iso-inequality contours in each case: observe that some - but not all - of them correspond to one particular transformation direction y for any $x \in X$. Although we present examples

---

[5]Cf Eichhorn and Gehrig (1982). See Amiel (1981) and Aczel (1987), pages 49-51 for a formal demonstration of this. In fact for virtually all standard types of inequality measure there remains a problem of discontinuity at one or more points in X as we shall see below. Also note that there is no problem with inequality measures being simultaneously scale- and translation-invariant in the sense of note 1: for example this property is possessed by the class of measures given by $\psi(I, \mu, n)$ where ψ is increasing in its first argument and I is either the Gini coefficient or the variance.
[6]For example Atkinson (1970) and Theil (1967) assume relativism; Kolm (1976b) argues in favour of absolutism.
[7]See Dalton (1920), pp.355-357.
[8]See Sen (1973), pp.60-61.

drawn for a two-person distribution the concepts can be extended to cases involving $n > 2$; however in such circumstances the transfer principle - as conventionally defined - may not always hold.[9]

Take first those cases where t is constant over $\mathbf{X}$. The iso-inequality contours in the conventional case of scale-independence are drawn in Figure 3 (relative inequality measures): equi-proportionate income changes do not affect inequality, but equal absolute additions to income reduce inequality (which can be checked by drawing a line parallel to the ray of equality and observing the successive intersections with the iso-inequality contours). Figure 4 depicts the iso-inequality contours for absolute measures (the case of translation independence): uniform absolute additions to income leave inequality unaffected and equi-proportionate additions to income will increase inequality (which can be checked by drawing rays through the origin and noting the successive intersections with the con-tours). The intermediate Bossert-Pfingsten approach is depicted in Figure 5: equi-proportionate additions to income will increase inequality, but equal absolute income additions will reduce inequality.

However, the Bossert-Pfingsten case is but one interesting generalization of scale- and translation-independence. The transformation type t and the transformation direction do not have to be constant over $\mathbf{X}$; equivalently the iso-inequality contours do not have to be straight lines. The class of measures with non-constant transformation direction includes some important cases. For example Figure 6 illustrates one case where both equal absolute and equal proportionate additions to income will reduce inequality: it is this type of pattern that corresponds to the views presented in Dalton (1920).[10] The opposite pattern in Figure 7: here both equi-proportionate and equal absolute income additions will increase inequality.

Many other interesting patterns are possible. Each of these distinct views about the structure of inequality may be internally consistent and defensible; and, of course, it is understandable that each observer will bring his own set of judgements and, as a result, will respond in different ways when confronted by inequality comparisons. But, one might wonder, what is the view that most people would reasonably adopt? Is there a consensus approach on the issue of income levels and inequality rankings? Would people conventionally conform to a particular transformation direction?

---

[9]On this point see Amiel and Cowell (1992).

[10]Notice that the case can be extended to situations where the iso-inequality contours (except for the equality contour) do not all pass through the origin.

FIGURE 10.1:
The Transformation Direction

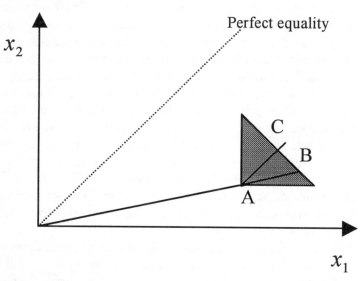

FIGURE 10.2:
Transformation direction-enlargement

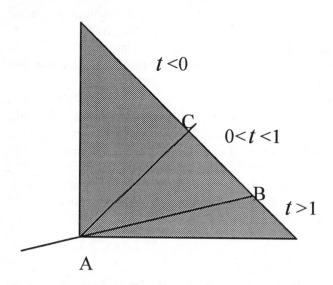

FIGURE 10.3:
Scale independence($t=1$)

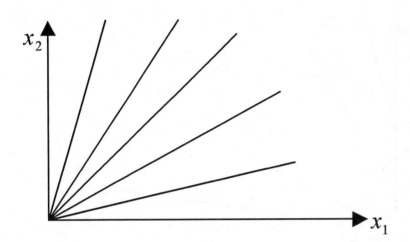

FIGURE 10.4:
Translation independence ($t=0$)

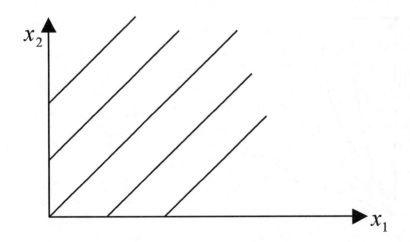

FIGURE 10.5:
Intermediate-transformation independence($0<t<1$)

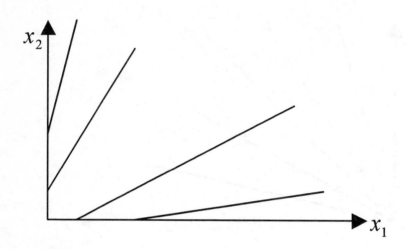

FIGURE 10.6:
The Dalton conjecture

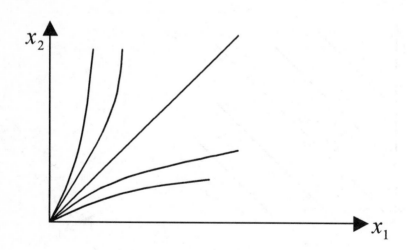

FIGURE 10.7:
The "Anti-Dalton" case

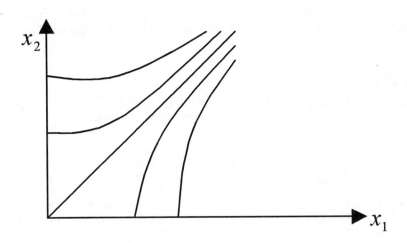

10.3   The Questionnaire Study

We obviously cannot provide a complete answer to such ambitious and general questions. Instead, we can offer here an analysis of the responses of students to our questionnaire which throws some light on how this one - possibly quite unrepresentative - group of individuals frame their views.[11]

We sought out the views of 186 Israeli students of various disciplines[12] using a questionnaire experiment. The general methodology is similar to that explained in Amiel and Cowell (1992). After presenting the student respondents with a short story we invited them to compare pairs of income distributions and to state which of them they consider to be the more unequally distributed. After this we asked a verbal question about their opinions on

---

[11]See Amiel and Cowell (1992) for a fuller discussion of the general nature of this approach. See also Harrison and Seidl (1994), Seidl and Theilen (1994) who adopt a similar methodology. Seidl and Theilen (1994) also discuss the issue of the transformation direction but their study does not adequately distinguish between income transformations and mean-preserving spreads.

[12]Economics, Sociology and Psychology.

inequality and gave them the chance to change their responses to the numerical questions in the light of their answers to the verbal questions. The full questionnaire is reprinted in the appendix.

Consider first the numerical part of the study. In the preamble to our questionnaire we introduced the respondents to a country called Alfaland and informed them of the country's average income (1000) and of the level of

TABLE 10.1:

Implied inequality change: responses to numerical question:

		(a) Adding a fixed absolute sum								
		question 1 A = (200, 400) B = (400, 600)			question 4 A = (600, 900) B = (900, 1200)			question 7 A = (1200, 1800) B = (1800, 2400)		
Class	N	Down	Up	Same	Down	Up	Same	Down	Up	Same
Psychology HU	49	86%	4%	10%	60%	12%	26%	49%	18%	31%
Econ. Ruppin	18	72%	22%	6%	67%	22%	6%	78%	11%	11%
Econ. Tel Aviv	62	86%	5%	10%	60%	15%	19%	60%	13%	24%
Econ. Tel Aviv	19	63%	32%	0%	47%	32%	16%	47%	32%	16%
Sociology HU	38	68%	11%	21%	42%	21%	37%	26%	50%	24%
All	186	78%	10%	11%	55%	18%	23%	51%	24%	23%
		(b) Adding a compromise sum								
		question 2 A = (200, 400) B = (400, 700)			question 5 A = (600, 900) B = (900, 1300)			question 8 A = (1200, 1800) B = (1800, 2550)		
Class	N	Down	Up	Same	Down	Up	Sam	Down	Up	Same
Psychology HU	49	71%	20%	8%	35%	53%	12%	41%	51%	8%
Econ. Ruppin	18	67%	33%	0%	44%	44%	6%	50%	50%	0%
Econ. Tel Aviv	62	74%	24%	0%	52%	42%	3%	53%	40%	5%
Econ. Tel Aviv	19	58%	37%	0%	37%	52%	5%	37%	58%	0%
Sociology HU	38	58%	39%	3%	29%	68%	3%	21%	71%	8%
All	186	68%	28%	3%	40%	52%	6%	41%	52%	5%
		(c) Adding a fixed proportionate sum								
		question 3 A = (200, 400) B = (400, 800)			question 6 A = (600, 900) B = (900, 1350)			question 9 A = (1200, 1800) B = (1800, 2700)		
Class	N	Down	Up	Same	Down	Up	Sam	Down	Up	Same
PsychologyHU	49	45%	33%	22%	25%	57%	18%	14%	67%	16%
Econ.Ruppin	18	28%	39%	28%	22%	56%	22%	22%	56%	22%
Econ.TelAviv	62	44%	21%	32%	21%	42%	37%	15%	45%	40%
Econ.TelAviv	19	26%	37%	32%	16%	58%	21%	26%	52%	16%
SociologyHU	38	42%	29%	29%	34%	63%	3%	13%	73%	11%
All	186	40%	29%	28%	24%	53%	22%	16%	59%	24%

income which would ensure a supply of basic needs anywhere in Alfaland (400). We then asked respondents to compare pairs of income distributions in various areas of Alfaland. Three pairs of distributions were constructed for the case of equal absolute additions to incomes ($t = 0$), three pairs that exhibited proportionate additions to income ($t = 1$), and three pairs that represented situations where the income additions lay "between" the cases of absolute and the proportionate transformations ($0 < t < 1$).

The results, presented in Table 1, reveal a consistent pattern of context-specific views about the effect of income transfers on inequality. Notice what happens as one switches the context of the question from relatively low incomes (the first column in the table) to relatively high incomes (the third column). There is a clear switch away from support for the view that an across-the-board addition to income (in any of the three directions) will reduce inequality as one looks at successively higher income levels. For proportionate or compromise additions to income (parts (b) and (c) of the table), the majority view is that at low income levels an income addition will reduce inequality, whereas at high income levels the same type of income additions will increase inequality. The results appear broadly consistent across the various subject-field subgroups of students of which our sample was composed.

The results in Table 1 can be usefully summarized in terms of the five standard patterns depicted in Figures 3 to 7, at each of the three income levels represented by questions 1-3, questions 4-6, questions 7-9; we may also identify other consistent response patterns that do not fit one of these five paradigms, and responses which are inconsistent.[13] We then have a distribution of responses across five standard categories (seven including the categories "other" and "inconsistent") for each of the institutions at three distinct income levels: "low" (clustering around the basic-needs income level), "medium" (above the basic-needs income level, clustering around the average income level) and "high" (well above the average income level). The distribution of

---

[13]Using the symbols D, U and S to correspond to the labels "Down", "Up" and "Same" for each set of responses (questions 1-3, questions 4-6, questions 7-9) in Table 1 the categorization into the seven possible cases is as follows

Anti-Dalton	UUU
Absolute	SUU
Intermediate	DDU,DSU,DUU
Proportional	DDS
Dalton	DDD
Other	DSS,SSS,SSU
Inconsistent	Other D-U-S combinations

FIGURE 10.8:

Pattern of responses depends on income level

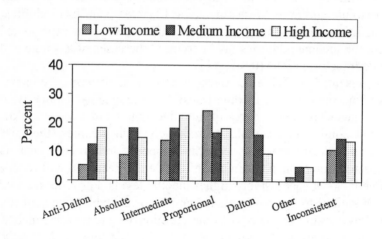

responses is shown in Figure 8: each triplet of bars shows the number of responses falling into each category at each income level. Immediately we see that at low incomes we have a remarkable result - the left hand bar in each triple becomes progressively larger over the five standard categories: there is consistently more support as one moves progressively from the "Anti-Dalton" to the "Dalton" position.[14]

The issue of the appropriate transformation direction can then be broken down into a number of questions. First, is there a consistent pattern of responses independent of income level? We can answer this by looking at the distribution of responses among the five main pattern-categories at each of the three income levels. It is clear from Table 2 that the χ^2 -test rejects the hypothesis that the distribution of responses amongst respondents is identical across the three income levels.[15] Secondly, is the result being driven by some

---

[14]Left and right on this figure correspond roughly to Kolm's "leftist" and "rightist" positions (Kolm 1976a).

[15]If we rework the analysis for all seven categories the value of the χ^2 -statistic is 71.664 which is significant at the 0.1 percent level with 12 degrees of freedom. Note also that the proportion of respondents whose views remained the same at all three income levels was quite small, as can be seen from the following table:

Anti-Dalton	1.61%
Absolute	2.69%

diversity within the sample? Does the distribution of responses differ by subgroup? A test across the three universities shows that, at each income level, the hypothesis that there is the same distribution of responses in each university subsample cannot be rejected.[16] We also have information about whether the individuals had already studied economics:[17] a test across "economics education" subsamples shows that the hypothesis that the distribution in the two subsamples is identical cannot be rejected at low income levels,[18] but is always rejected at medium and high income levels.[19] This suggests that the pattern of responses over the income levels may differ according to whether people have or have not studied economics before – see the lower χ^2-value for those in the "Studied economics" category in Table 2. As noted above, in addition to the indirect inferences drawn from the numerical responses we also asked our students a direct verbal question about the effect of changes in real incomes (question 10 in the Appendix). Table 3 reports the results. Note that the highest percentage support (41% overall) is for the opinion that "...inequality may remain unaltered: whether it does so depends not only on the change but also on initial and final levels of real income" - see the penultimate column. Apart from this, 32% supported scale independence and only 11% supported translation independence.[20]

Intermediate	4.30%
Proportional	8.06%
Dalton	3.23%
Other	0.00%
All	19.89%

[16]At low and medium incomes χ^2 = 11.423; 16.112, respectively (not significant at the 10% level); at high incomes χ^2 = 20:552 (significant at the 10% level, but not significant at the 5% level).

[17]124 students reported that they had not previously studied economics, 42 had studied before and 20 did not report. We carried out tests for all three categories and for the two-category case where the no-reports were grouped with those who had studied economics.

[18]The χ^2 -statistic is not significant at the 10% level.

[19]The χ^2 -statistic is significant at the 0.1% level.

[20]This result is consistent with our findings from other questionnaire studies. In Amiel and Cowell (1992) we report on a study of 1008 British, German, Israeli and US students. We found that an analysis of responses on numerical questions revealed that 37% were consistent with the principle of scale-independence, and 17% conformed to translation-independence.

TABLE 10.2:
Test for income-dependence of responses in five standard categories

	χ^2
Whole sample	63.405*
Hebrew University	50.118*
Ruppin Institute	42.552*
Tel Aviv	20.238**
Not studied economics	55.982*
Studied economics	16.917***

* significant at 0.1% level, d.f.=8
** significant at 1% level, d.f.=8
*** significant at 5% level, d.f.=8

TABLE 10.3:
"What income change will leave inequality unchanged?"

Class	N	Proportional additions	fixed sum	depends on levels	None of these
Psychology HU	49	27%	8%	55%	8%
Econ. Ruppin	18	28%	6%	33%	17%
Econ. Tel Aviv	62	37%	8%	37%	6%
Econ. Tel Aviv	19	16%	10%	47%	21%
Sociology HU	38	39%	21%	29%	5%
All	186	32%	11%	41%	9%

Notice that the wording of our investigation explicitly permits interpretation in terms of real incomes throughout. Apart from our explicit reference to this in the phrasing of the verbal question 10, the numerical questions also carry an implied "value" or "purchasing power" of the income concept that we have invented for our make-believe Alfaland. This specification is incorporated in the introductory clause "The average income in Alfaland by local currency is 1000 Alfa-dollars and the income which ensures a supply of basic needs is 400 Alfa-dollars." Had we not adopted this device, and had we wanted to ensure that the results are independent of changes in exchange rates or the price level, we might have had to accept the property of scale independence.

10.4 The Hypothesis of Dependence

Let us return to the issue that we raised earlier - whether translation independence or scale independence is the appropriate principle on which to base inequality comparisons that involve differing totals of income. This issue can be broken down into two components:
1. Is there a specific transformation direction y to which it is appropriate to refer when carrying out some income transformation on a particular distribution x?
2. If so, what is that direction?

Let us take a particularly simple case in which to represent this issue. Suppose that there are only two people in the economy with incomes x_1 and x_2 respectively, where $x_1 > x_2$. Suppose also that there is a given additional sum s, such that $s < x_1 - x_2$, which is to be divided between them so that person 1 will get s_1 and person 2 will get s_2, where $s_1 \geq 0$, $s_2 \geq 0$ and $s_1 + s_2 = s$.

It is obvious that giving all the sum to person 1 will increase inequality and giving all the sum to person 2 will decrease inequality. However, what distribution of s would keep inequality exactly unchanged? If we accept the transfer principle for a society consisting of two people, then there exists some value s such that for all $s_1^* < s_1 < s$ inequality will decrease. If it were always to be true that for
any arbitrary value of s

$$s_1^* = \frac{1}{2}s \qquad\qquad (10.1)$$

then we would have the property of translation independence. If it were always true that

$$s_1^* = \frac{x_1}{x_1 + x_2}s \qquad\qquad (10.2)$$

then we would have the property of scale independence. More generally if, for any such x_1 and x_2, it were always true that there existed a given number t and a number s such that

$$s_1^* = \frac{1}{2} \frac{x_1 t + 1 - t}{\frac{1}{2}[x_1 + x_2]t + 1 - t} s,$$
(10.3)

$$0 \le s_1^* \le 1$$
(10.4)

then we would have the property of inequality independence for transformation type t.[21]

However, it may be that no such pairs of values of s and t exist so as to determine a particular type of independence: s_1^* may depend in a more complex way on s, x_1, x_2 or on other features of the model. It is this more complex relationship that we shall refer to as the dependence hypothesis. Our questionnaire study specifically asked about the impact of income changes (such as s_1, s_2 above) and thus permits an examination of this hypothesis. We use Figures 9 and 10 to discuss the results. Along the horizontal axis of each of these figures we have put the reference income level x. On the vertical axis we plot the transformation type t: high positive values (above 1) represent situations where equi-proportional income additions will reduce inequality (the Dalton conjecture), negative values correspond to situations where even absolute additions to income will increase inequality ("anti-Dalton").

Recall that the transformation type t and the initial distribution fix a particular transformation direction y. The four curves in Figure 9 then depict four possible versions of the *income-transformation curve* - the relationship between Figure 9: Transformation type – independence transformation direction and income level - which would just leave inequality unaltered. If inequality rankings respect the principle of transfers then income additions which would decrease inequality can be represented in each figure as points below the income-transformation curve, and income additions which would increase inequality correspond to points lying above the curve. Of course this is just a simple attempt to capture a complex issue: to be realistic the approach would have to encompass other dimensions such as the effect of different total

---

[21] The argument generalises to the n-person case. The critical proportions for dividing the sum s (corresponding to equation 3) are:

$$s_i^* = \frac{s}{n} \frac{t x_i + 1 - t}{t \mu(\mathbf{x}) + 1 - t}$$

where $\sum_{i=1}^{n} s_i^* = s$.

FIGURE 10.9:
Transformation type-independence

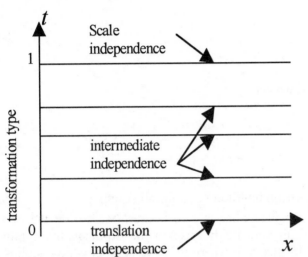

amounts added, the effect of different specific distributions of income additions and the like.

If the value judgment is that there is a specific transformation direction y, then the income-transformation curves will have slope zero as in Figure 9. So, for example, those who believe in scale independence will have their views represented by a horizontal straight line at $t = 1$; the views of those who believe in translation independence are represented by a line along the x-axis; the Bossert-Pfingsten case is a horizontal line at a height somewhere between 0 and 1. A constant value of t outside the [0; 1] interval (corresponding to a horizontal straight line below zero or above 1 in Figure 9) will produce a set of contours that exhibit logical inconsistencies somewhere on X as can be checked by referring back to Figure 1. However there is a deeper problem with the property of independence when applied to inequality contours: for any constant t different from 0 it turns out that there is a problem with the behavior of inequality orderings in the neighborhood of one critical point in X. By virtue of the symmetry property all straight line iso-inequality contours - including the line of equality – must intersect at the point $a(t)$, where each component of $a(t)$ is the number $1 - 1 = t$.

For scale-independent measures this means that the critical point is 0. The problem is that at a there is a fundamental discontinuity in the inequality map, except for trivial cases. Let I be an inequality measure and let $\mathbf{x}$ and $\mathbf{x}'$ be two distinct income vectors - each different from $\mathbf{a}$ - such that $I(\mathbf{x}) > I(\mathbf{x}')$. Construct the income vectors $\mathbf{x}_\alpha$ and $\mathbf{x}'_\alpha$ defined thus:

$$
\begin{aligned}
\mathbf{x}_\alpha &:= \alpha\mathbf{x} + [1 - \alpha]\mathbf{a} \\
\mathbf{x}'_\alpha &:= \alpha\mathbf{x}' + [1 - \alpha]\mathbf{a} \\
0 &< \alpha \leq 1
\end{aligned}
\tag{10.5}
$$

then, by definition of $\mathbf{a}(t)$, we get

$$
\begin{aligned}
I(\mathbf{x}_\alpha) &= I(\mathbf{x}) \\
I(\mathbf{x}'_\alpha) &= I(\mathbf{x}') \\
0 &< \alpha \leq 1
\end{aligned}
\tag{10.6}
$$

and so $I(\mathbf{x}_\alpha) > I(\mathbf{x}'_\alpha)$ in the neighbourhood of a for all strictly positive α. But if $\alpha = 0$ exactly at point $\mathbf{a}$ - inequality is zero because we are on the ray of perfect equality. The diffculty inevitably arises if the iso-inequality contours are straight lines, except for the case where they are parallel which applies in the case of $t = 0$.

Hence it is of particular interest to see whether there is empirical support for a constant value of t or, if not, what the shape of the iso-inequality contours is. Now it appears from the questionnaire evidence that independence of inequality under additions to income does indeed depend on the particular income level at which the inequality comparisons are being made. At a low level of income – at the income which will ensure a supply of basic needs for example - an addition of income to the poor is so important that even proportional additions to all incomes may actually decrease inequality overall. At a high level of income, proportional additions are perceived to give more to those who are already well-off so that such income additions will increase inequality. It is even conceivable that there may be people who consider that - at sufficiently high income levels - equal additions to income also increase inequality.

So Tables 1 and 3 suggest that the typical income-transformation curve usually has a negative slope, as illustrated in Figure 10. Notice that this does not entirely dispose of the problem of inconsistency in the neighborhood of 0 since, at low incomes, this form of the income-transformation curve corresponds to iso-inequality contours of the form depicted in Figure 6. Notice too that this dependence of inequality comparisons upon income has nothing to do with money illusion, since the problem of currency units has been disposed of in the way that we have framed the questions: fixing the mean and the basic-needs income level ensures that there is a concrete standard of reference within the simple economy discussed by the questionnaire. Rather, it appears to be the case that - as in the literature on poverty orderings - one ought to take into account both relative and absolute aspects of inequality. The combination of these two leads to a pattern that is quite different from most ready-made approaches to the topic of inequality measurement. It is even different from the compromise approaches of Kolm and of Bossert and Pfingsten.

FIGURE 10.10:
Transformation type – dependence hypothesis

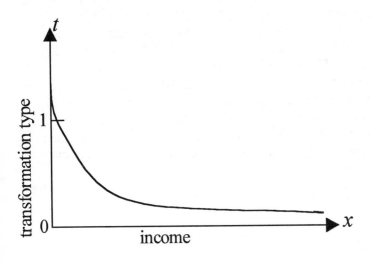

10.5   Conclusions

Economists often find it convenient to work with inequality measures that can be expressed as simple functional forms, but that permit a variety of views about inequality orderings out of a given total income - measures such as the Atkinson or Kolm family of indices. However the use of such a tool automatically imposes a particular system of "connecting up" inequality contours at different levels of income. In almost every case this system of connecting up the contours is, in some sense, independent of the level of incomes, because the connections are done according to one or other straight-line system.

But in addressing issues of inequality comparison, why should we think only in terms of straight lines? It is doubtful that there is any good reason for doing so other than convenience. Our questionnaire evidence suggests that people make inequality comparisons in different ways at different income levels - the hypothesis of dependence. So, although it may be convenient to use the inequality rankings implied by ready-made indices - or families of indices such as those of Atkinson and Kolm - as approximate parameterizations in situations where all distributional comparisons refer to the same income total, these standard tools are likely to be inappropriate when comparing distributions that differ substantially in their income level. Moreover if one does use such indices as convenient approximations for comparisons of distributions with the same level of total income, different parameterizations would be required at different levels of real income.

Our results help to clarify a question that has important policy implications. When there is a set of income changes - as a result of economic growth or of alterations in taxation, for example - in which direction should these changes be, if inequality is to be unaffected? The answer is a more complicated one than might be supposed, and one that should not be neglected by either economists or policy makers.

APPENDIX

INCOME INEQUALITY QUESTIONNAIRE

This questionnaire concerns people's attitude to income inequality. We would be interested in your view, based on hypothetical situations. Because it is about attitudes there are no "right" answers. Some of the possible answers correspond to assumptions consciously made by economists: but these assumptions may not be good ones. Your responses will help to shed some light on this, and we would like to thank you for your participation. The questionnaire is anonymous. Please do not write your name on it.

In Alfaland there are some areas with different levels of income. All areas have the same number of people which are identical except in their incomes. In each area half of the people have one level of income and the other half have another level of income. The average income in Alfaland by local currency is 1000 Alfa-dollars and the income which ensures a supply of basic needs is 400 Alfa-dollars. In each of the following questions you are asked to compare two distributions of income - one per each area. Please state which of them you consider to be the more unequally distributed by circling A or B. If you consider that both of the distributions have the same inequality then circle both A and B.

1) A = (200, 400)   B = (400, 600)
2) A = (200, 400)   B = (400, 700)
3) A = (200, 400)   B = (400, 800)
4) A = (600, 900)   B = (900, 1200)
5) A = (600, 900)   B = (900, 1300)
6) A = (600, 900)   B = (900, 1350)
7) A = (1200, 1800)   B = (1800, 2400)
8) A = (1200, 1800)   B = (1800, 2550)
9) A = (1200, 1800)   B = (1800, 2700)

In the next question you are presented with possible views about inequality comparisons labelled a,b,c,d. Please circle the letter alongside the view that corresponds most closely to your own. Feel free to add any comments which explain the reason for your choice.

10) Suppose we change the real income of each person in a society, when not all the initial incomes are equal.

a) If we add (or deduct) an amount to the income of each person that is proportional to his initial income then inequality remains unaltered.

b) If we add (or deduct) the same fixed amount to the incomes of each person inequality remains unaltered.

c) Inequality may remain unaltered: whether it does so depends not only on the change but also on initial and final levels of real income.

d) None of the above.

In the light of the above would you want to change your answers to questions 1-9? If so please note your new responses here:

1)   6)
2)   7)
3)   8)
4)   9)
5)

REFERENCES

[1] Aczel, J. (1987). *A Short Course on Functional Equations:Based upon recent applications to the social and behavioural sciences.* Dordrecht: D. Reidel.

[2] Amiel, Y. (1981). Some remarks on income inequality, the Gini index and Paretian social welfare functions. Technical Report 17-81, Foerder Institute for Economic Research.

[3] Amiel, Y. and F. A. Cowell (1992). Measurement of income inequality: Experimental test by questionnaire. *Journal of Public Economics* **47**, 3-26.

[4] Atkinson, A. B. (1970). On the measurement of inequality. *Journal of Economic Theory* **2**, 244-263.

[5] Blackorby, C. and D. Donaldson (1978). Measures of relative equality and their meaning in terms of social welfare. *Journal of Economic Theory* **18**, 59-80.

[6] Blackorby, C. and D. Donaldson (1980). A theoretical treatment of indices of absolute inequality. *International Economic Review* **21**, 107-136.

[7] Blackorby, C. and D. Donaldson (1984). Ethically significant ordinal indices of relative inequality. In R. L. Basmann and G. G. Rhodes (Eds.), *Advances in Econometrics*, Volume **3**, pp. 836. JAI Press.

[8] Bossert, W. and A. Pfingsten (1990). Intermediate inequality: concepts, indices and welfare implications. *Mathematical Social Sciences*, 117-134.

[9] Dalton, H. (1920). Measurement of the inequality of incomes. *The Economic Journal* **30** (9), 348-361.

[10] Eichhorn, W. and W. Gehrig (1982). Measurement of inequality in economics. In B. Korte (Ed.), *Modern Applied Mathematics -*

optimization and operations research, pp. 657-693. Amsterdam: North Holland.

[11] Harrison, E. and C. Seidl (1994). Acceptance of distributional axioms: Experimental findings. In W. Eichhorn (Ed.), *Models and Measurement of Welfare and Inequality*, pp. 67-99. Springer-Verlag.

[12] Kolm, S.-C. (1968). The optimal production of social justice. In J. Margolis and H. Guitton (Eds.), *Economie Publique*. Paris: CNRS.

[13] Kolm, S.-C. (1976a). Unequal inequalities I. *Journal of Economic Theory* **12**, 416-442.

[14] Kolm, S.-C. (1976b). Unequal inequalities II. *Journal of Economic Theory* **13**, 82-111.

[15] Kolm, S.-C. (1996). Intermediate measures of inequality. Technical report, CGPC.

[16] Krtscha, M. (1994). A new compromise measure of inequality. In W. Eichhorn(Ed.), *Models and Measurement of Welfare and Inequality*, pp. 111-119. Heidelberg: Springer-Verlag.

[17] Pfingsten, A. (1988). Empirical investigation of inequality concepts: A method and first results. Technical report, Karlsruhe University.

[18] Seidl, C. and A. Pfingsten (1994). Ray-invariant inequality measures. Diskussionsbeitrag aus dem Institut fÄ ur Finanzwissenschaft, Christian-Albrechs-UniversitÄ at zu Kiel, D-24098 Kiel, Germany.

[19] Seidl, C. and B. Theilen (1994). Stochastic independence of distributional attitudes and social status: a comparison of German and Polish data. *European Journal of Political Economy* **10**, 295-310.

[20] Sen, A. K. (1973). On Economic Inequality. Oxford: Clarendon Press.

[21] Theil, H. (1967). *Economics and Information Theory*. Amsterdam: North Holland.

Chapter 11

A NOTE ON THE GINI MEASURE FOR DISCRETE DISTRIBUTIONS

Robert L. Basmann
Department of Economics, Binghamton University, Binghamton,
NY 13851, USA

Daniel J. Slottje[*]
Department of Economics, Southern Methodist University, Dallas,
TX 75275, USA

11.1   Introduction

In abstract mathematics the *Gini coefficient* of concentration is one of several diverse measures of the degree of the concentration of a purely mathematical, or uninterpreted, distribution function. Camilo Dagum has provided a thoughtful perspective on analyzing the Gini that is unique among modern economists due to his personal relationship with Gini. Camilo does not have to "guess" what Gini meant in interpreting the Gini in a given context, because he actually worked side by side with Gini. A review of Camilo's Bibliography (at the beginning of this set of essays written in his honor) reveals the richness, diversity and dept of Camilo's work on that subject matter. We are pleased to present this essay on the Gini in Camilo's honor.

Like other measures of concentration of a purely mathematical distribution function, the Gini coefficient is a measure of *aggregate inequality* among the values of a density function derived from the distribution function in question. The abstract Gini coefficient serves as a useful "tool of thought" in the probing, refining and explicating of intuitive concepts of *substantive inequality* among real recipients of income and holders of wealth. The focal question of that empirical research effort is the nature of positive and negative analogies between the aggregative inequality among densities of abstract distribution functions and aspects of real, or substantive income inequality.

The Gini coefficient of concentration (or of inequality) of any distribution function has a unique numerical value. However, there is a considerable number of different formulas which express this unique Gini coefficient in terms of relevant observations. In several cases, the different formulas for the Gini coefficint reflect different lines of reasoning about substantive inequality, leading from different intuitive points of departure to equivalent computational formulas. This is also true of other measures of concentration, which do not produce those same values as does the Gini measure. Since economists and other social scientists have not yet reached a definitive concept of substantive inequality of income or wealth, familiarity with the alternative formulas and the lines of reasoning leading to them is essential for the user.

There is a vast literature on the Gini measure of income inequality, cf. Georgi (1993) and Lambert (1995). Many articles have presented the different extant formulas for the Gini measure and the alternative rules for its numerical computation, cf. Yitzhaki (1994). Nontheless, the existence of different formulas and computational rules is a source of confusion among users of the Gini measure. Usually the confusion centers on whether a discrete-based Gini measure overstates or understates the "true" Gini coefficient or is more greatly flawed by bias than a continuous-distribution-based estimator computed from the same batch of income data. Differences between expressions for Gini measures defined for discrete Lorenz income-share distributions and expressions of Gini measures defined for continuous approximations of Lorenz distributions compose of one important source of that confusion. Real income or wealth distributions are always discrete. That is the case for a complete census of income recipients as well as for samples of income recipients. This note focuses on the difference between the expressions of Gini measures for discrete Lorenz income-share distributions and the Gini measures that are computed from continuous approximations.

11.2 The Discrete Lorenz Distribution and the Gini Coefficient

We begin with a short account of the construction of a real Lorenz distribution and its Gini measure from data on a collection of n income recipients. It does not matter here whether the collection of income recipients constitutes the whole population or a proper subset of the population in question. We also begin by considering the case in which we want to assert that there is no *inequality* in the distribution of income, i.e., the n income recipients get equal shares of the group's total income. In this case, the real Lorenz distribution must be described by the *discrete uniform distribution function* and the Gini measure should be equal to zero. Consequently, the Lorenz distribution in this case is described by

$$L_1(z) = 0, z < 0;$$
$$= m/n, \quad (m/n) \le z < (m+1)/n, \qquad\qquad (11.1a\text{-}c)$$
$$= 1, \; z \ge 1.$$

It is reasonable to require that the proposed coefficient of income inequality depend on, and only on, the parameters of the distribution function that describes the distribution of income. In this case, the shares-weighted mean quantile of
(11.1a-c), namely,

$$\mu \sum_{m=1}^{n} (m/n)(1/n),$$

$$\qquad\qquad (11.2a\text{-}b)$$

$$= (n+1)/2n,$$

summarizes the parameters of (11.1a-c). The equal-share Lorenz distribution, (11.1a-c), has the smallest *share-weighted mean quantile* of all discrete Lorenz distributions.   This consideration, and the requirement that the proposed measure of income inequality be zero in this case, leads intuitively to the proposal that the proffered inequality measure of every Lorenz distribution depend directly and linearly on its share-weighed mean quantile, μ, i.e.,

$$G = K\,[(2\mu - 1) - (1/n)], \qquad\qquad\qquad (11.3)$$

where $K > 0$. K is a *normalizing factor* that depends on n.
    In order to determine the normalizing factor K in the definition (11.3), we consider the real-world situation in which one income-recipient gets the total income of the group and the remaining (n-1) recipients get nothing. This Lorenz distribution has the largest posible share-weighted mean, namely, $\mu = 1$. We will assign G ``` equation (11.3) - - - the value 1 in that case and, thereby, determine the value of K, In the case we are now considering, the Lorenz distribution is described by

L_2 (z) = 0, z < 1,   (11.4a-b)
$\quad\quad$ = 1, z ≥ 1.

The share-weighted mean of the distribution function (11.4a-b) is clearly equal to one. Setting $\mu = 1$ in the proposed inequality measure (11.3), we obtain

$$G = K(n-1)/n.$$ (11.5)

Since, for the conditions under consideration, the inequality measure is to be equal to one, we set
$\quad K = n/(n-1),$
thus completing the definition (11.3) as

$$G = (n/(n-1))[(2\mu-1) - (1/n)].$$ (11.6)

Notice that without the normalizing factor, K, the inequality measure for this case would be smaller than one, but increasing toward one as the population of income-recipients under consideration grows indefinitely large. The employment of the normalizing factor is open to challenge on substantive grounds, e. g., that substantive (real) economic inequality among recipients is dependent, in part, on the number of recipients. Successful challenge on collateral factual grounds would only entail removal of the normalizing factor from the expressions of the normalized Gini measure.

The final step in defining the Gini measure based on the share-weighted mean of discrete Lorenz distribution is to replace μ in (11.6) by its expression in terms of the latter. The expression for μ is

$$\mu = (1/n)\sum_{k=1}^{n} kq_k, \quad q_{k-1} < q_k,$$ (11.7)

where q_k denotes the income-share of the kth recipient (quantile). Making the substitution indicated, we obtain

$$G = 2(1/(n-1))\sum_{k-1}^{n} kq_k - (1+1/n).$$ (11.8)

There are many expressions of the Gini measure which are equivalent (produce the same numerical value) to the expression (11.8). Since the various equivalent expressions of the Gini measures may be arrived at, or inspired by different lines of intuitive thought concerning substantive economic inequality, it is important for users to be aware of them and the lines of reasoning that lead up to them.

11.3   A Continuous Approximation to the Discrete Lorenz Distribution

Another important expression of the Gini measure derives from consideration of a special *continuous approximating* of the discrete Lorenz distribution (11.7a-c). The discrete Lorenz distribution, $L(z)$, is described by the step function (with dotted "risers" and solid "treads". The "risers", or saltuses, q_k, $k=1,2,\cdots$, n, of any Lorenz function, $L(z)$, are nondecreasing. The continuous approximation, $L_{approx}(z)$, of $L(z)$, is represented by the dashed, kinked lines connecting the origin $(0,0)$ with the point $(1,1)$ and passing through the front edge of each step.

The most familiar lines of reasoning that leads to the Gini measure begins with the expectation that substantive income inequality would vary inversely with area, A, under the continuous approximation, $L_{approx}(z)$, of the real Lorenz distribution, $L(z)$. A further consideration leads to stipulation that the inequality measure be directly proportional to one minus twice the area A, i.e.,

$$G = 1 - 2A. \tag{11.9}$$

Upon substitution of the expression for A, we get the normalized measure of (11.9)

$$G = 1 - (2/(n-1)) \sum_{k=1}^{n-1} (n-k)q_k. \tag{11.10}$$

A similar line of reasoning leads to the representation of inequality by double the area enclosed by the continuous approximation $L_{approx}(z)$ and the straight lines connecting $(0,0)$ and (1.1). The normalized measure of inequality is expressed by

$$G = (n+1) / (n-1) - (2 / (n-1)) \sum_{k=1}^{n} (n - k + 1)q_k \qquad (11.11)$$

Continuous distribution functions are used as approximations of real discrete distributions in two chief ways. Continuous distribution functions, such as
$L(z;a) = 0, \; z < 0;$

$$\qquad = z^a, \; 0 \leq z < 1, \; a > 1; \qquad\qquad (11.12\text{a-d})$$

$$\qquad = 1, \qquad z \geq 1;$$

and its derived Gini coefficient

$$g(a) = a/(a+1), \qquad\qquad (11.12\text{e})$$

serve, respectively, as *idealizations* of some real, discrete, population Lorenz distribution and its mathematical derived Gini measure. In empirical work, a chief purpose of idealizations such as (11.12a-e) is to guide statistical estimation of the Gini measure. We now provide some additional representations of the discrete-based Gini for completeness.

11.4 Some Equivalent Representations for Grouped Data

There is no meaningful sense in which the formulas given above in section three for discrete Lorenz distributions understate the "correct" Gini measure for the data batch in question. The abstract (continuous) model and the discrete model are two different models. For large batch sizes, i.e., as n grows to infinity, the correction factors vanish and the calculated values of the discrete and abstract measures become identical. The Gini measure for grouped discrete data can therefore be expressed by,

$$G = 1 + (1/n) - \frac{2}{n} * \sum_{i-1}^{n} (n - i + 1)q_i \qquad (11.13)$$

where q_i is the ith quantile of income. Note that (11.13) is similar to the expression frequently used when individual observations are available,

$$G = 1 + \frac{1}{n} - \frac{2}{n^2 \bar{y}} [y_1, +2y_2 \cdots n\, y_n] \qquad (11.14)$$

(where $y_1 > y_2 > \cdots > y_n$, cf, Cowell (1977, p. 116).
Alternatively, we can rewrite (11.13) as

$$G = (1 - 1/n) - \frac{2}{n} * \sum_{i-1}^{n-1} (n-1)q_i \tag{11.15}$$

where $q_1 < q_2 < \cdots < q_n$.
the expression in (11.1a-c) can also be implemented by noting that the sum,

$$\sum_{m=1}^{n-1} L(m/n) = a + b + c + d \tag{11.16}$$

where $a = q_1, b = q_1 + q_2, c = q_1 + q_2 + q_3,$ and $d = q_1 + q_2 + q_3 + q_4$.
q_4.   The actual computation of (11.13), (11.15) and (11.16) all yield the same
Gini estimates. Therefore, any social scientist using (11.13), (11.15) or (11.16)
in empirical work has no reason for concern about the appropriateness of the
form used in analysis.

REFERENCES

[1] Basmann, R. and D. Slottje (1987), "A New Index of Inequality," *Economics Letters* 24, 385-389. (1987), "Errata," *Economics Letters* 25, 295-296.

[2] Basmann, R. L., K. Hayes and D. J. Slottje (1994), *Some New Methods for Measuring and Describing Economic Inequality*, Greenwich, Connecticut: JAI Press.

[3] Cowell, F. (1977), *Measuring Inequality*, Oxford: Phillip Allan.

[4] Giorgi, G. (1993), "A Fresh Look at the Topical Interest of the Gini Concentration Ratio," *Metron*, 51, 83-98.

[5] Lambert, P. (1995), The *Distribution and Redistribution of Income, 2nd Edition*, Oxford: Blackwell.

[6] Yitzhaki, S. (1994), "A Dozen Ways to Write the Gini," unpublished mimeo, Hebrew University.

Chapter 12

DISTRIBUTIONAL PREFERENCES AND THE EXTENDED GINI MEASURE OF INEQUALITY[*]

John Creedy

Department of Economics, The University of Melbourne, Parkville, Victoria, 3052, Australia

Stan Hurn

The University of Melbourne and Queensland University of Technology

12.1   Introduction

Much of the work that has been carried out since the early 1970s on the properties of alternative inequality measures has been concerned with the relationship between the inequality measures and basic value judgements. In the empirical measurement of inequality and in tax policy simulation analyses, such as the calculation of optimal tax rates, the usual approach is to explore the implications of using alternative value judgements. For example, in the context of the Atkinson (1970) inequality measure, this involves using a range of values of constant relative inequality aversion. The idea is to report results that are capable of representing a reasonably wide diversity of distributional views, so that different readers may form their own conclusions.

In contrast to the attention given to conceptual issues, there have been few attempts to quantify individuals' views on inequality aversion, so it is not clear just how representative are the value judgements used. Early questionnaire studies were carried out by Glesjer *et al.* (1977), and Gevers *et al.* (1979), although no attempt was made to estimate precise specifications of distributional preferences. Other approaches have involved attempts to impute a value of relative inequality aversion implicit in government tax decisions;

---

[*]We should like to thank Yoram Amiel, Mark Wilhelm and Diane Rogers for help with the Ruppin Institute and Pennsylvania State University surveys. This research was supported by a University of Melbourne Faculty of Economics and Commerce Research Grant.

see Mera (1969), Stern (1977), Christiansen and Jansen (1978), Moreh (1981) and Brent (1984).[1]

More recently, Amiel *et al.* (1996) provided a comparison of how well alternative social welfare function specifications reflect individuals' views on inequality aversion. They used data gathered from surveys of the attitudes to inequality of several different student groups in Australia and Israel, using an approach based on the famous 'leaky-bucket' experiment described by Atkinson (1973) and Okun (1975). Two main conclusions arose from this work. First, the students surveyed were found to have a much lower aversion to inequality than that used in the vast majority of applied studies of inequality and in theoretical public finance models such as optimal income tax models. Secondly, the distributional preferences of the students can be approximated more closely by a social welfare function based on the standard Gini measure of inequality, compared with the constant relative and constant absolute inequality aversion forms used in conjunction with the Atkinson inequality measure.

This paper seeks to extend the results of Amiel *et al.* (1999). In particular, it uses an extended data set, covering more groups of students including some from the US. More importantly, it compares the performance of a welfare function based on the standard Gini inequality measure with the use of the extended Gini specification discussed by, for example, Weymark (1981), Donaldson and Weymark (1980, 1983) and Yitzhaki (1983). The extended Gini measure allows for the use of an additional parameter which has a similar role to that of the inequality aversion parameter of the Atkinson inequality measure. In addition, the implications of adopting alternative social welfare functions are examine in the context of optimal income tax models.

Alternative social welfare functions are presented in section 2. The survey data and leaky-bucket conceptual experiment on which the questionnaires were based are described in section 3. The estimation method and empirical results are presented in section 4, and optimal tax comparisons are given in section 5.

---

[1]Questionnaires have also been used by Amiel and Cowell (1992, 1994) in order to investigate the extent to which respondants agreed with the major axioms used in the development of inequality measures.

12.2   Social Welfare Functions

12.2.1 Abbreviated welfare functions

In specifying distributional judgements, one way to proceed is to write down the form of a social evaluation, or welfare, function expressed in terms of arithmetic mean income, $\bar{y}$, and a measure of inequality, I, so that $W = W(\bar{y}, I)$. This is referred to as the abbreviated welfare function and directly expresses the willingness of the judge to trade-off equality and total income (usually expressed in terms of a trade-off between 'equity and efficiency'). For a given measure of inequality and form of W, the associated social indifference curves can then be derived. These describe, in the two-dimensional case, combinations of incomes for, say, persons i and j for which the value of W is constant.[2]

Two broad approaches to specifying the inequality measure and the abbreviated social welfare function may be distinguished. The first is simply to write down a functional form for $W(\bar{y}, I)$ using any chosen inequality measure, without reference to the fundamental value judgements that may be consistent with such a combination of welfare function and inequality measure. For examples of this type of approach, see Kondor (1975), de Graaff (1977), Blackorby and Donaldson (1978), Shorrocks (1988) and Atkinson (1992, pp.52-54).[3]

The second approach is to derive both the form of $W(\bar{y}, I)$ and simultaneously the measure of inequality directly from a statement of value judgements. This second approach is more demanding, but is perhaps more satisfying. The main results with regard to this approach concern the use of the Atkinson inequality measure and the standard Gini measure of inequality. These are considered briefly below.

12.2.2 Atkinson-based measures

Atkinson (1970) used an individualistic Paretean welfare function of the form $W = \sum_i U(y_i)$, with $U(y_i) = y_i^{1-\varepsilon}/(1-\varepsilon)$, for $\varepsilon \neq 1$ and $\varepsilon > 0$ Manipulation of

---

[2]For examples of such social indifference curves, see Creedy (1996 pp.13-22). For a detailed treatment of abbreviated welfare functions, see Lambert (1993, pp.109-138).
[3]de Graaff suggested the form $W = \bar{y}(1 - I)^{\theta}$ involving the use of a paramter, θ, while Shorrocks suggested the form $W = \bar{y} \exp I$.

this expression gives an abbreviated welfare function $W = U\{\bar{y}(1 - A(\varepsilon))\}$ with the measure of inequality, $A(\varepsilon)$ defined as $1 - y_e / \bar{y}$. The term y_e is the equally distributed equivalent income, the equal income which gives the same value of W as the actual distribution, and $\bar{y}$ is arithmetic mean income. The simpler form $W = \bar{y}(1 - A(\varepsilon))$ is usually used as it implies the same trade-off between 'equity and efficiency'. The value of ε reflects the constant relative inequality aversion, $-yU''(y)/U'(y) = \alpha$, of the judge. This influences the concavity of $U(y)$ and the convexity of social indifference curves relating to income transfers between individuals. The marginal rate of substitution, m, which reflects the (absolute) value of the slope of an indifference curve, is given by:

$$m = -\frac{dy_i}{dy_j}\Big|_w = (\frac{y_i}{y_j})^\varepsilon \qquad (12.1)$$

Hence ε is a measure of the constant elasticity of the marginal rate of substitution, m, with respect to the ratio of incomes, y_j / y_i so that:

$$(\frac{y_i / y_j}{m})\frac{\partial m}{\partial(y_j / y_i)} = -\varepsilon \qquad (12.2)$$

From 1 the slopes of social indifference curves are the same along any ray drawn through the origin.

In the case of constant absolute aversion, $-U''(y)/U'(y) = \alpha$, combine the same additive welfare function with the alternative form, $U(y) = 1 - e^{\alpha y}$ The marginal rate of substitution is therefore given by:

$$m = -\frac{dy_i}{dy_j}\Big|_w = e^{-\alpha(y_j - y_i)} \qquad (12.3)$$

Hence $-\alpha$ is a measure of the constant proportional change in the marginal rate of substitution with respect to the absolute difference between incomes, so that:

$$(\frac{1}{m})\frac{\partial m}{\partial(y_j - y_i)} = -\alpha \qquad (12.4)$$

The slopes of indifference curves are thus constant for a given absolute difference between two incomes.

Consider the alternative form of U given by $\{(y+y_0)^{1-\varepsilon}\}/(1-\varepsilon)$ for $\varepsilon \neq 1$, where y_0 is a fixed level of income; this was suggested by Kolm (1976). The marginal rate of substitution is thus:

$$m = -\frac{dy_i}{dy_j}\bigg|_w = (\frac{y_i + y_0}{y_j + y_0})^{\varepsilon} \tag{12.5}$$

and is constant for a constant value of the ratio $(y_i + y_0)/(y_j + y_0)$, and there is a common tangent to the social indifference curves along any ray from the point (y_0, y_0). This type of constant inequality aversion is to some extent intermediate between constant relative and absolute aversion. The relative aversion is $\varepsilon y/(y + y_0)$ which increases as y increases, while absolute aversion is $\varepsilon/(y + y_0)$, which falls as y increases.

12.2.3 Gini-based welfare functions

It is known that the Gini measure is not consistent with individualistic Paretean welfare functions which are increasing, symmetric and differentiable. But Sen (1973) showed that a 'pairwise maximin' criterion, according to which the welfare level of any pair of individuals is equal to the income of the poorest of the two, gives rise to average welfare across all pairs of $\bar{y}(1-G)$, where G is the standard Gini inequality measure defined by:

$$G = 1 + \frac{1}{N} - \frac{2}{(\bar{y}N^2)}\sum_{i=1}^{N}(N+1-i)y_i \tag{12.6}$$

where incomes are ranked such that $y_1 < y_2 < ... < y_N$. The abbreviated welfare function therefore takes the same convenient form as with the Atkinson measure. This result was extended by Lambert (1993, pp.125-129), who derived a social welfare function based on the standard Gini measure using two different arguments. One was based on the concept of relative deprivation, while the other was based on a form of altruism using the idea that U is a function of income and the individual's rank position. These approaches both give rise to the abbreviated form:

$$W = \bar{y}(1 - \kappa G), \qquad 0 \le k \le 1 \tag{12.7}$$

where κ is a parameter which combines with the Gini measure to reflect distributional judgments.[4] In Amiel et al. (1996), comparisons of the constant absolute and relative forms of the Atkinson-based welfare function were made with the Gini-based form in (7), and it was found that a slightly better fit was obtained for the latter specification. In each case, one parameter had to be estimated.

The Gini-based welfare function can be used with the extended Gini inequality measure. The form of the extended Gini is most easily be seen by first rewriting the standard Gini in covariance form using:

$$G = \frac{2}{y} Cov\{y, F(y)\} \tag{12.8}$$

where $F(y)$ is the distribution function of income. The extended form involves the introduction of a parameter, $v \ge 1$, such that

$$G(v) = -\frac{v}{\bar{y}} Cov\{y, (1 - F(y))^{v-1}\} \tag{12.9}$$

This function has $G(2) = G$, $G(1) = 0$ and $G(\infty) = (1 - y_m)/\bar{y}$, where y_m denotes the minimum income in the population.

Muliere and Scarsini (1989) showed, using an extension of Sen's 'maximin' criterion, that a rationale can be provided for the use of the welfare function $W = \bar{y}(1 - G(v))$. If the welfare of any v-tuple of individuals is equal to the income of the poorest person, then the average of the welfare of all v-tuples is $\bar{y}(1 - G(v))$; see also Lambert (1993, p.129).

The approach adopted in this paper is to investigate an extension of the welfare function in (7) by using the extended Gini measure instead of the standard Gini measure used above, and retaining the coefficient κ as used in the Lambert (1993) welfare function, so that:

$$W = \bar{y}\{1 - \kappa G(v)\} \tag{12.10}$$

---

[4]Another derivation was given by Kakwani (1986), and further references to papers in Italian are given in Dagum (1990). On welfare functions involving the Gini measure, see also Sheshinski (1972), Kats (1972), Chipman (1973) and Amiel and Cowell (1997).

However, the basic value judgements that give rise to such a welfare function have not been 'uncovered'. The approach may therefore be regarded as in some sense 'straddling' the two basic approaches discussed above.

Alternative forms of Gini-based welfare functions, based on explicit value judgements, have been proposed. For example, Kakwani (1980) derived a function of the form $W = \bar{y}/\{1+G\}$. Furthermore, Dagum (1990) derived two alternatives. In the first, the form $W = \bar{y}(1-G)/(1+G)$ is used in association with an inequality measure defined as $2G/(1+G)$; in the second form of welfare function, $W = \bar{y}(1-G)(1+\lambda G)/(1+G)$, where $0 \le \lambda \le 1$, and this is used in conjunction with the inequality measure given by $G(2-\lambda+\lambda G)/(1+G)$ The latter form therefore involves the use of an addition parameter. Preliminary analysis showed that these alternative Gini-based forms provide a relatively poor fit to the survey data, as they imply a larger degree of inequality aversion; results are therefore not reported here but these functions are discussed further in the Appendix C.

12.2.4 Marginal rates of substitution

As shown above, distributional preferences underlying a welfare function can usefully be summarised by the marginal rate of substitution relating to income transfers between two individuals. In the case of the welfare function $\bar{y}\{1-kG(v)\}$ used in this paper, the derivation of the marginal rate of substitution is somewhat more awkward than when the Atkinson inequality measure is used. It is obtained as follows.

First, the covariance in (9) can be written, making use of the fact that $f(y_i)=1/N$, as:

$$Cov(y,(1-F(y))^{v-1}) = \frac{1}{N}\sum_i y_i (1-\frac{i}{N})^{v-1} - \frac{\bar{y}}{N}\sum_i (1-\frac{i}{N})^{v-1} \qquad (12.11)$$

Hence the abbreviated welfare function, (10), can be written as:

$$W = \bar{y} + \kappa v[\frac{1}{N}\sum_i y_i (1-\frac{i}{N})^{v-1} - \frac{\bar{y}}{N}\sum_i (1-\frac{i}{N})^{v-1}] \qquad (12.12)$$

Differentiating this with respect to y_j gives:

$$\frac{\partial W}{\partial y_j} = \frac{1}{N} + \kappa v[\frac{1}{N}(1-\frac{j}{N})^{v-1} - \frac{1}{N^2}\sum_i(1-\frac{i}{N})^{v-1}] \tag{12.13}$$

Consider transfers between persons k and j (where $y_k > y_j$), such that the rankings do not change, that maintain W:

$$-\frac{dy_j}{dy_k}\bigg|_W = \frac{1+\kappa v[(1-\frac{k}{N})^{v-1} - \frac{1}{N}\sum_i(1-\frac{i}{N})^{v-1}]}{1+\kappa v[(1-\frac{j}{N})^{v-1} - \frac{1}{N}\sum_i(1-\frac{i}{N})^{v-1}]} \tag{12.14}$$

The right hand side of this expression gives the amount that must be given to person j if 1 dollar is taken from person k. This does not depend on the size of the transfer or the incomes, but on the ranks of the individuals. This contrasts with the corresponding result for the social welfare function based on the Atkinson inequality measure, reflecting the different perspectives of the two inequality measures. The Atkinson measure is said to reflect the 'wastefullness' of inequality, so that the rankings of the two individuals in the distribution do not matter, whereas the Gini measure is said to reflect the 'unfairness' of inequality.

In the special case of the standard Gini measure, $v = 2$ and using $\sum_{i=1}^{N}i = N(N+1)/2$, (14) becomes:

$$-\frac{dy_j}{dy_k}\bigg|_W = \frac{1+2\kappa[(1-\frac{k}{N}) - \frac{1}{2}(1-\frac{1}{N})]}{1+2\kappa[(1-\frac{j}{N}) - \frac{1}{2}(1-\frac{1}{N})]} \tag{12.15}$$

Furthermore, if $k = N = 2$, this reduces to:

$$-\frac{dy_j}{dy_k}\bigg|_W = \frac{1-\kappa/2}{1+\kappa/2} \tag{12.16}$$

and if $\kappa = 1$, it is simply 1/3.

Furthermore, substitution into the expression for the standard Gini measure gives, for the case of just two persons:

$$G = \frac{1}{2} - (\frac{y_1}{y_1 + y_2}) = \frac{1}{2}(\frac{\bar{y} - y_1}{\bar{y}}) \tag{12.17}$$

Consider another special case where $v = 2$, $\kappa = 1$ $k = N$ and $j = 1$, so that the transfer is from the richest to the poorest person. This implies that:

$$-\frac{dy_j}{dy_k}\bigg|_W = \frac{1}{(2N-1)} \tag{12.18}$$

and for large N simply confiscating the richest person's income, until it reaches the level of the next richest person, is tolerated. For $k = N/2$ (a transfer from the median person) and $j = 1$, then:

$$-\frac{dy_j}{dy_k}\bigg|_W = \frac{(1+N)}{(2N-1)} \tag{12.19}$$

and for large N a leak of half of the transfer is tolerated.

12.3 The Survey Data

The social welfare functions cannot of course be estimated from observed data. In order to evaluate individuals' distributional preferences in practice it is necessary to use a questionnaire approach. The approach used by Amiel *et al.*(1999) was to ask people their views about a series of discrete income transfers which differ in size. The questions were based on the well-known 'leaky-bucket' mental experiment, so that individuals were questioned about their tolerance for 'leaks' in making transfers between two individuals. Consider a transfer such that γ is taken from person k and θ is given to person j, where $y_k > y_j$, and there is no change in the rankings of any individuals in the population. Hence $\gamma - \theta$ is lost in the process. Under these circumstances, and in the case where $W = \bar{y}\{1 - \kappa G(v)\}$, the ratio, θ/γ can be obtained from the expression for $-\dfrac{dy_j}{dy_k}\bigg|_W$ given in (13). Given a set of questions where respondents give their hypothetical values of θ for various values of y and γ, expressions for θ/γ can be used to estimate values of the parameters κ and v

A questionnaire, shown in Appendix B, was completed by groups of students from the Ruppin Institute (Israel), the University of Melbourne

(Australia), and Pennsylvania State University (US).[5] It must be acknowledged at the outset that, since the population groups surveyed are all student groups, the results may not be representative of wider population groups.

Turning to the questionnaire in more detail, the first 15 questions concern just two individuals and give alternative income levels and amounts taken from the richer person. The second part, questions 16 to 27, gives the incomes of each of six members of society and considers transfers between different individuals. For each question the respondent is asked to state the minimum amount that must be given to the poorer person in order to make the transfer worthwhile.

Six questions in the second part of the questionnaire may involve changes in the rankings of the six individuals. In examining Gini-based welfare functions, however, the questions involving potential rank-order changes cannot be used. Hence these six questions were removed. Finally, it should be noted that respondents are told that all income levels are substantially above a poverty level, so that responses are not complicated by attitudes to poverty which may be distinct from those toward inequality.

The leaky-bucket experiment is particularly appropriate in the present context because it focuses directly on the trade-off between efficiency and equity of the social welfare function, with the questions making the efficiency loss explicit. However, some potential shortcomings of this approach are acknowledged. First, it may be that an alternative approach, perhaps placing less direct emphasis on the cost of redistribution, would elicit different responses. Second, the experiment makes no reference to non-income differences between individuals who may offer a rich range of issues over which potential respondents could express their attitudes toward inequality. Third, the transfers are described in a static framework, so that the attitudes towards dynamic factors such as the role of income mobility are ignored. It would be of interest to examine these wider issues in further research because the nature of the estimates of inequality aversion are likely to be influenced by the nature of the experiment; see also Cowell (1985, pp.574-5). Notwithstanding these difficulties, the experiment has been widely discussed (though not carried out) and it enables a comparison to be made of alternative social welfare functions.

---

[5]The Ruppin sample consists of first and second year students, formed by combining the two separate samples used by Amiel *et al* (1999). The US sample consists of several groups of third year students. The Melbourne groups are the same as those used by Amiel *et al* (1996).

TABLE 12.1:
Summary of Raw Data

Group	Mean	Std Dev	No.
Australia 1	0.702	0.226	56
Australia 2	0.710	0.258	272
Israel	0.771	0.231	78
US	0.729	0.268	73

12.3.1 Summary statistics

As explained above, that the questionnaire responses document the minimum transfer θ required to make the transaction worthwhile. Scaling this quantity by γ ensures that $0 \le \theta/\gamma \le 1$: the closer the ratio is to the upper bound the more tolerant the respondents are to income inequality (that is, inequality aversion is lower). In order to obtain a very preliminary insight into attitudes to inequality it is useful to consider the means and standard deviations of the ratio θ/γ over all questions and individuals for the various groups of students surveyed. These summary statistics are shown in Table 1, and immediately suggest that the average inequality aversion shown by all groups is similar, but the students from Israel are expected to have slightly lower aversion than that of the other groups. That of the US students is expected to lie between the Australian and Israeli values.[6]

12.4 Estimation and Results

12.4.1 Estimation procedure

The questionnaire was designed so that the minimum transfer, θ, is returned directly by respondents; these are the observed data. To the observed θ the model-based value $\hat{\theta}$, obtained from the appropriate expression, must be fitted by optimal choice of v and κ. The expected value of the minimum transfer, $\hat{\theta}$, is easily computed for given starting values of κ and v If q is the number of questions, then for each individual, $j = 1,...,N$, the appropriate parameter estimates were obtained by minimizing the following target function:

---

[6]The two Australian groups, 1 and 2, refer respectively to honors students and first-year commerce students respectively.

TABLE 12.2:
Distribution of Estimates for Individuals: Standard Gini-based Welfare

Group	Distributions of Parameters and Standard Errors[a]		
	1st Quartile	Median	3rd Quartile
Australia 1	0.213	0.226	0.578
	0.022	0.022	0.031
Australia 2	0.193	0.222	0.575
	0.009	0.010	0.014
Israel	0.109	0.216	0.574
	0.017	0.019	0.027
US	0.118	0.214	0.570
	0.01	0.020	0.028

[a]First row refers to distribution of parameter estimates and the second row to the distribution of standard errors

$$S = \sum_{i=1}^{q} \{\frac{\theta_{ji} - \hat{\theta}_{ji}}{\gamma_i}\}^2 \qquad (12.20)$$

using Broyden's (1967) variation of a quasi-Newton algorithm. The term γ appears in the target function in order to scale the residuals so that questions involving large transfers do not dominate. The standard errors were computed as the square root of the diagonal elements of the inverse Hessian matrix at the function minimum. During estimation, the parameters were constrained to be within relevant bounds; for example $0 \le \kappa \le 1$.

12.4.2 Empirical results

The first stage of the analysis involved the estimation, for each individual in each sample group, of the parameter, κ, in the standard Gini-based welfare function, using the target function in 19. This produced distributions of parameter estimates along with distributions of the associated standard errors. Summary measures of the separate distributions are shown in Table 2.[7] These results reveal a low dispersion of values, with broadly similar results across all four groups of students. In particular, the distribution of standard errors is typically very tightly clustered around the median value. As expected from the summary measures reported earlier, the values of κ are relatively low.

Although distributional judgements are clearly associated with individuals and there are well-known problems of aggregation, the distributions shown in

[7]The number individuals on the lower bound was 2, 39, 17 and 13 for the four groups (in the order in which they are listed in the table), and on the upper bound was 11, 56, 8, and 13.

Table 2 suggest that it is not unreasonable to carry out estimation over all individuals combined in each sample. This substantially reduces the results to be reported, particularly where it is required to make comparisons between alternative functional forms of the welfare function. Tables 3 and 4 therefore give the results of minimizing the modified target function:

$$S = \sum_{j=1}^{N} \sum_{i=1}^{q} \{ \frac{\theta_{ji} - \hat{\theta}_{ji}}{\gamma_i} \}^2 \qquad (12.21)$$

where summation over individuals has been added to 20. Table 3 shows considerable similarity across the four groups of students, with an estimated value of κ of 0.24 in each case. For each group, the minimum value of the target function and the standard error or the fit are lower when the extended Gini inequality measure is used.[8] It is of interest that the use of the extended Gini measure in Table 4 provides an additional degree of flexibility, so that some differences between groups emerge in the point estimates. However, only the Australian groups have values of that are significantly larger than that of Israel, and only Australia 2 has a value of v that is significantly larger than 2.

Based on the point estimates, the use of the welfare function associated with the extended Gini reveals slightly more aversion to inequality than is shown by the use of the standard Gini. Not only are the values of v in Table 4 slightly greater than 2 (the standard Gini case), but the values of κ are also increased, indicating that in the welfare function greater weight should be given to the measure of inequality. Both of these increases (in v and κ) imply a higher aversion to inequality.

TABLE 12.3:
Estimates: Standard Gini-based Welfare Function

Group	Parameter Estimate	Standard Error	Function Minimum	Standard Error of Fit
Australia 1	0.240	0.022	87.77	0.273
Australia 2	0.240	0.010	565.52	0.314
Israel	0.239	0.019	119.97	0.271
US	0.240	0.020	155.60	0.319

[8]Preliminary analyses showed that the addition of a parameter, y_0, to the Atkinson-based welfare function did not improve the fit compared with the use of Gini-based welfare functions.

TABLE 12.4:
Estimates: Extended Gini-based Welfare Function

Group	Sample Size	Point Estimate of κ	Point Estimate 0f v	SE of Fit	Function Minimum
Australia 1	56	0.356 (0.025)	2.040 (0.175)	0.255	76.27
Australia 2	272	0.334 (0.012)	2.334 (0.093)	0.303	523.40
Israel	78	0.252 (0.020)	2.293 (0.208)	0.269	118.61
US	73	0.307 (0.022)	2.176 (0.179)	0.313	149.82

12.5   Optimal Tax Comparisons

Having investigated the use of alternative social welfare functions, the aim of this section is to illustrate how results are in fact sensitive to the function used. It is well known that the rankings of income distributions often change when different inequality measures are used.[9] This section investigates instead the sensitivity of optimal linear income rates to the form of the social welfare function that is maximized. The standard approach to the analysis of optimal income taxation involves the maximization of a social welfare function specified in terms of individuals' utilities. In the vast majority of analyses, the welfare function used is that associated with the Atkinson inequality measure with constant relative aversion.[10] Within this framework it has been found that the optimal linear income tax rate is not very sensitive to the degree of relative inequality aversion, but is sensitive to the elasticity of substitution between leisure and consumption. This section uses instead the extended Gini-based welfare function.

Another issue concerns the use of individuals' utility in the welfare function. Even though it is known that results depend on the cardinalisation of individuals' utility functions used, very little attention has been given to the use of a money metric measure that is invariant with respect to monotonic transformations of utility.[11] The following examples therefore also use a

---

[9]There are many studies using the Atkinson measure, but for a rare set of comparisons using the welfare function using the welfare function $\bar{y}(1 - \kappa G)$, see Bishop *et al.* (1991).

[10]There is now an enormous literature on this subject, but see, for example, Atkinson and Stiglitz (1980, pp. 405-422), Heady (1993) and Creedy (1996).

[11]For a detailed treatment of this issue, see Creedy (1998).

money metric, based on the Hicksian concept of equivalent variations, that is usually referred to as 'equivalent income', following King (1983). This measures the income that, at some reference set of prices and wages, gives the same utility as an individual's actual income; it transforms utility into expenditure levels, and provides a particular form of indirect utility function. Welfare comparisons between different tax systems can be made for a fixed set of reference prices using equivalent income.

In the standard form of the optimal linear income tax problem it is required to select the values of the social dividend, a, and constant marginal tax rate, t, in order to maximize the social welfare function, W. In a pure transfer system this must satisfy the government's budget constraint that $a = t\bar{y}$, where $\bar{y}$ is arithmetic mean earnings. At the same time each individual is maximizing utility $U_i = U_i(c_i, h_i)$ where c and h respectively denote consumption (net income) and leisure, expressed as a proportion of total time available. If the price of consumption is normalized to unity and the wage obtained by person i is w_i, each individual's budget constraint is expressed as $c_i = w_i(1-t)(1-h_i) + a$. The `dual optimization' nature of the problem and the need to deal with corner solutions means that simulation methods have to be used in order to solve for the optimal tax rate. In view of the government's budget constraint, there is only one degree of freedom in the choice of tax parameters, so it is only necessary to search over values of the marginal tax rate, t. In specifying the extent of heterogeneity in the model, it is usual to assume that there is an exogenous distribution of wage rates, w_i, but that all individuals have the same tastes and face the same tax rates and commodity prices.

Suppose that in a simple single-period framework each person has constant elasticity of substitution preferences given by:

$$U = [\alpha c^{-\rho} + (1-\alpha)h^{-\rho}]^{-1/\rho} \tag{12.22}$$

where $\sigma = 1/(1+\rho)$ is the elasticity of substitution between c and h.

TABLE 12.5:
Optimal Linear Income Tax Rates: Utility

κ	1.5	2	2.5	3
0.2	0.39	0.43	0.43	0.45
0.4	0.42	0.48	0.50	0.52
0.6	0.47	0.52	0.55	0.57
0.8	0.50	0.56	0.59	0.61

TABLE 12.6:
Optimal Linear Income Tax Rates: Equivalent Income

κ	v			
	1.5	2	2.5	3
0.2	0.13	0.18	0.21	0.23
0.4	0.23	0.32	0.36	0.39
0.6	0.32	0.41	0.46	0.49
0.8	0.39	0.49	0.54	0.57

Simulations were carried out for a population size of 2000 individuals, for a pure transfer system. Wage rates were assumed to be lognormally distributed as $\Lambda(w|8,0.5)$, which implies an arithmetic mean wage rate of $\overline{w} = 3827.63$. In each of the simulations, $\sigma = 0.7$ and $\alpha = 0.9839$, which ensure that with no tax $(a = t = 0)$ an individual with the arithmetic mean wage, $\overline{w}$, spends 60 per cent of time working. Optimal marginal income tax rates, t, obtained using the extended Gini-based welfare function examined above, are given in Tables 5 and 6 for utility and equivalent income respectively.[12]

First, it can be seen that, contrary to the use of Atkinson-based welfare functions, the optimal linear tax rate is sensitive to the distributional preferences of the judge, as reflected in the parameters v and κ, even when utility is used.[13] The sensitivity of optimal t to these parameters is increased when equivalent incomes are used, particularly when lower values of t and κ are used. In view of the survey results summarised earlier in this paper, it is therefore suggested that in the analysis of public finance models it would be useful to investigate the effects of adopting a wider range of social welfare functions than is usual in the literature.

12.6 Conclusions

This paper has used questionnaire methods based on the idea of the 'leaky-bucket' experiment in order to investigate the distributional preferences of students from Australia, Israel and the US. It was found that a social welfare function based on the use of the extended Gini inequality measure provided a better fit to the data than a function using the standard Gini measure.

---

[12]In calculating equivalent income, the zero-tax prices and wages were used as reference prices.

[13]Furthermore, simulations also showed that the optimal tax rate shows very little variation in response to y_0, when using the extended version of the Atkinson-based welfare function.

Furthermore, the extended Gini-based welfare function was able to reveal differences between the student groups that were not shown when using the standard Gini-based function. For each group of students, the aversion to inequality was found to increase, associated both with a higher value of κ (the weight attached to inequality in the welfare function) and a value of v in excess of 2 (the value associated with the standard Gini measure). Simulations were used to examine the use of the extended Gini-based welfare function in optimal tax models. It was found that, in contrast to the use of the Atkinson-based welfare function typically used, the optimal linear income tax rate is sensitive to distributional preferences. Greater sensitivity was also found using a money metric utility measure rather than direct utility, which is commonly used despite the fact that results depend on the particular cardinalisation of utility that is used in the welfare function.

APPENDIX A:

Alternative Gini-based Welfare Functions

This appendix examines the alternative Gini-based welfare functions proposed by Kakwani (1980) and Dagum (1990), mentioned in section 2 above. The Kakwani form involves the abbreviated social welfare function:

$$W = \bar{y}/(1+G) \tag{12.23}$$

Using the definition of the standard Gini, G, given in (6), this welfare function can be rewritten as:

$$W = \frac{(\sum_i y_i)^2}{(2N+1)\sum_i y_i - 2\sum_i (N+1-i)y_i} \tag{12.24}$$

It is of interest to consider the form of social indifference curves for this function. As before, consider taking an amount γ from person k and giving θ to person j (with $k > j$), resulting in W'. Furthermore, write $a = \sum_i y_i$ and $b = \sum_i (N+1-i)y_i$ It
can be found that W' becomes:

$$W' = \frac{\{a - (\gamma - \theta)\}^2}{(2N+1)a - ab + \{(\gamma - \theta) - 2(\gamma k - \theta j)\}} \tag{12.25}$$

For the movement to be along an indifference curve, equate W and W' and solve the resulting expression for θ. This case is more awkward than the previous welfare functions, but it can be shown that θ is the positive root of the following quadratic:

$$A\theta^2 + B\theta + C = 0 \tag{12.26}$$

where:

$$A = (2N+1)a - 2b$$
$$B = (2a - 2\gamma)\{(N+1)a - ab\} - a^2(2j-1)$$
$$C = \gamma[\{(2N+1)a - ab\}(\gamma - 2a) + a^2(2k-1)]$$

(12.27)

The ratio θ/γ therefore takes a more complicated form than with the previous Gini-based welfare functions. In order to examine the indifference curves more closely, consider again the special case of just two persons, for which the Gini measure is given in equation (17). Appropriate substitution into (23) gives:

$$W = \frac{(y_1 + y_2)^2}{(y_1 + 3y_2)}$$

(12.28)

writing $\delta = y_2 / y_1$, the marginal rate of substitution is:

$$m = -\frac{dy_1}{dy_2}\bigg|_w = \frac{3\delta - 1}{5\delta + 1}$$

(12.29)

It can be seen that $dm/d\delta > 0$, showing that the indifference curves becomes steeper as the ratio of pre-transfer incomes increases.

A similar property is shared by the welfare function proposed by Dagum (1990, p.98) and given by:

$$W = \frac{\bar{y}(1-G)}{(1+G)}$$

(12.30)

For the special case of just two persons, this reduces to:

$$W = \frac{(3y_1 + y_2)(y_1 + y_2)}{2(y_1 + 3y_2)}$$

(12.31)

The equation of an indifference curve is therefore:

$$y_1 = [(2W - 4y_2) - \{(4y_2 - 2W)^2 - 12y_2(y_2 - 6W)\}^{1/2}]/6$$

(12.32)

John Creedy, Stan Hurn

Such indifference curves have the same general shape as those of the Kakwani abbreviated social welfare function $\bar{y}/(1+G)$, although they are much flatter, indicating a greater aversion to inequality.

Both the Kakwani and Dagum welfare functions therefore produce social indifference curves that are non-convex. However, this does not necessarily rule out their use, as they satisfy the condition of a 'locally equality preferring' function as defined and illustrated by Rothschild and Stiglitz$W$ (1973, p.195). Amiel and Cowell (1997, p.13) have argued that the Dagum form does not satisfy the axiom of monotonicity. Furthemore, preliminary investigations showed that neither of these forms fits the data as well as even the standard Gini-based function $\bar{y}(1-\kappa G)$ used above. Both imply 'too much' inequality aversion.

APPENDIX B:

The Questionnaire

The purpose of the survey is to obtain some information about your views on inequality, in particular, your attitudes towards income transfers between individuals. None of the questions involves calculations or a sequence of logical steps: they are designed to find out your personal views, so there are no 'right' or 'wrong' answers. Please do not write your name on this document.

THANK YOU FOR YOUR HELP.

Part A

In this part of the survey you are asked to consider a situation in which some money is taken from a 'rich' person (for example using a tax) and this is used to give some money to a poorer person, in order to reduce inequality. But the process involves some costs, so that some of the money is 'lost' in making the transfer. You are asked to give detail relating to the size of the loss that you are prepared to tolerate, for the transfer still to be worthwhile. Only the two individuals are affected by the change.

THE RICHER PERSON IS DENOTED BY THE LETTER R AND THE POORER PERSON IS DONOTED BY THE LETTER P.

1. R has twice as much as P, who has $10,000
   (a) If $1 is taken from R, what in your view is the *minimum* that needs to be given to P to make the transfer worthwhile?
   (b) What if $100 is taken from R?
   (c) What if $1,000 is taken from R?

2. R has four times as much as P, who has $8,000
   (a) If $1 is taken from R, what in your view is the *minimum* that needs to be given to P to make the transfer worthwhile?
   (b) What if $1,000 is taken from R?
   (c) What if $2,000 is taken from R?
   (d) What if $5,000 is taken from R?

3. R has five times as much as P, who has $10,000
   (a) If $1 is taken from R, what in your view is the *minimum* that needs to be given to P to make the transfer worthwhile?

(b) What if $1,000 is taken from R?
(c) What if $10,000 is taken from R?
(d) What if $15,000 is taken from R?

4. R has ten times as much as P, who has $5,000
  (a) If $1 is taken from R, what in your view is the *minimum* that needs to be given to P to make the transfer worthwhile?
  (b) What if $100 is taken from R?
  (c) What if $1,000 is taken from R?
  (d) What if $10,000 is taken from R?

Part B

In this part of the survey, you are again asked about transfers between pairs of individuals. Consider a society consisting of the following six person.

Person:	1	2	3	4	5	6
Income:	5,000	6,000	7,000	10,000	15,000	20,000

1. An amount equal to $1 is taken from person 4. What in your view is the *minimum* that needs to be given to person 1 to make the transfer worthwhile?

2. $1,000 is taken from person 4. What in your view is the *minimum* that needs to be given to person 1 to make the transfer worthwhile?

3. $2,000 is taken from person 4. What in your view is the *minimum* that needs to be given to person 1 to make the transfer worthwhile?

4. $1,000 is taken from person 4. What in your view is the *minimum* that needs to be given to person 2 to make the transfer worthwhile?

5. $2,000 is taken from person 4. What in your view is the *minimum* that needs to be given to person 2 to make the transfer worthwhile?

6. $5,000 is taken from person 6. What in your view is the *minimum* that needs to be given to person 4 to make the transfer worthwhile?

7. $5,000 is taken from person 6. What in your view is the *minimum* that needs to be given to person 1 to make the transfer worthwhile?

8. $2,000 is taken from person 6. What in your view is the *minimum* that needs to be given to person 2 to make the transfer worthwhile?

9. $5,000 is taken from person 6. What in your view is the *minimum* that needs to be given to person 3 to make the transfer worthwhile?

10. $3,000 is taken from person 5. What in your view is the *minimum* that needs to be given to person 1 to make the transfer worthwhile?

11. $5,000 is taken from person 5. What in your view is the *minimum* that needs to be given to person 1 to make the transfer worthwhile?

12. $5,000 is taken from person 3. What in your view is the *minimum* that needs to be given to person 2 to make the transfer worthwhile?

REFERENCES

[1] Amiel, Y. and Cowell, F.A. (1992) Inequality measurement: an experimental approach. *Journal of Public Economics* **47**, 3-26.

[2] Amiel, Y. and Cowell, F.A. (1994) Income inequality and social welfare. In *Taxation, Poverty and Income Distribution* (ed. by J. Creedy), pp. 193-219. Aldershot: Edward Elgar.

[3] Amiel, Y. and Cowell, F.A. (1997) Inequality, welfare and monotonicity. *LSE/STICERD Distributional Analysis Research Programme Research Paper*, **29**.

[4] Amiel, Y., Creedy, J. and Hurn, S. (1999) Measuring attitudes towards inequality. *University of Melbourne Department of Economics Reseach Paper*.

[5] Atkinson, A.B. (1970) On the measurement of inequality. *Journal of Economic Theory* **2**, 244-263.

[6] Atkinson, A.B. (ed) (1973) *Wealth, Income and Inequality*. London:Penguin.

[7] Atkinson, A.B. (1992) Measuring inequality and differing social judgements. In *Research on Economic Inequality* (ed. by D.J. Slottje and T.M. Smeeding), pp.29-56. New York: JAI Press.

[8] Atkinson, A.B. and Stiglitz, J.E. (1980) *Lectures in Public Economics*. New York; McGraw Hill.

[9] Bishop, J.A., Chakraborti, S. and Thistle, P.D. (1991) Relative deprivation and economic welfare: a statistical investigation with Gini-based welfare indices. *Scandinavian Journal of Economics* **93**, 421-437.

[10] Blackorby, C. and Donaldson, D. (1978) Measures of relative equality and their meaning in terms of social welfare. *Journal of Economic Theory* **18**, 59-80.

[11] Brent, R.J. (1984) On the use of distributional weights in cost-benefit analysis: a survey of schools. *Public Finance Quarterly* **12**, 213-230.

[12] Broyden, C.G. (1967) Quasi-Newton methods and their application to function minimization. *Mathematics of Computation* **21**, 368-381.

[13] Chipman, J.S. (1974) The welfare rankings of Pareto distributions. *Journal of Economic Theory* **9**, 275-282.

[14] Christiansen, V. and Jansen, E.S. (1978) Implicit social preferences in the Norwegian system of social preferences. *Journal of Public Economics* **10**, 217-245.

[15] Cowell, F.A. (1985) A fair suck of the sauce bottle, or what do you mean by inequality? *Economic Record* **61**, 567-579.

[16] Creedy, J. (1998) The optimal linear income tax: utility and equivalent income. *Scottish Journal of Political Economy*, (forthcoming)

[17] Creedy, J. (1996) *Fiscal Policy and Social Welfare: An Analysis of Alternative Tax and Transfer Systems.* Aldershot: Edward Elgar.

[18] Dagum, C. (1990) On the relationship between income inequality measures and social welfare functions. *Journal of Econometrics* **43**, 91-102.

[19] de V. Graaff, J. (1977) Equity and efficiency as components of the general welfare. *South African Journal of Economics* **45**, 362-375.

[20] Donaldson, D. and Weymark, J.A. (1980) A single parameter generalization of the Gini indices of inequality. *Journal of Economic Theory* **22**, 67-86.

[21] Donaldson, D. and Weymark, J.A. (1983) Ethically flexible indices for income distributions in the continuum. *Journal of Economic Theory* **29**, 353-358.

[22] Gevers, L., Glesjer, H. and Rouyer, J. (1979) Professed inequality
      aversion and its error component. *Scandinavian Journal of Economics*
      81, 238-243.

[23] Glesjer, J., Gevers, L., Lambot, Ph. and Morales, J.A. (1977) Professed
      inequality aversion among students. *European Economic Review* **10**,
      173-188.

[24] Heady, C. (1993) Optimal taxation as a guide to tax policy: a survey.
      Fiscal Studies, **14**, pp. 15-41.

[25] Kakwani, N.C. (1980) *Income Inequality and Poverty: Methods of
      Estimation and Policy Applications*. Oxford: OUP for the World Bank.

[26] Kakwani, N.C. (1986) *Analysing Redistribtuion Policies: A Study Using
      Australian Data*. Cambridge: Cambridge University Press.

[27] Kats, A. (1972) On the social welfare function and the parameters of
      income distributions. *Journal of Economic Theory* **5**, 377-382.

[28] King, M.A. (1983) Welfare analysis of tax reforms using household
      data. *Journal of Public Economics* **21**, pp. 183-214.

[29] Kolm, S.Ch. (1976) Unequal inequalities, I and II. *Journal of Economic
      Theory* **12**, 416-442 and **13**, 82-111.

[30] Kondor, Y. (1975) Value judgements imnplied by the use of various
      measures of income inequality. *Review of Income and Wealth* **21**, 309-
      321.

[31] Lambert, P.J. (1993) *The Distribution and Redistribution of Income: A
      Mathematical Analysis*. Manchester: Manchester University Press.

[32] Mera, K. (1969) Experimental determination of relative marginal
      utilities. *Quarterly Journal of Economics* **83**, 464-477.

[33] Moreh, J. (1981) Income inequality and the social welfare function.
      Journal of Economic Studies **8**, 25-37.

[34] Okun, A.M. (1975) *Equality and Efficiency: The Big Trade-off.* Washington: The Brookings Institution.

[35] Rothschild, M. and Stiglitz, J.E. (1973) Some further results on the measurement of inequality. *Journal of Economic Theory* **6**, 188-204.

[36] Sen, A. (1970) *On Economic Inequality.* Oxford: Clarendon Press

[37] Sheshinski, E. (1972) Relation between a social welfare function and the Gini index of income inequality. *Journal of Economic Theory* **4**, 98-100.

[38] Shorrocks, A.F. (1988) Aggregation issues in inequality measurement. In *Measurement in Economics: Theory and Applications of Economic Indices* (ed. by W. Eichhorn). Heidelberg: Physica-Verlag.

[39] Stern, N. (1977) Welfare weights and the elasticity of the marginal valuation of income. In Artis, M. and Nobay, R. (eds.) *Studies in Modern Economic Analysis.* Oxford: Basil Blackwell.

[40] Weymark, J.A. (1981) Generalized Gini inequality indices. *Mathematical Social Sciences* **1**, 409-430.

[41] Yitzhaki, S. (1983) On an extension of the Gini index. *International Economic Review* **24**}, 617-628.

Chapter 13

ON SOME IMPLICATIONS OF DAGUM'S INTERPRETATION OF THE DECOMPOSITION OF THE GINI INDEX BY POPULATION SUBGROUPS

Joseph Deutsch
Department of Economics, Bar-Ilan University, 52900 Ramat-Gan, Israel

Jacques Silber
Department of Economics, Bar Ilan University, 52900 Ramat Gan, Israel

13.1   Introduction

This paper has attempted to derive some implications from Dagum's (1997) recent proposal for a new interpretation of the decomposition of the Gini inequality index by population subgroups. His approach draws on his earlier work which stressed the importance in income inequality analysis of measures such as what Dagum called Relative Economic Advantage (REA) and income intensity of transvariation between subpopulations, the idea of transvariation being itself a concept originally invented by Gini (1916).

We have first attempted to show that Dagum's new interpretation of the between groups inequality and of the residual term of the decomposition of the Gini index allowed one in fact to determine the contribution of each population category to overall inequality. Moreover on the basis of Dagum's ideas we were able to analyze carefully the factors which may lead to a variation in income inequality over time as well as the specific impact of each population subgroup on such a change. We succeeded also, as far as the changes in the between groups inequality and the overlapping term are concerned, to estimate the influence each pair of groups had on these modifications. Finally an illustration based on Israeli data for the 1978-1994 period showed the fruitfulness of these developments, since new insights were derived on the factors which played a role in the change in inequality which was observed in Israel during this period.

In the vast literature which has appeared during the past thirty years on income inequality measurement, numerous papers have been devoted, at the theoretical as well as at the empirical level, to the breakdown of inequality by population subgroups. Several inequality indices have been used when making such decompositions although most often entropy based indices have been chosen because they can be easily decomposed into the sum of a between and a within groups inequality. When the Gini index is used, the breakdown leaves usually a residual for which, in the first studies which appeared on the topic, no intuitive interpretation could be given.

The first decompositions of the Gini Index by population subgroups seem to have been proposed by Bahattacharya and Mahalanobis (1969) as well as by Rao (1967) who showed that in the case of overlapping distributions ths breakdown of the Gini Index includes three elements: the between groups inequality, the within groups component and a residual.[1] This decomposition may be found in a way or another in several studies which were published later on (e.g. Mehran,1975; Piesch, 1975; Love and Wolfson, 1976; Pyatt, 1976; Fei, Kuo and Ranis, 1979; Silber, 1989). Some studies (e.g. Pyatt, 1976; Silber, 1989; Lambert and Aronson, 1993; Yitzhaki, 1994) managed to show that this residual term measured the degree of overlapping between the income distributions corresponding to the various population subgroups, so that a link was made between the analysis of income inequality and that, more common among sociologists, of stratification.

The importance of this concept of overlapping had, in fact, been stressed many years ago by Gini (1916) who then defined the notion of "Transvariazione" (on this topic, see also the works of Gini,1959, and Dagum, 1960). Dagum (1987) introduced also, when comparing the income distributions of two population subgroups, the interesting concepts of "Gross Economic Affluence" and "Net Economic Affluence" which are related to Gini's concept of "Transvariazione". Finally, in a recent study, Dagum (1998) made the link between these two concepts and two of the components of the breakdown of the Gini index by population subgroups. More precisely it can be shown that the between groups inequality is in fact a function of the "gross and net economic adavantages" which can be observed for each pair of groups while the residual is a function of what Dagum (1960) called the "intensity of transvariation" between the various pairs of subgroups.

---

[1]Bortkiewicz did work in the 1930s which may fact have been the first to propose such a decomposition but we did not have a copy of his work.

The purpose of the present paper is to derive some additional implications of this link between the breakdown of the Gini index by population subgroups and the concepts of intensity of transvariation, gross and net economic adavantage. The paper is organized as follows. Section II summarizes Dagum's (1997) most recent contribution. Section III shows then that Dagum's approach allows one to define the contribution of each population subgroup to the overall inequality and to its components (inequality between and within groups as well as overlapping term). In section IV a methodology is developed where the change in total inequality (or in one of its components) between two periods is broken down into basic components measuring the impact of changes in variables such as the population shares, the relative incomes of the groups distinguished, Dagum's relative economic advantage and his concept of income intensity of transvariation. Section IV defines also the contribution of each population subgroup to these changes in inequality. Section V presents an illustration based on Israeli data for the period 1979-1994 while concluding comments are given in section VI.

13.2 Dagum's Interpretation of the Decomposition of the Gini Index by Population Subgroups

One of the most popular algorithms to compute the Gini Index is defined as

$$I_G = (1/2)(1/n^2)(1/y_m)\Delta \tag{13.1}$$

where

$$\Delta = \sum_{i=1 \text{ to } n} \sum_{j=1 \text{ to } n} |y_i - y_j| \tag{13.2}$$

y_m is the mean income and n is the number of individuals in the population.

Let now m represent the number of population subgroups. Expression (13.2) may then be decomposed into the sum of two terms, Δ_A and Δ_W where Δ_A refers to what may be called the "across-groups inequality" while Δ_W measures the "within-groups ineqality", with

$$\Delta_W = \sum_{h=1 \text{ to } m} \sum_{i\in h} \sum_{k=h} \sum_{j\in k} |y_{ih} - y_{jk}| \tag{13.3}$$

and

$$\Delta_A = \Sigma_{h=1 \text{ to } m} \Sigma_{i \in h} \Sigma_{k \neq h} \Sigma_{j \in k} \mid y_{ih} - y_{jk} \mid \tag{13.4}$$

the second subindex (h or k) in (13.3) and (13.4) refering to the group to which the individual belongs.

Let us now assume that the groups are ranked by decreasing average income so that the mean income y_{mh} of group h is higher than the mean income $y_{m,h+1}$ of group (h+1). Expression (13.4) may then be written as

$$\Delta_A = \Delta_d + \Delta_p \tag{13.5}$$

with

$$\Delta_d = \Sigma_{h=1 \text{ to } m} \Sigma_{i \in h} \Sigma_{k \neq h} \Sigma_{j \in k} (y_{ih} - y_{jk}) \text{ with } y_{ih} > y_{jk} \tag{13.6}$$

and

$$\Delta_p = \Sigma_{h=1 \text{ to } m} \Sigma_{i \in h} \Sigma_{k \neq h} \Sigma_{j \in k} (y_{jk} - y_{ih}) \text{ with } y_{ih} < y_{jk} \tag{13.7}$$

Combining (13.6) and (13.7) we derive that

$$\Delta_d - \Delta_p = \Sigma_{h=1 \text{ to } m} \Sigma_{i \in h} \Sigma_{k \neq h} \Sigma_{j \in k} (y_{ih} - y_{jk}) \tag{13.8}$$

$$\leftrightarrow \Delta_d - \Delta_p = \Sigma_{h=1 \text{ to } m} \Sigma_{k \neq h} [\Sigma_{i \in h} (n_k \, y_{ih}) - \Sigma_{j \in k} (n_h \, y_{jk})] \tag{13.9}$$

$$\leftrightarrow \Delta_d - \Delta_p = \Sigma_{h=1 \text{ to } m} \Sigma_{k \neq h} [n_k \, n_h \, (y_{mh} - y_{mk})] \tag{13.10}$$

where n_h and n_k represent respectively the number of individuals in groups h and k.

Since the between groups Gini index I_B is obtained by giving each individual the average income of the group to which he belongs so that, using (13.1), I_B is expressed as

$$I_B = (1/2)(1/n^2) (1/y_m) \Sigma_{h=1 \text{ to } m} \Sigma_{k=1 \text{ to } m} n_h n_k \mid y_{mh} - y_{mk} \mid \tag{13.11}$$

we conclude, comparing (13.10) and (13.11) that

$$I_B = (1/2)(1/n^2)(1/y_m)(\Delta_d - \Delta_p) \tag{13.12}$$

Using (13.5), we observe that

$$\Delta_A = (\Delta_d - \Delta_p) + (2 \Delta_p) \tag{13.13}$$

Combining then expressions (13.1) to (13.5), (13.12) and (13.13), we conclude that

$$I_G = I_w + I_B + I_p \tag{13.14}$$

with

$$I_W = (1/2)(1/n_2)(1/y_m) \Delta_W \tag{13.15}$$

$$I_p = (1/2)(1/n^2)(1/y_m) (2 \Delta_p) \tag{13.16}$$

while I_B was defined in (13.11) and (13.12).
I_p which is the traditional residual term is therefore expressed as a simple function of all the "transvariations" which exist between all pairs of population subgroups.

The decomposition given in (13.14) may now be used to derive the contribution of a population subgroup to each one of the three components which appear on the R.H.S. of (13.14) as well as to the overall inequality (which shows up on the L.H.S. of (13.14)).

13.3 Using Dagum's Approach to define the Contribution of Each Population Subgroup to the Overall Inequality and its Components

Let us first take the within groups inequality. The contribution C_{wh} of group h to this component of the total inequality may be expressed, using (13.3) and (13.15), as:

$$C_{wh} = (1/2)(1/n^2)(1/y_m)[\Sigma_{i \in h} \Sigma_{j \in h} \mid y_{ih} - y_{jh} \mid] \tag{13.17}$$

Concerning the contribution of each group to the between groups inequality, we may observe that in (13.6) and (13.7) group h will appear $2(m-1)$ times.

Since there are only $m(m-1)$ terms in (13.6) or (13.7), the contribution C_{bh} of group h to the between groups inequality will be expressed, using (13.6), (13.7) and (13.12) as:

$$C_{bh} = (1/2)(1/n^2)(1/y_m)[\Sigma_{k\neq h} \Sigma_{i\in h} \Sigma_{j\in k} (y_{ih} - y_{jk})] \text{ for which } y_{ih} > y_{jk}$$
$$-(1/2)(1/n^2)(1/y_m)[\Sigma_{k\neq h} \Sigma_{i\in h} \Sigma_{j\in k} (y_{jk} - y_{ih})] \text{ for which } y_{jk} > y_{ih} \qquad (13.18)$$

Finally the contribution C_{ph} of group h to the residual I_p may be expressed, using (13.7) and (13.16), as:

$$C_{ph} = (1/2)(1/n^2)(1/y_m)[2\Sigma_{k\neq h} \Sigma_{i\in h} \Sigma_{j\in k} (y_{jk} - y_{ih})] \text{ for which } y_{jk} > y_{ih} \qquad (13.19)$$

Naturally the contribution C_h of group h to the overall inequality I_G may be written as:

$$C_h = C_{wh} + C_{bh} + C_{ph} \qquad (13.20)$$

and it can be easily proven that

$$I_G = \Sigma_{h=1 \text{ to } m} C_h \qquad (13.21)$$

We have therefore been able to determine the contribution of each population subgroup to the overall inequality as well as to each of the three components of this overall inequality, the between and the within groups inequality and the residual term. In the next section we will show how it is possible to combine the results of Sections II and III to analyze the change in inequality over time.

13.4   An Extension of Dagum's Approach: Analysing Changes in Inequality

To analyse changes in inequality over time, it will be convenient to use the notations and concepts developed by Dagum (1998) in his recent study.
Let us therefore call Δ_{hk} the Gini mean difference between groups h and k with

$$\Delta_{hk} = [\Sigma_{i=1 \text{ to } nh} \Sigma_{j=1 \text{ to } nk} |y_{ih} - y_{jk}|]/(n_h n_k) \qquad (13.22)$$

where n_h and n_k denote respectively the number of individuals in groups h and k.

Let also G_{hk} refer to the Gini ratio between populations h and k with

$$G_{hk} = \Delta_{hk} / (y_{mh} + y_{mk}) \qquad (13.23)$$

We also define the gross economic affluence d_{hk} between the population subgroups h and k as

$$d_{hk} = [\Sigma_{i=1 \text{ to } nh} \ \Sigma_{j=1 \text{ to } nk} \ (y_{ih} - y_{jk})] / (n_h \ n_k) \qquad (13.24)$$

for the cases where $y_{ih} > y_{jk}$ and $y_{mh} > y_{mk}$.
The first-order moment of transvariation p_{hk} between groups h and k will be defined as

$$p_{hk} = [\Sigma_{i=1 \text{ to } nh} \ \Sigma_{j=1 \text{ to } nk} \ (y_{ih} - y_{jk})] / (n_h \ n_k) \qquad (13.25)$$

for the cases where $y_{ih} < y_{jk}$. and $y_{mh} > y_{mk}$.

Dagum defines also the relative economic distance (or affluence) D_{hk} between groups h and k as

$$D_{hk} = (d_{ih} - p_{jk}) / \Delta_{hk} \qquad (13.26)$$

Calling respectively f_h and f_k the shares of groups h and k in the total population and s_h and s_k their share in total income, we may express (see Dagum, 1997) the between groups inequality I_B which was defined earlier as

$$I_B = \Sigma_{h=2 \text{ to } m} \ \Sigma_{k=1 \text{ to } (h-1)} \ G_{hk} \ (f_h s_k + f_k s_h) \ D_{hk} \qquad (13.27)$$

Similarly the contribution I_p of the income intensity of transvariation between the various subpopulations (which is in fact the residual of the decomposition of the Gini Index by population subgroups) may be expressed, using again Dagum's (1997) notations as

$$I_p = \Sigma_{h=2 \text{ to } m} \ \Sigma_{k=1 \text{ to } (h-1)} \ G_{hk} \ (f_h s_k + f_k s_h) \ (1 - D_{hk}) \qquad (13.28)$$

Finally, using (13.3) and (13.15), it is easy to show that the within groups inequality I_W may be expressed as

$$I_W = \sum_{h=1 \text{ to } m} f_h s_h I_{wh} \tag{13.29}$$

where I_{wh}, the within group h inequality is written as

$$I_{wh} = .(1/2)(1/(n_h)^2)(1/y_{mh}) [\sum_{i=1 \text{ to } nh} \sum_{j=1 \text{ to } nh} | y_{ih} - y_{jh} |] \tag{13.30}$$

Since $s_h = f_h (y_{mh}/y_m)$, we may rewrite expressions (13.29) to (13.30), using (13.23), (13.26) and (13.29) as

$$I_B = \sum_{h=2 \text{ to } m} \sum_{k=1 \text{ to } (h-1)} [f_h f_k] [(y_{mh} + y_{mk})/y_m] [\Delta_{hk}/(y_{mh} + y_{mk})]$$
$$[(d_{hk} - p_{hk})/\Delta_{hk}] \tag{13.31}$$

$$I_P = \sum_{h=2 \text{ to } m} \sum_{k=1 \text{ to } (h-1)} [f_h f_k] [(y_{mh} + y_{mk})/y_m] [\Delta_{hk}/(y_{mh} + y_{mk})][(2p_{hk})/\Delta_{hk}] \tag{13.32}$$

$$I_W = \sum_{h=1 \text{ to } m} [(f_h)^2] [y_{hm}/y_m)] [I_{wh}] \tag{13.33}$$

Note that the sum of expressions (13.31) to (13.33) is equal to total inequality (cf expression (13.14)). We may now use these results to redefine the contributions C_{bh} and C_{ph} of group h to the between groups inequality and to the overlap components and write that:

$$C_{bh} = (1/2) \sum_{k \neq h} [f_h f_k] [(y_{mh} + y_{mk})/y_m] [\Delta_{hk}/(y_{mh} + y_{mk})] [(d_{hk} - p_{hk})/\Delta_{hk}] \tag{13.34}$$

$$C_{ph} = (1/2) \sum_{k \neq h} [f_h f_k] [(y_{mh} + y_{mk})/y_m] [\Delta_{hk}/(y_{mh} + y_{mk})] [2p_{hk}/\Delta_{hk}] \tag{13.35}$$

Expressions (13.34) and (13.35), as well as expression (13.17).(which gave the contribution C_{wh} of group h to the within groups inequality) will be the basis of our analysis of the changes in inequality which may occur between two periods. We should first note that expressions (13.31) and (13.32) include on the R.H.S. four expressions under brackets which measure respectively the impact of the population shares and of the relative incomes of the two groups considered, the Gini ratio between them, and, in the case of I_B, Dagum's relative economic affluence between the two groups considered, in the case of I_P, Dagum's income intensity of transvariation between these two subpopulations (see Dagum, 1997). Expression (13.33) includes only three elements, a first one measuring (the square of) the population share of the group considered, a second one its relative income and a third one the Gini Index for this population subgroup. The appendix shows how it is possible to decompose the change in an expression which is the product of 2, 3 or 4 variables and the results obtained there will be applied to our case. [2]

Let the subscripts 0 and 1 refer to the period considered and use first expression (13.29) to analyze the change in within groups inequality. Calling $\Delta(I_W)$ this change, we derive

$$\Delta(I_W) = \sum_{h=1 \text{ to } m} (f_{h1} \, s_{h1} \, I_{wh1} - f_{h0} \, s_{h0} \, I_{wh0}) \tag{13.36}$$

$$\leftrightarrow \Delta(I_W) = \sum_{h=1 \text{ to } m} [((f_{h1})^2)(y_{mh1}/y_{m1})I_{wh1} - ((f_{h0})^2)(y_{mh0}/y_{m0})I_{wh0}] \tag{13.37}$$

Calling r_{ht} the ratio (y_{mht}/y_{mt}), t being equal to 0 or 1, and applying the algorithms defined in the appendix, we may express the difference defined in (13.37) as a weighted sum of three elements: the change over time in the (square of) the population shares f_{ht}, in the income ratios r_{ht} and in the within groups inequality I_{ht}.

In a similar way the change between periods 0 and 1 in the between groups inequality I_B as well as of the residual term I_p will be expressed as a weighted sum of the changes which occured in the population shares f_h, in the income ratios r_{ht}, in the Gini ratios between populations G_{hk} and in the relative economic affluence indices D_{hk}.

The next section presents an empirical illustration where the various methodological developments presented previously are applied to Israeli data for the period 1978-1994.

13.5 An Empirical Illustration: Income Inequality in Israel During the Period 1978-1994

In this empirical section we have used a traditional classification of the Israeli population into four population subgroups: Jews born in Asia or Africa (AA), Jews born in Europe, America or Australia (EA), Jews born in Israel (I) and Non-Jews (NJ). Neuman's (forthcoming) recent survey of the history of

---

[2] In the case of 3 variables there are in fact 3 possible decompositions while in the case of 4 variables there are 4 such decompositions. In each case we have taken the average of the different possible decompositions.

immigration in Israel shows the importance of this distinction between two categories of Jewish immigrants. This division of the Israeli population into four categories is used in most studies looking at ethnic groups in Israel. Sometimes six rather than four groups are used in so far as the group of the Jews born in Israel is broken down into three subcategories defined by the place of birth of the father (born in Israel, in Europe, America or Australia, and born in Asia or America). Table 1 shows that as a whole the weight in the total population of both subgroups of immigrants, those coming from Asia or Africa and those coming from Europe, America or Australia, decreased significantly over time while that of Jews born in Israel and of Non-jews increased. Note also the increase in the weight of the group EA between 1990 and 1994, a change which is evidently a consequence of the massive inflow of Jewish immigrants from the former U.S.S.R. during this period.

In Table 2 we have computed the relative income of the various population subgroups which have been distinguished, that is the ratio of the average income of the subgroup over the average income in the total population. In Section IV we have indicated that these ratios played a role in analyzing inequality changes over time. Table 2 indicates firstly that the relative income of the group AA increased significantly over the whole period: it was smaller than one in 1974 but higher than one in 1994. On the contrary that of the group EA delined, especially after 1990, a consequence again of the massive inflow of immigrants from the former U.S.S.R.[3]: it has even become smaller than one after 1992. The relative income of the group of Jews born in Israel did not vary very much over the period staying close to 1.05 while that of the Non-Jews has decreased significantly (from .83 to .70).

Let us now take a look at the results (see Table 3) of the traditional decomposition of the Gini Index into three elements: a between and a within groups inequality and a third component measuring the degree of overlap between the income distributions of the various population subgroups which have been distinguished (see Deutsch and Silber, forthcoming, for more details on this overlapping component). It appears that total inequality increased over time, this being also true for the within groups inequality. The between groups

---

[3]It is well known that new immigrants have a lower income than the local residents, among other reasons because they do not possess some human capital characteristics such as the language, the connections, etc...which have been shown to be important in determining the earnings of an individual (see, Neuman, forthcoming, for a short review of the literature on this topic)

inequality however decreased over time although it increased between 1978 and 1984. Given these trends in within and between inequality we should not be surprised to observe that the overlap component increased also over time.

How did the various population subgroups contribute to these trends in inequality. Results concerning total inequality are given in Table 4. The definition of these population specific contributions has been given previously in expressions (13.17) to (13.19). It appears that the contribution of the (Jewish) immigrants (the AA and the EA subgroups) to total inequality declined over time, while that of those born in Israel, whether Jewish (I) or Non-Jewish (NJ) increased. One could have thought that these differences are mainly a consequence of the changing population weight of these subgroups but Table 5 shows clearly, concerning the variation in total inequality, that over the whole period 1978-1994 the main impact was that of changes in the relative dispersions of the various distributions, whether on refers to the Gini index for the subpopulations (in computing the within groups inequality) or to the Gini Index between two subpopulations (see, Dagum 1998). Note however that during the subperiod 1984-1994, the factor which had the greatest impact on total inequality change was the change in population shares. The same remarks hold generally if one looks at the different types of inequality change. For the change in between groups inequality, Table 5 indicates that the variation in population shares or in the relative incomes of the groups did not play an important role. For the period 1978-1994 as a whole the main impact was that of changes in Dagum's "relative economic advantage", this being true also for the subperiod 1984-1994. During the period 1978-1984 the greatest modification occured in the Gini ratios between the distributions. If one looks at the inequality within groups, one may observe that for the period 1978-1994 as a whole as well as during the years 1978-1984, the main factor of change was the variation in the Gini indices of the different subgroups, although between 1984 and 1994 it was the change in population shares which affected mainly the inequality within groups. Finally concerning changes in the overlap component, it appears that for the years 1978-1994 as well as for the subperiod 1978-1984 the main factor of change was the variation which occured in the between groups Gini indices, while between 1984 and 1994 the main element of change was the variable measuring the income intensity of transvariation betweeen the subpopulations distinguished.

We now turn to an analysis of the results of Table 6 which gives the contribution of each population subgroup to the variation over time in total inequality or in its components. Concerning the changes in total inequality it appears that the main contribution is that of the group representing the Jews born in Israel, this being true for the period 1978-1994 as well as for the two subperiods which have been distinguished. The conclusions are different concerning the between groups inequality. During the first subperiod (1978-1984), a time when the between groups inequality increased, the main contribution to the change was again that of the group of Jews born in Israel. However during the second subperiod (1984-1994), as well for the whole period analyzed (1978-1994), the main role was played by the groups of Jewish immigrants born in Asia or Africa (AA) . Note that between 1984 and 1994 and during the total period 1978-1994 the between groups inequality decreased and this AA group precisely contributed positively to this decrease in between groups inequality. Finally the conclusions to be drawn from an analysis of the change in the overlap component are the same as those we reached when looking at the change in overall inequality in so far as here again the main contribution was that of the group of Jews born in Israel.

To get a better picture of the changes in the between groups inequality as well as in the overlap component we have presented in Table 7 the contribution of all the possible couples of population subgroups to these two components of inequality change. Concerning variations in the between groups inequality, we note for example that during the first subperiod, a time during which the between groups inequality increased, the main factor of change was the gap between the groups of Jews born in Europe , America or Australia and of those born in Israel, this gap having increased over the period considered. On the contrary between 1984 and 1994, a period during which the between groups inequality decreased, the main element of change was the closing gap between the groups of Jews born in Europe, America and Australia and that of Jews born in Asia or Africa, the same kind of conclusions holding for the overall period 1978-1994. If we look at modifications in the overlap component,, an element which as a whole increased during the period 1978-1994, we observe that during the first period the main factor of change was the increase in the degree of overlapping between the income distributions of the subpopulations AA and I, while during the second subperiod it is the increasing amount of overlapping between the subpopulations EA and I which played the main role. For the whole period 1978-1994 Table 7 indicates clearly that both the overlap between the subpopulations AA and I and that between the groups EA and I were the main elements contributing to the increasing degree of overlap between the income distributions of the different subgroups.

13.6 Conclusion

This paper has attempted to derive some implications from Dagum's (1998) recent proposal for a new interpretation of the decomposition of the Gini inequality index by population subgroups. His approach draws on his earlier work which stressed the importance in income inequality analysis of measures such as what Dagum called Relative Economic Advantage (REA) and income intensity of transvariation between subpopulations, the idea of transvariation being itself a concept originally invented by Gini (1916).

We have first attempted to show that Dagum's new interpretation of the between groups inequality and of the residual term of the decomposition of the Gini index allowed one in fact to determine the contribution of each population category to overall inequality. Moreover on the basis of Dagum's ideas we were able to analyze carefully the factors which may lead to a variation in income inequality over time as well as the specific impact of each population subgroup on such a change. We succeeded also, as far as the changes in the between groups inequality and the overlapping term are concerned, to estimate the influence each pair of groups had on these modifications. Finally an illustration based on Israeli data for the 1978-1994 period showed the fruitfulness of these developments, since new insights were derived on the factors which played a role in the change in inequality which was observed in Israel during this period.

APPENDIX

Let a and b be two variables whose subindices 0 and 1 will refer respectively to periods 0 and 1. If the rules of integration by parts are applied to the discrete case, it can easily be proven that:

$$(a_1 b_1 - a_0 b_0) = ((a_1 + a_0)/2)(b_1 - b_0) + ((b_1 + b_0)/2)(a_1 - a_0) \tag{13.A-1}$$

Expression (13.A-1) shows therefore that the change $(a_1 b_1 - a_0 b_0)$ is the weighted sum of two changes, one in the variable a and the other in the variable b.

The same decomposition principle may be applied in the case of three variables. We may for example write:

$$
\begin{aligned}
(a_1 b_1 c_1 - a_0 b_0 c_0) &= ((a_1 + a_0)/2)(b_1 c_1 - b_0 c_0) + ((b_1 c_1 + b_0 c_0)/2)(a_1 - a_0) = \\
&= ((a_1 + a_0)/2)[((b_1 + b_0)/2)(c_1 - c_0) + ((c_1 + c_0)/2)(b_1 - b_0)] + ((b_1 c_1 + b_0 c_0)/2)(a_1 - a_0) = \\
&= (1/4)(a_1 + a_0)(b_1 + b_0)(c_1 - c_0) + (1/4)(a_1 + a_0)(c_1 + c_0)(b_1 - b_0) + \\
&\quad + (1/2)(b_1 c_1 + b_0 c_0)(a_1 - a_0)
\end{aligned}
\tag{13.A-2}
$$

Naturally the decomposition given in (13.A-2) is not unique and by permuting a, b and c we can derive two additional decompositions. But in each case one would express the total change $(a_1 b_1 c_1 - a_0 b_0 c_0)$ in the weighted sum of the three changes $(a_1 - a_0)$, $(b_1 - b_0)$ and $(c_1 - c_0)$.

Finally in the case of four variables one would write:

$$
\begin{aligned}
(a_1 b_1 c_1 d_1 - a_0 b_0 c_0 d_0) &= ((a_1 b_1 + a_0 b_0)/2)(c_1 d_1 - c_0 d_0) + ((c_1 d_1 + c_0 d_0)/2)(a_1 b_1 - a_0 b_0) = \\
&= (1/4)(a_1 b_1 + a_0 b_0)(c_1 + c_0)(d_1 - d_0) + (1/4)(a_1 b_1 + a_0 b_0)(d_1 + d_0)(c_1 - c_0) + \\
&\quad + (1/4)(c_1 d_1 + c_0 d_0)(a_1 + a_0)(b_1 - b_0) + (1/4)(c_1 d_1 - c_0 d_0)(b_1 + b_0)(a_1 - a_0)
\end{aligned}
\tag{13.A-3}
$$

Here also (13.A-3) is not the unique decomposition. in fact by permuting a, b, c and d we can derive many other possible decompositions. But whatever the decomposition one choose, one obtains an expression which expresses the total change $(a_1 b_1 c_1 d_1 - a_0 b_0 c_0 d_0)$ as the weighted sum of the changes which occured respectivly in the variables a, b, c and d, the sum of the weights being generally not equal to one in this case either.

TABLE 13.1:

Share (in Percentage) in Total Population of the Various Groups Distinguished

Year[4]	AA (Jews born in Asia or Africa)	EA (Jews born in Europe, America or Australia)	I (Jews born in Israel)	NJ (Non Jews)
1978	33.7	38.9	25.1	2.4
1979	32.3	36.1	28.5	3.1
1980	32.0	35.4	29.4	3.2
1981	30.7	34.4	32.3	2.7
1982	30.6	34.4	31.6	3.4
1983	29.7	30.4	36.6	3.4
1984	29.7	30.3	36.3	3.6
1985	29.9	29.1	36.6	4.3
1987	28.3	26.9	40.1	4.7
1988	25.8	26.3	42.6	5.3
1989	24.9	25.7	44.4	5.0
1990	24.8	24.6	44.6	5.9
1991	23.1	27.2	44.1	5.6
1992	21.4	28.6	44.3	5.7
1993	20.1	30	43.8	6.1
1994	17.9	30.1	46.0	6.0

---

[4]No data are available for the year 1986

Joseph Deutsch, Jacques Silber

TABLE 13.2:
Relative Income[5] of the Various Population Subgroups[6]

Year[7]	AA	EA	I	NJ
1978	0.866	1.082	1.060	0.833
1979	0.873	1.072	1.077	0.774
1980	0.888	1.088	1.044	0.750
1981	0.876	1.087	1.053	0.630
1982	0.895	1.096	1.028	0.706
1983	0.902	1.095	1.027	0.676
1984	0.889	1.139	1.008	0.694
1985	0.886	1.103	1.052	0.698
1987	0.936	1.123	0.995	0.723
1988	0.903	1.099	1.035	0.679
1989	0.944	1.117	0.995	0.700
1990	0.984	1.114	0.996	0.661
1991	0.926	1.066	1.027	0.750
1992	0.930	1.038	1.050	0.702
1993	0.980	0.997	1.057	0.656
1994	1.056	0.947	1.052	0.700

---

[5]The relative income of a group is defined as being equal to the ratio of the average income of this group over the average income in the total population
[6]See Table 1 for a definition of the various population subgroups distinguished
[7]No data are available for the year 1986

TABLE 13.3:
Yearly Decomposition of Total Inequality into Between and Within Groups[8] Inequality and Overlap

Year[9]	Total Inequality	Within Groups Inequality	Between Groups Inequality	Overlap Component
1978	0.298	0.096	0.050	0.152
1979	0.315	0.099	0.049	0.167
1980	0.320	0.100	0.050	0.170
1981	0.324	0.102	0.053	0.169
1982	0.324	0.101	0.052	0.171
1983	0.323	0.102	0.049	0.172
1984	0.354	0.110	0.062	0.183
1985	0.327	0.101	0.056	0.170
1987	0.319	0.100	0.047	0.172
1988	0.316	0.102	0.052	0.163
1989	0.330	0.109	0.045	0.177
1990	0.325	0.106	0.043	0.177
1991	0.337	0.111	0.038	0.188
1992	0.346	0.115	0.037	0.193
1993	0.336	0.111	0.036	0.188
1994	0.359	0.122	0.039	0.197

[8]See Table 1 for a definition of the population subgroups distinguished
[9] No data are available for the year 1986

Joseph Deutsch, Jacques Silber

TABLE 13.4:

Yearly Decomposition of Total Inequality by Contribution of Various Groups[10]

Year[11]	Total Inequality	AA	EA	I	NJ
1978	0.298	0.091	0.122	0.078	0.007
1979	0.315	0.094	0.120	0.092	0.009
1980	0.320	0.095	0.118	0.097	0.009
1981	0.324	0.092	0.117	0.107	0.008
1982	0.324	0.092	0.118	0.104	0.010
1983	0.323	0.089	0.103	0.121	0.010
1984	0.354	0.097	0.114	0.131	0.012
1985	0.327	0.091	0.101	0.122	0.013
1987	0.319	0.085	0.092	0.128	0.014
1988	0.316	0.077	0.087	0.137	0.015
1989	0.330	0.079	0.091	0.147	0.014
1990	0.325	0.078	0.086	0.144	0.017
1991	0.337	0.074	0.097	0.150	0.016
1992	0.346	0.068	0.103	0.157	0.018
1993	0.336	0.066	0.101	0.151	0.018
1994	0.359	0.064	0.108	0.167	0.019

---

[10]See Table 1 for a definition of the various population subgroups distinguished
[11]No data are available for the year 1986

TABLE 13.5:

Analyzing the Components of the Change in Inequality Over Time[12]

Type of Inequality Change and its Components	Period 1978-1984	Period 1984-1994	Period 1978-1994
I) Change in Between Groups Inequality	1.1117	-2.2464	-1.1349
α) Contribution of changes in the population shares of groups	-0.2038	0.2532	-0.1312
β) Contribution of changes in the average incomes of groups	0.0118	-0.0540	-0.0299
γ) Contribution of changes in the relative dispersion of the groups distributions	0.9402	-0.0236	0.7267
δ) Contribution of changes in the index $((d-p)/\Delta)$	0.3635	-2.4220	-1.7005
II) Changes in Within groups Inequality	1.4285	1.1798	2.6082
α) Contribution of changes in the population shares of groups	-0.3596	1.0937	0.6940
β) Contribution of changes in the average incomes of groups	0.0887	-0.0078	-0.2039
γ) Contribution of changes in within groups inequality index	1.6994	0.0939	2.1181
III) Changes in Overlap Component	3.0918	1.4917	4.5835
α) Contribution of changes in the population subgroups	0.6583	-1.0839	-0.1557
β) Contribution of changes in the average income of the groups	-0.0065	0.0569	-0.1295
γ) Contribution of changes in the relative dispersion of the groups distributions	2.8035	0.0967	3.1682
δ) Contribution of changes in overlap indicator $(2p/\Delta)$	-0.3635	2.4220	1.7005
Total Inequality	5.6319	0.4251	6.0568
α) Total Contribution of changes in population shares	0.0949	0.2630	0.4071
β) Total contribution of changes in the average incomes of the groups	0.0940	-0.0049	-0.3633
γ) Total contribution of changes in relative dispersions of groups	5.4431	0.1670	6.0130

[12] All the numbers in this table are the original results multiplied by 100.

TABLE 13.6:
Contribution of the Various Groups[13] to the Change in Inequality Over Time[14]

Type of Change in Inequality and Group	Period 1978-1984	Period 1984-1994	Period 1978-1994
I) Change in Between Groups Inequality: Contribution of	1.1117	-2.2466	-1.1348
AA	-0.36495	-1.37295	-1.73785
EA	0.4969	-0.8710	-0.3741
I	0.5946	-0.3446	0.25005
NJ	0.38515	0.34195	0.7271
II) Change in Within Groups Inequality: Contribution of	1.4285	1.1798	2.6083
AA	-0.0588	-1.4338	-1.4926
EA	-1.3928	-0.3005	-1.6933
I	2.8620	2.8637	5.7257
NJ	0.0181	0.0504	0.0685
III) Contribution of Overlap Component: Contribution of	3.0917	1.4916	4.5833
AA	1.01745	-0.4658	0.55165
EA	0.03835	0.6285	0.66685
I	1.9172	1.02645	2.94365
NJ	0.1187	0.30245	0.42115
IV) Total Inequality Change: Contribution of	5.6319	0.4248	6.0568
AA	0.5937	-3.27255	-2.6788
EA	-0.85755	-0.543	-1.40055
I	5.3738	3.54555	8.9194
NJ	0.52195	0.6948	1.21675

---

[13] See Table 1 for a definition of the various population subgroups distinguished
[14] All the original numbers have been multiplied by 100

TABLE 13.7:

Impact of Various Pairwise Comparisons of Groups[15] on Change in Between Groups Inequality and in Overlap Component[16]

Change in Inequality Component by Type of Pairwise Comparison	Period 1978-1984	Period 1984-1994	Period 1978-1994
I) Change in Between Groups Inequality: Contribution of	1.1117	-2.2465	-1.1348
AA-EA	-0.5572	-1.6794	-2.2366
AA-I	-0.3739	-1.2361	-1.6099
AA-NJ	0.2012	0.1696	0.3708
EA-I	1.2725	-0.0150	1.2575
EA-NJ	0.2785	-0.0476	0.2309
I-NJ	0.2906	0.5619	0.8525
II) Change in Overlap Component: Contribution of	3.0918	1.4916	4.5835
AA-EA	-0.7380	-0.8036	-1.5418
AA-I	2.7502	-0.0362	2.7140
AA-NJ	0.0227	-0.0916	-0.0689
EA-I	0.8421	1.7267	2.5688
EA-NJ	-0.0274	0.3341	0.3067
I-NJ	0.2421	0.3624	0.6045

---

[15] See Table 13.1 for a definition of the various groups distinguished
[16] All the original numbers in this table have been multiplied by 100

REFERENCES

[1]   Bhattacharya, N. and B. Mahalanobis, "Regional Disparities in Consumption in India," *Journal of the American Statistical Association*, 62 (1967): 143-161.

[2]   Dagum, C., "Teoria de la transvariacion- Sus aplicaciones a la economia," *Metron* XX (1960)

[3]   Dagum, C., "Measuring the Economic Affluence between population of Income Receivers," *Journal of Business and Economic Statistics*, 5 (1987): 5-12.

[4]   Dagum, C., "A New Approach to the Decomposition of the Gini Income Inequality Ratio," *Empirical Economics,22 (1997)*.

[5]   Deutsch, J. and J. Silber, "The Decomposition of Inequality by Population Subgroups and the Analysis of Interdistributional Inequality," in J. Silber, editor, *Handbook of Income Inequality Measurement*, forthcoming, Kluwer Academic Publishers, Norwell, MA, U.S.A.

[6]   Fei, J.C.H., G. Ranis and S.W.Y. Kuo, *Growth with Equity* - The Taiwan Case, Oxford University Press, Oxford, 1979.

[7]   Gini, C., "Il Concetto di "transvariazione" e le sue prime applicazioni," *Studi di Economia, Finanza e Statistica*, editi del Giornali degil Economisti e Revista de Statistica (1916), reprinted in Gini, 1959.

[8]   Gini, C., *Memorie de Metodologia Statistica*: Volume Secondo - Transvariazione, Libreria Goliardica, Roma, 1959.

[9]   Lambert, P.J. and J.R.Aronson, "Inequality Decomposition Analysis and the Gini Coefficient Revisited," *Economic Journal* 103 (1993)

[10] Love, R and M.C.Wolfson, *Income Inequality: Statistical Methodology and Canadian Illustrations*, Statistics Canada, Ottawa, 1976.

[11] Mehran, F., "A Statistical Analysis on Income Inequality Based on a Decomposition of the Gini Index," *Bulletin of the International Statistical Institute* (1975).

[12] Neuman, S. "Immigration: The Israeli Case," forthcoming in K. Zimmermann editor, *European Migration: What Do We Know ?*, Cambridge University Press for the C.E.P.R.

[13] Piesch, W. *Statistiche Konzentrationsmasse*, J.C.B. Mohr (Paul Siebeck), Tubingen, 1975.

[14] Pyatt, G., "On the Interpretation and Disaggregation of Gini Coefficients," *Economic Journal*, 86 (1976): 243-255.

[15] Rao, V.M., "Two Decompositions of the Concentration Ratio," *Journal of the Royal Statistical Society*, series A, 132 (1969): 418-425.

[16] Silber, J. "Factor Components, Population Subgroups and the Computation of the Gini Index of Inequality," *Review of Economics and Statistics*, LXXI (1989): 107-115.

[17] Yitzhaki, S., "Economic Distance and Overlapping of Distributions," *Journal of Econometrics*, 61 (1994): 147-159.

Chapter 14

THE END OF SCIENCE?[*]

Mario Bunge

Foundations and Philosophy of Science Unit, McGill University,
Montréal, H3A 1W7, Canada

There has never been a dearth of prophets who announce the beginning or the end of something big. In recent years we have heard, among many other prophecies, the birth of the cybersociety and of a new world order, as well as the death of philosophy and even the end of science.

As a matter of fact there is a whole "end of" industry. Perusal of *Books in Print* show such titles as *The End of Art, The End of Beauty, The End of Culture, The End of Education, The End of Ideology, The End of love, The End of work,* and even *The End of Nature.*

Prophecies of this kind come cheap and sell well. Witness the sensational success of Christian eschatology, still on offer after two millennia. To make such prophecies, only three conditions are required: imagination, chutzpah, and ignorance about our nearly total ignorance of historical laws.

The end of science has been announced several times during what is known as the Age of Science. At the end of the 19th century, on the eve of the relativistic and quantum upheavals, and the birth of the synthetic theory of evolution and the biology of the mind, the eminent American physicist A. A. Michelson prophesied the end of great scientific discoveries. One century later his compatriot, the literary critic and journalist John Horgan, came out with his best-seller *The End of Science* (New York: Addison Wesley, 1996).

Unsurprisingly, this book was a hit with the antiscience crowd. It has reassured all those who cannot bring themselves to try and learn a bit of science. In particular, Horgan has earned the applause of New-Agers and

---

[*]Camilo Dagum, socioeconomist, statistician and philosopher, on his 70th anniversary.

postmoderns. He became an instant hero in faculties of arts all over North America. What a relief to be told that science is not worth the effort!

How did Horgan reach his alarming conclusion? Through studying the contemporary scientific problematics? On finding that, in fact, all the great scientific questions have already been answered, and that researchers are not coming up with any new important problems? Of course not: such investigation would require hard work by a multidisciplinary team of eminent scientists—who, if eminent enough, would be too busy doing science, to indulge in that exercise.

But Mr. Horgan is only one person, and moreover he is not a scientist: he has only a degree in English literature. Hence he cannot even read the specialized scientific literature. So, he is at the mercy of scientific popularizations—which are seldom faithful. He cannot read science but he can write for the rednecks who despise what they do not understand.

How did Mr. Horgan reach his devastating conclusion? Being a professional reporter, he interviewed a number of well-known scientists, some of them Nobel laureates, and most of whom made their mark long ago. He also interviewed a few philosophers. What can such specialists tell a journalist? Clearly, little more than some general impressions sprinkled with gossip, hopes and fears. They cannot explain to him any of the technical problems scientists are wrestling with, for fear of not being understood or, worse, of being badly misunderstood.

For instance, Mr. Horgan interviewed Nobel laureate Gerald Edelman, who is presently studying the brain mechanisms involved in conscious experience. He and other neuropsychologists are studying this question because, though several millennia old, it is yet to be solved. In fact, a lot is known about individual neurons, but very little about the way they interconnect constituting systems capable of having mental experiences. Neuropsychology is just at the beginning, not the end, of this great endeavor, which had formerly been in the hands of theologians, philosophers and speculative psychologists.

It would have been interesting if Mr Horgan had succeeded in explaining Professor Edelman's original and intriguing if somewhat unclear conjectures on the physiology of the mind. Instead, he informs us that he is an "ironic" scientist, that is, more speculative than empirical. And he adds that, regrettably, Professor Edelman lacks the required rhetoric skills. Required for what? To do research? Obviously not: An investigator need not know how to sell his product. He expects teachers and intelligent popularizers to take care of the marketing. So, Horgan blames Edelman for not doing the job that he, Horgan, is expected to do but does not do, presumably because he lacks the required scientific knowledge.

Mr Horgan cannot refrain from mentioning "chaos" theory, that dark albeit sexy newcomer. This is a difficult mathematical theory—or rather a collection of intriguing nonlinear differential and finite-difference equations with remarkable properties. It has attracted the attention of the public mainly because of its name, which wrongly suggests that the universe is not as lawful as it seemed. (Three decades ago something similar happened with singularity theory: by being misnamed "catastrophe theory", it suggested that revolution is more common than evolution.)

To write honestly about so-called chaos it is necessary to know something about nonlinear differential equations. And this subject can hardly be popularized, that is, translated into ordinary language. Whoever states lightly that the processes of financial or political turbulence are described by chaos theory risks being asked to write down some nonlinear differential equations, solve them, and compare the solutions with data about stock markets or political crashes or bubbles.

In any event, neither Horgan nor anyone else has made a case for the view that science is decaying and at the end of its tether. There is no such tether, or at least no one has proved that there are any limits other than budgetary and ideology constraints. On the contrary, science is booming, if the growing number of new scientific fields and the increasing volume of the scientific literature are any indications. To mention just two new fields with their own specialized journals: psychoneuroendocrinoimmunology and socioeconomics.

This is not to deny that there are some symptoms of malaise in the international scientific community. For example, theoretical particle physics is rather stagnant, due in part to a shortage of experimental data. In turn this shortage is due to the high cost of the experimental set-ups required to obtain those data.

Another reason for the stagnation of this particular field is that an excessive effort has been invested into the most fashionable theories, those of strings and superstrings, that have been around for a quarter of a century but have yet to yield any testable results. Nor are they likely to deliver them because they postulate that physical space has ten dimensions. (A dose of sound philosophy of science might have averted this costly experience.) However, this is but one of the branches of physics. All the others continue advancing, particularly in experimental matters.

Some of the recent advances in chemistry, particularly in the chemistry of proteins, are just as sensational. Those in biology, particularly in neuroscience, are even more so. Suffice it to recall that a number of brain mechanisms of mental functions are being uncovered; that mental processes are being imaged; and that mental disturbances that used to be the domain of shamans and psychoanalysts are now being treated medically with some success thanks to advances in psychoneurophysiology and psychoneuropharmacology.

A glance at such general scientific journals as *Science* and *Nature* , or even the science columns of good newspapers, should suffice to confirm the thesis that natural science as a whole is alive and well despite the occasional slowing down in this or that particular branch.

Admittedly, the social sciences are not doing so well. In particular, economic theory is not precisely booming. In fact, it is still in the throes of a century-old crisis, which may be dated to the so-called marginalist revolution. I regard this as a counter-revolution, in overlooking production and technology, and in being centered on the fuzzy notions of subjective utility and subjective probability, as well as in stubbornly refusing to admit that the postulate of maximizing behavior is far from having been empirically confirmed. Even worse, the pseudo-exact, narrow and aprioristic outlook of neoclassical microeconomics has lately spilled over into anthropology, sociology, political science, and even historiography.

Even so, there has been progress in the social sciences and technologies, particularly in anthropology, archaeology, economic history, economic sociology, descriptive macroeconomics, the sociology of the firm, and management science. One of the most interesting and promising new developments is perhaps the emergence of new intersciences, such as socioeconomics, sociolinguistics and political sociology. They are promising because, after all, they all study the same thing, namely society, from different but mutually complementary viewpoints.

Another symptom of malaise, though one limited to North America, is the declining interest in science on the part of students. Roughly half of the student body and the teaching staff in graduate programs is foreign. Moreover, for the first time in decades there is a significant number of unemployed scientists. A further indicator is this. Twenty years ago, every issue of the *Scientific American*, the most widely read of all semi-popular science magazines, had about 200 pages. Now it has only half as many, some of which are devoted to gossip. To top it all, John Horgan, of end-of-science fame, was a staff writer of this magazine for a while.

A third malaise symptom is the increasing pressure, on the part of some governments and university administrators, for scientists to do market-oriented work. This demand betrays an abysmal ignorance of both basic science and the psychological mechanisms of research. Basic science is the search for truth, not for utility. Scientists come up with findings, not designs. As for the psychological aspect, scientists and technologists are mainly motivated by curiosity. When commissioned to do something that does not interest them, they are bound to produce, at best, small advances. Great discoveries and inventions result from passionate quests for knowledge, not from the wish to comply with plans devised by myopic bureaucrats or businessmen.

Where does the idea of market-oriented science originate? It has several sources. One is straight philistinism: lack of interest in anything that cannot be priced. Another source is the popular confusion, fostered by pragmatist philosophers, between science and technology. A third is the constructivist-relativist school of sociology of science, according to which science is a mirror of society and a tool of political and economic power. According to these people, there is no such thing as a scientific discovery: the scientists or, rather, the scientific community, "construct" the facts. Moreover, scientists would not be driven by curiosity but by thirst for power instead.

Power, not truth, would then be the goal and trademark of science according to this school. Bruno Latour, one of its most prominent members, has said that scientific research is politics by another name. (This grotesque claim is not even original: it had been made earlier by Michel Foucault.) He has also claimed that, to understand science, it is best not to have studied it. He has even corrected Einstein, stating that the theory of special relativity, far from having to do with the electrodynamics of moving bodies, as its father had naively believed, is a trick for bringing back long-distance travelers. Latour must know, since he has a degree in French philosophy.

All this has come in the wake of the student revolt of the late 60s. Many of those students revolted not only against the so-called establishment but also against what they saw as its intellectual tools, namely science and technology. They rolled these two into one and fought what they saw as a solid block: the government-business-science-technology complex.

A number of philosophers helped, spreading the word that science and pseudoscience are the same, and that "anything goes": that is, that there are no rigorous standards of objective and cross-cultural truth. Obviously, if this is true, there is no scientific progress. Unsurprisingly, enrollment in science and technology faculties plummeted, while the arts faculties grew in numbers.

Another symptom of the malaise in question is the quick diffusion of the so-called "cultural studies". This line of work—to call it something—was started in France some three decades ago by such "postmodern" writers as Foucault, Barthes, Baudrillard, and Derrida. These are declared enemies of reason and, in particular, of science and technology. This movement is now flourishing in departments of English and Communications throughout the anglophone world. Their followers claim to engage in social studies, and specialize in science and technology bashing.

The central idea of this school is that whatever exists is both social construction and text. (This is why one of the main media of this movement is the journal *Social Text*, edited by two professors of English literature.) Thus the Moon would be a cultural object: it would exist only as a literary character. Presumably, famines and wars too are social conventions and texts. In particular, feeling hungry and being blown up by a land-mine would be misprints.

Now, if something is a text, then it has got to be interpreted. That is, the thing to do is hermeneutics, or general semiotics, as it is also called. And who more competent to accomplish this task that the literature specialist? Who can explain more authoritatively the origin of the lunar craters, of AIDS, of business cycles, and of political cataclysms? On second thought, I take this back, because the textualists do not frame hypotheses to explain anything: they limit themselves to asserting dogmatically that all science deals with symbols, which they claim to interpret.

The hermeneutic fraud made the front page of the *New York Times* on May 18, 1996. This newspaper reported that *Social Text,* the above-mentioned journal, had just published an article by Professor Alan Sokal, a physicist with New York University, titled "Transgressing the Boundaries: Toward a Hermeneutics of Quantum Gravity". This clever and hilarious spoof was written in the hermetic jargon of the hermeneutic school It held, among other things, that modern physics proves that, at bottom, physical reality is a social and linguistic construction—which is of course why it was accepted for publication.

Unbeknownst to the editors of the magazine, Sokal published in the academic journal *Lingua Franca* a paper revealing that the article in question had been a prank designed to expose the hermeneutic fraud. The hermeneuticists counter-attacked and accused the scientist of being "ill-read and half-educated". All this is very amusing, especially coming from scientific illiterates. But in the meantime thousands of unsuspecting students are being inoculated with the antiscience vaccine. And this not in the street but in the hallowed groves of academia, and often at the tax-payer's expense too.

This is not an isolated episode: it is only one battle in the unending war between science and obscurantism. The scientists have been winning the war over the past four centuries as long as they have been allowed to investigate and question, and as long as they have obtained the support they need. But people will not support scientific research unless they understand that scientific progress is needed not only to bolster productivity but also to go on being human. They will not support scientific research if they keep mistaking science for technology, and technology for business and government. People will not support science as long as scientists and philosophers do not react to the prophets of scientific doom. They will not support it as long as universities continue to shelter the enemies of reason and truth.

Nor will the taxpayers have any reason to support scientific research if the only products of research they have access to are social theories like rational choice models, which do not help to understand any social facts, or socioeconomic policies, such as neoliberalism, that only bring increasing economic inequality. If social scientists want public support for their work, they must not only come up with significant findings: they must also pressure their professional organizations to lobby for science just as effectively as the arms and tobacco lobbies.

To sum up: science keeps advancing on the whole even though some of its branches suffer occasional stagnation or even decline. The same holds for technology and the arts. Never before have there been so many outstanding problems waiting to be investigated with the help of so many powerful research tools. Hence, it is false that the end of science is in sight. However, there are reasons to fear a temporary slump due exclusively to social circumstances and, particularly, to public or governmental indifference or worse. After all, science has decayed before for lack of interest or support.

Remember four recent episodes: the nearly total destruction of basic science under Nazism; the destruction of genetics, psychology and social science under Stalinism; the severe cutbacks in social science research grants during the Reagan and Bush governments; and the near-total eclipse of science along with the collapse of the former Soviet Empire, where roughly half of the world's scientific and technological manpower used to be employed. These episodes should serve as reminders that not even mathematics, astrophysics, anthropology and history— some the purest of all sciences— are conducted in a social vacuum.

There is no law of automatic scientific progress. Whether or not science will continue to advance depends on the present generation of scientists as well as on governments. Science will keep going on if we fuel it with curious students and money, and protect academic freedom from religious and neoliberal zealots. It won't advance much further if the directly interested parties—mainly scientists and science teachers, technologists and innovative businessmen, concerned citizens and responsible civil servants—do not react in time to the philistines and the prophets of scientific doom.

The moral is that, if we want to allow science to keep going, and wish to preserve industrial civilization, we must work as citizens for an intensification of science education at all levels, as well as a vigorous public support of research.

Chapter 15

STATISTICAL INFERENCE AND INDUCTIVE PREVISION

Italo Scardovi

Statistical Sciences, University of Bologna, Via delle Belle Ari 41,
40126 Bologna, Italy

15.1 Introduction

It's a great honor for me to dedicate these scattered annotations (extracts from wider writings or simple discussion issues) to Camilo Dagum, great scientist and fraternal friend. They draw inspiration from the topics, we both started to debate a long time ago with our common master Corrado Gini. Under his guidance we learned to be wary of the widespread schemes of a certain philosophy of science still dealing with "ravens all black", "swans all white", "emeralds all green" (if not "grue").

In the most authoritative epistemological literature, scientific knowledge is assigned the task of describing, explaining and predicting events. There has always been much argument about describing and explaining, whereas the role of prevision seems to be beyond doubt. By assigning science a descriptive, non-explanatory task, Pierre Duhem (*La théorie physique*, 1906) identified the value of a theory with the features that make it appear a natural classification, endowing it with the power of "being ahead of experience". Thus, even in its narrowest expression, science must be able to anticipate events. Arguing as to whether this anticipation of empirical phenomena also entails an explanatory component lies beyond the scope of this discussion; on the other hand, we should focus our attention on the above-mentioned meaning of prevision.

It's necessary to distinguish – and this doesn't happen in epistemological literature - between prevision as "anticipation of experience", i.e. of a reality as yet unknown and prevision as "anticipation of the future" in its actual etymological meaning of what is to come. In the first instance, prevision virtually amounts to projecting known events in the form of hypothetical deduction from set laws; anticipation of an "explanandum", which does exist, although has not been acquired yet. In the second instance, prevision corresponds to visualizing an unknown "reality" which has not taken place yet.

And more: the notion of prevision as prefigurement of the future admits a further sub-distinction needs to be made. The world view and particular phenomenology can give rise to a deterministic-causal vision of facts; on this assumption, the future does not exist: it is, although hardly recognizably, in the present (and in the past as well, from which the present resulted); in an indeterministic view, on the contrary, the future is not concealed or lurking in past experience: looking ahead acquires the complete different meaning of a purely inductive deed, which dares to venture into empiricism. Things being so, there seems to be no reason at-all for it to be treated in the epistemological texts having induction as their subject matter.

The sort of previsions epistemology has traditionally been dealing with is the almost syllogistic inference of deterministic science and even though the blurred vagueness of some assumptions seems to suggest the anticipation of a future reality, its own paradigm is clear: future events are bound to take place as the necessary consequence of what is and has been, the integration of a theoretical system, the universality of a law. This philosophy does not appear to suit a science which came into being as a result of the collapse of the deterministic model, of the intellectual revolution, which meant that possibility could replace necessity, likelihood definiteness.

15.2   The Role of Deduction

When giving science a predicting task, the texts of epistemology also attribute to prevision the role of deduction with a view to reconciling the particular with the universal: the outcome is a kind of prevision which, at the same time, is evidence and discovery within one system. And although it may occasionally appear as a skillful inference based on calculation (as was the case with the deductive discovery of the planet Neptune, based on our previous knowledge of Newton's system), it is frequently a daring and ingenious concept (let's just think of Mendelejev's discovery of new chemical elements on the basis of his "periodic system", or of the intuitive guesswork underlying the discovery of Dirac's antiparticles, Pauli's neutrino or Yukawa's meson). A heuristic intuition, however, can enlighten even those inferences not derived by ingeniously and consistently extending a more or less well-established theory, but anticipations of events which might or might not take place in the future.

If the former can possibly fall into the top-rate category of the so-called "relations of ideas", the latter are no doubt to be counted among the untrustworthy "matters of fact". This is the basic distinction which Hume relied upon well over two hundred years ago in order to give a clear-cut profile to deduction and induction, thus destroying the illusion of the existence of a logical necessity in the transference from regularly observed occurrences to the notion of an underlying cause, which would strengthen its extrapolation into the future. "The contrary of every matter of fact is still possible" – the sceptic philosopher exhorted. (*An inquiry concerning human understanding*, 1758)

Since the times of Galileo and Bacon, or even earlier, a scientific law has consistently been regarded as such in so far as it has been able to anticipate events, i.e. to identify and define an ever-lasting order. This is the concept that over the centuries inspired philosophers and scientists. If in Hertz's view (*Prinzipien der Mechanik*, 1894) the major task of natural science is to predict future events; according to Peirce (*A theory of probable inference*, 1883), science aims at anticipating effects through a deductive process. Indeed, Popper (*Logik der Forschung* 1934) defines as "predictions" the deductive conclusions which can be drawn from a hypothesis or the individual assertions which can be deduced from a theory. Hempel (*Scientific explanation*, 1965) also describes as "prediction" nomological scientific deduction, thus relating it to the explanation. In Ayer's own words (*Language, truth and logic*, 1946), any scientific process is fully justified in so far as the predictions it implies do come true. Any scientist's foremost duty lies in prevision, claimed Poincaré (*La science et l'hypothèse*, 1902); he also reminded us that any generalization is a hypothesis and that there can be no science or prevision without a previous generalization. Mach (*Erkenntnis und Irrtum*, 1905) assigned experimental science a well defined task to lay down roles, even false ones, as long as they could reliably predict the outcome of future observations. Since this line of reasoning turned out to be extremely successful in physics, it soon became the science of certainties: this was a deductive sort of science, in that its conclusions were inherent in its premises.

Most passages we come across when going through the most significant papers of epistemology present induction as the inference of an unchanging world. It is in this framework that Hume sets inductive deeds, emptying them of any rational justifications: scientific induction relies on the assumption of an unchanging nature where a future is likely to the past. This is the picture of a non-evolutionary world, governed by timeless laws, where "before" and "after" are no phenomena at all, because phenomena do not undergo any development.

15.3   Event Regularities

If prevision is thought of as involving a regular recurrence of events, then the following inductive paradigm can be set: if all ravens observed so far are black, there are sound empirical reasons to expect other black ravens. This philosophy, however, seems to melt away as soon as a statement acquires a "statistical" character, instead of an "absolute" one, and the predictive inference, even though pertaining to a "single" event must deal with probabilities. However, one still finds it difficult to get the meaning of laws in which the cognitive interest shifts from the particular case to the wholeness of events, from individuals to populations. On the contrary, it is precisely this empirical inertiality of large numbers to provide a special inductive support for statistical laws. One obviously has to consider aggregates of sizes suiting the phenomenic variability. Keeping opposing the so-called "unexceptionable" laws to the statistical ones, though, amounts to knowing nothing of science, to an epistemological nonsense, to being unaware that even in the pluralistic dimension of events statistical laws are good and proper laws.

After describing prediction as the deduction of the conclusions drawn from an hypothesis, Carnap states that in many cases, the law involved may be "statistical" and the prediction will then be "only probable" (*Philosophical foundation of physics*, 1966). This instance conspicuously bears out how epistemology of a certain kind still hardly understands the meaning of a statistical law and barely grasps the concept that, the law being a statistical one, deduction and induction nearly become outgrown logical categories. Yet, there are empirical recurrences which can and others which cannot be projected into the future, retorts a certain type of logic, thereby almost realizing that the future can never be like the past and nature is not immutable, that the regular recurrence of events is the result of an abstract classification, of an eidetic-linguistical reduction of facts. Science means, first of all, searching for invariants, general principles and iterative patterns.

When defining prevision as the deduction of empirical conclusions drawn from a theory or when, going to the bottom of experience, it assumes the regularity and steadiness of given phenomena, of which Hume pointed out the unyielding uncertainty, a given sort of philosophy of science regards the future as an ascertaining proof of the past and, conversely, the past as an anticipation of the future. This is the future described by Laplace: rather than an "after", a "still". How can we - Hume asked - draw conclusions from past, experienced occurrences, which go beyond the latter? (*Treatise of human nature*, 1739). His answer to this question has become a philosophical landmark: habit is the only principle which makes experience useful and enables us to expect future events resembling the past ones.

Experience in itself, however, only justifies this inductive leap into the unknown from a natural standpoint, not a logical one. If we rationally want to exceed the limits of the known world, we need a theoretical scheme, which preserves its effectiveness beyond it. The unknown may turn out to be something never happened. Then, how can we anticipate events which still are to happen without, once again, assuming the existence of laws, the unchanging character of phenomena, the uniformity of nature? Even the strictest law enjoys actual confirmation if is based on the assumption of an alleged stability of events, which finds no rational justification. Scientific induction only mirrors the primordial instinct towards prevision, as a shield against the unknown: a heritage of the natural selection, a sort of response to the requirements of survival, which the methodological thought tries to convert into a conscious dead, a rational criterion, Jeffreys remarks that inference from observations of the past to the future "is not deductive" (*Scientific inference*, 1957).

There is no rational means, therefore, of anticipating historical future, any standard, any tool are "irrational" and are to be viewed as a direct result of "habit". The daily habit of living and acting, which leaves no room for any theoretical justification. On the other hand, if the purpose of science lies in prevision - as is claimed by a whole philosophical school, before and after Comte and Poincaré - a cause-effect mechanism always remains the most convenient and reliable implement. It satisfies a psychological need for necessity.

15.4   Causal Principles

Even the causal principle results from a classification process. Causes and effects are ideal representations, semantic categories set in the context of reality. Indeed, the principle of induction is to be found in the classification process by which the mind acquires empirical timeless uniformities and paves the way for the transition from quality to quantity, from unequal entities to the common noun and natural number. Any category embodies future and past at the same time; every single statistical case loses its historical individuality, things turn into ideas, confined within abstract paradigm: foreseeing means nothing but recognize the general applicability of the properties of each category. Precisely like the Galileian experiment, classification thus produces an artefact and nearly seems to equate induction concerning the future to deduction within an ageless syllogistic model.

Once the unchanging properties and laws have been identified, it is purely a matter of employing them to trace back past experience and anticipate future events. And if the future really is such, it can be predicted by deduction through a causal procedure. This also falls within the classic instance of inference from laws, it is the deterministic model of Galilei-Newton's mechanics and Lorentz-Maxwell's electrodynamics: a formal system in which - to say it in Max Planck's words (*Wege zur physichalischen Erkenntnis*, 1914) - "all processes taking place within it can be grasped in advance, thus making it possible to deduce the effect from the cause". This is once again a Laplacian view of the world: a mechanics in which time has no ontological meaning. When it comes to inferring the effect, the cause being known, prevision acquires the syntax of hypothetical assertion ("If A, then B") and antecedent and consequent follow in the sequence suggested by the causal relationship.

It seems only natural to wonder whether, beyond these two well-established logical figures, there is any point in looking for the foundation of prevision of an event, which is not only unknown (first figure) and non-happened (second figure), but also unnecessary. Matters of facts therefore: the causal principle does not hold true any longer and, what is even more important, any possible deterministic necessity fails to exist. What about, then, induction which project a factual picture and ventures into the future of an ever-changing world?

As a deductive inference consistent with a nomological system may or may not come true in reality (should it not come true, however, this by no means implies it is worthless, but only that it exceeded the boundaries of the system's validity scope), inductive inference relating to the future does not so much aim at fitting an empirical target, i.e. at finding a punctual confirmation in the time; its main reason lies in its method, in its attitude to turn initial circumstances into a non-incoherent picture of future. In matters of fact, the next time may always be different.

From this particular angle, prevision as the inductive inference of a tiny fragment of a future world, can be regarded as a hypothesis which still needs to be confronted with actual facts. Since Hume's age, both logic and science have been trying to give induction a rational foundation, partly by re-affirming the causal principle (as a necessary and sufficient condition), partly by detecting a new approach to the problem of induction in probability. At the same time, big efforts have been undertaken to bring inference concerning the future as close to deduction as possible, in a deterministic and timeless universe; to produce, in other words, an inference with all epistemological features. It is not by chance that Popper mentions a so-called "deduction of predictions". This is, so to say, a syllogistic prevision immersed in the historical flow of events; it depicts future, but nevertheless necessary, events.

A flawless philosophy, though imbued with determinism. In a prevision of facts based on facts, in an indeterministic design of events, initial conditions do not entail one future, but several futures. Because one thing is anticipating (causally) an event which must happen, another thing is anticipating (statistically) an event which might happen. The problem of establishing a relationship between acquired and virtual data varies according to the changes in the reference paradigm and in the individual or collective nature of the enunciation. Natural paradigms may be many and various: for example the "deterministic chaos" of dynamic systems, (i.e. the large effects of minimum variations), or the "random genetic drift" (i.e. the erratic casuality in small populations).

Ever beyond this, in the statistical intuition of nature emerged from Boltzmann's thermodynamics, Rutherford's radio-activity, Darwin's natural selection, Mendel's genetics, the problem of induction, as a cognitive and anticipative act, takes up an entirely new aspect. Uncertainty - which, starting from Plato's times, was thought to be ingrained in man's history as a heritage and limit of all so-called social sciences - also penetrates into natural phenomena thereby impairing a dogma which had been preserved as such over the centuries: the deterministic view of the world and the causal interpretation of its phenomena. It is the mechanics developed out of Planck's quanta which definitively leads to a crisis (expressed by Bohr's and Born's re-interpretation) of that glorious "natural philosophy": the cause effect model is lost in the description of microevents and the methodological impossibility of defining the present state of a particle makes its future unpredictable.

Should then science, and precisely this science, give up Comte's ideal of knowing in order to anticipate events? It shouldn't: what it should give up is a certain strict phenomenic mechanism in order to give prevision its most suitable shape: that of statistical assumptions and distributions of probability. The idea of cause - expressing the need to connect events - is flanked and then replaced by the idea of chance expressing contingent accidentality. Starting from Democritus, "chance" and "necessity" both in nature and in human life have acted and inter acted with alternate success. The basis of the new science is to be found in deriving laws from chance while the idea of cause was failing to properly describe actual circumstances and anticipate a necessary future out of them.

In the macroscopic order of magnitude, however, accidentality of an elementary event is not always mediated (and brought back to order: a collective order) by the empirical inertia of large numbers, as was stated by Laplace and Quetelet. The indeterminacy of an elementary event may happen to overcome the barrier of all other innumerable microprocesses because the system accepts and highlights its accidental innovative step. As the effects of that elementary leap emerge at a collective level, they break up the causal sequence of macrodimensional becoming and start another sequence. The deterministic chain of classical science which Laplace extended from large to small, from past to future, breaks down: one can, at most, identify separated finite fragments each of which can be deterministically represented and is valid in its own time.

One thing, therefore, is considering the sequence of events as univocal and necessary flow, and another thing is admitting its essential accidentality; one thing is anticipating a future set and another thing is anticipating a future which is not as such. If this statement has not yet become part of man's history, it has entered into the natural history of the species. Biological evolution is unpredictable, not so much because of our intellectual limits, but rather and above all because chance, which gives rise to variability, does not admit occult predestination, deterministic necessity and immanent aims: neither a direction nor a forced improvement. A deterministic theory of biological evolution would give it a one-way and necessary direction, considering that everything is inherent in the initial data, spontaneous variability would become a nonsense and it would be impossible to understand the existence of the unimplemented stock of accidental mutational variabilities which is compatible with the genoma of a species.

Without statistical intuition of the real, natural sciences would have never achieved their most important idea: the idea of evolution. They would have never seen a process of indeterministic becoming in life. Whereas Laplace's cosmology, Hegel's philosophy, Comte's sociology, Bernard's physiology, Quetelet's anthropometry and Kelvin's physic were dealing with a certain and planned reality, the theory of natural evolution suggested the alarming assumption of a non-necessary and non-predestined nature. The darwinian philosophy – more and before the theory of dynamic systems – has limited the laplacian view of the world.

One can therefore observe the unrepeatable succession of facts in the world and try to abstract categories, models, regular patterns out of them, so that phenomena become independent of space and time conditions: the principle of classification and the experimental canons thus identify the "universals" of science. On this basis, sciences are classified according to the degree of abstraction and atemporality of their assertions. It is true that the physical phenomenology has developed, by getting rid of contingencies, its own logical and deductive system in a body of laws which are valid independently of the initial conditions: the historical elements, the data of the problem; yet, it is true that the most revolutionary intellectual step taken by the sciences of life has been triggered off by the observation of living forms as becoming populations in a historical prospective: a statistical interpretation of the real fit into the becoming of events and aimed at renewing physical sciences before and more than social sciences. (This does not imply taking historicism as a dogma and fideistically seeing becoming as the fulfillment of a design and the inexorable success of necessity).

Therefore, deductive anticipations drawn from experience and relative to still unknown realities but yet inherent to a nomological system cannot be confused with the anticipation of the future, unless a strictly deterministic and fatalistic paradigm is taken. This is not meant to play down the extent and the audacity of so many deductive discoveries of science. Scientific knowledge develops above all (and Popper says only) by taking each theoretical system to its extreme critical consequences.

The point is that the truth entailed in an anticipation of experience, which is explicative of a theory, depends upon the domain of validity of a theory. Within that domain, anticipating means drawing consistent deductions and becomes the empirical corollary of a nomological system. The explanation for the irregularity of Mercury orbits given by means of a hypothetical planet no longer fall within the scope of validity of a paradigm which had until then been undisputed, i.e. Kepler-Newton's paradigm. A new paradigm, general relativity, in which the old one is preserved as a particular case, has proved that "anomaly" right. The degree of rationality of a predictive deduction is therefore not to be found in its becoming true: it rather lies in its consistency within a certain system. The prevision of an internal planet responsible for the precession of Mercury perihelion - though without grounds - was consistent with Newton's gravitation in the continuous three-dimensional aspect of Euclidean space; in the same way that Mercury orbit becomes no doubt consistent with the continuous four-dimensional aspect of space and time in Reimann's geometry. (When certain epistemology textbooks skim over the subject of prevision and the nomic explications of a system are considered, one can find such statements as - in the case of Neptune discovery - that the fact that Adams and Leverrier's calculations anticipated "a future". What could be described as future was the discovery and not the existence of the planet!).

The heuristic aspect of prevision as "anticipation of experience" is found in the control of explicative limits of a theory: it remains mere hypothesis until it becomes true in our observations. Before Galle trained his telescope, the existence of a celestial body disturbing Uranus orbit was a mere hypothesis; now the assumption of a curved, closed and infinite universe is a mere hypothesis as well as the idea of a proton made up by "quarks" kept together by a not yet breakable force or the idea of a neutrin having a mass. All these hypotheses have sprung out of creative intelligence, brave imagination and critical approaches, despite the fact that they heuristically turn into previsions of going-on realities, consistent with a hypothetical-deductive system.

The knowledge of the innate casuality of the entire microworld (from Boltzmann to Heisenberg, from Mendel to Monod) has freed scientific thought from a deterministic methodology aimed at codifying the single event, its causal necessity and the predictability of its recurrence. The existence of individual variability offers new connotations to the statistical inductive process, at the same time giving a meaning to statistical probability.

15.5   Statistical Prevision

In statistical methodology, a distinction is usually made between "deterministic" and "statistical" prevision. This is a vague dualism if one does not describe the sense in which a prediction is considered "statistical" and the implicit scientific paradigm is not defined. In both cases the act of anticipating is based upon the pre-assumption that the phenomenic conditions remain unchanged and that the laws (whatever they are) persist in time: this certainty becomes less and less sure the more prevision stretches forward losing in terms of empirical necessity and exposing itself to Hume's uncertainty of the matters of fact.

The obvious and sad conclusions are that predictions can be successful only in an ordered, isolated and indifferent world; yet an ordered, isolated and indifferent world needs no predictions. There is another and deeper reason for a contradiction: an explicative model is more explicative if an artefact is simple, well-designed and articulated on essential variables; a predictive model is, theoretically, bound to take all possible variables into account to decrease the degrees of freedom of the system, so that the risk of failure is reduced to a minimum degree. Yet the higher the number of variables, the more a model can become useless and not only because of the difficulty in describing the initial conditions.

The antithesis (typical of econometric research) between explicative and predictive capacity of a model reflects a more general epistemological antinomy. In Hempel's view, explanation and prediction have the same logic structure and differ only in their pragmatic aspect: what is unknown in the one case is known in the other one and vice versa: each suitable explanation is a potential prediction; and each suitable prediction is a potential explanation (*Aspects of scientific explanation*, 1965). It is worth observing that this is true in a strictly deterministic context but not for science which has made statistics a universal code of interpretation and postulates a more and more indeterministic grammar, in an attempt at unifying phenomenology of matter and life. Only if historical past is reduced to a pre-set pattern, explanation amounts to prediction. A borderline condition which is almost impossible to find when analyzing the social phenomena. Even more so in the operative framework, where it is not the rational structure of the model which is given the preference to, but its concrete effectiveness. These two aspects do not always go along well with each other. All the more so, if one adds notions of value and decisionalistic assumptions.

Doubts can be cast on the logical equivalence - put forward by Hempel and repeated by others - between "prevision" and "post-vision", justified by the symmetry of plurivocal outcomes. It is true that in the history of thought, the understanding of nature has always been and still is characterized by a continuous debate between possible paradigms of the past (think of the disputes between Vulcanists and Neptunists, Uniformists and Catastrophist, Creationists and Transformists; think about the long "querelle" concerning spontaneous generation and the alternative pathways in the descent of man; think about the theoretical debate on the origin of life in a reduced primitive atmosphere or on the beginning of the Universe ...); however, choosing between various possible future alternatives is not the same as choosing between various possible past alternatives, because one past has already occurred and one future is still to take place and at present seems to be non-univocal, non-necessary and non-determined.

Uncertainty as to the past is lack of information, whereas uncertainty as to the future (when strict deterministic views are no longer true) is something more and something different. The variety of possible past alternatives is - so to say - a kind of "Laplacian"" plurality around the truth, though it still is to be identified. The plurality of possible future alternatives is a sort of "Darwinian" plurality. Confronted with this plurality, decision-makers aim at identification and scientists do not. It is, once again, a matter of premises.

15.6   Statistical Prediction

Calling a prediction statistical and taking probabilities into account is not enough to make a non-deterministic choice. Above all, one should not see "statistical prediction" as a makeshift solution due to the fact that certain branches of knowledge lack in nomological system and therefore no deductive predictions are possible. It is once again a matter of general paradigms: from the one of classical physics (in which chance is the expression of the epistemic limits of human mind) to Darwin-Mendel's one where chance is phenomenic, evolves in time and plays with necessity. Darwin's time is no longer the time of the philosophies of history of his age. It is a phenomenic time; the time of non-deterministic and non-finalistic becoming. No goal and no plan: only an adaptation to changing situations in organic structures and institutions, in species and society. A new concept of historicity thus penetrates into science together with an accidental and contingent element which wipes out all forms of teleology and mythology, in spite of the new barriers created between natural becoming and man's history by idealistic historicism. The time of biological evolution is the time of a nature becoming history and evolving through the populations.

It is always, then, a problem of hypotheses. Hypotheses are the canons of all research, even in social sciences: there is always a conceptual reference system, often in the form of ideology. There are those who see the revelation of an aim and of a providential design in human history; there are those who deny such a design but believe in the existence of historical laws accounting for the succession of events in the past and capable of directing us towards the future. Even in natural sciences we have seen the succession of teleological paradigms (universe as the achievement of a target) and causal paradigm which was determinant in inspiring centuries of scientific discoveries. One sees, almost in all sciences, an accidentalist paradigm due to the statistical interpretation of the indeterminacy inherent in the unpredictable becoming of the species.

Among the magnitudes of this new science probability comes into play; and these are phenomenal probabilities rather than gambling odds: here there lies the irreconcilable antithesis between the subjectivism of those who consider probability as a wholly personal evaluation and scientific realism of those who profess to derive probability from events. After the crisis in classical determinism scientists see probability in Nature and not only in the epistemic limitations of the human mind. But, to the subjectivist, scientific practice appears a conventional and superstitious manner of founding a logic of uncertainty. Yet these same "superstitious probabilities" are those of the physicist, the biologist, probabilities on which it was possible to build sciences such as statistical mechanics or population genetics. The laws of these sciences, said Einstein, hold for multitudes and not for individuals. But the laws of multitudes are statistical laws and the probabilities within these laws are a consequence of a process of abstraction and classification, lacking which there is no science. Hans Reichenbach considered the probability theory in the science as "the tool of prediction". We make use - he explained - of probabilistic statement to "predict future frequencies" (*Experience and prediction*, 1938). Postulating the empirical limit of a frequency therefore amounts to anticipating a future: thus geneticists, physicists, economists and demographers have to make extrapolations and are almost unaware of the question David Hume posed for over two centuries. Actually, the stability of a frequency is and still remains, whatever Bernoulli may say, a matter of fact.

In scientific practice, statistic frequencies identified in inertial systems are interpreted as inductive probabilities, called "probabilities of sciences" by Carnap. All elementary probabilities of classic and population genetics are relative frequencies from which other probabilities are drawn by applying the sum and product principles. To the subjectivist, however, the statistical identification of probability seems too restrictive. He sees probability in terms of belief, a personal expectation of the single event: an expectation determined in terms of betting, like a price to be paid. In fact, we already find Kant measuring the degree of belief in terms of risking money. (*Kritik der reinen Vernunft*, 1781).

Subjectivists view each event as a "unicum" and emphasize the conventional character of "objectivistic" criteria which base probability on an empirical sample. It is true that the categorical repetitiveness of the world's facts is a classificatory abstraction, linguistic artefact, semantic allegory. But it is also true that rational knowledge began when facts were reduced into classes (as symbols of conceptual categories), with the search for laws which transcend the unique event. Whereas Leonard Savage asserts that probability must refer to the single case in which a decision is involved and, as such, cannot be resolved within the frequentist definition, the physicist and genetist can reply that the single case, in itself, does not make science: it is, rather, a particular case of an operative choice, of a utilitarian gamble. Especially in the empirical field of immanent variability.

Bertrand Russell points out that, all knowledge we possess is either "knowledge of single facts" or "scientific knowledge". In reality, neither Galileo's artefact, typified by the experiment, nor the statistical event, referring to populations, can be called "particular facts". By considering each event to be unique, probabilistic subjectivism runs the risk of falling into a form of solipsistic idealism and becoming isolated from science: a science which has matured by abstracting "the singular", dealing with variability, identifying statistical group properties, with probability distribution of the arrival point of experimental process. Herein lies the statistical foundation of scientific probability; and, perhaps, this is where we find the solution to the divergence between a concept of probability based in a phenomenology arising from natural variability and the one depending on the activities connected to the man's hedonistic choices; between a context of knowledge and that of decision. Although a heated debate, it seems to bypass the important role of the inductive and hypothetical deductive principles of statistics in the growth of knowledge; it seems to ignore the contribution of the statistical "modus operandi" in the progression of scientific thought, which tends more and more to make the statistical intuition of reality its own "modus intellegendi". Then it's a new paradigm: a statistical paradigm.

In a finalistic paradigm it is the future which, in a sense, "determines" both the present and the past; in the classical causal paradigm the past determines the present and the future; in the statistical paradigm each present is compatible with many "futures" and the link between what has been and what will be is mediated by chance: it is no possible to forecast the events, but only their probability. Therefore, looking for a mathematical law in a historical series (the aim of many statistical procedures) is like putting forward again Newton-Laplace's system, where the future is the image of the past. Yet, if future is thought to be innovative and non-univocally determined by the past - because "natura facit saltus" - the closer the model reproduces the past, the less it can pre-figure the future. The most intuitive example is the dynamical exponential divergence, from Poincaré's three-body problem to deterministic chaos of Lorenz. (Evocative theses are in *From being to becoming* (1978) by Ilia Prigogine and in *Chaotic evolution* (1987) by David Ruelle).

Statistical techniques and probabilistic models respond to conceptual paradigms which are not always resorted to by even the most careful manipulators of algorithms. The dominating factor is the search for a "generating model" of a historical series so that its process turns into an explicative formal tool which is inherent in it. Within a single "causal chain", the model of the past series maybe viewed as a way to predict the coming series; this is not true if one goes beyond those limits. Maybe the current distinction between short-term and long-term predictions accounts for an implicit acknowledgment of the existence of non-unlimited deterministic chains. One cannot even think of, always and in any way, drawing the parameters of the model from a long sequence of historical data. The longer the sequence, the more it is exposed to changes in the variables which can alter its explicative significance.

Once again we have to deal with the primary problems of understanding, which are at the origins of the statistical method and which, nowadays, we tend to forget, maybe because they are hidden behind a technicalism which prevents us from distinguishing the means from the end, knowledge from its tools. It is certainly inappropriate to look upon certain formal developments as to a way of concealing the void of ideas behind the veil of algorithmic embroidery; it is worth wondering what is the nature of the asserted non-determinism of certain techniques. Is it the indeterminism of individual events which is determinism in the large numbers? Is it the indeterminism of groups, that is the statistical indeterminism of processes? Is it indeterminism of non-linear dynamical systems and indeterminism of biological evolution, in which becoming may have an outcome external to any space of probabilized events?

In certain models the so-called "stochastic component" seems to lead the (predarwinian) view of external variability to the profoundest laws of nature. If one does not precisely define it, "stochastic" may become an ambiguous adjective: it cannot at the same time characterize the aleatory additive of a non-erratic variable, that is the accidental element of a process tending towards stabilization in the aggregates, and the phenomena which cannot be brought back to the stability of frequency and parameters by the determinism of large number. Adding to the variables of a model an accidental enigmatic component meant as a capricious variable which can impair their predictive capacity, is like postulating an "indeterminism" which is such only in that the precise value of all system coordinates are not know: once these unknown elements are no longer so, all uncertainties will become untrue. This is like going back to Laplace.

Maybe there is a certain resistance against indeterministic intuition because one rather tends to believe - from Einstein to Thom - that the values of probability conceal undeciphered causal laws and parameters, which, once unveiled, would cause phenomenology to become deterministic again as classical physics was (and as, after all, also relativistic physics is). In all empirical sciences, however, one finds a sort of statistic determinism juxtaposed to a more radical indeterminism which upsets collective equilibrium and plural regularities. Once they have got used to variability, the sciences of matter and life have given a non-contraddictory framework to necessity and accidentality paving the way to a new era of human thought and offering a universal methodological code; more than anything else, they reflect the premises of the distinction between anticipation of an experience and prediction of a future, between explanation of a law in facts and induction of facts which have not occurred, yet.

Certainly, natural sciences have drawn advantages from the setting up of large timeless system. We know the meaning of reexamining Linnaeus' system in the framework of the macroevolutionary process of becoming and also the meaning of seeing the historical plot of the universe stages in the star classification according to the spectrum (from red to white light). In the case of stars as well as human beings, knowledge steps forth through the systematic order of simultaneous processes and through the time genesis of phenomena. After Hubble's spectrum observations, the sky has a measurable history, as was the case with the living species, after Darwin's voyage. This is not the reason why astronomy has given up its deterministic laws and why evolutionistic genetics has given up translating its Darwinian and Mendelian assumptions into the "principle of allelic and genotypic equilibrium" (the so-called "theorem of Hardy-Weinberg": a fundamental probabilistic proposition).

In the sciences which have not become nomological systems, should the inductive anticipation of what will take place remain confined to operative and strategic activities? It does not seem so, as its aim is not that of reproducing a more or less near future, but rather that of "unwrapping" the present, of "explaining" the data of reality intended as becoming. As such, prediction may become almost a methodological canon of non-strictly experimental disciplines, with a view at "accelerating" the present by understanding its trends and contradictions. In non-natural sciences you can see statistic prediction as an observation in limit conditions, as a sort of accelerator. It is significant that one of the great thinkers in statistical interpretation of quantum mechanics, Werner Heisenberg, defined particle accelerators as "philosophical machines".

Prevision can be seen as an experiment of non-experimental sciences, as historicization of an assumption, as diachronic representation of the coordinates of reality. In human sciences, where it is even truer that prevision is anticipation of what is possible, the ontological premise of scientific tradition, the idea of a regular and structural reality, vanishes. Yet, the more reality seems to be disordered and accidental - which is not a limit of social phenomena only - the more it amounts to postulating forcedly isolated systems: a fictitious nomology smoothed out by aleatory components. However, no model will ever be capable of harnessing the unpredictable. In this view, if predictions with strategic and decision-making aims tend to come as close to future reality as possible, latter will eventually become true, scientific predictions have a different justification and their possible failure does not condemn them as theoretical choice: they expressed a kind of hypothetical statement of the type of "If A, then $B_1 \cup B_2 \cup ... \cup B_m$, with probability p_1, p_2, ..., p_m, respectively". And, if the expected consequent does not become true in reality, this means that the antecedent or the rational connection between antecedent and consequent should have been different; or, finally, it proves the occurrence of a new fact, of an amplified quantum jump.

Of course, if the statement accounts for a theoretical system in which the antecedent is made up of laws and the consequent is nothing but the hypothetical-deductive translation of that system (more or less complex and articulated but always liable to being proved) through a hypothesis which extends it to an unknown phenomenic setting. But, as the whole reality undergoes the process of becoming, each theory is a classification-abstraction, an experimental artefact, a conceptual theory which becomes explicit in a future of facts: the occurrence of predicted events is a stage in the empirical test of theory and the experimental confirmation of its scope of validity in space and time.

In this respect, prediction is the ideal configuration of a possible justification, of empirical trial which may even not become true, of the "per mentem" experiment followed by Bacon, or of the "Gedankenexperimente" which Einstein called "free inventions of human intelligence" and which are at the basis of science, from the principle of inertia to general relativity. The laws of science are therefore true for ideal phenomena and prediction - in the sense of an experiment - is idealization. This is true of the theories which are classified as abstract and independent of empirical evidence but, even more, for those which have found or still find their significance in facts. Their becoming explicit in a more or less circumscribed future always performs, however, an instrumental function: in terms of extension of the present aimed at identifying its variables, at unwinding its internal dynamics. A prediction which therefore has a value of its own, regardless of whether it becomes true. Since Hume understood the logic jump between experience and prediction, inductive inference cannot be asked to ensure success in any phenomenic setting, and even less so in sciences which are far from a nomothetic stage and in which the scope of validity of a law ends when becoming starts, when abstraction dissolves in history. Even more so in the case of social phenomenology.

The theme of recognizing scientific laws in the social framework bounces from Comte to Spencer, from Marx to Weber, from Pareto to Neurath, from von Mises to Hempel in the perspective of methodological unity between human and natural sciences. Hempel believes in the possibility of general laws in history, viewed as universal enunciation capable of connecting events in explicative and predictable models: enunciations in a universal conditional form which are to be compared with facts. Prediction - as was said - may have an explicative function rather than divinatory. The lack of universal abstracts does not role out, in the social framework, the "raison d'être" of the projective extrapolation of a reality not only as a technical fact but, even more, as a hypothesis consistent with an interpretation of reality.

15.7 Conclusions

When natural or social phenomenology is expressed by statistical laws, then the prevision becomes statistical inference. The Bayes-Laplace formula reflects the essential algorithm of inductive inference, the probabilistic scheme defining the semantic link between experience and reason: the formulation of a "final" probability from an initial one with a factor of likelihood. It reflects furthermore the role of "a priori" knowledge, showing its adaptability to the touchstone of experience. The history of scientific methodology is one with the long debate on the role of preliminary knowledge and pre-existing paradigms (whether theoretical systems, working hypotheses or preconceptions...): a radical rethinking of the dialectic relationship between reality and paradigm, empirical world and conceptual scheme, fact and fantasy, and a continual illusion regarding the possibility of an abstract codification of a heuristic relationship between theoretical scheme and empirical evidence. However, the relevance of general knowledge cannot help but be subject to change in keeping with historical transformations.

Almost alien to scientific thought, utilitarian and subjectivistic conceptions lead in their extremes to a managerial transposition of inductive inference: probability as a convenient gamble, statistical induction as the choice of the most profitable solution. The encounter between de Finetti's and Savage's subjectivism and Wald's decisionism gave rise to a transformation of statistics into a "managerial" form of mathematics, under the impulse of a utilitarian philosophy which regards an entire critical tradition as an immense prehistory.

Rather than offering actual rules, or a recipe to replace other recipes, the formula of inverse probability serves to demonstrate that facts win out over preliminary positions. It enables the emergence of statistical laws in large numbers, given that other alternatives are not a priori excluded: when, that is, the "a priori" unitary probability is not all attributed to a single hypothesis. Indeed, the mind of the species appears to be modeled by large numbers. This is an attitude produced by the experience of phylogenesis and ontogenesis, also liable to Hume's sceptical question which would be posed today in new terms: 'What rational foundation has the empirical regularity of large numbers?'

There is only one answer: chance; which is interpreted as objective indeterminacy, not only subjective uncertainty. It is difficult to say how much that is not rational is concealed by this enigmatic word, defined by Cassirer as a chameleon, always taking on new colors. There are those who (like Planck, Schroedinger, de Broglie, Einstein) consider chance to be a provisional convention while waiting to decipher "hidden variables" and others who (like Bohr, Heisenberg, Born, Pauli) view it as an intellectual "point of no return". But the "man of the abacus", like myself, looks to the most ancient and vivid definition: "Nothing which is due to chance occurs for something" - Aristotle said as much twenty four centuries ago.

However, he was far from any idea of an empirical pattern in the casual event, of an unsuspected natural order in the results of purposeless occurrences. Such an order was to make itself manifest to the author of "theorem H", when he observed the entropic time pattern of reversible and unpredictable molecular mechanics, within a superior thermodynamic regularity which was both predictable and irreversible. Boltzmann became convinced that "probabilistic hypotheses" reflect the "natural reality". After the decline of classic determinism, the scientist is left asking Poincaré's question if the chance is really any different thing from the name we give to our ignorance.

Yet, it is not the same thing to class prevision as a problem of logical induction or one of optimization; and neither can a scientist's conjecture be put in the same class as a gambling bet. We must also not ignore the alien nature of strategic thought to a scientific mode of thought: the former seeks the most useful solution, the latter, the most truthful; the former minimizes a function of loss, the latter admits no form of penalization except for a back tracking over hypotheses and evidence. Prevision may be a probable act, but this is no reason to reduce it to the terms of "Pascal's gamble" which proves it is always useful to believe in God: if he exists, to believe in him is highly advantageous; if he does not exist, nothing has been lost. Rather than a methodology of knowledge, this is an opportunist canon of a methodology of convenience in which utility has supremacy over truth, decision over induction.

Even should we choose to replace knowledge with decision, hypothesis with gamble, probable induction with strategic opportunity, we must ask ourselves whether it is the same to "play" with a nature which "chooses" once and for all or with a nature whose destiny is determined at the moment it is wrought, with no necessity in the emerging reality, it being just one of the many possible realities. After the darwinian *"Origin"* (1859) and the mendelian *"Versuche"* (1866), this becomes the intellectual (and moral) code of naturalistic knowledge, finding itself up against an evolving reality expressed by individual variability and the accidentality of the processes involved (*Le hasard et la nécessité* (1970) by Jacques Monod and *La logique du vivant* (1970) by François Jacob proves this argument).

Even in reducing a problem of inductive logic to one of optimization, we still have to adopt a canon with which to interpret phenomena as it is clearly not the same to bet on a necessary reality as it is to bet on a contingent reality: a reality which is, and might not have been. Once again, it is question of general hypotheses. We must draw a distinction between the uncertainty regarding an event, whose occurrence cannot be predicted exactly as not all the initial data are known, where probability is used due to a lack of information, and the state of uncertainty regarding a phenomenon, the occurrence of which is not implicit in the initial conditions, where unpredictability is immanent to the phenomenon itself: a reality which is variability, an immanence which becomes contingent.

Chapter 16

THE SCIENTIFIC TRAINING[*]

Maurice ALLAIS

Editor's Note: Professor Allais's contribution is a bit different than the other chapters, we will present it as he sent it.

16.1   Introduction

Defining the conditions of the scientific training is a vast and fundamental subject. While a thorough and complete analysis of that subject is impossible, a very brief analysis may be very useful. In this paper, I shall limit myself to defining what is the scientific mind and to stating a few fundamental principles which should be applied for the scientific training.

16.2   The Scientific Mind

How first can we define the scientific mind? What are the fundamental principles of the scientific process? What are the perversions of science which are all too often encountered?

16.2.1 What is science?

Model building

• The prerequisite for any science is the existence of *regularities* which can be analyzed and forecast.

Any science is based on models, and every model entails three distinct stages: starting with well specified hypotheses, deducing all the implications

---

[*] English translation of my paper *La Formation Scientifique* (the French text is available on request)

from these hypotheses and nothing but the implications, and confront the implications with observed data.

Of the three stages, only the first and the third – elaborating hypotheses, and confronting their implications with the observed data – are of interest for the analysis of reality. The second stage is purely logical and mathematical, that is tautological, and is only of mathematical interest.

• Abstraction plays an essential role in the elaboration of theories and their models. The role of science, in fact, is to simplify and to choose: to reduce facts to significant data and to seek their fundamental interdependencies.

Any science is a compromise between concern for simplification and concern for resemblance. Great simplicity is convenient, but carries the risk that the picture which emerges does not sufficiently resemble the facts; a more exact resemblance makes the model too complex and unusable in practice.

Creative intuition

In developing a science, i.e., in constructing the theories and the models which represent them, *creative intuition is always the factor which plays the determining role*. It is this intuition which, on the basis of existing knowledge, generates *the selection of the concepts* and of the relations between these concepts which makes it possible to represent the essential features of reality.

The observation of facts

Mere logical, or even mathematical deduction, remains worthless in terms of the understanding of reality if it is not clearly linked to reality.

Submission to experimental data is the golden rule which dominates any scientific discipline. This rule is the same in all sciences. No theory whatever can be accepted unless it is verified by empirical evidence.

The use of mathematics

As a tool for testing the logical coherence of a theory and bringing out its essential significance when the phenomena under consideration are bound together by fairly complex relationships, mathematics is irreplaceable.

The inestimable advantage of a mathematical formulation is that it requires from the mind both, reflection and precision. It provides a tool for discovering *all the consequences of the assumptions made, and those consequences only*, and therefore for bringing their effective content to light.

Nevertheless, every author who uses mathematics *should always apply himself to express in plain language* the meaning of the assumptions and results he obtains. *The more abstract the theory, the more imperative this obligation.*

In fact, mathematics is only a tool to explore reality. *In this exploration, mathematics cannot be an end in itself. It is and should only be a means.*

16.2.2 The fundamental principles of a scientific process

What are the fundamental principles of the scientific process? At least three seem essential: unconditional submission to the observed data, an indispensable critical mind, and a clear understanding of the nature of theory.

Unconditional submission to observed facts

The first principle of the scientific process is that of *an absolute predominance of observed facts over theoretical analyses.*

Observed facts are the only ones which have physical reality, and true physical reality only rests on experimental results. According to a famous statement: *"Experience is the only source of truth; it is the only one that can teach us something new; it alone can give us certainty".*

Only concrete phenomena can decide whether a theory should be accepted or rejected. There are no other criteria of the truth of a theory other than its more or less perfect agreement with reality. Too many theoreticians too often tend to neglect those facts which contradict their convictions.

An indispensable critical mind

The second principle of a scientific process is *an indispensable critical mind.*

The distinctive feature of error is the belief in being true, and the one who makes a mistake, is making a double mistake: he makes a mistake, and he does not know that he is making a mistake. The stronger our beliefs the more we must be convinced of the relativity of our beliefs, and the more we must be ready to accept opinions that differ from ours.

In science the notion of *"truth"* is, in fact, very relative. No theory or model can claim to represent *"absolute truth"* and, if such truth exists, it will certainly always remain inaccessible to us. There are only models which are more or less well verified by observed data.

The history of physics shows that the same facts can be explained by completely different theories. Therefore, *the empirical verification of a theory, at a given time, cannot prove its definitive validity.*

Understanding the real nature of theories: the fallacious opposition between theory and practice.

The third principle of a scientific process is *a clear understanding of the nature of theories.*

A contrast is often made between theory and practice, in such statements as "theory is one thing, practice another", or "theory by reason of its very abstraction, is remote from reality".

Such opposition is completely unjustified, for *a theory is valid only insofar as it provides a condensed representation of reality.* A theory that does not do this is a pure figment of the imagination, an artificial creation which, from a scientific point of view, has no value at all. If, on the contrary, a theory does provide an effectively condensed representation of reality, it is extremely useful, for it reduces a mass of information of all kinds about the observed phenomena into a concentrated and easily usable form.

16.2.3 The negation of the scientific mind: the perversions of science

In fact two perversions have constantly hampered the development of science; the abuse of mathematics and the dogmatic tyranny of "established truths".

The abuse of mathematics

Firstly, in any science, the rigor of the deductions of mathematicians should not lead to any illusions.

When reading certain papers, one can only be struck by the growing abuse of mathematical formalism. There is a tendency to forget that *true progress never lies in purely formal exposition; it is always to be found in the guiding ideas which underlie any theory.* First and foremost, these ideas must be made explicit and discussed, instead of sealing them up behind a more or less hermetic veil of symbols.

In fact, in all disciplines, the contemporary literature presents innumerable examples of the aberrations which can result from the neglect of the fundamental principle that a theory is valid only to the extent that it agrees with observed facts, and that *the only source or truth is experience.*

The dogmatism and tyranny of "established truths"

The history of science shows that new ideas have always been fought against and rejected by the tyrannical power of *"established truths"*. At any time, narrow, intolerant dogmatism has never stopped to undermine the progress of science, opposing the revision of the postulates of accepted theories when new facts have invalidated them. One could very well say that *the history of science boils down to the history of the errors of "competent" men.*

Universal consensus, and *a fortiori* that of a majority, can never be considered as a valid criterion for truth. *In the final analysis, the essential condition for progress in science is a complete submission to the teaching of experience, the only real source of knowledge.* There is not, and there cannot be, any other test of the truth of a theory than its more or lest perfect conformity with concrete phenomena.

In fact, sooner or later, the facts finally prevail over the theories which deny their existence. Science is in perpetual transformation. It invariably sweeps away *"established truths"*. And it is the future which finally judges works and men.

16.3 The Acquisition of The Scientific Mind

If we consider what does constitute the scientific mind, what should be the *most appropriate* form of teaching for the young to acquire the scientific mind?

Six conditions at least should be met: - teaching always based on the concrete; - teaching always based on general views; - teaching always based on critical analyses; - teaching of mathematics always considered as a tool; - teaching always based on an active participation; - teaching always decentralized and always founded on selection.

16.3.1 Teaching based on the concrete

• Teaching must be based on the concrete. Abstraction is undoubtedly necessary, but it can be justified only as far as it rests on the concrete and prepares the explanation of phenomena and their uses.

For example, classical mechanics is taught on the basis of innumerable theoretical calculations but only a derisory part is devoted to fundamental experiments supporting the general principles of mechanics.

In fact, any course on classical mechanics *ought to start by commenting on some basic experiments* such as those of the spinning-top or on Foucault's pendulum. It is said that in 1560 during an eclipse of the sun, Tycho Brahe, aged fourteen, was stunned by the accuracy by which the ephemeredes had announced the event and that it was that which determined his vocation as an astronomer.

• What is valid for teaching at the college or university level is equally valid for secondary and elementary education. *Teaching must start from the concrete and lead to the concrete.*

16.3.2 Indispensable overviews

To be efficient, any teaching must be accompanied by overviews, giving the main guiding lines of the subject, its historical development and its link with the general principles of the philosophy of sciences.

In any form of teaching, the guiding principles and general ideas are the most difficult to grasp. But the general ideas and principles are the most important for a full comprehension of the questions to be dealt with. Nevertheless, they are too often neglected.

16.3.3 The need for critical analyses

• All teaching must also be accompanied by critical analyses on the significance and scope of the experiments and corresponding models and theories.

What is essential in all teaching is a thorough discussion of the primary hypotheses, comments on the methods of the resolution, interpretation of the results, an understanding of the orders of magnitude, and examples of application.

• At higher levels of education, considerable attention should be given to discussing facts which are contradictory with or unexplained by accepted theories.

Too often, teaching takes on a dogmatic and definitive form. There is nothing more contrary to the scientific mind, nothing more opposed to scientific progress than this reduction of science to dogmatic teaching.

• Let us consider, for example, the Newtonian theory of universal gravitation which has been extraordinarily verified through the centuries. However, it is based on hypotheses, of which at least one is false, *that of the instantaneous transmission of attracting forces at a distance without any intermediary medium.* As a matter of fact, the falsity of this hypothesis is not really discussed in the works of classical mechanics. *It has always remained insufficiently analyzed.*

16.3.4 The teaching of mathematics directed towards applications

• In fact, the teaching of mathematics always tends to be too abstract, and geared to training pure mathematicians. However, for most students, its prime objective should be to prepare their minds for its understanding and use, which is quite different.

• Naturally, the teaching of mathematics must be governed by great intellectual rigor, but such rigor must be focus essentially on understanding the meaning of hypotheses and the interpretation of results. It must never be a pretext for doing mathematics for its own sake.

Mathematics must be taught in such a way as to be seen as a useful tool for exploring reality. Its purpose should primarily be a very clear understanding of *the link that can be established between the abstraction and the reality thanks to mathematics.*

16.3.5 Teaching with the active participation of students

Necessary dialogue

Teaching cannot be efficient if it is not accompanied by written texts. Classwork should be used primarily to comment on these written texts and to exchange views with the students.

In point of fact, the only real advantage of oral teaching is the presence of a teacher who can answer the students' questions and comment on the difficulties of the questions dealt with.

If students are to be trained efficiently, what really matters is the ability of the teacher much more than the content of the course; it is not so much what is taught but how it is taught.

Preparation for ulterior personal work

The main object of all teaching is to prepare students to be capable of analyzing efficiently and thoroughly any questions that may arise during their professional careers.

For that purpose, teaching must give priority to intuitive and creative analyses of experimental results. But at the same time it should help students to be able to work in the future on any question in a rigorous and deep manner, and to make effective use of any study, even at a very high level.

Too often students are not taught how to organize their personal work efficiently. However, this is one of the most needed and useful things that can be taught.

16.3.6 Teaching based on decentralization and selection

Necessary decentralization

Scientific training *must be decentralized* everywhere.

Only decentralization, i.e. the granting of complete academic autonomy, can stimulate high standards of teaching and research, and thus, scientific training. Developing diversity, not uniformity, can ensure scientific training of a high standard.

Indispensable selection

Scientific training of a high standard requires being very selective in choosing students as well as teachers.

To provide scientific education to the masses while attempting to maintain high standards is not an achievable goal. The outcome of such an objective will only be a mediocre level in the average standard of the students and academic staff alike.

Indeed, to refuse selection can only compromise the promotion of the elites from all social backgrounds; therefore to refuse selection is fundamentally anti-democratic.

Those are the conditions that I consider essential for scientific training. If we ignore them, we can only undermine the progress of science and the training of all those who must secure its future.

REFERENCES

1954 *Puissance et dangers de l'outil mathématique en économique*
Econometrica, 22 (1), pp. 58-71.

1967 *L'Economique en tant que science*
Collection of studies of the "Institut Universitaire de Hautes Etudes Internationales", Genève, 1968, n° 6, 26 p.
and Revue d'Economie Politique, January 1968, pp. 5-30.
   English translation:
Economics as a Science
Collection of studies of the "Institut Universitaire de Hautes Etudes Internationales", Geneva, n° 7, 24 p.
and Cahiers Vilfredo Pareto, 1968, pp. 5-24.

1988 *Les lignes directrices de mon œuvre*
Nobel Lecture, 9 décembre 1988, Nobel Foundation, Les Prix Nobel 1988, pp. 357-371.
   English translation:
An Outline of my Main Contributions to Economic Science
Nobel Foundation, *The Nobel Prizes 1988*, pp. 372-391.
and The American Economic Review, December 1997, Vol. 87, n° 6, pp. 3-12.

1989 *La Philosophie de ma Vie*
Revue d'Economie Politique, Vol. 99 (1), pp. 28-54.
   English translation:
My Life Philosophy
The American Economist, Vol. XXIII, n° 2, pp. 3-17.

1989 *Autoportraits. Une vie, une œuvre*
Paris, Montchrestien, 150 p.

Chapter 17

A FAMILY OF MULTIDIMENSIONAL POVERTY MEASURES

François Bourguignon
EHESS and DELTA (Joint research unit CNRS-EHESS-ENS), Paris, France

Satya R. Chakravarty
Indian Statistical Institute, Calcutta, India

17.1   Introduction

Removal of poverty has been and continues to be one of the primary aims of economic policy in many countries. Two important questions that arise in this context are: What exactly do we mean by poverty? In what sense do we say that poverty of a nation has increased or decreased over a certain time period? The first question addresses the problem of 'perception of poverty'. The second question deals with 'measurement of poverty'. In this paper we are interested in the measurement aspect of poverty. Since the efficacy of an antipoverty policy is evaluated by observing changes in the level of poverty, the way poverty is measured is important both for an understanding of poverty and for policy applications.

Evidently, the problem of poverty arises from insufficiency in quantities of different basic needs or attributes that are necessary to maintain a subsistence standard of living. Examples of such basic needs are housing, literacy, health, income, and so on. In other words, we say that poverty is a multifaceted phenomenon and insufficient income is just one indicator of poverty. In fact, use of inadequate income as the sole indicator of poverty may be quite misleading. A number of goods have no market prices (for instance, we can think of supply of pure drinking water) and therefore cannot be evaluated in terms of income. But even when evaluation at market prices is possible, the condition that a person is non-poor with respect to income does not ensure that his consumption of different attributes are at or above thresholds in terms of subsistence. This suggests that poverty should be viewed multidimensionally as the failure to reach 'minimally acceptable' or subsistence levels of different income as well as non-income attributes of well-being, e.g. indicators of distribution of per capita expenditure on all market goods and services, indicators of access to non-market attributes such as health services, and indicators of intrahousehold distribution such as child nutritional status (see Ravallion, 1996)[1].

It should be noted that the poverty thresholds or subsistence levels of different indicators are determined independently of the distributions. In this sense the notion of poverty measurement we adopt in this paper is of *absolute* type and departs from the concept of 'social disutility' from poverty or 'loss function' that C. Dagum introduced in the inequality measurement literature - see Dagum (1990, 1995). When it is defined in the single dimension of income or expenditure, poverty may be defined in relative terms, for instance, by defining the poverty limit relatively to some quantile of the distribution in the whole population. Such a definition would be consistent with Dagum's idea of considering the social evaluation of individual welfare as depending on both absolute income and rank in the whole income hierarchy. In a multidimensional context, however, defining such a relative poverty or welfare position of a person becomes problematic because of the multiplicity of viewpoints which may be taken for definitional purpose.

While the research on single dimensional, more precisely, on income based poverty measurement, has flourished in the last two decades [2], the multidimensional poverty measurement remains an important area to be explored. The purpose of this paper is to suggest a family of multidimensional measures of poverty. The suggested family generalizes the single dimensional, subgroup decomposable Foster-Greer-Thorbecke (1984) class of poverty measures by incorporating the elasticity of substitution between relative shortfalls of attributes from respective subsistence quantities. Thus, our measures explicitly take into account the notion of substitutability among attributes, an important issue associated with multivariate measurement. More general issues associated with the measurement of multidimensional poverty are considered in Bourguignon and Chakravarty (1998).

The paper is organized as follows. The next section discusses the problem of identifying the set of poor. Section 3 suggests the properties that should be fulfilled by a measure of multidimensional poverty obtained by aggregating the

---

[1]Ravallion (1996) and Bourguignon and Chakravarty (1998) provide further rationales for viewing poverty in a multidimensional framework.
[2]See Zheng (1997), for a recent review of income based poverty measures.

characteristics of the poor. Section 4 presents the family of measures and section 5 concludes.

17.2 Identification of the Poor

As Sen (1976) pointed out, there are two stages in the construction of a poverty measure. The first step is to identify or to count the number of poor. In the case of income-based poverty measures, the counting problem involves the specification of a threshold income level, referred to as the poverty line. A person is called poor if his income falls below the threshold level. Thus, the poverty line is a line of demarcation in the sense that it distinguishes the group of poor people from the rest of the population. Once the identification problem is solved, the second step is to aggregate the information available on the poor into an overall indicator of poverty.

Since we deviate in this paper from income based measurement and adopt a multidimensional approach, the identification problem is also of mutidimensional nature. For simplicity of exposition, we assume that there are only two attributes, 1 and 2. For instance, attribute 1 can be life expectancy and attribute 2 can be a composite good reflecting all other basic needs of life. However, the formal discussion easily generalizes to more than two-attribute case.

Now, in a population of size n, the ith person possesses a 2-vector of attributes $(x_{i1}, x_{i2}) = x_i \in R^2_+$, the non-negative part of the 2-dimensional Euclidean space. The vector x_i is the ith row of an $n \times 2$ matrix $X \in M^n$, where M^n is the set of all $n \times 2$ matrices whose elements are non-negative real numbers. We regard each individual as a separate entity and can therefore assume that x_i's are independent. Let $M = M^n$, $n \in N$ where N is the set of natural numbers.

In the multidimensional framework, instead of setting a poverty line, a threshold level is determined for each attribute. These levels represent minimal quantities of the two basic needs necessary for a subsistence standard of living. Let $z = (z_1, z_2) \in Z$ be a vector of thresholds, where Z is a nonempty subset of the positive part of R^2_+.

In this two-attribute structure, person i is certainly poor if $x_{ij} < z_j$ for j=1,2. Since in this case person i's quantities of both the attributes fall below corresponding thresholds, we refer to the associated attribute space, which is a subset of R^2_+, as the 'two-dimensional poverty area' (TDPA). Now, it may be the case that person i has one attribute, say life expectancy, above its threshold but the other attribute, say income, is below the corresponding threshold. Evidently, this person cannot be regarded as rich because of his longevity. We will therefore say that person i is poor if $x_{ij} < z_j$ for at least one j. On the other hand, person i is nonpoor if $x_{ij} \geq z_j$ for all j. It is supposed that any attribute matrix $X \in M$ can be written as $X = (X^P, X^r)$, where $X^P(X^r)$ is the attribute matrix of the poor (rich). This should be possible by a simple rearrangement of the rows of X.

For any $X \in M$, we denote the corresponding population size by n(X) (or n) and the number of persons who are poor with respect to attribute j by $q_j(X)$ (or, q_j). The attribute space corresponding to the set of persons who are poor in terms of one attribute only will be called 'single dimensional poverty area' (SPDA). Let S_1 and S_2 be these two regions. Adding together the number of poor in these two areas $(q = q_1 + q_2)$ for calculating the total number of poor would clearly lead to double counting. Bourguignon and Chakravarty (1998) suggested a more sophisticated way of obtaining the number of poor in the multiattribute structure that avoids this double-counting problem.

17.3   Properties for a Measure of Poverty

A multidimensional poverty index is a function $P : M \times Z \to R^1$. Given any $X \in M$ and $z \in Z$, P(X ; z) indicates the degree of poverty intensity associated with the basic need matrix X and subsistence levels z. Therefore, for a given poverty measure and vector of thresholds, each basic need matrix is assigned a numerical number, or poverty value.

The functional form of a poverty index depends to a large extent on how we view poverty. One needs to specify the purpose of measurement and then find a suitable measure within the corresponding framework. The axiomatic approach adopted by Sen (1976) fits this structure. He observed that the two well-known income based measures, the head count ratio (proportion of population below the poverty line) and the income gap ratio (proportionate gap between the poverty line and the average income of the poor) remains invariant under a redistribution of income among the poor and the former is also insensitive to monotonic changes of a poor person's income. He argued that poverty measurement should consider distributional sensitivity in addition to counting the number of poor and calculating their average income gap.

The two axioms suggested by Sen for an income based poverty measure are (i) the monotonicity axiom, which requires poverty to increase if there is a reduction in the income of a poor, and (ii) the transfer axiom, which demands that poverty should increase under a transfer of income from a poor person to anyone who is richer. Following Sen, many additional axioms and variants of the two above axioms have been proposed in the literature (See, for example, Foster, Greer and Thorbecke, 1984; Donaldson and Weymark, 1986; Chakravarty, 1990; Foster and Shorrocks, 1991; and Bourguignon and Fields, 1997).

The properties we suggest below for a two-dimensional poverty index P are straight generalizations of different postulates proposed for an income based index.
- **Weak Focus (WF)**: For any $X \in M$, $z \in Z$, P does not depend on x_{ij} if $x_{ij} \geq z_j$ for $j=1,2$.
- **Strong Focus (SF)**: For any $X \in M$, $z \in Z$, if person i is in S_1 (S_2) but not in $S_2(S_1)$, then P should not depend on $x_{i2}(x_{i1})$.
- **Monotonicity (MN)**: For any given $X \in M$, $z \in Z$, if $x_{ij} < z_j$, then an increase in x_{ij} should not increase P, where i and j are arbitrary.
- **Continuity (CN)**: For any $z \in Z$, P is continuous on M.
- **Principle of Population (PP)**: For any $X \in M$, $z \in Z$, $P(X ; z) = P(X^1, X^2..., X^k ; z)$ where each $X^i = X$, i=1, 2,..., k and $k \geq 2$ is arbitrary.
- **Symmetry (SM)**: for any $X \in M$, $z \in Z$, any reordering of the rows of X does not change P.
partitioned into $m \geq 2$ subgroups so that $X = (X^1, X^2,..., X^m)$, then
- **Subgroup Decomposability (SD)**: For any $n \in N$, $X \in M^n$, $z \in Z$, if the population is

$$P(X ; z) = \sum_{i=1}^{m} \frac{n_i}{n} P(X^i ; z),$$

where X^i is the attribute matrix of subgroup i and n_i is its population size.

Before we suggest further properties for a multidimensional poverty measure, let us discuss the ones considered above. Note that the efficiency and justification of the axioms for a measure of a poverty are quite important since various axioms are used to construct and evaluate poverty measures. WF requires poverty measures to be independent of basic need levels of nonpoor. If we view poverty as deprivation of the poor in terms of shortfalls of basic need quantities from respective thresholds, then this axiom is quite appropriate. Evidently, WF does not rule out the possibility that the number of nonpoor (and therefore total population size) is relevant to the measurement of poverty. According to SF if person i is poor with respect to one attribute say, life expectancy, but rich with respect to the other (a composite good), then the poverty index does not depend on the composite good of this person. Thus, this axiom implicitly assumes that the composite good cannot be traded off for life expectancy in the single dimensional poverty area associated with life expectancy. This is equivalent to assuming some complementarity between the two attributes. More or less of the composite good above the threshold is of no use if life expectancy is below its own threshold. Note, however, that this does not rule out substitutability when *both* attributes are below their thresholds. A complete discussion of this point is provided in Bourguignon and Chakravarty (1998).

The next axiom is quite appealing. Other things being given, an increase in the quantity of an attribute of a poor should not increase poverty. This axiom as well implies that if there is a reduction in an attribute level of such a person, then poverty should not decrease. Since under monotonicity the benefeciary may become rich with respect to the attribute considered, it should be clear that axioms SF and MN imply WF.

Basic need data are often subject to observational errors. It is reasonable to expect that such errors will not generate an abrupt jump in the numerical value of the poverty index. Continuity takes care of this.

The Principle of Population (PP) demands that if a basic need matrix is pooled several times, then poverty of the pooled matrix is the same as that of the original matrix. Thus, technically this axiom means that the poverty index is expressed as an average function. Now, given that any two different-sized basic need matrices can be replicated to the same size, we can compare their poverty. Therefore, PP is helpful for intercountry comparisons of poverty and also for intertemporal poverty comparisons of the same population.

According to symmetry any rearrangement of the rows of the basic need matrix does not change poverty. Since the rows represent basic need quantities of different individuals, under symmetry any characteristic other than these quantities, e.g., names of the individuals, is irrelevant to the measurement of poverty.

The subgroup decomposability axiom is quite attractive from a policy point of view. This axiom says that given a partitioning of the population into different subgroups with respect to some homoneneous characteristic - age, sex, race, region, religion etc.- the overall poverty is the population share weighted average of subgroup poverty levels. The contribution of subgroup i to total poverty is $n_i P(X^i ; z)/n$ and this is precisely the amount by which national poverty will reduce if poverty in the subgroup is eliminated. $100 \, n_i \, P(X^i ; z)/n \, P(X ; z)$ is subgroup i's percentage contribution to total poverty. Thus, axiom SD enables us to identify the subgroups that are most susceptible to poverty and to implement efficient antipoverty policies. We, however, note that this notion of policy prescription is contingent on the implicit valuation of the poverty index.

Clearly, using SD, we can write $P(X ; z)$ as

$$\frac{1}{n} \sum_{i=1}^{n} P(x_i ; z).$$ (17.1)

Since $P(x_i ; z)$ depends only on person i's attribute levels, we can interpret it as individual poverty function.

While the properties suggested above are easy generalizations of a desiderata for a single dimentional poverty measure, the next postulate, which deals with redistribution of attributes, is somewhat less straightforward.

- **Multidimensional Transfers Principle (MT)**: For any $z \in Z$, X, $Y \in M$, if $X^p = BY^p$, where $B = (b_{ij})$ is some bistochastic matrix and BY^p is not a permutation of the rows of Y^p, then the poverty level associated with X is not higher than that associated with Y, that is, $P(X ; z) \leq P(Y ; z)$.

This multidimensional transfers principle is concerned with equity of attributes among the poor. Intuitively, it says that it is possible to go from Y^p to X^p by some equalizing operation so that the distribution of attributes under X^p becomes less concentrated, that is, more equal than that under Y^p. MT implies that each row of X^p is an average, that is, a linear convex combination, of the rows of Y^p. Given SD, MT holds if and only if the individual poverty function is convex (Kolm, 1977).

We will now consider an important property which is apparently of less importance in characterizing multidimensional poverty measures but of very much practical importance. It is that of correlation between attributes and the way it affects poverty. In order to understand this, let us consider, for simplicity, the two-person two-attribute case, where $x_{ij} < z_j$ for i, j = 1,2. Suppose that initially $x_{11} > x_{21}$ but $x_{12} < x_{22}$. Now, consider a switch of attribute 1 between the two persons, that is, after the switch person 1 gets x_{21} and person 2 gets x_{11} units of attribute 1. Thus, person 2, who had more of attribute 2, has now more of attribute 1 also, and as a result correlation between the attributes has gone up. Evidently, poverty should increase or decrease under a correlation increasing switch according to whether the two attributes display similar or different aspects of poverty, that is, whether they are substitutes of complements (Atkinson and Bourguignon, 1982, and Bourguignon and Chakravarty, 1998). We state this principle formally for substitutes as:

- **Nondecreasing Poverty under Correlation Augmenting Switch (NDP)**: For any $z \in Z$, $X \in M$, if $Y \in M$ is obtained from X by a correlation increasing switch of an attribute between two poor, then $P(X ; z) \leq P(Y ; z)$, if the attributes involved in the switch are substitutes. The corresponding property that demands nonincreasingness of poverty under such a switch, when the attributes are complements, is denoted by NIP.

Since in view of NDP or NIP, we want attributes to be substitutes or complements, the poverty index should incorporate a parameter to reflect this. This is captured by the following postulate.

- **Constant Elasticity of Substitution of Shortfalls (CS)**: For any individual i, the elasticity of substitution between the relative shortfalls of the basic needs from the corresponding thresholds is a constant.

The consideration of the elasticity of substitution between proportionate gaps of the two basic needs from respective thresholds shows that there is some degree of substitutability between the attributes for any person. This is quite a standard assumption about a person's behaviour in a multi-attribute set up. The constancy of the elasticity will cover a very wide class of measures. It must be noted, however, that CS is not equivalent to assuming a constant elasticity of substitution between attributes. We shall see that the reason behind CS is essentially analytical convenience. Note also that, taken together with SF, CS should apply only to the TDPA.

17.4   The Family of Poverty Measures

We now examine a family of poverty measures which satisfy most of the preceding properties while being roughly homogeneous in the well-known Foster-Greer-Thorbecke measure.

First, in order to use CS let us define the following CES type aggregator function of the shortfalls of the two attributes:

$$A(x_i; z, \beta, B) = \left[\left(1 - \frac{x_{i1}}{z_1} \right)^\beta + B \left(1 - \frac{x_{i2}}{z_2} \right)^\beta \right]^{1/\beta}$$

where β and B are positive constants. This basic transformation essentially aggregates two individual shortfalls into a single linearly homogeneous shortfall which, up to the β-power function and up to a constant, is simply a weighted average of them. If we denote this 'aggregate' shortfall by $(1-y_i)$, then it is simply defined by:

$$(1-y_i)^\beta = \frac{(1-x_{i1}/z_1)^\beta + B.(1-x_{i2}/z_2)^\beta}{1+B}$$

Of course, this aggregation can only work in the TDPA where there may be some trade-off between the two attributes.

If we now combine this aggregate shortfall for the poor in the TDPA using the same functional as employed by Foster-Greer-Thorbecke in the case of (single-dimensional) income poverty, we obtain after a suitable redefinition of the constant B:

$$P(x_i; z, \alpha, \beta, b) = (1-y_i)^\alpha = \left[\left(1-\frac{x_{i1}}{z_1}\right)^\beta + b^{\beta/\alpha}\left(1-\frac{x_{i2}}{z_2}\right)^\beta \right]^{\alpha/\beta}$$

(17.2)

$$x_{i1} < z_1, x_{i2} < z_2.$$

$$P(x_i; z, \alpha, \beta, b) = \left(1-\frac{x_{i1}}{z_1}\right)^\alpha \quad, \quad x_{i1} < z_1, x_{i2} \geq z_2,$$

(17.3)

$$= b\left(1-\frac{x_{i2}}{z_2}\right)^\alpha \quad, \quad x_{i1} \geq z_1, x_{i2} < z_2,$$

where the positive parameter α can be interpreted as in the single-dimensional case as the aversion of society against poverty. The continuous extension of P in (2) to SDPAs (under SF) is simply:
so that the general expression of the family of two dimension poverty measures

$$P(X; z, \alpha, \beta, b) = \frac{1}{n}\sum_i \begin{cases} \left(1-\frac{x_{i1}}{z_1}\right)^\alpha &, \quad x_{i1} < z_1, x_{i2} \geq z_2 \\\\ \left[\left(1-\frac{x_{i1}}{z_1}\right)^\beta + b^{\beta/\alpha}\left(1-\frac{x_{i2}}{z_2}\right)^\beta\right]^{\alpha/\beta} &, \quad x_{i1} < z_1, x_{i2} < z_2 \\\\ b\left(1-\frac{x_{i2}}{z_2}\right)^\alpha &, \quad x_{i1} \geq z_1, x_{i2} < z_2. \end{cases}$$

(17.4)

In this expression, aversion toward poverty, α is assumed to be greater than or equal to unity to guarantee that the individual poverty function is convex and hence fulfils MT in SDPAs. Given $\alpha \geq 1$ we need $\beta \geq 1$ for MT to hold in TDPA. The parameter β represents curvature of the isopoverty contour in TDPA and is therefore related to the trade-off between attributes -see figure 1. For any finite $\beta \geq 1$, the isopoverty contours are convex to the origin. Given other things, an increase in the value of β makes the contours more convex. The elasticity of substitution between relative shortfalls corresponding to two attributes is $1/(\beta - 1)$. Finally, $b > 0$ reflects the importance attached to the poverty associated with attribute 2 relative to that attached to attribute 1. Evidently, 2 gets more, equal or less weight according as $b \gtrless 1$.

$$P(X; z, \alpha, 1, b) = \frac{1}{n} \sum_i \begin{cases} \left(1 - \frac{x_{i1}}{z_1}\right)^\alpha, & x_{i1} < z_1, \ x_{i2} \geq z_2 \\ \\ \left[\left(1 - \frac{x_{i1}}{z_1}\right) + b^{1/\alpha}\left(1 - \frac{x_{i2}}{z_2}\right)\right]^\alpha, & x_{i1} < z_1, \ x_{i2} < z_2 \\ \\ b\left(1 - \frac{x_{i2}}{z_2}\right)^\alpha, & x_{i1} \geq z_1, \ x_{i2} < z_2 \end{cases} \qquad (17.5)$$

The first and third expressions in (4) are the Foster-Greer-Thorbecke (FGT) indices in the two SDPAs. Therefore, our suggested family appears as a straight generalization of the single dimensional FGT index to the bivariate case. While the FGT function entails only one parameter α, the generalized family involves two additional parameters β and b. In the case where $\beta = 1$, there is perfectly elastic trade-off in TDPA and the overall poverty index becomes

For any $\beta \in [1, 2]$, the two attributes and/or shortfalls are substitutes and measures in (4) satisfy NDP. On the contrary, they satisfy NIP if $\beta \in [2, \infty]$ since the two attributes are then complements.

$$P(x; z, \alpha, \infty, b) = \frac{1}{n} \sum_i \left[1 - \min\left(1, \frac{x_{i1}}{z_1}, \frac{x_{i2}}{z_2}\right)\right]^\alpha \qquad (17.6)$$

$$= \frac{1}{n} \sum_i \left[\max\left(0, 1 - \frac{x_{i1}}{z_1}, 1 - \frac{x_{i2}}{z_2}\right)\right]^\alpha \qquad (17.7)$$

In the extreme case when $\beta \to \infty$, the resulting poverty index is given by

FIGURE 17.1:
Shape of the iso-poverty contours of meas

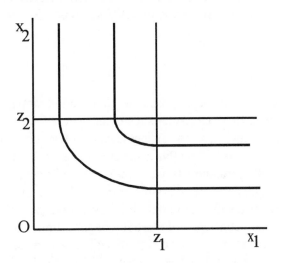

Thus, in this perfect complementarity situation the poverty index simply aggregates the maximum of relative shortfalls of different persons. The extreme parsimony of this index should be observed. It only needs information about threshold levels, quantities of different attributes, and, of course, poverty aversion. This index, which has a rectangular isopoverty contour, satisfies NIP.

The family of measures P in (4), and hence its particular cases (5) and (6), are (strongly) focussed, monotonic, symmetric, population replication invariant and bounded between zero and one, where the lower bound is achieved if there is no poor person in the society. On the other hand, the family reaches its upper bound if nobody possesses a positive quantity of any attribute, that is, $x_{ij} = 0$ for all i, j. Further, it satisfies a scale invariance condition also - when all quantities of an attribute, as well as its threshold level, are multiplied by a positive scalar, poverty remains unchanged.

In one of the very few articles dealing with multidimensional poverty measurement, Tsui (1994) suggested a poverty index that involves unit constant elasticity of substitution between attribute quantities, actually aggregating attributes into a scalar through a Cobb-Douglas transformation and defining single dimensional poverty measures on that scalar. The aggregation in our case is less simple because: a) it distinguishes between TDPA and SDPAs; b) constant elasticity is not necessarily equal to one; c) constant elasticity is defined between shortfalls rather than attributes. The latter choice is justified by observing that, constant elasticity different from one between attribute levels makes a continuous extension of the underlying measure from TDPA to SDPAs impossible.

17.5   Conclusions

In income based poverty measurement it is assumed that the individuals in a society are identical with respect to all characteristics other than income. But in addition to low income, a person may have insufficient levels of other attributes of life, e.g., literacy or health care. Consequently, a genuine measure of poverty should include monetary as well as nonmonetary indicators of well-being. In this paper, for simplicity, we consider the two-variable framework and provide a detailed discussion of the properties that an underlying poverty measure should fulfill. A family of measures using constancy of elasticity of substitution between proportional shortfalls of attributes from respective thresholds, which represent subsistence quantities of the attributes, has been suggested. Examination of the properties of this general family and its various limiting cases has been made in detail.

REFERENCES

[1] Atkinson, A.B., and F. Bourguignon (1982), The Comparison of Multidimensioned Distributions of Economic Status, *Review of Economic Studies*, 49, 183-201.

[2] Bourguignon, F., and S.R. Chakravarty (1998), The Measurement of Multidimensional Poverty, Mimeographed, DELTA, Paris.

[3] Bourguignon, F., and G.S. Fields (1997), Discontinuous Losses from Poverty, Generalized $P_\square$ Measures, and Optimal Transfers to the Poor, *Journal of Public Economics*, 63, 2, 155-175.

[4] Chakravarty, S.R. (1990), *Ethical Social Index Numbers*, Springer-Verlag, London.

[5] Dagum, C. (1990), Relationship Between Income Inequality Measures and Social Welfare Functions, *Journal of Econometrics*, 43, 1-2, 91-102

[6] Dagum, C. (1995), Income Inequality Measures and Social Welfare Functions: a Unified Approach, in C. Dagum and A. Lemmi (Eds), *Income Distribution, Social Welfare, Inequality and Poverty*, JAI Press, London, England

[7] Donaldson, D., and J.A. Weymark (1986), Properties of Fixed Population Poverty Indices, *International Economic Review*, 27, 667-668.

[8] Foster, J.E., J. Greer and E. Thorbecke (1984), A Class of Decomposable Poverty Measures, *Econometrica*, 52, 761-766.

[9] Foster, J.E., and A.F. Shorrocks (1991), Subgroup Consistent Poverty Indices, *Econometrica*, 59, 687-709.

[10] Kolm, S.C. (1977), Multidimensional Egalitarianisms, *Quarterly Journal of Economics*, 91, 1-13.

[11] Ravallion, M. (1996), Issues in Measuring and Modelling Poverty, *Economic Journal*, 106, 1328-1343.

[12] Sen, A.K. (1976), Poverty: An Ordinal Approach to Measurement, *Econometrica*, 44, 219-231.

[13] Tsui, K.Y. (1994), Multidimensional Poverty Indices, Mimeo., Chinese University of Hong Kong.

[14] Zheng, B. (1997), Aggregate Poverty Measures, *Journal of Economic Surveys*, 11, 123-162.

Chapter 18

INDEPENDENCE AND CHANGES IN THE SIZE DISTRIBUTION OF INCOME

Philip Rothman

Department of Economics, Brewster Building, East Carolina University,
Greenville, NC 27858, USA

18.1   Introduction

It has been suggested that the size distribution of income follows a pure random walk. If true, this has serious implications for the effectiveness of U.S. Government income transfer policies. In this paper the random walk hypothesis is addressed by examining whether changes in the size distribution of income are independent. Conventional linear second-order time series analysis suggests that the first differenced series indeed are white noise processes. Results obtained with Mizrach's SNT test, based on developments in the recent literature on nonlinear dynamics, strongly reject the independence null for changes in each of the income inequality measures examined. While this suggests that year-to-year shifts in the income distribution are not random, it does not show that U.S. Government income redistribution policies have been either efficient or effective.

Since the onset of Lyndon Johnson's "War on Poverty" in the mid-1960s, the U.S. Government has spent trillions of dollars in income transfer payments so as to shift the distribution of income. In an intriguing paper, Hayes *et al.* (1990) present evidence suggesting that U.S. time series data on the size distribution of income follow pure random walks. From the policy perspective this finding is intriguing. If measures of the size distribution of income are truly random walk processes, then the net aggregate result of U.S. income transfer programs is that the distribution of income is annually shifted in only a random fashion, despite the best intentions of policymakers.

The Hayes *et al.* unit root results are based upon calculation of the Dickey and Fuller (1979) and Phillips (1987) test statistics. It is well-known, however, that Dickey-Fuller type tests have low power against stationary alternatives (see, e.g., DeJong *et al.* [1992]). It has also been argued that such tests tend to have low power against segmented trend stationary processes (see, e.g., Perron [1989]).

To this effect, Raj and Slottje (1994) and Rothman (1998) explore the robustness of the Hayes *et al.* unit root findings by applying the Zivot and Andrews (1992) and Kwiatkowski *et al.* (1992) testing procedures, respectively. Raj and Slottje reject the unit root null hypothesis in favor of a breaking trend alternative for time series data on the size distribution of income. Reversing the Dickey-Fuller approach by considering a stationary null hypothesis, Rothman fails to reject the null that the income inequality data considered are stationary time series.

The purpose of this paper is to cast aside formal unit root testing and study the random walk behavior of income inequality data directly by examining a simple implication of the pure random walk model: if the pure random walk model is true, the changes in the series are independent. In this paper, then, the random walk hypothesis for various income inequality measures is examined by testing whether the respective time series of first differences exhibit significant departures from independence.

Two classes of procedures are applied to explore the independence of changes in the size distribution of income. First, the second-order properties are examined with conventional time series tools. The second-order results presented below all suggest that the changes in the income inequality series are white noise processes. To the extent that these time series are Gaussian, the first-differenced series appear to be independently and identically distributed stochastic processes using standard linear time series diagnostics.

The analysis is carried out with annual postwar data covering the interval 1947-1989. For samples of this size, however, it is well-known that the second-order diagnostic procedures employed, e.g., Ljung-Box portmanteau statistics and tests based on the periodogram, tend to have low power against non-independent linear alternatives. Thus, the low sample size may explain the inability to reject the random walk hypothesis for these data.

Another potential explanation of the failure to reject the pure random walk model is that these second-order tests have no power against uncorrelated but nonlinear time series processes. The main substantive contribution of this paper is to explore such a possibility and show that when appropriate techniques are employed, there is very strong evidence against the claim that the size distribution of income follows a pure random walk.

The evidence of non-random walk behavior is produced through use of Mizrach's (1995) simple nonparametric test for independence (SNT). The SNT is a product of the recent research program in nonlinear dynamics which has focused on the search for hidden structure in time series with the spectra of white noise. It's closest antecedent is the BDS test due to Brock *et al.* (1987). Computationally much simpler, the SNT exhibits a great deal less size distortion in small sample sizes relative to BDS. When properly sized, Mizrach also shows that it typically is more powerful against non-independent alternatives. Evidence presented in this paper confirms Mizrach's power comparisons in so far as the SNT rejects independence for the changes in each of the eight income inequality series examined while the BDS rejects independence for only one such series.

The paper proceeds as follows. The alternative measures of income inequality are defined and the second-order results are presented in Section 2. The SNT test is described and applied in Section 3. Section 4 concludes.

18.2   Second-Order Properties

18.2.1 The data

The time series studied consist of annual observations from 1947-1989 for eight measures of income inequality based on transformations of the underlying data on the quintile shares of income. The quintile data are published in the *Current Population Report* by the U.S. Bureau of the Census. Several alternative measures are used since each particular measure captures a different aspect of inequality. A simple test of robustness, then, is provided through consideration of these individual series.

The summary measures examined are: the Gini measure (G), the Kakwani measure (K), the Relative Mean Deviation measure (R), the Theil Entropy measure (T) and four of Atkinson's social welfare measures. See Cowell (1977), Kakwani (1980), Theil (1967), and Atkinson (1970) for detailed descriptions of these measures; Raj and Slottje (1994) present a useful short summary. These eight are the most popular nonparametric characterizations of income inequality used in the literature. The four Atkinson measures were calculated by setting the "inequality aversion" parameter to 0.5, 0.95, 1.5 and

2.0. The corresponding Atkinson index series are labeled A1 through A4, respectively.

18.2.2 Correlation structure of changes in income inequality

Since much of the inference in this paper is carried out under the maintained hypothesis that the underlying data are draws from a Gaussian probability distribution, this assumption is tested first.   Table 1 reports p-values for Kolmogorov-Smirnov D statistics to test the null hypothesis that the first differenced series for each income inequality measure is normally distributed. While there is a good deal of variation across the different series, all p-values for the normality null are greater than 0.15. There is thus no strong evidence for rejecting the Gaussian assumption.

The estimated autocorrelation functions for the first differences of these eight income inequality series were calculated and at all lags the estimated autocorrelations are within the 95% confidence intervals. The p-values for Ljung-Box portmanteau Q statistics, evaluated for the first 4, 8, and 12 lags, for each of the series are reported in the third column of Table 2. All p-values for these Q statistics are above 0.50.

The estimated spectra for these first-differenced series were also computed. Each periodogram was smoothed with a Parzen window to produce consistent estimates of the spectral density functions.   For a white noise process the spectrum is completely flat. All the estimated ordinates are extremely small, on the order of 10^{-5} or less, suggesting that the true spectral density functions indeed are flat. Formal tests, Fisher's kappa, and Bartlett's test statistic, for these frequency domain results are reported in Table 3. Fisher's kappa is the largest periodogram ordinate divided by the average of these ordinates. Bartlett's procedure examines the normalized cumulative periodogram, which is a uniform $(0,1)$ variate under the null hypothesis of Gaussian white noise. The p-values for both tests are substantially higher than 0.10 for each of the eight income inequality series.

Thus, linear second-order analysis suggests that the first differences of the income inequality measures are white noise processes.   Together with the evidence in favor of the Gaussian model, the conventional analysis suggests that these series are independent and therefore offers no evidence against the claim that the levels of these series follow pure random walks.

18.3 Nonlinear Diagnostics

18.3.1 Squared autocorrelations

The estimated autocorrelation function of the square of a time series is often examined for identification of uncorrelated but nonlinear dependence. The McLeod-Li (1983) test is commonly used for this purpose. Introduced as a general test of linearity, the McLeod-Li test is based on a portmanteau statistic which consists of the Ljung-Box Q statistic calculated on the estimated autocorrelations for the square of a series.

P-values for the McLeod-Li linearity test, evaluated at the first 4, 8, and 12 lags, for the first differenced income inequality measures are reported in the fourth column of Table 2. For all but one series, the *p*-values are near 0.30 and above. Departure from linearity appears to be strongest for the first differenced Relative Mean Deviation series, with a *p*-value for the corresponding McLeod-Li Q(4) statistic slightly above 0.10. On the whole, then, the McLeod-Li nonlinear diagnostics do not provide evidence against the random walk model for the inequality series.

18.3.2 Two tests of independence

The BDS statistic has its origins in the empirical literature on testing for low-dimensional chaos in economic and financial data. For a time series $\{x_t\}$ with T observations, the BDS statistic is formed as follows

$$w_m(\varepsilon, T) = \sqrt{T}\,[C_m(\varepsilon, T) - C_1(\varepsilon, T)^m] / \sigma_m(\varepsilon, T), \qquad (18.1)$$

where $C_m(\varepsilon, T)$ is the sample correlation integral at embedding dimension m and scaling parameter ε, and $\sigma_m(\varepsilon, T)$ is the estimated standard deviation of the BDS statistic under the null hypothesis of independence. Brock, et al. (1987) show that $w_m(\varepsilon, T)$ is distributed asymptotically as N(0,1) under the null hypothesis that $\{x_t\}$ is independently and identically distributed.

Since it's introduction, the BDS statistic has been widely used as a test for independence (see, e.g., Chen and Tsay [1993] and Tsay [1991]). One drawback in the case of testing the income inequality measures is that for low sample sizes the BDS statistic is very poorly sized. This has been noted, for example, by Brock, et al. (1991), Mizrach (1995), and Rothman (1992). For example, at sample size 100 for embedding dimension 2, the BDS statistic rejects from 22 to 11 times more often than it should, across different values of ε, for the standard normal independently and identically distributed case.

Mizrach (1995) recently introduced a much simpler test of independence. Requiring calculations of order T, as opposed to T^2 for BDS, it is computationally less demanding. More important for analysis of the income inequality measures, he shows that his new test has much better size and power properties relative to BDS for small sample sizes. Further, his test is potentially far more useful in identifying a model, relative to the BDS and other tests, since it helps characterize the order of dependence in the underlying series.

The Mizrach simple nonparametric test of independence (SNT) is based on the notion of *local independence of order p* for a stochastic process $\{x_t\}$ which implies the equality of the conditional and unconditional probabilities

$$\text{Prob}[x_{t+p} < \varepsilon \,|\, x_t < \varepsilon] = \text{Prob}[x_{t+p} < \varepsilon], (18.2)$$

for arbitrary ε. Under local independence of order p, for arbitrary embedding dimension m

$$\text{Prob}[x_{t+(m-1)p} < \varepsilon, x_{t+(m-2)p} < \varepsilon, ..., x_t < \varepsilon] = (\text{Prob}[x_t < \varepsilon])^m \qquad (18.3)$$

To estimate the joint and marginal distributions in (3), introduce the kernel function $h:\Re \rightarrow \Re$

$$h(x_t) = I[x_t < \varepsilon] = \left(\begin{array}{l} 1, \text{if } x_t < \varepsilon \\ 0, \text{otherwise} \end{array} \right) \equiv I(x_t, \varepsilon) \qquad (18.4)$$

A consistent estimator of the joint unconditional probability that m leads of the x's are less than ε is given by the U-statistic

$$\theta(m, N, \varepsilon) = \sum_{t=1}^{T} \prod_{i=0}^{m-1} I(x_{t+ip}, \varepsilon)/N, \qquad (18.5)$$

where $N = T - (m-1)p$. The Mizrach SNT independence statistic is formed as follows

$$\sqrt{N} \frac{[\theta(m, N, \varepsilon) - \theta(m-1, N, \varepsilon)\theta(1, N, \varepsilon)]}{[\theta(m-1, N, \varepsilon)\theta(1, N, \varepsilon)(1 - \theta(m-1, N, \varepsilon)(1 - \theta(1, N, \varepsilon))]^{0.5}} \qquad (18.6)$$

Mizrach shows that the asymptotic distribution of the SNT statistic is $N(0,1)$.

18.3.3 The BDS and SNT results

Simulation results have shown that the size and power properties of the BDS statistic are best, at any sample size and across embedding dimensions, when the scaling parameter ε is set equal to one sample standard deviation of $\{x_t\}$. For this value of ε, the BDS statistic was calculated at embedding dimensions 2, 3, 4, and 5, for the first differences of each of the eight income inequality measures. The results are reported in Table 4.

Given the significant size distortions of the BDS test at low sample sizes, hypothesis testing for independence was based on estimated critical values obtained through Monte Carlo simulations for the standard normal case. When properly sized, then, at embedding dimension 2 there is no evidence against the null of independence for any of the first-differenced income inequality series. For the changes in the Relative Mean Deviation series, the independence null hypothesis can be rejected at the 0.05, 0.05, and 0.01 significance levels for embedding dimensions 3, 4, and 5. For none of the seven other series can independence be rejected at these embedding dimensions.

Results for the SNT test for the first-order, i.e., $p = 1$, independence null hypothesis at embedding dimensions 2, 3, 4, and 5, are reported in Table 5. For each test the kernel function (18.4) was calculated with ε set equal to the sample mean.

Mizrach (1995) reports small size distortions for the SNT tests at low sample sizes. To properly size the tests, estimated critical values for the independently and identically distributed standard normal case were also used to carry out hypothesis testing for the SNT results. At embedding dimension 2, the independence null can be rejected at the 0.05 significance level for all first-differenced income inequality series. None of the SNT statistics reject the first-order independence null at embedding dimensions 3, 4 or 5. Mizrach reports that the SNT statistic tends to be most powerful at embedding dimension 2. Accordingly, the $m = 2$ SNT results strongly suggest that the levels of all the income inequality measures do not follow pure random walks.

18.4   Conclusions

The purpose of this paper was to explore the random walk behavior of income inequality measures by examining whether the changes in these series exhibit departures from independence. Conventional linear second-order time series analysis suggests that the first-differenced income inequality series are white noise processes. For seven out of the eight series, the BDS test also fails to reject independence.

Strikingly different results emerge when the independence null is examined through Mizrach's SNT statistic. For each of the eight first-differenced income inequality measures, the SNT rejects independence. The SNT also indicates that the dependence for all of the series is present at the 1st lag. This may prove useful in identifying a statistical model for these series.

To return to the substantive policy question addressed by this paper, the SNT results strongly suggest that the income inequality measures do not follow pure random walks. These findings, however, do not imply that past U.S. Government income redistribution schemes have been efficient or were in any fundamental sense effective. Whether or not public policy has played a decisive role in shifting the income distribution would require analysis with a model specified to explicitly capture the interaction between the policy variables and the income inequality measurements.

Construction of such a structural model is beyond the scope of the current paper. The time series analysis presented here was limited to investigation of an important implication of the Hayes et al. unit-root results for data on the U.S. size distribution of income. The Mizrach SNT tests show quite strongly that this implication, i.e., independence of year-to-year changes in income distribution measures, is rejected by the data.

TABLE 18.1:

Kolmogorov-Smirnov Goodness of Fit D Statistics for Null Hypothesis of Normality for Changes in Income Inequality Measures

Series	D Statistic	*P*-value for D Statistic
A1	0.133	0.444
A2	0.174	0.156
A3	0.151	0.295
A4	0.171	0.172
G	0.106	0.733
K	0.116	0.626
R	0.122	0.559
T	0.121	0.574

Table presents Kolmogorov-Smirnov D statistics for testing the null hypothesis of normality for first differences of the Atkinson A1-A4, Gini (G), Kakwani (K), Relative Mean Deviation (R) and Theil Entropy (T) income inequality measures.

TABLE 18.2:
P-values for Ljung-Box Q(m) Statistics for Income Inequality Measures

Series	m	ΔX_t	$(\Delta X_t)^2$
	4	0.947	0.698
A1	8	0.794	0.900
	12	0.724	0.871
	4	0.857	0.653
A2	8	0.749	0.905
	12	0.720	0.868
	4	0.659	0.476
A3	8	0.636	0.843
	12	0.667	0.814
	4	0.507	0.297
A4	8	0.537	0.721
	12	0.612	0.714
	4	0.946	0.449
G	8	0.760	0.644
	12	0.666	0.736
	4	0.968	0.655
K	8	0.801	0.854
	12	0.715	0.849
	4	0.886	0.106
R	8	0.772	0.232
	12	0.702	0.447
	4	0.965	0.638
T	8	0.778	0.842
	12	0.679	0.849

Table presents *p*-values for the portmanteau Ljung-Box Q(m) statistics, evaluated at lags 1,...,m, for the first differences ΔX_t and squared first differences $(\Delta X_t)^2$ for the Atkinson A1-A4, Gini (G), Kakwani (K), Relative Mean Deviation (R) and Theil's Entropy (T) income inequality measures.

TABLE 18.3:

Fisher's kappa and Bartlett's Test Statistics for Null Hypothesis of Independence for Changes in Income Inequality Measures

Series	Fisher's kappa	Bartlett's Test
A1	1.265	0.042
A2	1.398	0.044
A3	1.532	0.047
A4	1.610	0.058
G	1.276	0.051
K	1.195	0.042
R	1.355	0.054
T	1.238	0.047

Table shows Fisher's kappa and Bartlett's periodogram test statistics for first differences of the Atkinson A1-A4, Gini (G), Kakwani (K), Relative Mean Dispersion (R) and Theil Entropy (T) income inequality measures. The critical values for Fisher's kappa are 4.862, 5.408 and 6.594 for significance levels of 0.10, 0.05 and 0.01, respectively. The .05 critical value for Bartlett's test is 0.189.

TABLE 18.4:

BDS Tests for Changes in Income Inequality Measures at $\varepsilon/\sigma = 1.00$

Series	m=2	m=3	m=4	m=5
A1	1.787	1.604	1.787	2.420
A2	1.128	1.201	1.599	2.162
A3	0.575	0.839	1.229	1.731
A4	0.078	0.548	0.754	1.120
G	2.076	2.666	2.824	4.032
K	2.059	2.076	1.989	2.772
R	3.701	5.217 [b]	5.696 [b]	8.350 [c]
T	2.145	2.569	2.451	3.302

[a] m = embedding dimension
[b] Significant at the 5% level.
[c] Significant at the 1% level.

Table presents BDS statistics evaluated at $\varepsilon = \sigma$, where σ is the sample standard deviation of the series, for embedding dimensions m = 2,...,5, for the first differences of the Atkinson A1-A4, Gini(G), Kakwani, Relative Mean Deviation (R) and Theil Entropy (T) income inequality measures. Hypothesis tests based on estimated critical values tabulated in Mizrach (1995), Table 7.

TABLE 18.5:
Mizrach First-Order SNT Statistics for Changes in Income Inequality Measures

Series	m=2 [a]	m=3	m=4	m=5
A1	-3.536 [c]	0.606	0.000	-1.016
A2	-3.536 [c]	0.606	0.000	-1.016
A3	-2.679 [b]	0.371	0.694	-1.066
A4	-2.566 [b]	0.260	0.783	-1.118
G	-2.679 [b]	0.371	0.694	-1.066
K	-3.536 [c]	0.606	0.000	-1.016
R	-2.679 [b]	0.371	-0.694	-1.066
T	-3.536 [c]	0.606	0.000	-1.016

[a] m = embedding dimension
[b] Significant at the 5% level.
[c] Significant at the 1% level.
Table presents Mizrach SNP test for first-order independence, at embedding dimensions m = 2,...,5, for the first differences of the Atkinson A1-A4, Gini(G), Kakwani, Relative Mean Deviation (R) and Theil Entropy (T) income inequality measures. Hypothesis tests based on estimated critical values tabulated in Mizrach (1995),

REFERENCES

[1]   Atkinson, A.B. (1970), "On the Measurement of Inequality," *Journal of Economic Theory*, 2, 244-263.

[2]   Brock, W.A., W.D. Dechert, and J.A. Scheinkman (1987), "A Test for Independence Based on the Correlation Dimension," working paper, Department of Economics, University of Wisconsin. [Revised version, Brock, W.A., W.D. Dechert, J.A. Scheinkman, and B. LeBaron (1996), *Econometric Reviews*, 15, 197-235.]

[3]   Brock, W.A, D.A. Hsieh, and B. LeBaron (1991), *Nonlinear Dynamics, Chaos and Instability*, Cambridge, MA: MIT Press.

[4]   Chen, R. and R.S. Tsay (1993), "Functional-Coefficient Autoregressive Models," *Journal of the American Statistical Association*, 88, 298-308.

[5]   Cowell, F. (1977), *Measuring Inequality*, London: Wiley and Sons.

[6]   DeJong, D.A., J.C. Nankervis, N.E. Savin, and C.H. Whiteman (1992), "Integration Versus Trend Stationarity in Time Series," *Econometrica*, 60, 423-433.

[7]   Dickey, D.A. and W.A. Fuller (1979), "Distribution of the Estimators for Autoregressive Time Series with a Unit Root," *Journal of the American Statistical Association*, 74, 427-431.

[8]   Hayes, K., D.J. Slottje, S. Porter-Hudak, and G. Scully (1990), "Is the Size Distribution of Income a Random Walk?" *Journal of Econometrics*, 43, 213-226.

[9]   Kakwani, N. (1980), "On a Class of Poverty Measures," *Econometrica*, 48, 437-446.

[10]   Kwiatkowski, D., P.C.B. Phillips, P. Schmidt, and Y. Shin (1992), "Testing the Null Hypothesis of Stationarity Against the Alternative of a Unit Root: How Sure are we that Economic Time Series have a Unit Root?" *Journal of Econometrics, 54, 159-178.*

[11] McLeod, A.I. and W.K. Li (1983), "Diagnostic Checking ARMA Time Series Models Using Squared-Residual Autocorrelations," *Journal of Time Series Analysis*, 4, 269-273.

[12] Mizrach, B. (1995), "A Simple Nonparametric Test for Independence," unpublished working paper, Department of Economics, Rutgers University.

[13] Perron, P. (1989), "The Great Crash, The Oil Price Shock and the Unit Root Hypothesis," *Econometrica*, 57, 1361-1401.

[14] Phillips, P.C.B. (1987), "Time Series Regression with a Unit Root," *Econometrica*, 55, 227-302.

[15] Raj, Baldev and Daniel J. Slottje (1994). "The Trend Behavior of Alternative Income Inequality Measures in the United States From 1947-1990 and the Structural Break," *Journal of Business and Economic Statistics*, Vol. 12, pp. 479-488.

[16] Rothman, P. (1992), "The Comparative Power of the TR Test Against Simple Threshold Models," *Journal of Applied Econometrics*, 7, S187-S195.

[17] Rothman, P. (1998), "Is the Size Distribution of Income Stationary?" *Research on Economic Inequality*, 8, 1-12.

[18] Theil, H., (1967), *Economics and Information Theory*, Amsterdam: North Holland.

[19] Tsay, R.S. (1991), "Detecting and Modeling Nonlinearity in Univariate Time Series Analysis," *Statistica Sinica*, 1, 431-452.

[20] Zivot, E. and D.W.K. Andrews (1992), "Further Evidence on the Great Crash, the Oil-Price Shock, and the Unit Root Hypothesis," *Journal of Business and Economic Statistics*, 10, 251-270.

Chapter 19

NECESSARY AND SUFFICIENT CONDITIONS FOR DOMINANCE USING GENERALIZED LORENZ CURVES

Shlomo Yitzhaki

Dept. of Economics, Hebrew University, Jerusalem 91905, Israel

Almost all functions used in economics are concave, but there are important examples of convex functions, e. g., cost functions and poverty or concentration indices. In these cases one can choose between working with convex or concave functions (e.g., poverty indices or welfare functions).

The aim of this chapter is to derive the connections between necessary and sufficient conditions for dominance of convex and concave functions.

Let X, Y be two continuous random variables with cumulative distributions $F_X(\ )$ and $F_Y(\ )$ respectively. It is assumed that the expected value of the distributions is bounded ($\mu_X < \infty$; $\mu_Y < \infty$). Let U be the class of increasing concave functions and V be the class of increasing convex functions. We say that X dominates (by second-degree stochastic dominance) Y for concave (convex) functions if:

$$E\{u(X)\} \geq E\{u(Y)\} \qquad \text{for all } u_\varepsilon U . \tag{19.1}$$

$$E\{v(X)\} \geq E\{v(Y)\} \qquad \text{for all } v_\varepsilon V . \tag{19.1'}$$

The following proposition has been proved by several investigators:

Proposition 1:
(1) holds iff $_{-\infty}\int^z [F_Y(t) - F_X(t)]dt \geq 0$ for all z.
(1') holds iff $_z\int^\infty [F_Y(t) - F_X(t)]dt \geq 0$ for all z.

A proof of the first part of the proposition (for concave functions) can be found in Hanoch and Levy (1969), Rothschild and Stiglitz (1970) and of the second part (for convex functions) in Spencer and Fisher (1990).

Conditions (19.1) and (19.1') are related to each other by:

$$\int_{-\infty}^{z}[F_Y(t) - F_X(t)]\,dt + \int_{z}^{\infty}[F_Y(t) - F_X(t)]\,dt = \mu_X - \mu_Y. \tag{19.2}$$

It is easy to see that if $\mu_X = \mu_Y$ then

$$\int_{-\infty}^{z}[F_Y(t) - F_X(t)]\,dt \geq 0 \text{ for all } z \text{ iff } \int_{z}^{\infty}[F_Y(t) - F_X(t)]\,dt \leq 0 \text{ for all } z, \tag{19.3}$$

and we may conclude that the rules are symmetric in the sense that if X dominates Y for concave (convex) functions this also means that Y dominates X for convex (concave) functions. However, if $\mu_X \neq \mu_Y$, this symmetry need not hold. That is, X may dominate Y for concave functions, without Y dominating X for convex functions. To formally prove the asymmetry note that $\mu_X \geq \mu_Y$ is a necessary condition for dominance in both cases. Hence, if $\mu_X > \mu_Y$ then X may dominate Y for concave or convex functions while Y cannot dominate X for both types of functions.

Further insight into the origin of the asymmetry can be gained by presenting the necessary and sufficient conditions in terms of generalized Lorenz curves. The generalized Lorenz curve is defined by

$$A(p) = \int_{-\infty}^{z} t\, f(t)\, dt,$$

where $z = F^{-1}(p)$ and $f(\ )$ is the density function.

Proposition 2 states the necessary and sufficient conditions for dominance of concave functions in terms of generalized Lorenz curves.

Proposition 2:
$A_X(p) \geq A_Y(p)$ for all $0 \leq p \leq 1$ iff $\int_{-\infty}^{z} [F_Y(t) - F_X(t)]\, dt \geq 0$ for all z.

For proof see Shorrocks (1983), Lambert (1993) or Yitzhaki and Olkin (1991).

To construct necessary and sufficient conditions for dominance of convex functions in terms of generalized Lorenz curves it is convenient to define the Lorenz curve in terms of $h = 1-p$. Under this formulation the observations are sorted in descending (instead of ascending) order. Then, the generalized (descending-order) Lorenz curve portrays the cumulative value of the largest h percent of the population (the appropriate Lorenz curve is above the diagonal). In this case, the generalized (descending-order) Lorenz curve, $D(\ )$, is a mirror image of the conventional generalized Lorenz curve:

$$D(h) = \int_{z}^{\infty} t\, f(t)\, dt \quad \text{where } z = H^{-1}(h) = 1 - F^{-1}(h). \tag{19.4}$$

Proposition 3 states the necessary and sufficient conditions for dominance of convex functions:

Proposition 3:
$D_X(h) \geq D_Y(h)$ for all $0 \leq h \leq 1$ iff $\int_z^\infty [F_Y(t) - F_X(t)] \, dt \geq 0$ for all z.

Proof:
(a) Sufficiency: We have to prove that if the integral is non-negative for all z, then $D_X(h) \geq D_Y(h)$ for all h.
Using integration by parts we can write

$$\int_z^\infty [1 - F(t)] \, dt = -H(z) \, z + \int_z^\infty t \, f(t) \, dt = D(h) - z \, h \;, \tag{19.5}$$

where $H(z) = 1 - F(z)$ and $h = H(z)$. Therefore

$$\int_z^\infty [F_Y(t) - F_X(t)] \, dt = D_X(h_1) - z \, h_1 - D_Y(h_2) + z \, h_2 \;, \tag{19.6}$$

where $h_1 = H_X(z)$; $h_2 = H_Y(z)$ and $D_X(h_1)$ denotes the generalized Lorenz curve of X, evaluated at $h_1 = H_X(z)$.
Two additional properties of generalized Lorenz curves are required to complete the proof:

$$\partial A(p)/\partial p \, |_{p=F(z)} = z \quad ; \quad \partial D(h)/\partial h \, |_{h=H(z)} = z$$
$$\partial^2 A(p)/\partial p^2 \, |_{p=F(z)} \geq 0 \quad ; \quad \partial^2 D(h)/\partial h^2 \, |_{h=H(z)} \leq 0 \, .$$

Using these properties (19.6) can be written as:

$$\int_z^\infty [F_Y(t) - F_X(t)] \, dt = D_X(h_1) - h_1 \, \partial D_X/\partial h \, |_{h=h1} + h_2 \, \partial D_Y/\partial h \, |_{h=h2} - D_Y(h_2) \,, \tag{19.7}$$

where $h_1 = H_X(z)$; $h_2 = H_Y(z)$. That is, the integral on the left hand side of (19.7) is equal to the difference between the two generalized Lorenz curves evaluated at an equal-slope points *plus* a term which is based on the derivative of the curves. Figure 1 portrays the term of equation (19.7). Let OC be D_X and OD the curve D_Y (the curves are concave because the figure plots the generalized (descending) Lorenz curves, that is, h_1 represents a percentage of the highest observations and h_1C is the cumulative value of variate of those observations). The points C and D are with the same slope. Hence the first term represents OA while the second term is OB. Since (at points D and C) the derivatives of the curves are equal (and equal to z) we may write (19.7) as

$$_z\!\int^\infty [F_Y(t) - F_X(t)]dt = D_X(h_1) + \partial D_Y/\partial h \; [h_2 - h_1] - D_Y(h_2) \; . \qquad (19.8)$$

Note that $D_Y(h_2) + \partial D_Y/\partial h \; [h_1 - h_2]$ is the first-order approximation of $D_Y(h_1)$, approximated from h_2. Since D_Y is concave, $D_Y(h_1)$ is smaller than its first-order approximation. Therefore,

$$_z\!\int^\infty [F_Y(t) - F_X(t)]dt \le D_X(h_1) - D_Y(h_1) \; . \qquad (19.9)$$

Since the relationship holds for all z, it also holds for all h.   QED.

(b) Necessity:
      We have to prove that if $D_X(h) \ge D_Y(h)$ for all h then $_z\!\int^\infty [F_Y(t) - F_X(t)]dt$ for all z.
Using (19.8) it is sufficient to prove that if $D_X(h) \ge D_Y(h)$ then there exists z such that

$$D_X(h_1) + \partial D_X/\partial h \; [h_2 - h_1] - D_Y(h_2) \; \ge 0 \; .$$

Since $D()$ is concave
$D_X(h_1) + \partial D_X/\partial h \; [h_2 - h_1] \ge D_X(h_2)$,
hence
$D_X(h_1) + \partial D_X/\partial h \; [h_2 - h_1] - D_Y(h_2) \ge D_X(h_2) - D_Y(h_2) \ge 0.$ QED.

      The necessary and sufficient conditions for dominance for convex functions are stated in terms of (descending-order) generalized Lorenz curves while those for concave functions are stated in terms of generalized Lorenz curves. Both state that dominance means that one generalized curve cannot intersect the other. Hence, the only difference between the conditions for concave and convex functions is the definition of the generalized Lorenz curve. This difference also shows up in forming necessary conditions. A necessary condition for dominance is that the area below the dominating curve cannot be smaller than the area below the dominated curve. As shown in Yitzhaki (1982) this means that $\mu_X \ge \mu_Y$ and $\mu_X(1-G_X) \ge \mu_Y(1-G_Y)$ (G is the Gini coefficient) are necessary conditions for dominance of X over Y for concave functions. By exactly the same method one can show that $\mu_X \ge \mu_Y$ and $\mu_X(1+G_X) \ge \mu_Y(1+G_Y)$ are necessary conditions for dominance of X over Y for convex functions. Needless to say, these are not necessary conditions for first degree stochastic dominance (FSD) because FSD allows dominance by partially convex and partially concave functions.

Figure 19.1:
Generalized Lorenz Curves

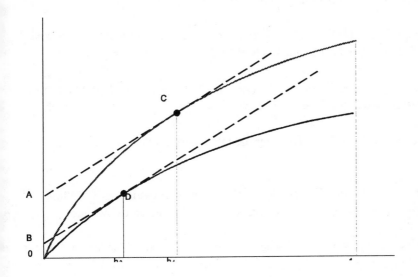

REFERENCES

[1]   Hanoch, G. and Levy, H. (1). "The Efficiency Analysis of Choices involving Risk, " *Review of Economic Studies*, 36: 335-346.

[2]   Lambert, Peter (1993). *The Distribution and Redistribution of Income*. Manchester: Manchester University Press.

[3]   Rothschild, M. and Stiglitz, J. E. (1970). "Increasing Risk I. A Definition, " *Journal of Economic Theory*, 2: 225-253.

[4]   Shorrocks, A. F. (1983). "Ranking Income Distributions," *Economica*, 50: 3-17.

[5]   Spencer, B. D. and Fisher, S. (1990). "On Comparing Distributions of Poverty Gaps," Northwestern University, Dept. of Statistics, Mimeo.

[6]   Yitzhaki, S. (1982). "Stochastic Dominance, Mean Variance and Gini's Mean Difference," *American Economic Review*, 72 (March): 178-85.

[7]   Yitzhaki, S. and Olkin I. (1991). "Concentration Indices and Concentration Curves," in Karl Mosler and Marco Scarsini (eds.) *Stochastic Orders and Decisions under Risk*, Institute of Mathematical Statistics: Lecture-Notes Monograph Series, 19: 380-392.

CAMILO DAGUM

SCIENTIFIC PUBLICATIONS

1949

"La Funcion de Demanda, Su Elasticidad, Flexibilidad del Precio", **Revista de la Facultad de Ciencias Economicas** (Universidad Nacional de Cordoba), Vol. II, No. 2-3, 1949, pp. 355-405.

1951

"Sistema de Patron Compuesto", **Revista de la Facultad de Ciencias Economicas** (Universidad Nacional de Cordoba), Vol. IV, No. 1-2-3-4, 1951, pp. 5-28.

1952

"Estadistica y Economia", **Revista de Economia** (Banco de la Provincia de Cordoba), Vol. IV, No. 7, 1952.

"Distribucion de Poisson", **Revista de Economia** (Banco de la Provincia de Cordoba), Vol. IV, No. 8, 1952.

"El Plan Economico y la Teoria Cuantitativa de la Moneda", **Revista de la Facultad de Ciencias Economicas** (Universidad Nacional de Cordoba), Vol., V, No. 1-4, 1952.

1953

"Elasticidad Ingreso del Consumo - Flexibilidad Ciclica y Flexibilidad Estructural de los Precios", **Estocastica**, Revista de la Sociedad Argentina de Estadistica - Vol. II, No. 3, 1953.

1954

Base Tecnicas y Calculos Actuariales para la Creacion de la Seccion Vida de la Compania de Seguros "El Comercio de Cordoba", Mimeographed document, Cordoba, 1954.

1955

"La Funcion de Demanda de Algunos Bienes de Consumo de la Republica Argentina: Su Elasticidad - Flexibilidad del Precio", **Revista de la Facultad de Ciencias Economicas** (Universidad Nacional de Cordoba), Vol. VIII, No. 1-2, 1955.

"Presentacion del Profesor Corrado Gini de la Universidad de Roma", **Revista de la Universidad de Cordoba**, 1955.

1956

Bases Tecnicas y Estructura Legal de la Prevision Social para la Provincia de Cordoba, (Co-author). Mimeographed documents, Gobierno de la Provincia de Cordoba, 1956.

1957

"Varianza e Covarianza del Momento Misto dei Campioni di Una Variabile Casuale a K-Dimensioni", **Atti della XVII Riunione Scientifica della Società Italiana di Statistica**, Roma 1957.

1958

"Comentarios Sobre la Situacion Financiera de la Caja Provincial De Jubilaciones y Pensiones de Cordoba", **Memoria de la Caja Provincial de Jubilaciones y Pensiones**, 1958.

"Varianza y Covarianza del Momento Producto de las Muestras de una Variable Aleatoria K-Dimensional", **Revista de Economia y Estadistica** (Universidad Nacional de Cordoba), Vol. II, 1958.

"Comentario del libro de C. Gini: Patologia Economica", **Revista de Economia y Estadistica**, Vol. 2, No. 3, 1958, pp. 403-408.

"Evolucion Logica del Metodo Estadistico y Analisis de los Modelos de Comportamiento de los Sujetos de la Actividad Economica", **Revista de Economia y Estadistica** (Universidad Nacional de Cordoba), Vol. II, No. 4, 1958, pp. 283-304.

1959

"Transvariazione fra più di Due Distribuzioni", in C. Gini, ed., **Memorie di Metodologia Statistica**, Vol. II, **Transvariazione**, Libreria Goliardica , Roma 1959, pp. 608-648.

1960

Teoria de la Transvariacion, Sus Aplicaciones a la Economia, Metron, Rome University, 1960, 206 pages.

Bases Tecnicas y Estructura Legal para la Seguridad Social del Cuerpo Docente de la Universidad Nacional de Cordoba, (Co-author). Mimeographed document, Universidad Nacional de Cordoba, 1960.

"Comportamiento de los Depositos del Banco de la Provincia de Cordoda", **Revista de Economia** (Banco de la Provincia de Cordoba), Vol. II, No. 17, 1960.

"Ecuaciones en Diferencias Finitas - Su Aplicacion a la Solucion de los Modelos de Harrod - Domar, Samuelson, Hicks y otros", **Universidad Nacional de Cordoba**, 1960.

"Transvariacion entre Mas de Dos Distribuciones", **Studi in Onore di Corrado Gini**, Istituto di Statistica, Università di Roma , Vol. 1, Roma, 1960, pp. 53-92.

"Zonas de Libre Comercio", **Revista Rotaria**, Illinois, U.S.A., 1960.

1961

"Transvariacion en la Hipotesis de Variables Aleatorias Normales Multidimensionales", **Proceedings of the International Statistical Institute,** Vol. XXXVIII, Book 4, Tokyo, 1961, pp. 473-486.

1962

"Universidad y Revolución Social Latinoamericana", **Cuadernos Americanos,** Vol. 19, 1962, pp. 74-85.

1963

"Sociedad de Masas y Tecnica Social", **Cuadernos de los Institutos,** Instituto de Sociologia, "Raul A. Orgaz", Facultad de Derecho y Ciencias Sociales (Universidad Nacional de Cordoba), No. 67, 1963, pp. 3-34.

"François Perroux, Doctor Honoris Causa de la Universidad Nacional de Cordoba", **Revista de Economia y Estadistica** (Universidad Nacional de Cordoba), Vol. VII, No. 3-4, 1963.

"Fundamentos para la Modificacion de la Escala de Jubilaciones en la Provincia de Cordoba", (Analisis Economico, Estadistico, Demografico y Social). **Revista Seguridad Social,** Consejo Federal de Seguridad Social de la Rep. Argentina (COFESES), No. 8/11, Noviembre 1962 - Junio 1963, pp. 1-12.

"Corrado Gini, Doctor Honoris Causa de la Universidad Nacional de Cordoba", Actas del XX°. **Congreso del Instituto Internacional de Sociologia,** Vol. I, 1963, and Revue Internationale de Sociologie, Série II, Vol. 2, No. 2, 1965, pp. 24-31

1964

"La Integracion y el Crecimiento Economico en America Latina", **Desarrollo Economico,** Revista del Instituto de Desarrollo Economico y Social, Buenos Aires, Vol. 4, Nos. 14-15, 1964.

1965

"Teoria de los Modelos y Analisis Economico", Volumen en Homenaje al Profesor Benjamin Cornejo, **Revista de Economia y Estadistica** (Universidad Nacional de Cordoba), Vol. IX, 1965, pp. 51-53.

"Probabilité et Intensité de la Transvariation dans l'Espace à N Dimensions", **Économie Appliquée**, Revue de l'Institut de Science Économique Appliquée (ISEA), No. 4, 1965, Paris, pp. 507-538.

"Théories des Modèles et Modèles avec Retards Distribués dans l'Analyse Économique", **Économie Appliquée**, Institut de Science Économique Appliquée (ISEA), No. 4, 1965, Paris, pp. 539-556.

"Corrado Gini, Doctor Honoris Cause de la Universidad Nacional de Cordoba", **Revue Internationale de Sociologie**, Série II, Vol. 2, No. 2, Rome, 1965.

1966

"In Memoriam - Corrado Gini" (23-5-1884/13-3-1965), **Revista de Economia y Estadistica**, (Universidad Nacional de Cordoba), Vol. X, No. 1-2, 1966, pp. 1-2.

"Distribucion del Rezago y Dinamica Economica", **Revista de Economia y Estadistica** (Universidad Nacional de Cordoba), Vol. 10, No. 3-4, 1966, pp. 101-110.

"Bases y Principios para la Elaboracion de Modelos en la Ciencia Economica", Atti del Simposio Internazionale sul tema, "La Statistica Come Metodologia delle Scienze Sociali", **Metron**, Vol. XXV, No. 1-4, Istituto di Statistica e Ricerca Sociale "C. Gini", Università di Roma, 1966, pp. 401-435.

"Wahrscheinlichkeit und Ausmass Der Transvariation Im N-Dimensionalen Raum", **Statistische Hefte**, Internationale Zeitschrift für Theorie and Praxis, Westdeutscher Verlag, Köln und Opladen, 7 Jahrgang, 1966, Heft 1-2, pp. 3-29.

"L'intégration et la Croissance Économique en Amérique Latine", **Tiers Monde**, Revue de l'Institut d'Étude du Développement Économique et Social de l'Université de Paris, Tome VII, No. 25, 1966, pp. 113-138.

"Principes pour l'Élaboration de Modèles en Science Économique : Une Approche Économétrique", **Tiers Monde**, Revue de l'Institut d'Étude du Développement Économique et Social de l'Université de Paris, Tome 7, No. 2, 1966, pp. 481-510.

"Bases y Principios para la Construccion de Modelos en la Ciencia Economica: Un Enfoque Econométrico", **Estadistica Espanola**, Revista del Instituto Nacional de Estadistica, No. 31, 1966, p. 5-33.

1967

"Bases y Principios para la Elaboracion de Modelos en la Ciencia Economica", **La Scuola in Azione**, Scuola Enrico Mattei di Studi Superiori Sugli Idrocarburi, E.N.I., Giugno 1967, pp. 82-119.

"On Deterministic and Stochastic Structures", Research Memorandum No. 92, **Econometric Research Program**, Princeton University, December 1967, 22 pp.

1968

"El Concepto de Permanencia Estructural", **Revista de Economia**, No. 100, Madrid, 1968, pp. 25-31.

"Nonparametric and Gaussian Bivariate Transvariation Theory: Its Application to Economics", Research Memorandum No. 99, **Econometric Research Program**, Princeton University, June 1968, 56 pp.

"Multivariate Transvariation Theory among Several Distributions and its Economic Applications", Research Memorandum No. 100, **Econometric Research Program**, Princeton University, June 1968, 39 pp.

"Consecuencia de la Introduccion del Concepto de Estructura en la Teoria del Comercio Internacional", **El Trimestre Economico**, Vol. XXXV, No. 138, 1968, pp. 237-255.

"On Method and Purposes in Econometric Model Building", **Zeitschrift für Nationalökonomie**, No. 4, 1968, pp. 381-398.

1969

Un Analisis Econométrico de la Oferta y Demanda de Energéticos en Mexico, Mexico: Instituto Mexicano del Petroleo, 1969, 208 pages.

El Problema de la Prediccion en Ciencias Sociales (Co-author). Mexico: National University of Mexico (UNAM) Press (Instituto de Investigaciones Sociales), 1969, 228 pages.

"Conséquence de l'Introduction du Concept de Structure dans la Théorie du Commerce International", **Économie Appliquée**, Tome XXII, No. 12, 1969, pp. 65-88.

"El Capital de Infraestructura y la Tecnologia Nuclear en la Integracion de America Latina" (co-author), **El Trimestre Economico**, Vol. XXXVI, No. 142, 1969, pp. 197-214.

"Inflazione, Efficienza Economica e Benessere Sociale", in: **Idee sull'America Latina**, Edizioni della Nuova Antologia, Arnoldo Mondadori Editore, Milano, pp. 178-188, 1969.

"A New Approach to Inflation Through the Joint Analysis of Economic Efficiency and Social Welfare, A case Study: Argentina", **Zeitschrift des Instituts für Weltwirtschaft an der University Kiel**, Band 102, Heft 2, 1969, pp. 197-213.

"Stuctural Permanence. Its Role in the Analysis of Structural Dualisms and Dependences and for Prediction and Decision Purposes", **Zeitschrift für die Gesamte Staatswissenschaft**, Band 125, Heft 2, 1969, pp. 211-235.

"Universidad y Desarrollo Economico", IX Congreso Latinoamericano de Sociologia: Mexico, 21-25, November 1969, in **Investigacion Economica**, Universidad Nacional de Mexico, Vol. XXX, No. 118, 1970, pp. 255-267.

"Inflacion, Eficiencia Economica y Bienestar Social, Un Analisis de Causalidad Estructural. Estudio de un caso: Argentina", **Investigacion Economica**, Vol. XXXIX, No. 114, 1969, pp. 257-273.

"A Logistic Decision Model for Stability and Development", **Proceedings of the 37th Session of the International Statistical Institute**, Volume XLIII, Book 2, London, 1969, pp. 14-16.

"Inflacion Estructural y Modernizacion: Notas para Una Teoria Socio - Economica de la Inflacion", **Actes du XXII Congrès de l'Institut International de Sociologie**, Rome 1969, **Revue Internationale de Sociologie**, Série II, Vol. VII, No. 1, 1971, pp. 664-676.

1970

"Le Concept de Permanence Structurale et l'Analyse Économétrique", **Série Économie Mathématique et Économétrie, Économies et Sociétés**, Cahiers de l'I.S.E.A., Tome IV, No. 3, 1970, pp. 457-479.

"Oskar Morgenstern: Su contribucion a la construccion de la economia matematica y la teoria economica del siglo XX", **Investigacion Economica**, Universidad Nacional Autonoma de Mexico, Vol. XXX, No. 118, 1970, pp. 245-254.

"Les Modèles Économétriques dans la Prévision et la Décision", **Série Économie Mathématique et Économétrie, Économies et Sociétés**, Cahiers de l'I.S.E.A., Tome IV, No. 3, 1970, pp. 481-495.

"L'Inflation Structurelle : Un Modèle Économétrique", **Série Économie Mathématique et Économétrie, Économie et Sociétés**, Cahiers de l'I.S.E.A., Tome IV, No. 3, 1970, pp. 497-517.

"Un Modelo Econométrico sobre la Inflación Estructural", **El Trimestre Economico**, Vol. 37 (1) , No. 145, 1970, pp. 39-58.

1971

Introduccion a la Econometria, Co-author with Estela Bee Dagum, Mexico: Siglo XXI, 1971, VIII-255 pages, 11th reimpression, 1986.

"A Decision Function for Macroeconomic Decision Units", **Proceedings of the 38th Session, International Statistical Institute,** Washington, D.C., V. 44, Book 2, 1971, pp. 152-156.

"Un Modèle Économétrique de l'Offre et de la Demande de Produits Énergétiques. Étude d'un cas concret: Le Mexique", **Série Économie Mathématique et Économétrie, Économies et Sociétés,** Cahiers de l'I.S.E.A., T.V., No. 8, August 1971, pp. 1393-1420.

"Un Modelo Econometrico de la Oferta y la Demanda de Energéticos (Estudio de un caso: Mexico)", **El Trimestre Economico,** V. 38 (2), No. 150, 1971, pp. 275-300.

"Un Modèle Stochastique de Répartition Fonctionnelle du Revenu", Série Économie Mathématique et Économétrie, **Économies et Sociétés,** Cahiers de l'I.S.E.A., T.V., No. 10, 1971, pp. 1729-1750.

"Un Modèle de Décision pour une Redistrubution Fonctionnelle du Revenu", **Série Économie Mathématique et Économétrie, Économies et Sociétés,** Cahiers de l'I.S.E.A., T.V., No. 10, 1971, pp. 1751-1768.

"Multivariate Transvariation Theory Among Several Distributions and its Economic Applications", **Studi di Probabilità, Statistica e Ricerca Operativa in Onore di Giuseppe Pompilj,** Gubbio: Oderisi, 1971, pp. 1-33.

"Characteristics of Economic Model-Building", (co-author with E. B. Dagum), Working Paper Series No. 71-26, The University of Iowa, 1971, 38 pages.

"The Logical-Empirical Process in Econometric Model-Building", (co-author with E. B. Dagum), Working Paper Series No. 71-28. The University of Iowa, 1971, 42 pages.

1972

An Econometric Analysis of the Central American Common Market, SIECA/UNCTAD, United Nations, 1972, 101 pages.

"The Meaning of "Theory" and "Model" in the Social Sciences", (co-author with E. B. Dagum), Working Paper Series No. 72-11, The University of Iowa, 1972, 35 pages.

"Elements of an Economic Model", (co-author with E. B.Dagum), Working Paper Series No. 72-11, The University of Iowa, 1972, 35 pages.

"Une Fonction de Décision pour l'Approvisionnement en Produits Énergétiques le cas Particulier du Mexique", **Revue Européenne des Sciences Sociales**, T. X, N. 26, 1972, pp. 193-221.

"A Stochastic Model of the Functional Distribution of Income", in, **International Economics and Development. Volume in Honor of R. Prebisch**, L.E. Di Marco, ed., New York: Academic Press, 1972, pp. 245-265.

1973

"Théorie des Jeux et Répartition Fonctionnnelle du Revenu : Une Approche Structurelle", **Économie Appliquée**, Tome 26, 2-3-4, 1973, pp. 817-842.

"Un Modèle Nonlinéaire de Répartition Fonctionnelle du Revenu", **Économie Appliquée**, Tome 26, 2-3-4, 1973, pp. 843-876.

1974

Construction de Modèles et Analyse Économétrique, Co-author with Estela Bee Dagum. Collection Économies et Sociétés, Paris, Série EM no. 5, 1974, 498 pages.

"Un Modelo Estochastico Sobre la Distribucion Funcional del Ingreso", in, L.E. Di Marco (editor): **Economia Internacional y Desarrollo, Estudios en Honor de Raul Prebisch**. Buenos Aires: Ediciones Depalma, 1974, pp. 273-294.

"Un Modelo No-lineal Generalizado de la Distribucion Funcional del Ingreso", **El Trimestre Economico**, Vol. 41, No. 163, 1974, pp. 483-520.

"Une Classe de Fonctions de Production avec Elasticité de Substitution Variable et ses Applications à l'Économie International", **Économie Appliquée**, Tome XXVII, No. 2-3, 1974, pp. 373-398.

1975

"On Constant and Variable Elasticity of Substitution Production Function. A New Approach and an International Comparision**", 3rd World Congress of the Econometric Society**, Toronto, August 1975, 29 pp..

"A Model of Income Distribution and the Conditions of Existence of Moments of Finite Order". **Proceeding of the 40th Session of the International Statistical Institute**. Vol. XLVI, Book 3, Warsaw, 1975, pp. 196-202.

1976

"Teoria dei Giuochi e Ripartizione Funzionale del Reddito (Un Approccio Strutturale)", **Rassegna Economica**, Napoli, Anno XL, No. 6, Novembre-Décembre 1976, pp. 1395-1424.

1977

"Idéologie et Méthodologie de la Recherche en Science Économique", **Économies et Sociétés**, Série "Philosiphie et Science de l'Homme", Cahiers de l'ISMEA, Tome XI, No. 3, 1977, pp. 553-586.

"Analyse régionale de la répartition du revenu au Canada", **Économie Appliquée**, Tome XXX, No.2. 1977. pp. 285-302.

"A New Model of Personal Income Distribution: Specification and Estimation", **Économie Appliquée**, Paris, Tome XXX, No. 3, 1977, pp. 413-437.

"El Modelo Log-Logistico y la Distribucion del Ingreso en Argentina**", El Trimestre Economico**, Mexico, Vol. XLIV(4), No. 176, 1977, pp. 837-864.

"La grande nécessité, c'est d'être", **Mondes en Développement**, No. 19, 1977, pp. 495-498.

1978

"A Measure of Inequality Betwen Income Distributions", invited paper, International Meeting on **L'idée de régulation dans le mouvement des sciences**, Paris, December 5-10, 1977, in **Économie Appliquée**, Tome XXXI, No. 3-4, 1978, pp. 401-413.

"The Impact of the Composition of Income upon the Size Distribution of Income", **Pionneering Economics, Studi in Onore di G. Demaria**, Padova: CEDAM, 1978, pp. 239-258 (co-author with C. Théoret).

"Toward a General Model of Production and Distribution", **Hommage à François Perroux**, Grenoble : Presses Universitaires de Grenoble, 1978, pp. 539-553.

"On Economic Structure, National Economic Spaces and the Theories of Comparative Advantage in International Trade", **Mondes en Développement**, No. 21, 1978, pp. 11-32.

"Un Nuevo Modelo Descriptivo de la Distribucion Personal del Ingreso", in L. Di Marco (ed.): **La Distribucion del Ingreso en la Argentina**. Buenos Aires: Editorial El Coloquio 1978, pp. 43-58.

1979

Metodologia y Critica Economica, (Ed.), Mexico: Fondo de Cultura Economica, 1979, 611 pages.

"A Mean Generating Function for the Assesment of Estimator Biases", **Économie Appliquée**, Special issue on Time Series Problems, Tome XXXII, No. 1, 1979, pp. 81-93.

"Specification and Identification of a Distributed Lag Model", **Journal of the College of Administration and Economics**, Al-Mustansiryah University, Vol. 111, 1979, pp. 3-10.

"Comments on N. Georgescu-Roegen's Methods in Economic Science", **Journal of Economic Issues**, Vol. XIII, no. 2, 1979, pp. 387-390.

"Specification and Identification of a Distributed Lag Model", **Économie Appliquée**, Tome XXXII, No. 2-3, 1979 pp. 527-533.

1980

"La stucture du pouvoir et le secteur agricole en Argentine. Un essai d'interprétation historique", **North-South, Canadian Journal of Latin American Studies**, Vol. V, No. 9, 1980, pp. 11-30.

"Measuring the Economic Distance Between Income Distributions", in **Reflection on Canadian Incomes**, The Economic Council of Canada. Hull: Government of Canada Publishing Centre, 1980, pp. 545-556.

"Mesure de la Distance Économique entre Répartitions du Revenu", in **Observations sur le Revenu au Canada**, Conseil Économique du Canada. Hull : **Centre d'édition du Gourvernement du Canada**, 1980, pp. 599-612.

"Inequality Measures Between Income Distributions", **Econometrica**, Journal of the Econometric Society, Vol. 48, No. 7, 1980, pp. 1971-1803.

"The Generation and Distribution of Income, the Lorenz Curve and the Gini Ratio", **Économie Appliquée**, Vol. XXXIII, No. 2, 1980, pp. 327-367.

"Sistemas Generadores de Funciones de Distribucion del Ingreso y la Ley de Pareto", **El Trimestre Economico**, Mexico, Vol. 47, No. 4, October-December 1980, pp. 877-917.

"Generating Systems and Properties of Income Distribution Models", **Metron, An International Journal of Statistics**, Vol. XXXVIII, No. 3-4, 1980, pp. 69-87.

1981

"Elements for a New World Order", **Proceedings of the 1980 International Conference of Professors and Scholars: In Search of a New World Order.** Taipei: Pacific Cultural Foundation, 1981, pp. 243-253.

"L'axiomatique du comportement de l'être humain en science économique", **Mondes en Développement,** IX, 35, 1981, pp. 33-46.

"La structure du pouvoir et le secteur agricole en Argentine : un essai d'interprétation historique", in L.R. Alschuler, avec la collaboration de J. Gélinas, T.B. de Hollanda et A. Winberg: **Développement Agricole Dépendant et Mouvements Paysans en Amérique Latine.** Ottawa : Éditions de l'Université d'Ottawa, 1981, Chapitre 4, pp. 69-87.

"Jacques Maritain and Human Rights", **University of Ottawa Quarterly,** 51(4), 1981, pp. 663-668.

"Sistemas Generadores de Distribution de Ingreso y la Ley de Pareto", **Estadistica, Journal of the Inter-American Statistical Institute,** XXXV, 125, 1981, 143-183.

"Structural Stability and Catastrophes in Economics", **Institute for International Development and Cooperation,** University of Ottawa, 1981, 88 pages.

1982

"L'axiomatique du comportement de l'être humain en science économique", **Carrefour,** Revue de la société de Philosophie de l'Outaouais, 4 (1), 1982, pp. 70-88.

"Index Numbers", **Encyclopedia of Economics,** D. Greenwald (Editor-in-Chief). New York: McGraw-Hill Book Co., 1982, pp. 495-498 (co-author with E. B. Dagum).

"Secular Trend", **Encyclopedia of Economics**, D. Greenwald (Editor-in-Chief). New York: McGraw-Hill Book Co., 1982, pp. 848-851 (co-author with E. B. Dagum).

"Male-Female Income Distribution in Canada", **Proceedings of The American Statistical Association, Business and Economics Section**, 142nd Meeting, 1982, pp. 426-430.

"Elements for a New World Order", **International Social Science Review**, 57(3), 1982, pp. 149-153.

1983

"Male-Female Income Inequality by Employment Status in Canada", **Revista de Econometria**, 3(1), 1983, pp. 63-82.

"On Structural Stability and Structural Change in Economics", **Proceedings of the American Statistical Association, Business and Economics Section**, 143rd Meeting, 1983, pp. 654-659.

"Income Distribution Models", **Encyclopedia of Statistical Sciences**. N.L. Johnson and S. Kotz (Editors-in-Chief). New-York. John Wiley and Sons, Vol. 4, 1983, pp. 27-34.

"Income Inequality Measures", **Encyclopedia of Statistical Sciences**. N.L. Johnson and S. Kotz (Editors-in-Chief). New York: John Wiley and Sons, Vol. 4, 1983, pp. 34-40.

"Medida de la differential de ingreso entre familias blancas, negras y de origen hispanico en los Estados Unidos", **El Trimestre Economico** (Special Issue in celebration of the 50th Aniversary of this Journal), 50(2), No. 198, 1983, pp. 963-990.

"Econometric Package for Income Distribution (EPID)", co-author, Ottawa: **University of Ottawa and Time Series Research and Analysis Division, Statistics Canada**, 1983, 87 pages.

1984

"Male-Female Income Distribution in Four Canadian Metropolitan Areas: An Application Using Personal Income Tax Data", W. Alvey and B. Kills (eds.), **Statistics of Income and Related Administrative Record Research**: 1984, U.S. Internal Revenue Service, 1984, pp. 103-110 (co-author with G. Grenier and M. Bédard).

"Male-Female Income Distribution in Four Canadian Metropolitan Areas: An Application Using Personal Income Tax Data", co-author with G. Grenier and M. Bédard. **Proceedings of the 144th Meeting of the American Statistical Association, Survey Research Methods**, 1984, pp. 164-169.

"Stabilità strutturale, mutamento strutturale e previsione economica", **Rassegna Economica**, Vol. XLVIII(1), 1984, pp. 7-28.

"Male-Female Income Differential Among Canadian Employers and Employees", in Y.P. Chaubey and T.D. Dwivedi, eds., **Topics in Applied Statistics**. Montreal: Concordia University, 1984, pp. 239-256.

1985

"Lorenz Curve", **Encyclopedia of Statistical Sciences**, S. Kotz and N.L. Johnson (Editors-in-Chief). New York: John Wiley and Sons, Vol. V, 1985, pp. 156-161.

"Analyses of Income Distribution and Inequality by Education and Sex in Canada", **Advances in Econometrics**, Vol. 4: **Economic Inequality, Survey, Methods and Measurements**, R.L. Basmann and G.F. Rhodes, Jr., Editors, Greenwich, Connecticut: JAI Press Inc., 1985, pp. 167-227.

"Structural Stability, Structual Change and Economic Forecasting", **Optimalité et Structures, en Hommange à Edouard Rossier**. G. Ritschards et D. Royer, editors, Paris: Economica, 1985, pp. 153-171.

"Measure de la distance économique entre distributions de revenu", **Croissance, échange et monnaie en économie internationale. Mélanges en l'honneur de Jean Weiller**, Paris: Economica 1985, pp. 51-65.

"The Definition and Measurement of Poverty and Income Inequality over Time and Space", A Centenary Meeting of the International Statistical Institute, **Proceedings of the International Statistical Institute**, Vol. LI, Book 5, Amsterdam, 1985, pp. 83-86.

"Measuring the Economic Affluence Between Populations of Income Receivers", N. 130 in the Series of **Working papers in Economics and Econometrics**. Faculty of Economics and Research School of Social Sciences, Australian National University. 1985, 33 pages.

1986

"Economic Model, System and Structure, Philosophy of Science and Lakatos' Methodology of Scientific Research Programs", **Rivista Internazionale di Scienze Economiche e Commerciali**, Anno XXXIII, No. 9, 1986, pp. 859-886.

"Répartition du revenu selon le sexe dans quatre agglomérations urbaines du Canada: exemple d'application de données des déclarations de revenu des particuliers," **L'Actualité économique**, Vol. 62, No. 1, 1986, pp. 23-42 (co-author with G. Grenier et M. Bédard).

"Economics, Education and Development", **Proceedings of the Seminar Argentina Today and Canada-Argentina Relations**, University of Ottawa, 1986, pp. 111-113.

"The Distribution of Income and Wealth: Measurement Problems, Inequality Dynamics, Social Policy Impacts: A Comment", **Proceedings of the XXXIIIrd Scientific Meeting of the Italian Statistical Society**, Bari, 1986, pp. 12-16.

"Analyzing Rational and Adaptive Expectations Hypotheses and Model Specifications", **Economies et Sociétés**, T. XX. EM 10, 1986, pp. 15-34.

1987

"Measuring the Economic Affluence Between Populations of Income Receivers", **Journal of Business and Economic Statistics**, **American Statistical Association**, Vol. 5, No. 1,　　　　January 1987, pp. 5-12.

"Gini Ratio", in J. Eatwell, M. Milgate and P. Newman (editors), **The New Palgrave: A Dictionary of Economics**, London, MacMillan Press, Vol. 2, 1987, pp. 529-532.

"Corrado Gini", in J. Eatwell, M. Milgate and P. Newman (editors), **The New Palgrave: A Dictionary of Economics**, London, MacMillan Press, Vol. 2, 1987, p. 529.

"Mouvements cycliques et changements structurels des économies contemporaines: une introduction", **Économie Appliquée**, Tome XL, No 4, 1987, pp. 625-639.

1988

"Factor Shares in Canada, the United States, and the United Kingdom", in A. Asimakopulos (editor), **Theories of Income Distribution**, Hingham, Ma., Kluwer Academic Publishing, 1988, pp. 199-223.

"Economic Model, System and Structure, Philosophy of Science and Lakatos' Methodology of Scientific Research Program", in **Essays in Memory of Tullio Bagiotti**, Padova: CEDAM, 1988, pp. 331-357.

"Trend", in S. Kotz and N. L. Johnson (Editors-in-Chief). **Encyclopedia of Statistical Sciences**, New York, John Wiley and Sons, Vol. 9, 1988, pp. 321-324 (co-author with E.B. Dagum).

"Struttura Causale e Specificazione della Funzione Generatrice del Reddito nell'Esperienza Italiana", **Studi & Informazioni**, XI(2), 1988, 45-55 (co-author with A. Lemmi).

"Proposta di Nuove Misure della Povertà con Applicazioni al Caso Italiano in Anni Recenti, **Note Economiche**, 1988, N. 3, 74-97 (co-author with A. Lemmi and L. Cannari).

"Scienza è Libertà", Academic Lecture given in occasion of being awarded the degree of Doctor Honoris Causa (Statistics and Economics) by the University of Bologna, Italy, 1988. University of Bologna Press, **Quattro Lauree Ad Honorem**, 1991, pp. 27-41.

"Universidad, Economia y Sociedad", Academic Lecture given in occasion of being awarded the degree of Doctor Honoris Causa by the National University of Cordoba, Argentina, 1988. Cordoba: National University of Cordoba, 48 pages.

1989

"Poverty as Perceived by the Leyden Evaluation Project. A Survey of Hagenaars' Contribution on the Perception of Poverty", **Economic Notes**, No. 1, 1989, pp. 99-110.

"A Contribution to the Analysis of Income Distribution and Income Inequality, and a Case Study: Italy", in **Research on Economic Inequality**, D.J. Slottje, ed., 1989, Greenwich, CN: JAI Press, Vol. 1, pp. 123-157 (co-author with A. Lemmi).

"Maurice Allais, Prix Nobel de Sciences Économiques 1988", **Canadian Journal of Development Studies**, Vol. X, No. 2, 1989, pp. 171-176.

"Hommage à Maurice Allais", **L'Actualité Économique**, Vol. 65, No 3, 1989, pp. 351-357.

"Scientific Model Building: Principles, Methods and History", in Herman Wold (editor), **Theoretical Empiricism: A General Rationale for Scientific Model Building**, New York: Paragon Press, 1989, pp. 113-149.

"Expectations and Rational Expectations Models and Bernd Schips on Estimation of RE-Models", in Herman Wold (editor), **Theoretical Empiricism:**

A General Rationale for Scientific Model Building, New York: Paragon Press, 1989, pp. 103-112.

1990

Income and Wealth Distribution, Inequality and Poverty, C. Dagum and M. Zenga, eds., Berlin: Springer-Verlag, 1990, XIII-415 pp.

"On the Relationship Between Income Inequality Measures and Social Welfare Functions", **Journal of Econometrics**, Vol. 43, No. 1/2, 1990, pp. 91-102.

"Fondamenti di Benessere Sociale delle Misure di Disuguaglianza", **Note Economiche**, 1990, No 1, pp. 1-16 (co-author with G. Tatullo).

"A Model of Wealth Distribution Specified for Negative, Null and Positive Wealth", in **Income and Wealth Distribution, Inequality and Poverty**, C. Dagum and M. Zenga, editors, Springer-Verlag, Berlin, 1990, pp. 42-56.

"Generation and Properties of Income Distribution Functions", in C. Dagum and M. Zenga, eds., **Income and Wealth Distribution, Inequality and Poverty**, Berlin: Springer-Verlag, 1990, pp. 1-17.

"On Structural Adjustment and Stabilization: A Comment", in **Strucutral Adjustment and Social Realities in Africa**, G.E. Bourgoignie and M. Genné, eds, Ottawa: University of Ottawa Press, 1990, pp. 87-93.

1991

Renta y Distribucion de la Riqueza, Desigualdad y Pobreza: Teoria, Modelos y Aplicaciones. Cuaderno No. 22, Vitoria-Gasteiz: Instituto Vasco de Estadistica, 1991, 75 pp.

"Genera I Wlasciwosci Funkcji Rozkladu Dochodow", **Polskie Towarzystwo Statystyczne Rada Glowna**, Seria Tlumaczenia, Warszawa, 1991, pp. 1-39.

1992

"Scientific Realism and Idealism in Economics", **Asian Journal of Economics and Social Studies,** Vol. 11, N. 1, 1992, pp. 40-54 (co-author with F. Carlucci).

"New Approaches to the Measurement of Poverty", in **Poverty Measurement for Economies in Transition in Eastern European Countries,** Warsaw: Polish Statistical Association and Central Statistical Office, 1992, pp. 201-225 (co-author with R. Gambassi and A. Lemmi).

1993

"The Social Welfare Bases of Gini and Other Income Inequality Measures", **Statistica,** Anno LIII, N. 1, 1993, pp. 3-28.

"The Social Welfare Bases of Income Inequality Measures", **Proceedings of the 49th Session of the International Statistical Institute,** Contributed Papers Volume, Florence, 1993, pp. 307-308.

"A General Model of Net Wealth, Total Wealth and Income Distribution", **Proceedings of the American Statistical Association, Business and Economics Section,** 153rd Meeting, 1993, pp. 80-85.

"Fundamentos de bienestar social de las medidas de desigualdad en la distribuciòn de las renta", **Cuadernos de Ciencias Economicas y Empresariales,** Universidad de Malaga, Vol. 17, n. 24, 1993, pp. 11-36.

1994

"Index Numbers", **Encyclopedia of Economics,** 2nd. Edition, Douglas Greenwald, Editor-in-Chief, McGraw Hill, New York, 1994, pp. 513-517 (co-author with E.B. Dagum).

"Secular Trend", **Encyclopedia of Economics,** 2nd Edition, Douglas Greewald, Editor-in-Chief, McGraw Hill, New York, 1994, pp. 901-904 (co-author with E.B. Dagum).

"Economia e Statistica: riflessioni ontologiche, metodologiche ed epistemologiche", in **Conferenze di statistica**, Siena: La Nuova Immagine, 1994, pp. 35-54.

"Human Capital, Income and Wealth Distribution Models with Applications", **Sociedad Argentina de Estadistica**, Cuaderno n. 11, 1994, pp. 1-18.

"Measuring Poverty in the Countries in Transition, the Case of Poland: a Comment", **Statistics in Transition, Journal of the Polish Statistical Association**, vol. 1, n. 5, 1994, pp. 637-639.

"Human Capital, Income and Wealth Distribution Models with Applications", **Proceedings of the Business and Economics Section, American Statistical Association**, 154th Meeting, 1994, pp. 253-258.

"A Dual Relationship Between the Spaces of Income Inequality Measures and Social Welfare Functions", in **Scritti di Statistica Economica**, Claudio Quintano, editor, Napoli: Rocco Curto Editore, 1994, pp. 89-111.

"Un modello generale della distribuzione della ricchezza netta, della ricchezza totale e del reddito con applicazioni", in **Scritti di Statistica Economica**, Claudio Quintano, editor, Napoli: Rocco Curto Editore, 1994, pp. 113-126.

1995

Income Distribution, Social Welfare, Inequality and Poverty, C. Dagum and A. Lemmi, eds. JAI Press, Greenwich, CN, U.S.A., Vol. 6, 1995, XVII, 406 pages.

Quantitative Methods for Applied Sciences, C. Dagum, P. Barbini, A. Lemmi and C. Provasi, eds. Siena: Nuova Immagine, 1995, 427 pp.

"The Scope and Method of Economics as a Science", **Il Politico**, Università di Pavia, Anno LX, N.1, Gennaio-Marzo 1995, pp. 5-39.

"Income Inequality Measures and Social Welfare Functions: A Unified Approach", in **Income Distribution, Social Welfare, Inequality and Poverty**,

C. Dagum and A. Lemmi, editors, JAI Press, Greenwich, Connecticut, U.S.A., 1995, pp. 177-199.

"The Scope and Method of Economics as a Science", **in Quantitative Methods for Applied Sciences**, C. Dagum, P. Barbini, A. Lemmi and C. Provasi, eds., Siena: La Nuova Immagine, 1995, pp. 28-69.

"Analyse Interrégionale des distributions des salaires français", **Economie Appliquée**, 48(3), 1995, pp. 103-133 (co-author with F. Guibbaud-Seyte et M. Terraza).

"Alcance y método de la economìa como ciencia", **El Trimestre Economico**, Vol. 62(3), N. 247, 1995, pp. 297-336.

1996

"Il costo del lavoro e la distribuzione del reddito familiare e del reddito individuale per condizione professionale e per sesso in Italia", **Problems of the Modern Labor Economics**, Accademia Nazionale dei Lincei, Roma, 1996, pp. 113-185 (co-author with M. Costa).

"A Systemic Approach to the Generation of Income Distribution Models", **Journal of Income Distribution**, 1996, Vol. 6, No. 1, pp. 105-126.

"Human Capital Measurement and Distribution". **Proceedings of the Business and Economic Statistics Section, American Statistical Association**, 156th Meeting, 1996, pp. 194-199 (co-author with G. Vittadini).

"Quelques réflexions sur les fondements micro de la macroéconomique et les fondements macro de la microéconomique", Academic Lecture given in occasion of being awarded the degree of Doctor Honoris Causa by the University of Montpellier I, France, **University of Montpellier I**, 1996, pp. 11-18.

1997

"A New Approach to the Decomposition of the Gini Income Inequality Ratio", **Empirical Economics**, 1997, Vol.22(4), pp.513-531.

"Decomposition and Interpretation of Gini and the Generalized Entropy Inequality Measures", Proceedings of the **American Statistical Association, Business and Economic Statistics Section,** 157-th Meeting, 1997, pp.200-205.

"Universidad, Economia y Sociedad", **Statistica,** Vol.LVII(2), 1997, pp.239-260.

"Scomposizione ed interpretazione delle misure di disuguaglianza di Gini e di entropia generalizzata", **Statistica,** Vol.L VII(3), 1997, pp.295-308.

"Fondements de bien-être social des mesures d'inégalité du revenu", en **Mélanges en Honneur d'Henri Bartoli,** 1997, pp. 283-306.

1998

"Measures de l'inégalité du revenu et fonctions de bie-ètre social: une approche unifiée", **L'économie, une science pour l'homme et la société,** Mélanges en l'honneur d'Henri Bartoli, F. Michon, coord., Paris: Publication de la Sorbonne, 1998, pp.283-306.

"Répartition personnelle et fonctionnelle du revenu: une approche integrée", **Etudes Internationales,** Vol.XXXIX(2), 1998, pp.239-265.

"Fondements de bien-être social et décomposition des mesures d'inégalité dans la répartition du revenu", Tenth Invited Lecture in Memory of François Perroux, Collège de France, **Economie Apliquée,** Vol.LI(4), 1998, pp.451-484.

"Linking the Functional and Personal Distribution of Income", **Handbook of Income Inequality Measurement,** Jacques Silber, editor, Boston-Dordrecht: Kluwer Academic Press, pp.101-128.

"Analysing the functional and the personal distributions of income and the size distributions of human capital, net wealth, total wealth, and total debt", Invited Lecture in Memory of Luigi Solari, Département d'Econométrie, Université de Genève, **Cahiers Vilfredo Pareto,** forthcoming.

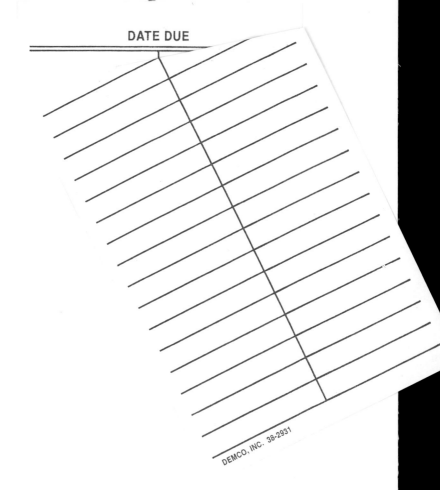

DATE DUE

DEMCO, INC. 38-2931